Passive Voices
(ON THE SUBJECT OF
PHENOMENOLOGY AND OTHER
FIGURES OF SPEECH)

SUNY series, Intersections: Philosophy and Critical Theory

Rodolphe Gasché, editor

Passive Voices
(ON THE SUBJECT OF
PHENOMENOLOGY AND OTHER
FIGURES OF SPEECH)

Kristina Mendicino

Cover image: Chromatic Penumbra of Thought. Photograph by Marta Machabeli, 2015. Owned by Marta Machabeli.

Published by State University of New York Press, Albany

© 2023 State University of New York

All rights reserved

Printed in the United States of America

No part of this book may be used or reproduced in any manner whatsoever without written permission. No part of this book may be stored in a retrieval system or transmitted in any form or by any means including electronic, electrostatic, magnetic tape, mechanical, photocopying, recording, or otherwise without the prior permission in writing of the publisher.

For information, contact State University of New York Press, Albany, NY
www.sunypress.edu

Library of Congress Cataloging-in-Publication Data

Name: Mendicino, Kristina, author.
Title: Passive voices : (on the subject of phenomenology and other figures of speech) / Kristina Mendicino.
Description: Albany : State University of New York Press, [2023] | Series: SUNY series, Intersections: Philosophy and Critical Theory | Includes bibliographical references and index.
Identifiers: ISBN 9781438491974 (hardcover : alk. paper) | ISBN 9781438491981 (ebook) | ISBN 9781438491967 (pbk. : alk. paper)
Further information is available at the Library of Congress.

10 9 8 7 6 5 4 3 2 1

Contents

Acknowledgments — vii

Introduction: Principally Unprincipled; or, Speaking of "Beginnings" — 1

1 "Self"-Citations in Husserl and Augustine — 23

2 Provocations: "I," Husserl, and the Passive Voices of Phenomenology — 47

3 Parsing Pairing: George Bataille and the Scripts of Subjectivity — 73

4 Writing Out of Sight: On the Papers and Traces of Kafka — 99

5 Passive Voices: Echoes, Blanchot — 129

Postscript — 163

Notes — 169

Works Cited — 273

Index — 291

Acknowledgments

I do not know how to begin giving the thanks owed to others for the conversations that have sustained me through this study of the "passions of the voice." The subject speaks in advance against the very attempt to acknowledge all debts: it could go on indefinitely, and it would certainly exceed the bounds of this book.

But for now, I would like to thank my colleagues from the Department of German Studies, the Department of Comparative Literature, and the Pembroke Center for Teaching and Research on Women at Brown University for creating the atmosphere of spirited inquiry that has sustained me in writing this book. I would like to thank those students who patiently and passionately read Husserl with me over the past semesters, and especially Emma Schneider, whose findings as a research assistant have enriched so many of the pages to come. I am grateful for the years of collaboration on phenomenology and literature that I have shared with colleagues from other institutions, above all Philippe P. Haensler and Rochelle Tobias, whose work has taught me so much about the texts addressed in this book. My sincere gratitude goes to Rodolphe Gasché and Rebecca Colesworthy from SUNY Press for their unwavering commitment to this project. I thank Marta Machabeli for her permission to reprint her "Chromatic Penumbra of Thought" on the cover of this volume. I would like to thank Kelly McCullough for the countless lessons in strength and flexibility. I would like to thank those dear friends of (and with) whom I am always thinking, however often or intermittently we may hear from one another. Special thanks go to Rainer Nägele, without whom the readings offered in this book would not have been possible. My deepest gratitude goes again to Marta Machabeli, Joan Mendicino, Joseph Mendicino, and Dominik Zechner for being my closest conversation partners and *compagnons de route* through the turbulent times when this book was first drafted.

Introduction

Principally Unprincipled; or, Speaking of "Beginnings"

At the latest since Aristotle's *Peri hermeneias*, there has been talk of the pathos of language: "There are, then, things in vocal-sound that are symbols [σύμβολα] of the affections [παθημάτων] in the soul," Aristotle writes, and while voicings may vary, he asserts that the "affections" or "passions" of which they are the "signs [σημεῖα]" are the same for all, as are those things of which the passions are the "similitudes [ὁμοιώματα]."[1] Before there can be any articulate thought, that is to say, something must have been suffered in a way that marks the mind, which Boethius reiterates when he translates Aristotle's σύμβολα with *notae*, suggesting that the voice must itself undergo an inscription in order to render what the soul has undergone.[2] Thomas Aquinas interprets the passivity at the core of language and thought as a sign for the "deficiency" of the human intellect, which, unlike divine intellect, needs sense impressions and phantasms in order to act and understand.[3] And before these commentators, Augustine—who will confess to studying Aristotle's *Categories*, if not *Peri hermeneias*[4]—recalls learning language as his first memory in terms that repeat and elaborate upon Aristotle's formulation perhaps more than they comment upon any experience of his own: "What [the adults] wanted was clear, for they used bodily gestures, the natural words of all peoples [*verbis naturalibus omnium gentium*], such as facial expressions or glances of the eyes or movements of other parts of the body, or a tone of voice, indicating *the affection of the soul* [*affectionem animi*] concerning those things that they sought, wished to hold on to, rejected or shunned altogether."[5]

The notion that there could be neither discourse nor thought without affection would be reprised in even the most rigorous modern investigations of transcendental subjectivity, from the role that receptivity (*Empfindung*) plays in Immanuel Kant's *Critique of Pure Reason*, to the passive syntheses of hyletic data that Edmund Husserl situates at the foundation of conscious apprehension in and beyond his lectures on passive synthesis from the 1920s. Yet something strange happens in Husserl: just as he seeks to articulate a phenomenological understanding of passivity that would be pure of the metaphysical, scientific, and sensualistic prejudices that he finds in his predecessors,[6] Husserl describes the passive operations of consciousness as responses to the appeals—and the protests—that issue from the material givens. As he will concisely put it in one exemplary passage: "That which is experienced each time has the character of one who is calling [*den Charakter des Anrufenden*]"; and in another passage, he will speak of the "protests" that certain associative formations may give against the tendency of other associative formations to assimilate them.[7] These turns of phrase are most likely meant to emphasize the subjective character of even the most inchoate "stuff [*Stoff*]" that enters consciousness[8] and thus to indicate Husserl's distance from anything like the suggestion that sensory data may be "proper material substances": "Sense-data, sense-complexes," as he would insist elsewhere, "are only thinkable as perceived, as conscious in a subject."[9] Even the foreign matter of "I-less [*ichlosen*]" formations is only thinkable, in other words, when it is understood to speak to, and therefore like, "me."[10] By casting the subject matter in this way, however, Husserl does not so much offer a rigorously phenomenological formulation "that does nothing further than lend expression to such givens through [. . .] exactly commensurate meanings,"[11] as he returns to the trope or fiction that had already figured in Augustine's *Confessions*, where, beside the voice of reason, the mind was said to be solicited by both the "messengers [*nuntios*]" of the senses,[12] as well as the unsolicited memories that call attention to themselves, "saying, as it were, 'are we not [what you are seeking]?'"[13] That is to say, the imaginary calls Husserl cites may themselves be fictive citations and citations of fiction, without any foundation in the "givens" of intuition. But this is also not to say that Husserl's or Augustine's "personifications" are mere figures of speech. To the contrary, they are themselves traces of an affection or passion, which shows both writers to be drawn by the appeal of appeals whose occurrence could be neither intuitively founded nor otherwise substantiated. And in this respect, the voices that Husserl invokes also bear associations with those of Augustine's oeuvre, rendering their respective voices passive in yet another way that none could claim to experience:

for insofar as each writer echoes the other, their voices undergo a mutual inscription independently of their knowledge. Hence, the unverifiable yet repeated appeals of sensory and memory impressions may always resonate further, through to the passage from Eugene Ionesco's *The Bald Soprano* that Emmanuel Levinas will recite in order to exemplify the structure of the trace—"Someone rang, and there is no one at the door: did anyone ring?"[14]—or the still more enigmatic, because fragmentary, phrase that appears isolated in italics in Maurice Blanchot's *The Step Not Beyond*: "*As if there would have reverberated, in a muffled way, a call*"[15]; or the call of the castle official, Klamm, who is said in Franz Kafka's *The Castle* to have summoned a woman named Frieda but whose speech also may not have been intended to address anyone at all, rendering his summons, at the limit, a call that can barely still be called "calling": "And the fact that he sometimes called Frieda need not at all have the meaning that one may wish to ascribe it; he simply called the name Frieda—who knows his intentions?—while the fact that Frieda naturally rushed to come was her issue [. . .] but one cannot exactly maintain that he exactly called her."[16]

The foreign instances of speech that are called to mind in Husserl's and Augustine's oeuvres, among others, suggest that the pathos grounding first-person discourse and experience is not merely a matter of those corporeal affections that the *cogito* might eventually grasp in conscious acts. Rather, they indicate that affections are already structured like a language and that language would therefore need to be suffered before any thought, recollection, or meaning could be recognized or voiced by "me." The linguistic pathos that is registered within texts such as Augustine's *Confessions* and Husserl's manuscripts thus calls for different readings of passion and passivity than recent theories of affect have tended to offer.[17] For it is not merely a matter of describing what the affective contingencies of memory, cognition, and signification may mean for rethinking the supposed agency of the intellect or the embodied nature of experience. It is a question of how language affects the experience, sense, signification, and expression of the subject of speech, before any *logos* or *autos* of cognition; and in the last analysis, it is a question of how language could respond to these questions of language.

These are the questions that are addressed in *Passive Voices (On the Subject of Phenomenology and Other Figures of Speech)*, beginning with those linguistic interventions that are not only said to affect the transcendental subject in Husserl's descriptions of passive synthesis but that also enter into his rhetorical performance through the citations, echoes, and protests that traverse his writing and resist assimilation to its epistemological aims. Other voices will play critical roles in this study, including those of Augustine, as well as literary writers from the twentieth century, whose fictive experiments echo the thinking of Husserl and Augustine, while exceeding the more restrictive fictions of phenomenological "science." *Passive Voices* addresses, that is to say, an affective corpus of philosophical and literary writings whose repetitions and variations testify to the manifold ways in which speech occurs in the passive voice, affecting even the most reduced claims to experience. Already those echoes that let Aristotle speak with Augustine and Augustine with Husserl, expose each of their voices to be passively disposed toward others whom none could have intended or precluded—and thus to speak otherwise than anyone may have pretended to do himself. Yet unlike the phenomenological exercise of imaginative variation, where individual givens are imagined otherwise so as to disclose invariant structures, the passive experiences of language surpass the limits of possible experience from the outset, soliciting further examination through literary fictions, which are beholden to no ontological or epistemological premises but permitted to "say anything, accept anything, receive anything, suffer anything, and simulate everything."[18] The passive dimensions of both philosophical literature and literary fiction call not for a phenomenological investigation but for a "philological labor [. . .] which necessarily complements the philosophical one and indicates its limits."[19]

It is phenomenology, however, that marks an exemplary point of departure for approaching linguistic pathos because and not despite of the fact that it was never intended to do so. Because, in other words, Husserl most insistently calls for the radical reduction of all sensible and speakable experience to subjective consciousness, the passive relationship between subject and language that his texts nevertheless register gives one of the most radical testimonies to the irreducible alterity and priority of language to subjectivity and knowledge. In an age where notions of agency, power, and truth are in a crisis at least as troubling as the one which Husserl had confronted when he wrote *The Crisis of the European Sciences*, a reduction to the contingent and passive foundations of "experience" in language may be more crucial than the reduction of the modern sciences to life that Husserl more expressly retraces in that work—not in order to know the world we will have made but to advocate for the others whom we speak with, unbeknownst to ourselves. It is for this other reduction that phenomenological writing also speaks, when diverse voices and fictions cross Husserl's lines against his better knowledge, and it is for the sake of such speaking that this philological study draws out those traces of passion in the voice, which testify to modes of experience and community that would rest upon no common ground and no ego-subjects, but would rather hold open indefinitely for others.

Long before Husserl's lectures on passive synthesis, the project of phenomenology is marked by this passive "experience" beyond experience, from the "beginning." For the epistemological "principle" that Husserl states toward the outset of his *Ideas Pertaining to a Pure Phenomenology* is not simply "intuitive." The often-cited "principle of all principles" reads: "that every originarily giving intuition is a legitimizing source of knowledge."[20] To be sure, this statement would at first seem to affirm the unconditional priority and validity of intuitive givenness, as an authentic occurrence that "affects" consciousness from within its immanent stream and therefore as an originary presence beyond a shadow of a doubt.[21] And even for many subsequent thinkers who would shift the emphasis of phenomenological discourse to other traits of experience than those which Husserl underscores in his explications of subjective constitution, the implications of his statement on principle would appear to remain decisive. It was by reinterpreting Husserl's "idea of an 'originary' and 'intuitive' grasp and explication of phenomena" that Martin Heidegger would understand phenomenality as the disclosure of "beings [. . .] themselves [. . .] in the way of access that genuinely belongs to them"—and would thereby begin to approach the question of being that opens through a return "to the things themselves."[22] It was in taking up the primacy of "*giving* intuition" that Jean-Luc Marion would elaborate givenness as the condition of possibility for all appearance that precedes even "intuition and intention."[23] And it was with attentiveness to the "pathos" implied in "givenness" that Bernhard Waldenfels would insist upon the alterity that conditions the origin of subjective experience, where "we are struck [*betroffen*] *by something*," in advance of all (self-) awareness, which can neither be "founded on the previous 'what,'" nor "sublated into a subsequently accomplished 'for what.'"[24]

But Husserl's statement of principle is followed nearly as soon as it is offered with a remark on language that doubles it, troubling its claim to priority—and thereby introduces a duplicity or discrepancy from the "beginning": "Every statement [*Aussage*]," Husserl adds, "that does nothing further than lend expression to such givens through mere explication and exactly commensurate meanings, is therefore really [. . .] an absolute beginning, called upon [*berufen*] to lay the ground, a principium in the genuine sense of the word."²⁵ Thus it would seem that intuitive evidence could not "really" mark the beginning of knowledge, nor could "givens" fully be granted at first since the "absolute beginning" is said to arrive only when given intuitions are lent words. Husserl's articulation of "beginnings" thus anticipates both Tilottama Rajan's observation that "the linguistic is already embedded in phenomenology,"²⁶ as well as Michael Marder's more recent arguments that "Husserlian 'original experience' presages the deconstruction of pure origins that are inconsistent with phenomenology."²⁷ But beside these general insights into the linguistic and historical character of phenomenological knowledge, Husserl's particular formulations also indicate that the lending of words takes place as an operation which principal statements are themselves "called" ("berufen") to perform, recalling or anticipating the "calls" that Husserl would invoke in his descriptions of passive synthesis. Although the source for this call does not seem to lie in the appeals of hyletic data, moreover, Husserl's usage of the (grammatical) passive voice suggests that it issues from an experience that does not belong primarily to "me," which is made still more pronounced by the fact that the authority of said experience is, according to Husserl, itself an anonymous "assertion [*Behauptung*] drawn immediately from general insight."²⁸ The givens of intuition thus call for corresponding linguistic expressions in a manner that is already an "assertion" of sorts, rendering all further speech provoked in advance by this prior yet unspoken claim. An ambivalent, citational character thereby comes to mark every "beginning"—whether it be called an "originary" intuition or the "expression" that intuition will have originally called for—and this ambivalence is registered still more emphatically, when Husserl places "beginnings" in quotation marks in another iteration of this thought. Only those "findings," he asserts, "which are carried out" in such a way where what is "directly given in intuition" is brought "to faithful expression," are "real 'beginnings' [*wirkliche 'Anfänge'*]."²⁹ On these terms, too, it is hardly evident where the "beginning" of phenomenological thinking begins. And even if it should be objected that intuition should remain prior to expression—it is intuition, after all, that each "expression" should faithfully translate and repeat—or if it should be objected that Husserl's word of "beginnings" has less to do with phenomenological insight per se than with its intersubjective, mundane appearance,³⁰ there remain fundamental differences among intuitive givens, their solicitations for expression, and the expressions that are given to them, whose descriptions provide no evidence that the expression of any given intuition could not, in principle, fail its initial calling or fall from faithfulness.

The "beginnings" of phenomenological insight are thus not only already a recital of but also subjected to the epochal suspension that "quotation marks [*Anführungszeichen*]" will signify in Husserl's thought,[31] and this suspension is not so much enacted by the transcendental subject of phenomenology, as it occurs as an effect of the language of "principle." How could any commensuration between an expression and an intuition be asserted, if not in "quotation marks," when intuition is already understood to speak for itself, on the one hand, and when this silent speech nonetheless calls for expression, on the other, with the consequence that there could be no common measure between intuition and expression—or between unspoken "assertion" and verbal "expression"—that would not repeat their irreducible difference? How could any but a "suspended" position be taken toward statements that pretend to do "nothing further than lend expression" to the givens, when the latter require repetition in order to "begin,"[32] to say nothing of the fact that any terms that may lend themselves to expressing intuitions will have themselves already come before "I" could have a say?[33] It is in "response" to such questions that Marder calls for ongoing "critiques of *logos* by phenomena and of phenomena by *logos*,"[34] yet the logic of Husserl's critical remarks on intuition and expression suggests that "we are not" ever "sufficiently sure of what terms like reason, reasonable, rational, intuition, faith, truth signify in order to commence by way of them," as Brice Parain would write in his *Recherches sur la nature et les fonctions du langage*, which may also be read as an answer to the phenomenological investigations of Husserl.[35]

This passive *epoché* is not, however, the only trait of Husserl's formulations that testifies to an experience of language that eludes and affects what will be called "subjective experience." Husserl's "principle" remarks are themselves reiterations of a dilemma that will have long since marked the thought of intuition in texts such as Gottfried Wilhelm Leibniz's "Meditations on Knowledge, Truth, and Ideas," where "symbolic" knowledge is synonymous with "blind" cognition and where "signs" are said to be used "in the place [*loco*] of things" that they do not replace, so much as they allow us to operate upon the fiction or belief that we know what we are talking about, at a remove from any question of reference or referent. It was already within this tradition that Husserl's understanding of "signitive" meanings had inscribed itself,[36] despite the purely descriptive method that

Husserl announces,[37] when he observes in his *Logical Investigations* that understanding is a "descriptive trait in the experience of the intuitionless, yet understood sign."[38] Nor would Leibniz fail to characterize what Husserl will call the "act-experience [*Akterlebnis*]" of signitive understanding through a first-person performance of his own:[39] "Either knowing or believing [myself] to have" the explication of signs "in [my] power, I remember that I know the signification of the words [*memini me significationem istorum vocabulorum habere*]."[40] Since, however, remembering oneself to have explanatory knowledge does not necessarily mean that one still has it or that one has ever had it, Leibniz's formulation also implies that any "memory" marked in this way could always be a sort of screen memory or fiction of knowledge effected by memorized signs.[41] He nearly says so explicitly, when he claims that what is initially recalled in using signs is not any grasp of their meaning but the belief that no "interpretation" or "explication" of them "is necessary for the present judgment [*nunc judicio necessariam non esse*]."[42] It was with an eye to this structural trait of language that G. W. F. Hegel would posit the mechanical memorization of signs as the critical juncture between reproductive imagination and discursive thought in the evolution of subjective spirit,[43] and that Husserl would later call for the thorough investigation of historically "sedimented" meanings on the grounds that any "judgments" that take place on their basis cannot but rest upon blind and unthought "prejudice," so long as they have not been traced back to their intuitive origins.[44] But insofar as each reduction to an intuitive ground would have to be iterable in order to offer any verifiable insight, and insofar as its verification could not be affirmed without recourse to signs, each reduction necessarily remains blind on at least two counts, as Jacques Derrida has argued at length: as an iterable ideal, it necessarily exceeds immediate intuition in order to be what it is—and is therefore always already "(no-) more-sight [*plus-de-vue*]"[45]—and as a linguistic formulation, it opens the phenomenon in question to "an infinite discursiveness" from the "beginning."[46] All of these intersecting voices, fictive constructions, and unresolved problems contaminate Husserl's appeals to pure intuition in his *Ideas Pertaining to a Pure Phenomenology*, whose formulations cannot but run the risk of repeating the very sort of prejudice they seem meant to speak against, of erring on the side of speaking otherwise than intended and thus of speaking in the passive voice, which would here signify the incapacity of speech to exclude such repeated risks.

For this very reason, Husserl's language exposes itself to further and other associations, including associations with those writers of confession, theory, and fiction who would rearticulate intuition and evidence, phenomenality and light, through a discourse of blindness. Georges Bataille, for example, would characterize "experience" in *Guilty* (*Le Coupable*) as an ecstatic movement that escapes the one who lives it, which he illustrates by invoking "a blind man's motions, eyes wide open, arms stretching out, staring at the sun, and inside he's turning to light himself."⁴⁷ The phenomenological of tropes of vision and immanence, as well as the ideal of adequation, are all evoked in this passage where outer and inner luminosity coincide, but they are also all displaced. Far from offering any promise of an "originarily giving intuition," the moment that Bataille describes would remain beyond the scope of the one who lives through it as well as his witness, who could not approach an illumination like the one that he relates without becoming blind to it himself. In Bataille's scenario, blindness and evidence can *either* be lived through *or* "known" and "spoken," and by exposing the insuperable disjunction that renders vision inaccessible to cognition, and vice versa, the text thus draws *the* operative metaphor of phenomenology "to the edges of the blind spot that constitutes it" as Rodolphe Gasché has brilliantly shown Bataille's writing to do in other contexts.⁴⁸ Yet what also renders the passage from *Guilty* a most powerful indication of the blindness that would affect all signs of "intuition" are the ways in which Bataille's words on blind motion become themselves impossible to fix, locate, or trace. For although one could object that the above-cited passage could be contrasted with others, more favorable to the notion of evidence, or that Bataille may not have intended his text to be a critical response to phenomenological insight, the testimony to blindness that it gives is not dependent upon authorized intentions but emerges through echoes that expose not only Husserl's but also Bataille's vocabulary, among others, to unforeseeable associations. Within the context of Bataille's corpus alone, his lines repeat the portrayal that he had provided of his blind and syphilitic father in the postscript to the *Story of the Eye* (*Histoire de l'oeil*),⁴⁹ whether or not they were meant to evoke or overwrite the paternal figure from his novel. At the same time, moreover, they resonate with the evocation of a benighted eye that takes place toward the opening of Maurice Blanchot's *Thomas the Obscure*: "His eye, useless for seeing, took on extraordinary proportions, developed beyond measure, and, extending over the horizon, let the night penetrate into its center to create an iris."⁵⁰ Yet even beyond these nearly contemporaneous passages, Bataille's words also distantly recall the illustration that Augustine offers for the simultaneous presence of God to man and absence of man to God, which is similar to "the way that a blind man is posed in the sun, and the sun is present to him, but he is absent to the sun [*quomodo homo positus in sole caecus, praesens est illi sol, sed ipse soli absens est*]";[51] as well as the fragment on truth that Franz Kafka would draft during a period of convalescence in Zürau: "Our art is a being-blinded-by-the-truth [*ein von der Wahrheit Geblendet-Sein*]: The light upon the grimacing visage that draws back is true, nothing else."[52] And finally, all of these passages take another turn with the helio-tropism of Husserl's *cogito*, whose acts are said to radiate like the sun, but whose luminosity is itself left unclarified and obscure: "In every actual cogito a radiating 'look' [*ausstrahlender 'Blick'*] is directed from the pure Ego to the 'object.'"[53] Each of these writers will be explicitly cited elsewhere in Bataille's oeuvre,[54] but because there is no clear evidence that Bataille had any of them in mind when he recorded the motions of a blind man in *Le Coupable*, there is also no way to decide the extent to which his lines may be borrowed, spliced together, or severed from those others in this indefinitely culpable (*coupable*) and cuttable (*coup-able*) text. In lieu of any unequivocally original or citational formulation, a vacancy thus opens through Bataille's words—which he pronounces "void" himself: "so many empty words [*autant de mots devenus vides*]"[55]—and it is this linguistic vacancy, like the eyes of Bataille's blind man, which blindly admits all possible associations and "interferences."[56] It is a blind and passive movement of language that is traced through Bataille's words of light and sight, which leaves room for other articulations of those phenomena and lets various voices resonate with—and without—one another.[57]

It was precisely under the sign of such blind and passive movements that Jacques Derrida would write in his *Memoirs of the Blind* (*Mémoires d'aveugle*): "Language is spoken / speaks to itself [*Le langage se parle*], that is to say, *from / of blindness* [de l'aveuglement]. It always speaks to us *from / of the blindness* that constitutes it."[58] Drawing together both Husserl's signature notion of "constitution" and Heidegger's famous dictum, "language speaks [*die Sprache spricht*],"[59] Derrida rearticulates these phrases along the lines of the destitution "from" and "of" which language speaks, and he does so without compensating for the lack of vision or intuition that "his" language makes pronounced. His citational "language" on language emphasizes instead the difference between language and intuition, which entails, on the one hand, that no speech could make up for its intuitive deficit but could only repeat a variation upon its constitutive blindness; while on the other hand, it entails that language could never speak "itself," either, without withdrawing from evidence and remaining blind to its senses. As it echoes and alters the phenomenological vocabulary of Husserl and Heidegger, however, Derrida's passage also shows words to be excessive beyond measure: "tropes [*tropes*] of [. . .] rhetorical supplementarity" that "always lead us [. . .] too far [*trop loin*]."[60]

Faithful to this counter-intuitive language, the narrative performance that Derrida goes on to sketch in his *Memoirs* offers an indirect yet critical commentary on the conscious and lucid ego of phenomenology—upon the premises Derrida sketches, there could be no other way[61]—by drawing the tropes of vision and first-person figures of speech that mark phenomenological investigation into a thoroughly citational portrait of "personal" experience. This "portrait," in turn, exposes the radical alterity of the scripts for vision and self alike. Early in his *Memoirs*, for example, Derrida will confess to "insinuating an oblique or distracted reading" of Bataille's *Story of the Eye* into the "story of the eye"[62] that he will call his own, which intersection of readings and writings, of proper titles (*Story of the Eye*) and common names (*story of the eye*), would alone cross through the "proper" claims to experience that found Husserl's theory of the "I." Derrida's passing remark on Bataille's *Story of the Eye* also bears out further, however, as Derrida develops his "self-portrait of a blind man."[63] For just as Bataille's story will be traced back to "Réminiscences" that are not initially remembered by himself[64] but first recalled by photographs from "an American magazine,"[65] even the most personal confessions of Derrida's *Memoirs* turn out to be entangled with other narrative scripts and contingent encounters. From the first, the partially recorded dream that Derrida relates of two elderly dueling blind men will prompt the recollection of a plethora of elderly blind men from Greco-Roman and biblical antiquity: Oedipus, Tiresias, Homer, Isaac, and Tobit, among others.[66] Associations prescribed by an archive, rather than any sensed or remembered data, are what form the composite images that make up his mind and do not portray thought as a *"free-floating* [. . .] play of self-destructive signs,"[67] as critics such as William Spanos have asserted of Derrida's writing, but rather expose the passive constitution of subjectivity through language, without which there could be no coming to terms with "ourselves." The fact, moreover, that Derrida, like Bataille, introduces his oneiric text not as one that he recalls directly but one that he only remembers recording in the dark—that is, without a glimmer of knowledge as to its contents—not only inscribes his dream *ab initio* into a tradition of manuscripts and copies but also shows this tradition to be the only chance for getting a grip: "And so on the night of July 16th of last year, without turning on the light, barely awake, still passive but careful not to chase away an interrupted dream, I felt around with a groping hand beside my bed for a pencil, then a notebook."[68]

What Derrida "remembers" writing in the dark figures in no process of lending words to an "originarily giving intuition": there is no "absolute beginning,"[69] but an abyssal gap that absolves both scribe and inscription from every memory on the record, thus letting speech take (their) place in the passive voice. Hence, when Derrida goes on to write, "Upon awakening, I deciphered this [*ceci*], among other things," he characterizes the dream-text that will have only later become apparent to him as though it were originally drafted in a foreign hand. Beyond the propositional content of this confession, moreover, the very word for "this" ("ceci") literally points to the "blindness" (*cécité*) of both its writing and written protagonists. In these ways and more, Derrida thereby disowns the ocular subject of his (and Bataille's) "story of the eye,"[70] while his emphasis upon the eye shifts the sight, vision, regard, aims, and acts of the (phenomenological) subject out of focus. Yet it is also in these ways that the dream-text produced by groping in the dark exposes the passive history of an experience that could never be appropriated but remains open to the vicissitudes of whatever is written of it, thus marking out a space where the "heterogeneity of the invisible to the visible can haunt the visible as its very possibility."[71]

Derrida's writing offers some of the most far-reaching commentaries on the blindness and passivity that will have marked the language of subjectivity, experience, truth, and knowledge, not only in the study of Husserl's *Logical Investigations* that he would set under the sign of *Speech and Phenomena* or in his introduction to Husserl's "Origin of Geometry" but also in the confessional rhetoric and literary fictions that are explored in, among others, *Memoirs of the Blind*, *Circonfessions*, and *Demeure: Maurice Blanchot*. In these works, first-person speech figures not in the form of the knowing *cogito* but in the performative modus of testimony, which "always goes hand in hand with at least the *possibility* of fiction, perjury, and lie"—with "the *possibility*," in a word, "of literature."[72] In its "own" way, of course, phenomenological writing, whose eidetic descriptions depart from the exemplary evidence of what is given to "me," also presents itself as a sort of testimony.[73] But the "literary" effects that may at all times dispose the phenomenologist to speak in a manner that is shaped by archives, tropes, coincidences, and contingencies that surpass his capacity to know or to tell—that is, to speak in the passive voice—tend to be understated, if not left out of the picture. Thus, if Derrida offers articulations of experience that exceed the scope of phenomenology—articulations "where," as John D. Caputo has written, "experience does not mean phenomenological seeing but running up against the unforeseeable"[74]—then his polyvocal first-person performances draw the furthest consequences of his readings in Husserl. As Derrida had written in his earlier study of Husserl's *Logical Investigations*, "The primordially repetitive structure" that Husserl assigns to "signs in general" means that the sign is—like testimony—"*originally wrought by fiction* [travaillé par la fiction],"[75] and that no sign could enable one to tell between "reality and representation, between the veridical and the imaginary, and between simple presence and repetition,"[76] even when "I tell myself 'I am.'"[77] This inability to tell is a consequence of the passivity to which all acts of speaking and writing are exposed; and it is what structurally allows each voice and trace to recall others, permitting passive associations that belong to no subject of experience but to the experience of language. The lineage that readers such as Rajan have drawn from phenomenology to deconstruction and literature may thus be traced back to the passive character of (linguistic) experience.[78] Language is, in a word, "a matter of the passivity of passion before or beyond the opposition between passivity and activity," as Derrida would write, echoing similar remarks by Emmanuel Levinas and Maurice Blanchot but also Husserl, whose writings on the so-called appeals and protests of passive synthesis will have said much the same.[79] But language is also, for the same reason, a matter of the affect that precedes the distinction between fact and fiction and that is therefore exposed most emphatically not in Derrida's commentaries on fiction, citation, and passivity but in the more citational and fictional traits of his written performance.[80] Hence, it is the less evidently phenomenological texts of Derrida that set the example for this book, where the "same" quotations and motifs will be read through various confessional, fictive, and philosophical contexts, so as to draw out those resonances that render their passive character pronounced and to unfold their implications for the thought of self-knowledge, testimony, and community, among others.

Departing more often from Blanchot and Levinas than from Husserl, scholars over the past several decades such as Steven Shapiro, Ann Smock, and Thomas C. Wall have sought to elaborate what could be called the transcendental passivity of language.[81] Yet the elucidating commentaries that they offer through readings of not only Blanchot and Levinas but also Georges Bataille, Samuel Beckett, and Herman Melville solicit further and other readings, not least because the implications of linguistic passivity, as opposed to those of an eidetic structure, cannot be formalized. Rather, they emerge each time anew through singular contingencies and associations across texts that escape intentionality and cannot themselves be fixed once and for all. In particular, *Passive Voices (On the Subject of Phenomenology and Other Figures of Speech)* retraces how the subjects of phenomenology—in the first instance, "I"—are figures of speech and thus disposed to be affected at every turn by aleatory signifying effects, "citational" associations, and asignificant echoes. The first chapter takes up where the *Cartesian Meditations* leave off, namely, with an exceptional string of citations that begins with the Delphic oracle, "Know thyself," and that ends by lending Augustine the last word of Husserl's book. Following this indication that Augustine introduces the motifs that would prove decisive for phenomenology, the chapter pursues a reading of Augustine's articulations of self, truth, knowledge, and language, along the lines of his "own" recitations and exegeses of the Delphic inscription, "Know thyself." To the extent that Augustine appears as the last speaker of Husserl's text, the *Cartesian Meditations* calls for this preliminary detour through Augustine's oeuvre, whose relevance to phenomenological thought has, to be sure, been underscored by other phenomenological thinkers such as Martin Heidegger, Jean-Luc Marion, Jean-Louis Chrétien, and James K. A. Smith.[82] Yet whereas numerous readings of Augustine and Husserl will have centered upon the significance of confession, memory, and prayer for the thought of the self, the permutations throughout Augustine's oeuvre of the particular syntagm that Husserl cites—namely, "Know thyself"—solicit further elaboration of the consequences of originally receiving word of a "self" from another, as a linguistic event that occurs to "me" before "I" know myself to be at all. Thus, although Augustine calls himself into question in his *Confessions*—"I have been made a question for myself [*mihi quaestio factus sum*]"[83]—he also suggests that self-knowledge could not even begin to be questionable without the language of another, rendering the question of alterity all the more urgent than any concerning "myself." These observations prepare for an analysis of Augustine's descriptions of language acquisition and infancy in the *Confessions* and *De trinitate*, which show that the experience of alterity and the alterity of language do not cease to affect the voice, and in ways that are not quieted or settled with the responses that Christian doctrine may have been seen to provide to the question of the self.

Reading backward from the *Cartesian Meditations* to Augustine may seem initially to lead away from Husserl, yet it is a similarly unsettling experience of language that takes shape through Husserl's analyses of passive synthesis, where voices of alterity are said to be what first calls the *cogito* to life. The second chapter thus furthers the discussions of Augustine by registering the ways in which Husserl's writings on passive synthesis and intersubjectivity testify to appeals and associations that precede intentional acts and expressions of consciousness. In other words, consciousness is affected by the language of others before anyone can know it, let alone know (of) a self. Yet as the readings of Husserl in this chapter also show, the language of alterity does not merely affect whatever may come to be known as "I" but also provokes decisive alterations to the language of phenomenology: for Husserl finds himself compelled to resort to fictions that are unfounded in intuition in order to describe it, while at the same time, his "descriptions" themselves assume the shape of convoluted rhetorical figurations that do not allow for distinctions to be fixed between self and other, *comparatum* and *comparandum*. Especially in drawing out these latter traits of Husserl's analyses of passive synthesis, the chapter complements those elucidating studies that largely underscore embodiment and gesture, such Maurice Merleau-Ponty's *Phenomenology of Perception* and, more recently, Natalie Depraz's *Transcendance et incarnation: Le statut de l'intersubjectivité comme altérité à soi chez Husserl*—as well as those interventions that decenter the cogito by turning to the question of being (Martin Heidegger), the transcendence of the Other (Emmanuel Levinas), the revelation of givenness (Jean-Luc Marion), the pathos of auto-affection (Michel Henry), and the desire that troubles every sign of cognition (Jean-François Lyotard). Taking Husserl's rhetoric for passivity as the subject of inquiry, in particular, allows for critical implications to be unfolded from both Husserl's less-studied manuscripts and more well-known texts, such as the *Cartesian Meditations*, where, for example, the overlapping that is said to take place whenever similar data "recall" or "remind" of one another is characterized as a "living, reciprocal [*wechselseitiges*] awakening-of-one-another; a reciprocal, overlapping [*überschiebendes*] overlaying-upon-one-another [*Sich-Überdecken*] according to their objective sense [*gegenständlichen Sinn*]."[84] In this passage, the changing (*Wechsel*) of sides (*Seiten*) that the very word for "reciprocal [*wechselseitig*]" indicates is at once amplified and crossed through with a hyperbolic "overlaying" that is itself "overlapping," yielding an "over"-perplexing dynamic of communication that can originate from no single, recognizable "side," because each is already "over" with the other to begin with.

If this strange language should render the foundational conditions for not only the associative developments of "objectival sense," but also intersubjectivity and verbal intercourse, as Husserl will imply that it does, then it also "says" that the phenomena of association, intersubjectivity, and verbal communication would be originally unsettled by a passive and arational mode of relating that is carried out among the givens themselves. Since this relationship is characterized as their "awakening" to one another, moreover, their (and, indirectly, "my") first experience of language is thereby also marked off as one that would undo categorial formations before they can be formed: for this awakening is also an initial provocation whose approximation in Husserl's text pushes the categories of syntax—to say nothing of the categorial intuitions upon which they are supposed to be based—to the breaking point. In passages such as this one, Husserl's writings not only found the logos of the subject but also bring it to the founder in advance, deconstructing the structures they appear designed to support, as Jean-François Lyotard would also insist in his critique of Maurice Merleau-Ponty's approach to passivity.[85] And ultimately, those writings may therefore be found to reduce "I" to an unstable figure of speech, among others, whose truth would lie not in the correspondence between intentions and intuitions but in the variable and figural associations that will have exposed every one and every other to a language that none could truly own but only ever share in the passive voice. Before any word can be given of an intersubjective community, the presubjective, anonymous work of language will have brought "us" in touch and entangled "us" with other others than we could know for all our more and less wakeful lives. The rhetorical reading of Husserl that is performed in this chapter thus describes how passive synthesis opens phenomenological study to "the poetic value of passivity" that Derrida had evoked in the contrastive comparison he once drew between Husserl and Joyce.[86] It also opens the question, however, as to how testimonies, conversations, and common speech would need to be read and heard otherwise, from out of their abyssal, passive grounds.

By indicating how language suspends and disrupts the very orders of experience that it otherwise seems to express, Augustine's and Husserl's meditations approach a limit that may be further probed through an examination of writings that register religious and phenomenological thought, while calling the operative notions of those discourses into question through written performances whose infra- and intertextual echoes exceed every single persona and authority. Precisely because an attentive reading of Husserl's rhetoric discloses its eccentricities not to be external to its central themes and claims but to affect it at its (Augustinian) foundations, his writing also speaks to oeuvres other than those he names: for example, writers such as Georges Bataille, Franz Kafka, and Maurice Blanchot, whose prose responds to the problems of phenomenology in the improper, passive, and fictive modes of speaking that will have always more or less implicitly marked it. Along similar lines, Leslie Hill describes Bataille's, Pierre Klossowski's, and Blanchot's writing as interventions "in the discourse of philosophy from a place that hitherto has been relegated outside philosophy,"[87] taking inspiration from a 1978 interview in which Michel Foucault had spoken of the ways in which these writers "shattered" the "founding self-evidence of the subject."[88] Yet before this interview, Foucault would name a slightly different triad of writers toward the end of *The Order of Things*, where he addresses the unthought dimensions of thinking and language that phenomenology and psychoanalysis will have broached:

> And as if this experiencing of the forms of finitude in language were insupportable, or inadequate [. . .] it is within madness that it manifested itself—the figure of finitude offering itself [*se donnant*] in language [. . .] but also before it, preceding it, as that formless, mute, unsignifying region where language can liberate itself. And it is indeed in this space thus disclosed that literature, first with surrealism [. . .] then, more and more purely, with Kafka, with Bataille, with Blanchot, offered itself [*s'est donné*] as experience: as experience of death (and in the element of death), of unthinkable thought (and in its inaccessible presence), of repetition (of original innocence, always there at the nearest and yet always the most distant term of language); as experience of finitude (captured in the opening and the constraint of that finitude).[89]

The emphasis that Foucault places upon "offering" or "giving" (*se donner*) repeats the critical term of phenomenological description; yet here, what is said to offer or give itself as finitude and experience is received by no subject but registered in language. "Experience" could therefore no longer signify anything of the order of conscious knowledge or intuition; rather, it would indicate what occurs through language and to language, whose role as a nonagent and nonpatient in any usual sense of the words also means that its element is death, that its thought is not thought by it, and that its finitude or closure remains indefinitely open.[90] Hence, it is not even Kafka, Bataille, or Blanchot themselves but "*with* Kafka, *with* Bataille, *with* Blanchot" that literature is said to give itself (as) an experience in Foucault and to let this experience alter the way in which (literary) language speaks. Such modes of givenness, experience, alteration, and alterity imply in yet another way that language speaks not only blindly, as Derrida had said, but also and initially in the passive voice, where speech undergoes its (self-) alteration. What Foucault's rhetorical gestures indicate still more pronouncedly than his arguments, however, is that the passivity and alterity of speech also could not be adequately characterized or conceptualized in general but only expressed and "experienced" through singular written performances. The following three chapters of this book therefore seek to address the implications of passive voices for experience, both singular and shared, through the language of selected fictions penned by each of the writers whom Foucault names, drawing the consequences of not only Foucault's, but also Husserl's, Augustine's, and Derrida's writings on the subject. At the same time, the readings that are offered of Bataille's *L'Abbé C.*, Kafka's *The Castle*, and Blanchot's *Aminadab*—and especially, the readings that are offered of their reciprocal overlapping—accentuate the passive voices of these texts in new ways for readers of literature.

The first of these chapters retraces the ways in which Bataille's notion of scissiparity modifies Husserl's notion of intersubjective "pairing," when it comes to articulating the structures of identity and alterity. Unlike the presupposition of a primordial proper sphere from which Husserl departs when it comes to "my" engagement with another "I," Bataille borrows the foreign term for unicellular reproduction, showing through both his terminology and argumentation how the identity of each living being would have to be cut through with difference. This difference is necessarily suffered in a way that could never be assimilated into conscious experience, since it cannot "itself" be identified for thought: no traditional logic can accommodate the notion that one being may double by being split, or that replication both eliminates the original and leaves two of the "same" in its place. In formal terms, scissiparity would translate to the impossible equation: $a = a' + a'' = -a + -a$. If scissiparity could hardly be thinkable, however, it can nonetheless be imparted in writing, as Bataille's literary prose indicates perhaps more precisely than his theoretical essays, and especially the fiction of autobiographical testimony that plays out in his novel about two identical and self-divided twins, *L'Abbé C*. The chapter concludes with a reading of the divisions that mark not only the embedded and discordant first-person narratives that make up the text but also the narrating voices themselves, which repeatedly suffer breaches and allow others to cut in.

The structural plurivocity of Bataille's novel would, as such, have to extend beyond the nominal personae who figure within it, which trait becomes perhaps most pronounced in a remarkable passage toward the end of *L'Abbé C.*, where one of the twin protagonists entertains and then rejects the thought of burning the scattered papers that his deceased twin had left behind. The initial thought occurs to the surviving brother as if from out of nowhere, marking Bataille's fiction with an especially pronounced trace of foreignness that invites associations with other texts, such as Max Brod's afterword to Kafka's *The Trial*, where Brod pleads his case for not burning Kafka's manuscripts, despite documents testifying to Kafka's wish that he destroy them. This split from within *L'Abbé C.* is the point of departure for the next chapter, where the bifurcation that opens Bataille's oeuvre to Brod's and Kafka's writings is explored as a more radical instance of "scissiparous" language than those that more obviously appear to affect Bataille's fictive personae. Its radicality emerges from and not despite the fact that the resemblance between the words of Bataille's narrator and Brod's afterword is neither authorized nor precluded by Bataille's language but merely admitted at the limit of his narrative logic. Beyond any dichotomy between the archival preservation of papers and their annihilation, the traces of Kafka and Brod in Bataille's novel thus occur in a way that can neither be confirmed nor denied on the basis of evidence—not unlike the constitutive blindness of testimony, as Derrida would describe it.

But Bataille's literary fiction does not merely offer exemplary instances of the split and passive character of narrating voices; for it also echoes what he would elsewhere say of Kafka's novels: "They are books for the fire [*pour le feu*], objects for which the truth of being on fire is lacking; they are there, but they are there in order to disappear [*pour disparaître*], as though they have already been annihilated."[91] This succinct commentary prepares a way to approach Kafka's fictional writing along the lines of its vanishing traces, its withdrawal from evidence, its effacement of subjective authority, and its indefinite splitting of voices. These issues already emerge through the diary entries and aphorisms where Kafka—at times in the first person—broaches the notion of "inner" experience that had been developed by the major figures in proto-phenomenological empirical psychology whom he had studied during and beyond his university years. Subjective interiority figures in Kafka's notes as the unsteady, if not fictive, effect of external resonances and inscriptions, whose repercussions will be multiplied perhaps most dramatically when these quasi-personal records give way to the novelistic fiction of *The Castle*, where the initial "I" is crossed through and replaced with the signature "K." From the outset, namely, the first-person subject appears placed under erasure, just as "I" or "K." is about to cross a bridge into the realm of the eponymous "castle"; but this effacement of the subject is precisely what allows the text to give testimony to another experience of language, where no single instance of speech or narration could be decisive. Hence, as many perceptive readers such as Charles Bernheimer, Stanley Corngold, Malte Kleinwort, Henry Sussman, and Joseph Vogl have recognized, K.'s trajectory bifurcates into "a" story of multiple circulating legends, none of which is or could be privileged upon the basis of experience or evidence.[92] Yet what is less often explored are the consequences of the fact that the equally plausible and mutually incompatible variants of "K.'s" story are not only told *of* K. but are also told *to* K., yielding paradoxical situations that expose what it would mean for a "subject" to be constituted—and deconstructed—through encounters that cast him as a variable figure of speech.

The plurality of voices that intersect and interfere with one another in Kafka's various fictions of the subject provokes the question of the truth that may nevertheless lie in a collection of passive voices: the truth that Aristotle presupposes when he asserts that the passions of the soul are the same for all and that Kafka more tentatively approaches with an aphoristic remark on confession: "Confession and lie are alike. In order to be able to confess, one lies. One cannot express that which one is, for one is just that: one can only impart that which one is not, that is, a lie. A certain truth may lie only in a chorus."[93] Once the possibility of knowing, confessing, or expressing oneself is excluded in this way, however, choral truth could be predicated upon neither subjective certitude nor a certain intersubjective basis. Its chances would instead rest solely in the cumulative utterance of that which no one could utter alone or even know oneself to have said in part. The rumors and stories of K. that circulate throughout *The Castle* already expose the fragility of this chance for shared truth, but it is Maurice Blanchot's early novel from 1942, *Aminadab*, which still more vocally places choral truth at stake in ways that are analyzed in the last chapter. Both in its broader strokes and specific lines, *Aminadab* has been read as a further permutation of the language, logic, and situations that play out in Kafka's *Castle*, whether their more or less pronounced similarities are interpreted as an effect of imitation, as Jean-Paul Sartre suggested in his review of *Aminadab*,[94] or whether they are taken for indications of what Paul Davies has characterized as Kafka's and Blanchot's "apprenticeship" in the indefinite "movement" of writing.[95] But among those traits which Blanchot's and Kafka's novels share, the most marked one may be the openness of their writing to echoes, which Blanchot amplifies by setting his novel in a boarding house described as an "immense sonorous cage."[96] This sonorous enclosure opens to any number of voices, but unlike the house of language that Heidegger would famously address, it unsettles everyone and everything that may seem to speak or be: instead, each utterance rebounds with repercussions that yield a situation where there is no first-, second-, or third-person speech that is not passively disposed toward echoes and distortions from the outset. Hence, it is not only that no one could answer but also that no one could ask the question, "Who are you?" that reverberates through *Aminadab* like a parody of the proverbial imperative "Know thyself," or the less proverbial aphorism, "Confession and lie are alike." Yet it is because and not despite of the fact that echoes proliferate in lieu of personal questions and claims that *Aminadab* opens a literary space for exploring the chances for choral truth that Kafka had invoked.

The movements of language that are traced, imparted, echoed, and parsed through Blanchot's writing expose what the texts of Augustine, Husserl, Bataille, and Kafka will have indicated for their part as well: namely, that language abandons its speakers to occurrences of pairing and parting that cross the limits of subjective experience and intersubjective communication and that thus come to pass with every instance and figure of speech as a passion that no subject could know to suffer. But as the unprincipled contingencies of language dispossess speakers of the very words that escape them, they also hold speech open for alterity, for speaking otherwise, and for impossible encounters that may put them in touch beyond all appearance and to no one's knowledge. Drawn together, the writings of Augustine, Husserl, Bataille, Kafka, and Blanchot thus trace an exemplary history of those encounters that can only take place in the passive voice.

Chapter 1

"Self"-Citations in Husserl and Augustine

After introducing the idea of science, the principle of evidence, the structure of intentionality, the phenomenological reduction, the genesis of the concrete ego, and the constitution of an alter ego, Edmund Husserl's *Cartesian Meditations: An Introduction to Phenomenology* conclude with a final return not to the self of the meditations, properly speaking, but to the word of "self" that is given in famous passages drawn from early and late antiquity: "The Delphic saying, 'Know thyself!' has won a new meaning. Positive science is a science lost in the world. One must lose the world through the epoché in order to win it again by a universal self-examination. 'Noli foras ire,' says Augustine, 'in te redi, in interiore homine habitat veritas.'"[1] (Das Delphische Wort γνῶθι σεαυτόν hat eine neue Bedeutung gewonnen. Positive Wissenschaft ist Wissenschaft in der Weltverlorenheit. Man muß erst die Welt durch ἐποχή verlieren, um sie in universaler Selbstbesinnung wiederzugewinnen. *Noli foras ire*, sagt Augustin, *in te redi, in interiore homine habitat veritas*.)[2] With this flourish of quotations, Husserl's "introduction to phenomenology" ultimately leads beyond the field of transcendental subjectivity that can be accessed through the "systematic self-investigation [*systematische Selbstbesinnung*]" of the "pure ego [*reine[n] ego*]" alone.[3] To be sure, certain impurities were implicit in Husserl's "systematic self-investigation" long before his conclusion, insofar as the *Cartesian Meditations* were never meditations per se but a script for thinking, whose specifically phenomenological sense would need to be constituted by each reader anew: as Husserl's assistant Eugen Fink would write in his *Sixth Cartesian Meditation*, "reports of phenomenological research [. . .] can only be 'read' at all by re-performing the investigations themselves."⁴ Hence, all phenomenological writings would be other than the mind of which they speak and foreign to any "self," both before and after any self-investigations that they may provoke or guide. Yet it is when Husserl claims that the "meaning" of traditional philosophical sayings has been renewed through the meditative performance that he has just spelled out that the historical and linguistic dimensions of "subjective" immanence are rendered most pronounced. For if these hitherto unspoken sayings were at stake all along, then each reiterated call to turn inward also recalls that phenomenology will have never been "pure" of the "sedimented forms" that make up both the terms of everyday speech and the history of European philosophy, whose examination Husserl will later designate "the philosopher's genuine self-reflection [*echte Selbstbesinnung*]" in his posthumously published *Crisis of the European Sciences*. "Genuine self-reflection," in other words, would always have to begin elsewhere than with any "self" and entail other voices than one's "own" from the outset.⁵

What is not said, however, through either Husserl's final gestures of citation in the *Cartesian Meditations* or his discussions of tradition in *The Crisis of the European Sciences*, is what citations would mean for phenomenological writing when they are not subject to analysis but interwoven into the texture of phenomenological thought in an unthematic way. Even if Husserl's conclusion to the *Cartesian Meditations* should anticipate his later claims that phenomenology not only retraces the operations of the "pure ego" but also "inquir[es] back into the primal establishment" of traditional "forms,"⁶ the rhetorical implications of his *cento* exceed any implicit archaeology of meaning they may be meant to exemplify. Beyond any single ideal or contextual sense they may have borne, for instance, the disparate phrases that Husserl weaves together also suggest that the *logos* of phenomenology transcends not only disparate times but also divergent linguistic idioms, from Ancient Greek to postclassical Latin. At the same time, Husserl's specific appeal to the "Delphic saying, Know thyself!" implies the more dramatic claim that phenomenological philosophy provides the ultimate answer to the one of first oracular words of wisdom to be recorded in the West—that the cognizing "I" of Husserl's *Meditations* answers the "thy" of the Delphic imperative—as if Husserl were following Aristotle's advice on the rhetorical use of commonplaces: "It is also necessary to speak words of wisdom against popular sayings ([. . .] such as 'know thyself' and 'nothing in excess'), whenever one's character would likely appear better."⁷And in addition to those marked quotations that draw the texts of Husserl, the Delphic oracle, and Augustine into "direct" dialogue, the resonance between

Husserl's last words of "winning" and the final lines of *The Communist Manifesto*, "The proletarians have nothing to lose but their chains. They have a world to win [*eine Welt zu gewinnen*],"[8] further suggests that it is not historical dialectics but the science of phenomenology that promises to revolutionize the world, as Husserl's more politically minded admirer Arnold Metzger had emphatically argued in 1919.[9]

Without directly stating these claims, let alone arguing for them, the final paragraph of Husserl's *Meditations* nevertheless allows them to suggest themselves through those citations which, as such, open his text to associations that diverge from the lineage of philosophical "self-reflection" he may have intended to trace. Beyond what it manifestly says, the text may thus convey a prophetic or revolutionary pathos that could neither be confirmed nor denied, precisely because it is not of the order of the proposition but rather emerges as a possible rhetorical effect. In this way, the citations that mark "Husserl's" last words also mark a departure from the strict expression of intuitive evidence that he otherwise recommends, while betraying the ambivalence to which all intentional acts of exposition cannot but be passively exposed. Husserl's "introduction to phenomenology" thus introduces the vicissitudes of language that render the phenomenological subject a figure of speech, called upon by gestures of direct address ranging from the Delphic oracle to Augustine and Marx. Whatever Husserl may or may not have had in mind in writing the conclusion to the *Cartesian Meditations*, taking him at "his" word thus indicates that an approach to phenomenology, as well as the new "meaning" that it will have given old words, solicits an examination that leads back to the other voices, texts, topoi, and tropes that are placed at stake and set in play within it. And if such a reduction would seem to lead away from the pursuit of "self"-knowledge that transcendental phenomenology was designed to undertake, an outward turn is nonetheless demanded by the inward turn that Husserl enjoins his readers to take via Augustine, just as the cited imperative to "Know thyself" demands coming to terms with the citational character of "self-knowledge."

As Husserl's last words of the *Cartesian Meditations* suggest, the imperative to mind yourself and know your mind will have made its mark on thinking with those minimal, commanding words inscribed on the temple at Delphi—"know thyself," γνῶθι σεαυτόν, *nosce te*—which called upon a "self" to be the object of knowledge before any metaphysical, critical, or phenomenological theory of the "subject," and which rendered theoretical insight secondary to a practical, do-it-"yourself" project.[10] In the *Charmides*, Plato's dialogue on σωφροσύνη or "moderation"—if that is what the Greek word should mean—Critias interprets the Delphic inscription to be mean "be temperate [σωφρόνει]," and to function not as a bidding, but as a "greeting," like the quasi-imperative "welcome! [χαῖρε]": "this inscription," he says, "appears to me to have been dedicated for the following purpose, as though it were a greeting from the god to those coming in in place of the usual 'Hail' [χαῖρε], as though to say 'hail' were an incorrect greeting, but we should rather urge one another to 'be temperate' [σωφρονεῖν]."[11] The unclarified virtue of σωφροσύνη is thus said to translate the unclarified inscription on self-knowledge, which should itself transcend any single speaking instance, if it is true that those who enter the temple are meant to "urge one another" in this way, thereby making both "be moderate [σωφρόνει]" and "know thyself [γνῶθι σεαυτόν]" into excessive and deficient scripts—at once redundant and in need of repetition—while rendering "self-knowledge" as well as its more "moderate" variant all the more obscure.[12]

Centuries later, Augustine returns to the oracular dictum in his early Cassiacum-dialogues;[13] his *Confessions*;[14] and, most notably, his discussions of noesis in *De trinitate*, where "Know thyself [*Cognosce te ipsam*]" is understood as a reminder of the presence of mind to the mind. "Not as if absent should [the mind] seek to perceive itself [*cernere*]," he admonishes, "but [it] should take care to discern [*discernere*] itself as present."[15] Such passages as this one reflect the close attention that Augustine not only demands but also devotes to the immanent evidence of mental life, whose proximity to phenomenological thought is made explicit not only through Husserl's recourse to Augustine at the close of the *Cartesian Meditations* but also through his praise for Augustine's investigations into time at the opening of his lectures on internal time-consciousness,[16] and again through his recitation of Augustine's words on the primacy of love in his manuscripts on ethics: "Augustine: only love makes one have the power of sight—for value and ideal. No one is known if not by friendship."[17] Unlike the Cartesian certitude of the mind that Husserl would renew, however, Augustine reduces the mind to its life,[18] which the mind does not own or give itself but rather owes to God beyond its comprehension. Hence, as Jean-Luc Marion argues, Augustine describes a mind that "knows itself certainly to be and to exist, but so as to sense all the more evidently that this Being and this existence, no more than the thought that assures it of them, do not give it to a self or give a *self* to it."[19] Or, as it said more concisely "in the beginning" of the Gospel of John and recited in Augustine's *De trinitate* "in Him was life, and life was the light of men, and the light shone in the shadows, and the shadows did not comprehend it."[20] In Augustine's oeuvre, the imperative to "know thyself" thus translates to an imperative to turn oneself to God, in distinction to both the public orientation that Critias describes in Plato's dialogue on σωφροσύνη, as well as the transcendental turn that the phrase will take in Husserl.

None of these divergent diagnoses is excluded, strictly speaking, by the at once cryptic and gnomic inscription, "Know thyself," which gives no word to clarify who is meant by "you," or what it means to "know." The oracular saying instead makes next to nothing known, except that the knowing in question has yet to be done; that self-knowledge could therefore be no automatic given; and that the imperative of another is what solicits "self" and "knowledge" alike, which would otherwise be unspeakable, if not unthinkable, if it were not for the language that first allows for them to be addressed. Hence, when Marcus Tullius Cicero interprets the "self" that is invoked by the Delphic maxim to signify the "soul" in his *Tusculan Disputations*—a mediating text between Plato, with whom Cicero's writing is in explicit dialogue, and Augustine, who will repeatedly recur to Cicero's oeuvre—he speaks to the dialogic character of the original inscription, writing, "We are not bodies, nor do I speak to your body in speaking to you. Thus when [Apollo's precept] says, *know thyself*, it says: *Know your soul* [*Nosce animum tuum*]."[21] But if the gesture of address thus receives greater emphasis in Cicero than it had in Plato, Cicero does not address the further implication of the imperative as such: namely, that self-knowledge may depend not only upon another self but also upon the language that allows for the self to be called and that differs from any self to speak of. Instead, Cicero passes over the self-less trait of the Delphic inscription that his formulation had nonetheless drawn out as he shifts attention to the soul's "power of memory, mind, and thought,"[22] and as he goes on to deny the receptivity of the soul that Apollo's precept presupposes, casting the body as "a sort of vessel or receptacle for the soul," while reiterating the active character of the latter: "from out of your soul, whatever is enacted, it is enacted from out of you."[23] It is in this way that Cicero avoids entering into the consequences of the notion that the soul may be affected by other matters such as words, but in so doing, he leaves an unresolved tension between the contingent situation that he cites as evidence for the identity of self and soul—"when [Apollo's precept] says, *know thyself*"—and the essential properties the soul should innately know itself to have: "Thus the soul senses itself being moved, and when it senses that, it senses this: that it is itself moved of its own force, not another, nor can it befall it that it deserts itself. From this, [its] eternity follows."[24]

Yet even though Cicero appeals only in passing to the language of address that "Know thyself" asks one to understand—before and beside oneself—the suggestion is nevertheless offered that the Delphic inscription solicits one to consider not only oneself but also itself and, with it, the relation between such a scripted imperative and the self-knowledge that it seems to command. It is this complex relation that Augustine will address at length, when he echoes the language of both the Delphic inscription and Cicero's *Tusculan Disputations* in the tenth book of *De trinitate*:

> Not then, as if being absent should [the mind] seek to perceive itself, but [it] should take care to discern itself as present. Not as if it did not know itself should it seek to recognize itself, but it should diagnose of itself what it knows to be other. For when it hears this itself [*Ipsum enim quod audit*]: *know thyself* [*Cognosce te ipsam*], in what way will it take care to act, if it does not know either what *know* is, or what *thyself* is? But if it knows both of the two, it also knows itself, since it is not said to the mind, *Know thyself*, as if it were said, "Know the cherubim and seraphim"; for of these absent things we hold beliefs according to what has been said before [*praedicantur*]: that they are certain celestial powers. Nor as if it were said, "Know the will of that man," which for us is in no way present to be sensed or understood, if not by bodily signs that are given out, and even at that, it is such that we believe more than we understand. Nor is it so, as if it were said to a human: "See your face," which cannot be done, unless in a mirror. For even our own face is absent from our look, since it is not where [our look] can be directed. But when it is said to the mind: *Know thyself*, in the same stroke [*eo ictu*] it understands what is said with *thyself* [*te ipsam*] and knows itself [*cognoscit se ipsam*], not on account of anything other than what is present to it. If, then, this is said and not understood, then surely it is not done. This, then, is made precept for [the mind] [*praecipitur ei*], so that it does what it [is told] when it understands the precept itself [*praeceptum ipsum*].[25]

> Non itaque velut absentem se quaerat cernere, sed praesentem se curet discernere. Nec se quasi non norit cognoscat, sed ab eo quod alterum novit dinoscat. Ipsum enim quod audit: *Cognosce te ipsam [mentem]*, quomodo agere curabit si nescit aut quid sit: *cognosce*; aut quid sit *te ipsam*? Si autem utrumque novit, novit et se ipsam; quia non ita dicitur menti: *Cognosce te ipsam*, sicut dicitur: "Cognosce cherubim et seraphim"; de absentibus enim illis credimus secundum quod caelestes quaedam potestates esse praedicantur. Neque sicut dicitur: "Cognosce voluntatem illius hominis," quae nobis nec ad sentiendum ullo modo nec ad intellegendum praesto est nisi corporalibus signis editis; et hoc ita, ut magis credamus quam intellegamus. Neque ita ut dicitur homini: "Vide faciem tuam," quod nisi in speculo fieri non potest. Nam et ipsa nostra facies absens ab aspectu nostro est, quia non ibi est quo ille dirigi potest. Sed cum dicitur menti: *Cognosce te ipsam*, eo ictu quo intellegit quod dictum est: *te ipsam*, cognoscit se ipsam; nec ob aliud quam eo quod sibi praesens est. Si autem quod dictum est non intellegit, non utique facit. Hoc igitur ei praecipitur ut faciat quod cum praeceptum ipsum intellegit facit.[26]

Taking up the precept that was hitherto attributed Apollo, Augustine presents the well-known dictum, "Know thyself," as the anonymous and iterable phrase that it always must have been, had it ever been read and understood. He thus makes no reference to a particular source—Apolline or otherwise—since it is not primarily the wisdom of a god that the phrase imparts. Rather, the focus is on "you," whose knowledge "you" are merely reminded to recall, while the imperative demands nothing other than a hearing. For its aim will have been fulfilled "in the same stroke [*eo ictu*]" that it reaches "you," presuming that "you" do not miss a beat in comprehending each word, or at the very least, "thyself." Unlike the words for "cherubim and seraphim" or the will of another mind, which may command belief but must remain inaccessible to direct knowledge—unlike words which convey "signitive intentions," but permit no originary intuitive fulfillment,[27] as Husserl would argue—the occasional expression "thyself" means the subject to whom it is addressed, and for whom self-awareness should have always already been intuitively given, through the prereflexive, unthematic consciousness that Immanuel Kant, Franz

Brentano, and Husserl would later find again to accompany every act of mind.[28] If the utterance of *Cognosce te ipsam* effectively does anything—if it is "made precept" in order to "make" something occur—then it is the sheer fact, Augustine suggests, that it calls oneself to mind, whenever it is encountered.[29]

The closer one attends to this "precept," then, the more it appears to be utterly superfluous for those in the know, who are also the only ones to whom this tautology of self-knowledge—this tautology of autology—could ever speak. In this respect, the sign for "thyself" says nothing new; rather, it presupposes knowledge of its referent, as Augustine elsewhere insists that all words do, if they should "teach" us anything, rather than demanding mere belief. "When, namely, a sign is given to me, if it finds me not knowing the thing whose sign it is, it can teach me nothing [*Cum enim signum mihi datur, si nescientem me invenit, cuius rei signum sit, docere me nihil potest*],"[30] Augustine tells his son Adeodatus in his earlier dialogue, *De magistro (On the Teacher)*. Yet it is this very structure of presupposition that, upon closer analysis, complicates the automatic fulfillment that appears to be self-evident from Augustine's claims on self-knowledge. On the one hand, as scholars such as Phillip Cary have argued, Augustine's remarks on signs appear to show "the notion that I learn things from signs [to be] entirely backwards"[31]: if signs nonetheless play a role in teaching, as Augustine insists, then they can do so only insofar as teachers use them to "show you where to look by asking you questions and getting you to rethink your answers until you see the point for yourself."[32] On the other hand, this assumption that signs serve only a mnemonic or admonitory function merely defers the question as to where our innate memory and knowledge should come from, whose further elaborations in Augustine's corpus will suggest that the mind neither eventually nor initially sees anything for itself. As Augustine will reiterate in and beyond *De magistro*, the inner illumination that permits us to judge not only the "reports" of the senses but also the verbal messages that we receive[33]—and that allows us to intuit eidetic structures such as "unity and equality" as well[34]—comes from "the Truth within, which is Christ."[35] Inner illumination thus ultimately rests upon faith, with the consequence that insight into the truth would always be itself unverifiable, however surely one might believe oneself to know it.[36] This is most likely why even Augustine's teaching on "Truth" is itself not a claim that he offers from personal insight but that he recites from the Gospel of Matthew: "Neither call yourselves teachers since your one teacher is Christ [*nec vocemini magistri quia magister vester unus est Christus*" (Mt. 23.10).³⁷ And it is similarly in light of the alterity that turns out to be at the origin of *both* signs *and* intuitive insights that Jacques Lacan would draw an analogy between Augustine's dialogue on "teaching" and the "dialectic of truth which lies at the heart of the analytic discovery": "In the presence of speech which we hear," namely, "we find ourselves in extremely paradoxical situations—not knowing if they are true or not, whether or not to stand by truth, to refute them or accept them, or to put them in doubt."³⁸

As with our knowledge of self, the most intimate truth places us in the "paradoxical situation" where only external sources let it be divined. But by implicating "truth" and "self" in citational rhetoric—in all senses of "citation," from "summons" to "quotation" and "reference"—Augustine's oeuvre also prompts questions concerning signification and selfhood that permit a radical reexamination of the subjective foundations of phenomenology from out of the abyssal area that opens within language. What sort of knowledge would correspond to this dilemma of our lives? Is the "self" ever truly "self"-evident, or would this truth likewise be a matter of faith in the end? If consciousness could ever be certain of itself, then why would this certitude not simply go without saying? Why do "I" need to be cited and summoned through "you" in order to find myself?

Given the linguistic point of departure he adopts, it is accordingly a proto-phenomenological description not of immanent experience but of different instances of verbal understanding that initially allows Augustine to suggest that self-knowledge is uniquely privileged, as he distinguishes "Know thyself" from imperatives to know of beings that transcend intuitive experience, such as angels and other minds. At the same time, however, Augustine will also set "thyself" apart from those perceptible matters that may be known through the senses: if the mind were, he argues, made up of fire or air as the Stoics had claimed it to be,³⁹ then "it would know" fire or air "otherwise than the rest [. . .] by some interior [. . .] true presence," which it does not in fact do: instead, Augustine observes, no corporeal things are held in the mind as such, but only their mental simulacra.⁴⁰ What is signified with "thyself" is therefore not something that can be pointed out, like "fire" or the "head," whose reiterated pronunciation, accompanied with demonstrative gestures, is described in *De magistro* to exemplify the teaching of signs.⁴¹ Not even particular lived experiences could be known "otherwise" than our representations of other things, as Brian Stock shows in his commentary on Augustine's *Confessions*, where the "life-informing *process*" of interpretation takes precedence over "the *content* of [the] narrative," and where remembrance itself unfolds as a primarily "interpretive process" that yields no certitude but rather requires "faith [. . .] in inner discourse."[42]

The verbal gestures that Augustine recites thus approximate a self whose memories and experiences largely withdraw in this way from the scope of evidence. But if this withdrawal would therefore seem to render one's own mind more similar than Augustine may seem to admit to the unknowable will of another man, he will go on to argue that the very operations that the mind performs in understanding the phrase, "Know thyself," would not only certify that one exists and lives but also indicate that the life of the mind consists of the "remember[ing], and understand[ing], and will[ing]" that it will have done in the process, irrespective of any other matters that one may remember, understand, or will.[43] And if these operations would also be at work in understanding any other phrase—including expressions of self-doubt[44]—it is the imperative to "know thyself" alone that should call nothing else to mind but its own doing, which cannot itself be expressed but only realized in response. It is, moreover, no mental lapse but the perpetual involvement of memory, intellect, and will that renders the life of the mind impossible to express or expose. For on the one hand, every outward sign that one may give of one's mind could only be understood through mental acts on the parts of others, which would attest to their presence of mind but could not guarantee one's own. And on the other hand, the self-involvement of our respective remembering, understanding, and willing could not be thought in separation from the mental life that they make up, nor could they be made into an object or contrasted with another state of mind without being implicated themselves. The mind thus works incognito as it keeps to itself,[45] which is also why "thyself" cannot be spoken of but only spoken to when Augustine addresses the mind;[46] just as it is why Augustine cannot exclude the possibility that the message, "Know thyself," may always be missed: "If, then, this is said and not understood, then surely it is not done."[47]

But this is also not to say that the words "Know thyself" are not imperative for the realization of what we really are and really do all time, often unbeknownst to ourselves. Early in his discussion of the subject, Augustine explicitly addresses the question, "Why, then, is it a precept for [the mind] that it know itself?"[48] And he proceeds to respond by drawing a distinction between knowing and thinking—"it is one thing not to know oneself, another not to think oneself"[49]—which difference opens the possibility for the mind to know itself, even as it directs its thoughts elsewhere, to the point where the *cogito* can confuse itself beyond all recognition with the other things it thinks about. "So great is the force of love," he explains, "that [the mind] attracts to itself those things which it has thought for a long time with love and to which it has adhered with the glue of care [*curae glutino*], even when it returns in some way to think itself."[50] As Marion has argued at length, love and desire exercise a privilege over thinking for Augustine, as that which orients the direction of thought and thus decides its intentionality before any possible conscious decision on its part.[51] The effects of desire are so far-reaching that the mind sticks to what it loves and mistakes itself its love objects, even when it thinks that it is thinking of itself. Thus, self-reflection becomes indefinitely more complicated than phenomenological thought could intuit: if Husserl had sought to unearth those historical sedimentations that accumulate and affect the notions of everyday life and modern science, Augustine implicates the mind itself in a process where the agglutination of love objects covers over its proper awareness and fashions its self-perception in their likeness. And once consciousness itself accrues "sedimented" meanings in this most intimate way, then it is no longer able to reenact the original constitution of those meanings "through its own self-reflection," as Husserl presumes every "autonomous thinker" or "self-thinker [*Selbstdenker*]" to be at least capable of doing.[52] More radical than even the "radical skeptical epoché" that Husserl attributes to Descartes,[53] Augustine's meditations lead to the recognition that the mind can always fail to acknowledge itself and default to others in its very "presence," unless, perhaps, it is called out: "Know thyself."

Because the preeminent "presence" of mind to itself consists in what the mind does when it remembers, thinks, and loves, it should be logically and ontologically anterior to every other presence or absence of which it could be cognizant—"Nothing is more present [*praesentius*] to the mind than itself,"[54] Augustine insists—but because this "presence" is ignored as the mind gets caught up in its acts, he will also call it not "consciousness," but "memory," upon the premise that the mind will have "never desisted" from being in store for itself, even when its thoughts are directed elsewhere and it knows not what it does.[55] This "memory" therefore does not comprise past impressions but a sort of knowledge that belongs to all times and no time, present or past: "In no way could [Ulysses] have remembered himself if present things did not pertain to memory,"[56] Augustine explains in a gloss on Virgil's lines from Book 3 of the *Aeneid*, "Nor did Ulysses suffer such things, nor did the Ithacan forget himself in so great a danger."[57] Such is the "memory of the present" with which Étienne Gilson finds Augustine to modify the Platonic notion of "anamnesis" and to approach the Freudian notion of the unconscious but that Augustine founds neither in a Platonic myth of preexistence nor in the experiences of involuntary memories.[58] Instead, this memory is founded in the "inner master" of Christ, who is thought to make up the life, being, and truth of the mind.[59] Thus, Augustine explicitly derives human memory from the Trinity, or the divine "memory, intelligence, [and] love or will" in whose "image" man was made,[60] where "memory" should refer not to any latent knowledge, but to the "principle"[61] or "essence"[62] of the coeternal Word, wisdom, and knowledge that the Father eternally "begets" with love.[63]

But whereas God can therefore always say of himself, "I am who I am [*ego sum qui sum*],"[64] "I" need to be told to know "myself," since God's mind is eternally one, while "my" mind is divided at all times between the unconscious scope of "my" knowledge and "my" present gaze;[65] since "my" memory of "my" being would therefore be the more or less unthought dimension of "my" ever-changing mind; and since "my" divergent desires may draw "my" attention away again at any given moment. With this structure in mind, it would thus seem that precisely when I would need it most, no reminder of "my" presence could be recalled on "my" part, because "I" would be lost in other thoughts. And it may even be further testimony to the contingency of immanent "memory" upon external reminders that Augustine does not speak of it from experience in *De trinitate* but deduces it through an analysis of verses from Virgil's *Aeneid*: just as insight into Christ as our inner teacher is cited from the gospels in *De magistro*, and the recollection oneself is excited through the imperative-citation, namely, "Know thyself." Within the broader context of Augustine's thinking, then, it could be said that any hearing and understanding of the latter phrase in "the same stroke [*eo ictu*]" neither coincides with the arrival of new knowledge[66] nor confirms familiar thoughts: instead, this invocation of "my" ever-immanent yet forgotten memory would mark a cut in the present of "my" thinking and being, breaking "my" current train of thought and splicing together "my" realization with the "self" which will have been latent to "me." What forms a substantial union in the God of the Trinity, in other words, can only occur to "me" in the form of a "syncope" that is analogous to the combination of "putting-together" and "cutting [. . .] away" which Jean-Luc Nancy would articulate in his reading of Descartes's famous dictum, "I think, I exist."[67] There, too, self-knowledge is affected by the difference language makes, as "the subject identifies itself with the (thinking) substance and distinguishes itself from it *at the same time*" through the "first-person statement that alone makes the position possible: I am me who is substance."[68] In the situation that Augustine describes, however, it is a question of rejoining "myself" in "my" thought upon the injunction of another, whose intervention renders the Augustinian "mind" more explicitly exposed to alterity than the "ego" of Descartes's first-person speech. For besides the contingency of self-cognizance upon another instance of speech,[69] there is the "stroke" (*ictus*) of the address that one must suffer, whose impact is independent of both speaker and addressee, rendering the experience of self and language irreducible to any meaning that could be identified or comprehended and affecting both with a passion which opens the moment of self-recollection to indefinite possibilities of default and dispersion.[70]

What Augustine's words suggest is that there could be no memory of a time before language,[71] no minding of knowledge before admonishment, and therefore no instance of thinking that is not affected by the striking words of others, as well as gestures of signification that may be other than words. This thought will become more pronounced, when Augustine considers infants in the fourteenth book of *De trinitate*, whose flesh responds to all varieties of sensual solicitation, yet without so much as the slightest awareness of being glued to those attractions: "They do not know of their own interior, nor can they be admonished so that they do so, since they do not know the signs of admonition, where words hold the principle place."[72] The infant's need for "signs of admonition" is especially acute, since infantile oblivion turns out to be unlike any other. Adults may forget various things, including the present moment, as when I have read "a page or a letter but did not know what I was reading," because "the memory was not applied to the sense of the body as the sense itself is applied to the letters."[73] But this lacuna in memorable experience would not be possible if the adult mind were not occupied with other memories that divert it from the current, passing moment: as Augustine puts it, my "will" gives its "nod of assent [*nutu voluntatis*]" to other things.[74] Memory is therefore not only "the condition of present thought" for Augustine, as scholars such as David Tell have similarly observed;[75] it is also the condition of forgetting as we know it; and it consists in the retention of referential traces—the "notation [*notare*]" of significant impressions[76]—which renders memory a structure whose linguistic character would be illegible to infants.[77] The immemorial character of infantile life even renders uncertain the immanent "memory" of oneself that Augustine otherwise insists upon but that could not be tested, let alone affirmed or denied, concerning that forgotten age: "But let us omit this age, which cannot be questioned about what goes on within it, and which we have forgotten [*obliti sumus*] to a great extent."[78] This oblivion instead marks the radical hiatus that Giorgio Agamben would ascribe to human history from its infancy: "The enigma which infancy ushered in for man" entails that "[h]istory cannot be the continuous progress of speaking humanity through linear time, but in its essence is hiatus, discontinuity, *epoché*."[79]

Thus, even as an infant may appear to be "excessively" intent upon certain things such as a "night-light [*nocturnum lumen*]," which "it begins to sense through the bodily senses with all the more pleasure, the more that the pleasure is new,"[80] each present sensation would also be lost on it every time; its activity would be a passionate dispersion; and the so-called novelty that it seeks would name no sensible quality but would signify the correlate to its void and "avid [*auida*]" mind. The attraction to nocturnal luminosity that Augustine evokes here would thus be itself benighted,[81] closer to the abyssal gaze that Maurice Blanchot describes toward the beginning of his novel *Thomas the Obscure* than to light and life of God that Augustine will elsewhere recite from Scripture: "His eye, useless for seeing, took on extraordinary proportions, developed beyond measure, and, extending over the horizon, let the night penetrate into its center to create an iris. And so, through this void, it was sight and the object of sight which mingled together."[82] In order for even a first glimmer of illumination to be possible, let alone any self-recollection, the infant would need to note the difference, repetition, and reference that constitute the first signs of memory and that organize Augustine's articulation of love as well: "Just as a word indicates something and indicates itself as well, but a word cannot indicate itself unless it indicates itself indicating something; so too does love love itself, but unless it loves itself loving something, it does not love itself with love."[83]

The more that Augustine indicates the iterative, indicative, differentiating—and therefore linguistic—structure of memory, thought, and love, however, the more urgent it is to ask what their condition of possibility could be, when infantile minds appear to lack language entirely and therefore seem to be deficient beyond recall. Nor can the aporia be overcome by appealing to faith, as scholars such as Miles Burnyeat have found Augustine to do:[84] for the fact that the transition from infancy to speaking will have been lived through, unlike other matters of faith such as "cherubim and seraphim,"[85] suggests that a phenomenological approach to the dilemma would not only be possible, but also necessary according to the nature of the subject. It is just such an approach, moreover, that Augustine prepares with the description of infantile life that he offers in *On the Trinity* before his proposal to omit further inquiry: since he finds infants to be utterly absorbed in sensual life, this observation alone suggests that no acquisition of language could be possible without an initial experience of separation from those sensations that render infants glued to outside matters to the point of being out of their minds. And since this separation would be the opening *for*, rather than the content *of* any speech or memory,[86] it would have to differ "in the same stroke [*eo ictu*]" from sensible things as well as from any memorable words that may be beaten into "you."[87] Augustine's description thus indicates that the condition for the linguistic conditions of mental life would be a thoroughly unconstituted and deconstituting traumatic occurrence that is outside any sensible experience, meaning, or thesaurus of memory. In other words—and in something other than words—the event that creates an opening for language would necessarily be prior to and other than any language that is known to be spoken, not unlike the "*experimentum linguae*" that Agamben will characterize as "an impossibility of speaking *from the basis of language*" and ascribe to "the infancy which dwells in the margin between language and discourse."[88] It would be an experience of language, not as it is spoken and understood, but as it strikes and affects before it can mean and thus strikes itself through with a trait that is irreducible to any sense. As Blanchot would write elsewhere: "There is language because there is nothing in 'common' between those who express themselves: a separation that is presupposed—not surmounted, but confirmed—in all true speech."[89] But Augustine also says nothing less than this when he describes "Know thyself" as a striking instance of speech whose stroke necessarily differs from what it "says," separates the mind from its absorption in other matters, and thus exposes the alterity of language to "mind" and "language" itself.

The scenario of language acquisition that Augustine elaborates in the *Confessions*, however, speaks still more acutely than the passages cited above to the alterity of language, the speechlessness of speech, and the externality of memory to "oneself."[90] To begin, when Augustine recalls his first memory—which is his memory of learning to speak—traces of rupture mark his narration throughout. No sooner does he claim, "I remember this [*memini hoc*]," than he admits to learning of his learning only after the fact: "and later I turned my attention to the way in which I had learned to speak [*et unde loqui didiceram, post adverti*]."[91] Although this development differs, then, from the first stages of life that Augustine relates upon hearsay—the "period of my life which I did not live, and that has been reported to me,"[92] as Jean-François Lyotard describes it—it is nevertheless as though Augustine's first memory were not present to him at the time it was forged but contingent upon a later turn of attention whose condition and structure remain to be seen.[93] But if the exceptional character of this inaugural-yet-belated memory should seem to owe itself to the fact that memory presupposes language, and thus becomes possible only after his learning experience, Augustine also goes on to confess that the desire to speak his mind was what first motivated him to "grope for memory [*prensabam memoria*]": "I [taught] myself, using my own mind which you gave me, my God, since I wanted to give forth the senses of my heart with groans and various voicings and various movements of my members, so that obedience to my will would manifest, but I prevailed neither in all that I willed nor with all that I willed; and so I groped in my memory" (*ego ipse mente quam dedisti mihi, deus meus, cum gemitibus et vocibus variis et variis membrorum motibus edere vellem sensa cordis mei, ut voluntati pareretur, nec valerem quae volebam omnia nec quibus volebam omnibus, prensabam memoria*).[94] Just as Augustine's initial lack of memory implied a need for speech, so too does his inability to speak imply a need for memory—"infancy and language seeming to refer back to one another, in a circle,"[95] as Agamben has written in another context—and ultimately, the will to speak that Augustine remembers turns out to be deficient as well: for his impersonal, passive construction, "so that obedience to my will would manifest [*ut voluntati pareretur*]," omits to mention any addressee, while his admission, "I prevailed neither in all that I willed nor with all that I willed [*nec valerem quae volebam omnia nec quibus volebam omnibus*]," similarly fails to name any object of volition, alternating between *omnis* ("all," "every") and *qui* ("which," "what") in a pronomial language for a language before language and a will before will: or, for a sheer wanting to want-to-say that is itself wanting.[96] It could hardly be otherwise, so long as memory will have not yet taken hold in order to make the presence or absence of another subject or object significant, let alone desirable to him. If the period that Augustine describes nonetheless differs from the sheer oblivion and speechlessness of infancy, then it is not because memory, language, and will were experienced as present but because they were experienced in the modus of radical privation, where even the subject and objects of privation were unknown to him.

This sheer privation, which Augustine's self-canceling affirmations betray, could have been the traumatic experience of language that renders speech, memory, will, and thought possible: an experience that is more like the stroke, *ictus*, or syncope that "Know thyself" brings about, than like any speakable or thinkable expression. In a series of remarks on infancy in another context, Christopher Fynsk will speak of an "experience with language (before phenomenological experience)," which "must have opened if there is to be anything like thought and anything like language as we know it."[97] And it would then be because and not despite of its linguistic character that such an experience of privation would also be impossible to name, narrate, or confirm as such: for it would be neither a word nor a memory nor a thought, but the "naught" which first makes room for something to be seen and said but that itself cannot be said and cannot be. Or, as Augustine would write in *De magistro*, "naught" signifies at most "some affection of the soul [*affectionem animi quamdam*], when it does not see a thing."[98] Either way, however, the transition from infancy to speech entails an experience of want, which for want of words could only be broached in the way that Augustine does though his writing: through the aporetic ruptures in logic that are registered with the mutual presupposition of memory and speech that renders both impossible, or with the frustrated desire to speak without object or addressee. Besides even these details, moreover, there is the further fact that, precisely when Augustine's will to speak is said to have arisen, there was also "nothing" wanting: as he had confessed just before, he was fully satisfied at the time: "You also gave [*dabas*] me the will to not want more than you gave [*dabas*]," he says in praise to God, "and [you gave] to my nurses the will to give [*dare*] me what you gave [*dabas*] them."[99] Amidst these gifts, the sense of want that will move him to want to speak is therefore utterly gratuitous, which Augustine also suggests when he aligns this lack with the gift of mind: "I [taught] myself, using my own mind which you gave [*dedisti*] me, my God, since I wanted to give forth [*edere*] the senses of my heart."[100] What is lacking, in other words, is the ability to give, and this lack is itself a gift of grace that gives away the irreducible alterity of both word and mind, exposes the self to be wanting, and thereby decisively alters in advance the "self-givenness" or "Selbstgebung" that Husserl would eventually describe as the foundation of experience.[101]

This original alterity becomes more pronounced when Augustine claims to have "groped" in his "memory" ("prensabam memoria"), and when the recollection that he grasps is said to consist in the repetitions that adults will have performed of certain vocal and corporeal gestures: "When people called an object by some name, and while saying the word moved their bodies towards something [*corpus ad aliquid movebant*], I watched and held in mind [*videbam et tenebam*] that they used that sound when they wanted to show [*ostendere*] that thing."[102] In this situation, it is the adults' reiteration of certain gestures that both effects and effectively stands in for Augustine's retention of the same, as their voices and movements make memorable impressions, shape his memories in their likeness, and imprint the iterable character of memory upon him. Inner recognition and outer repetition thus overlap in such a way where there could be no telling precisely when Augustine's passage from sight to comprehension begins, which his initial confusion between direct and belated memory had also implied: "I remember this [*memini hoc*], and later I turned my attention [*post adverti*] to the way in which I had learned to speak."[103] Hence, Augustine will similarly explain in *De magistro* that only the indefinitely extended performance of speaking can teach someone what speaking "is," as opposed to all other subjects of learning that may be shown or explained through signs, since there could not be any sign for speaking in signs beside speaking itself: "In order to teach him, it is necessary to speak [*loquar necesse est*] [. . .] until I have made plain to him what he wants [*donec ei planum faciam quod vult*]."[104] And when Augustine speaks of reading Scripture in yet another context, he will again underscore the contingency of verbal understanding upon those verbatim repetitions from which it is, strictly speaking, indistinct: "What those who fear God and have a docile piety are looking for in all these books is the will of God [*uoluntatem dei*]. The thing to observe in this laborious work is [. . .] to know these books, and even if not yet so as to understand them, all the same by reading them to commit them to memory [*legendo tamen uel mandare memoriae*], or at least not to have them be entirely unknown [*uel omnino incognitos non habere*]."[105] In all of these passages, the thought that Augustine repeats presses the point: it is the scripts and scriptures of external "memory" that give rise to a mental archive, whose original separateness and foreignness to thought also entail that no assurance could ever be given that their sense is, was, or will be internalized and understood. As Jacques Derrida would write in confessions of his "own": "I wonder what I am looking for with this machine of avowal, beyond knowledge and truth, which has nothing to do with it here."[106]

The privation of language that Augustine had initially sensed would thus characterize the having of language as well, since language and memory alike give no sign to differentiate imitation from intention. Instead, both begin and survive through this very undecidability, which allows the one to coincide with and substitute for the other at all times, which contaminates the voice of every one with indefinitely many others and thus inscribes an incapacity to speak within speaking as such. Because, moreover, it could neither be ascertained nor expressed without its affirmation or expression being exposed to the same uncertainties, this trait of linguistic experience is more radically passive than even the passions that Augustine goes on to read in adult language and gesture: "What [the adults] wanted was clear, for they used bodily gestures, the natural words of all peoples [*verbis naturalibus omnium gentium*], such as facial expressions or glances of the eyes or movements of other parts of the body, or a tone of voice, indicating the affection of the soul [*affectionem animi*] concerning those things that they sought, wished to hold on to, rejected or shunned altogether [*in petendis, habendis, reiciendis fugiendisve rebus*]."[107] Here, Augustine would seem to characterize the "affections of the soul" as the universal, a priori foundation for language, which allowed him to read the gestures and voices of the adults around him. Yet Augustine's interpretation of gestures and enunciations presupposes their repeated performance and recognition, which in turn expose the fundamental indeterminacy of even these "natural words," whose invocation itself echoes Aristotle's famous opening lines from *De interpretatione*, at least as much as it would seem to convey a direct observation on Augustine's part: "There are, then, things in vocal-sound that are symbols of the affections in the soul [. . .] those things of which these are firstly signs, the affections of the soul, are the same for all."[108] Because we only ever speak "from memory [*memoriter*],"[109] and because our memories are made of others' speech, Augustine's words on affect, which may themselves be unmarked "citations," imply that all ostensible gestures of affection testify to the effects of repetition in addition to—and perhaps in lieu of—anything else that could affect us. Before and beside any provocations to seek or shun other things, there is the impact of language, which is why words themselves may burn—"How I did burn [*quomodo ardebam*],"[110] Augustine says as he recalls reading Cicero's *Hortensius*—and it is also why each ardor may be but a scripted performance for its own sake: as Lyotard writes on the *Confessions*, "One is led to suspect that such a decorous language, a language so full of pathos, is yielding to the pleasure of length, to its being drawn out."[111] Or, as Bataille would write in his very different confessional, first-person performance: "Thus we are nothing, neither you nor I beside burning words [*paroles brûlantes*] which could pass from me to you, imprinted on a page."[112] Whatever we may do or say about our feelings, however, those affections which draw or repel us—the affections concerning those things we will have "sought, wished to hold on to, rejected or shunned altogether"[113]—would be as impossible to tell apart from the language of desire as the unspeakable motives that drive the *ab-* and *ad-*version of infants would be impossible to address without speaking of language: here, too, it is an issue of that which "offends through the flesh or solicits it [*per carnem offendit aut allicit*]."[114] And the same uncertainty would go for all other selves as well, which Augustine implies through the sheer fact that his first memories of other persons coincide with his first impressions of language, exposing the contingency of their self-manifestation upon those motions and vocalizations by which they point not toward but away from themselves. What Lacan concludes from Augustine's teaching in *De magistro* thus also speaks to Augustine's learning from infancy: "So speech, as much taught as teaching, is located in the register of the mistake, of error, of deception, of the lie. Augustine takes it a long way, since he even places it in the domain of ambiguity, and not only of semantic ambiguity, but of subjective ambiguity. He admits that the very subject who is telling us something very often does not know what he is telling us."[115]

Along the lines of Augustine's most radical reduction—namely, to infancy—the very makeup of our minds would depend still more intimately upon the language of others than any teacher and any pivotal precept such as "Know thyself" could say. For what this reduction exposes is that the only "self" and "knowledge" to which one could turn would be those figures of speech and gesture that will have made an impression but whose meanings and motives therefore remain fundamentally obscure. Within Augustine's oeuvre, the "Delphic saying, 'Know thyself!'" thus wins "a new meaning" that Husserl could hardly have known himself to evoke when he repeated those words, among others, at the close of his *Cartesian Meditations*.[116] For at bottom, "know thyself" could only mean: go through the unfathomable alterity of language that each attempt to understand these words exposes and that renders every affection and expression of a "self" other than oneself, other than all others, and other than whatever it may seem to say itself. Augustine will say nothing less than this later in the *Confessions*, when he interprets the waters of creation at the opening of Genesis to signify the obscure affective flux of creaturely life, which he arrives upon through the equally abyssal impulse to address it:[117]

> To whom should I speak, and how express myself, about the passion that drags us headlong into the abrupt abyss [*abruptam*

abyssum], and the charity that uplifts us through your Spirit, who hovered over the waters? To whom should I say this, and in what terms? These are not literally places into which we plunge and from which we emerge: what could seem more place-like than they, yet what is in reality more different? They are affects, they are loves [*affectus sunt, amores sunt*]. One is the uncleanness of our own spirit, which like a flood-tide sweeps us down, in love with restless cares; the other is the holiness of your Spirit, which bears us upward in a love for peace beyond all care, that our hearts may be lifted up to you, to where your Spirit is poised above the waters, so that once our soul has crossed over those waters without substance [*sine substantia*] we may reach all-surpassing repose [*supereminentem requiem*].[118]

And he will reiterate this abyssal character of life and language still more pronouncedly in his commentary on the forty-first Psalm, where the verse on self-reflection speaks not of self-knowledge but of turmoil—"Turning towards myself, my soul is in turbulence [*Ad meipsum anima mea turbata est*]"[119]—and where this inward turn turns out to recall an abyss: "Abyss invokes abyss, in the voice of your cataracts [*Abyssus abyssum invocat, in voce cataractarum tuarum*]."[120]

Departing from the patristic tradition of interpreting this double abyss as a figure for the relation between the Old and New Testaments,[121] Augustine goes on to read it as a sign for the abyssal, because impenetrable character of the human mind.[122] But insofar as the "abyss" is said to do nothing other than invoke and be invoked, Augustine's words on the unfathomability of the "heart" speak more initially to the abyssal foundations of our linguistic life. Hence, just after calling the "human heart [*cor hominis*]" an "abyss [*abyssus*],"[123] Augustine goes on to explicate further: "Humans can talk; they can be seen through the operation of their limbs, heard in their speech, but whose thought is penetrated, whose heart inspected? [*Loqui homines possunt, uideri possunt per operationem membrorum, audiri in sermone, sed cuius cogitatio penetratur, cuius cor inspicitur?*]," and he thus calls into question the constative force of the very vocal and gestural movements that he had characterized in his *Confessions* as the "natural wording" of the soul.[124] If these remarks might seem nonetheless to suppose a singular, albeit unknown, self at the source of each utterance, then this self would have to be as much a question of faith as God, who is also the only one "for whom 'the abyss of human consciousness' is an open book," should we take Augustine's word for it.¹²⁵ Only God knows whether "I" will ever have spoken, as Augustine suggests in his commentary on another verse from the Psalms, which reads: "I have cried out, since you heard me [*Ego clamaui, quoniam exaudisti me*]."¹²⁶ Or, as Jacques Derrida would write on *Circumfession*: "A confession is never mine [. . .]. It is always the other in me who confesses."¹²⁷ This is not to say that "I" am not, or that "I" play no role in speaking, but that "I" am not able to know who "I" am, nor could anyone know where to draw line between "you" and "me," as well as any number of present and absent others, each time "we" believe ourselves to invoke one another. It is for this reason that Kafka would insist, more categorically, "Confession and lie are alike. In order to be able to confess, one lies. One cannot express that which one is, for one is just that; one can only impart that which one is not, that is, a lie."¹²⁸ But whether the accent is placed upon the "other" or the "lie," Derrida and Kafka are perhaps more faithful to the unsettling character of faith and language that Augustine exposes than those commentators who would affirm faith in faith and cast the "soul"—as well as the word—"in God's 'image and likeness.'"¹²⁹ For writings such as Kafka's and Derrida's emphasize, in more or less close proximity to Augustine, the ways in which each subject of speech and belief is subject to flux and to the possibility of withdrawal at any time, leaving every feeling and confession radically precarious for subject and audience alike. It is most likely for this reason that, when Augustine describes the way in which abysses "invoke" one another, he will claim that they do so not knowingly or expressly—it is not done by "mak[ing] a speech," he says—but in the manner that one "invokes" death, that is, by "living in such way that one calls death upon oneself [*ut mortem ad se uocet*]."¹³⁰ And he will add, "It is in this way that wisdom is taught, and in this way that faith is taught [*Sic discitur sapientia, sic discitur fides*]."¹³¹

Such is the teaching of the precept, "Know thyself": the "systematic self-investigation [*systematische Selbstbesinnung*]" of both the "pure ego" and the "sedimented forms" that it invokes traces back from the subject of Husserl's *Cartesian Meditations* to Augustine's words on the "self," and it issues into this abyss of anonymous invocations.¹³² Rather than disclosing the fundament for knowledge, the various articulations of the "self" that thereby emerge expose the turbulence and obscurity of language, which allows various instances of speech to surface and intersect but permits none to rest assured and lets no claims be settled. In the first and last analysis, language would mean the death of "oneself" as much as it makes up the life of the mind, whose most vital and lethal experiences alike would depend upon nothing known to be lived or spoken, but the unpredictable, syncopated movements that render words striking, that mark us to the core, and that leave us wanting for words as we speak.

Chapter 2

Provocations

"I," Husserl, and the Passive Voices of Phenomenology

An anonymous flux of invocations is what Edmund Husserl describes when he approaches the syntheses that take place at the passive level of experience. Whether his investigations are primarily oriented toward the perceptual present, the associations of memory, or the apperception of another subject, he will repeatedly take recourse to gestures of speaking that arrive before the apparition of any speakable object or any "I" to speak of. In the introduction to his lecture course on passive synthesis from the early and mid-1920s, Husserl writes:

> In every moment of perceiving, the perceived is what it is in its mode of appearance [as] a system of referential implications [*Verweisen*] with an appearance-core upon which appearances have their hold. And it calls out to us, as it were, in these referential implications [*Verweisungen*]: "There is still more to see here, turn me so you can see all my sides, let your gaze run through me, draw closer to me, open me up, divide me up; keep on looking me over again and again, turning me to see all sides. You will get to know me like this, all that I am, all my surface qualities, all my inner sensible qualities," etc.[1]

In a later manuscript on intersubjectivity from 1932, he would reiterate: "That which is each time experienced has the character of one who is calling [*Charakter des Anrufenden*], of one who is exerting stimuli upon the I."² Beyond "that which is each time experienced" in the present, moreover, those movements of appeal and referral that characterize the passive foundation of perception will also be said to occur whenever a present perception calls forth the memory of a prior experience: "Something present recalls something reproductively presentified, which is to say, there is a tendency that is directed from the former to the latter," Husserl writes, before reformulating: "We, as attentive egos, look from this to that by being referred from the one to the other; and we can also say: The one points to the other—even though there is still not an actual relation of indication by signs and designation."³ With or without "an actual relation of indication by signs," in other words, "affective communication" comes to pass across both temporally near and remote hyletic data,⁴ as they "resonate" with one another,⁵ forging each time an anachronistic "synthesis of coinciding in distance [*Synthese der Deckung in Distanz*]."⁶ Whatever does not give forth any appeal, on the other hand, will be said by Husserl to be "entirely without language [*im Ganzen Sprachlosen*], a night that is silent, that exerts no call and harbors no call in itself."⁷

This preverbal, passive "language" of association is, to be sure, radically improper, but not in the sense that Husserl's "figurative" manner of speaking may be opposed to more "authentic" expressions. It is instead "improper" in the more fundamental sense of a language that is inappropriable for any subject of enunciation. For insofar as passive constitution precedes cognizing activity, it necessarily escapes any "'real' genesis or chronology,"⁸ as Françoise Dastur has argued. It is in view of this dilemma that Bruce Bégout suggests that Husserl's analyses of passive synthesis proceed "as if the reflexive spirit deduced that which arrives in advance of it, departing from its proper affective-active experience," while surreptitiously "dissimulat[ing] [. . .] the deductive character of the originary."⁹ Yet even if passivity could only be deductively rather than "originarily" accessed, Husserl's various formulations for it nevertheless testify to an original linguistic pathos—a pathos that moves him to address passive syntheses as linguistic movements¹⁰—and they underscore its foreignness from the "proper" activity of the ego through a rhetoric that is itself foreign to logic as well as to phenomenological description. In this way, Husserl's writing lends a certain truth to the otherwise unfounded premise that resonances make up the initial "draw of affections [*Zug der Affektionen*],"¹¹ which first allows a perception to be consciously posited or "the unity of a 'proposition' [*eines 'Satzes'*]" to grow from "out of manifold positings [*aus mannigfaltigen Setzungen*]."¹² And although he does not positively say so, Husserl thereby indicates as well that those associative resonances, which at once found and exceed "the simple constitution of a noema,"[13] would expose every conscious position to other voices that may also unsettle or depose it.

Although the linguistic traits that Husserl ascribes to passive synthesis could seem to align it with the *logos* of conscious experience, then, its unsettling implications for phenomenology are also drawn out, the more that affections are described along the lines of instances of speech that may be utterly unlike "me"—"ich-los," as Husserl often puts it—whose calls for attention multiply (within) "my" experience before "I" can have a word. Anne Montavont summarizes Husserl's remarks on the appeals of passive experience: "All comes to pass as if the relation of the ego and the non-ego were a relation of dialogue."[14] Unlike a dialogue whose terms and subjects are supposed to be known, however, the "dialogue" that should lay the ground for all further dialogue begins without "me"—before the activity of the *cogito*—and thus leaves open the possibility that the affective appeals, references, and reminders that it comprises need not be consonant ("zusammenstimmend"), like the "world" as "I" would eventually wish to have it. For all that "I" may know, the affective appeals that forge associations may be a far cry from the "univocity [*Einstimmigkeit*]" that constitutes the criterion for experiential truth in Husserl,[15] while remaining at least as remote from the "inner monological thinking [*innere[s] monologische[s] Denken*]" that Husserl will ascribe—more than problematically, as it will turn out—to the *cogito*.[16] However near or distant it may be from the ideal of univocity, moreover, each tentative call would be structurally exposed *ab initio* to dissonance and interference, as Husserl suggests when he speaks of the ways in which the same sensory data may appear to solicit divergent apprehensions, whose ambiguity derives from the fact that a still more ambiguous "something" is felt to "speak" alternately "*for* and *against*" the one and the other apprehension.[17] Nor is ambiguity the only trouble here: for since this "for" and this "against" would also precede any sense of 'something' one may form—since dissimilar data would "protest" against their assimilation into a unified whole[18]—there would initially be no object for these prepositional announcements, and no criterion for determining what should found a "for" or an "against" when they first make themselves felt.

The language of passive association that Husserl addresses thus resists the grammar of language as we know it and withdraws from the attempt to approximate it in various passages from his oeuvre. These preliminary signs alone suggest that it would not only provide the prepredicative foundation for conscious modalities of positivity, possibility, and doubt, as Husserl will claim it does in, among others, the *Cartesian Meditations*,[19] but would also show this foundation to consist of inconsistent prelogical and alogical modulations, as he will make more explicit in his manuscripts from the early 1930s on time-consciousness: "It would have to be said that affections [. . .] can inhibit one another, stand in dispute with one another, and in this sense, they therefore have modalities" themselves.[20] The extent to which affective associations trouble rather than assure the constitutive functions of transcendental subjectivity becomes perhaps most pronounced, however, when they return in Husserl's writings on the apperception of an alter ego. This time, the appeals of alterity that forge passive experience emerge as that which affects not only the constitution of other minds as well as the world of perception, but also the development of "my" own self-awareness. For Husserl's formulations for intersubjectivity, which will be analyzed in greater detail below, suggest that neither the selfhood of the ego nor the alterity of the alter ego is initially thought, so much as they are undergone through a process of pairing inaugurated by the appearance of some body like mine, whose apparent likeness consists solely in indications that "something psychical [. . .] must now step forth in original experience."[21] The realization of these promising indices is necessarily inhibited by the fact that "my" sensory fields do not extend to those of the other;[22] and more initially, it is the inhibition of certain passive associations that lets our respective bodily limits become apparent. A dialogue thus plays out not between "you" and "me" but among the hyletic givens that speak with and against one another concerning our "selves." It is their dissonance that eventually allows us to appear separately, while it is their consonance—Husserl will speak of "consonant 'gesturing' [*zusammenstimmenden 'Gebaren'*]"—that attunes "ego" to "alter ego" in such a way that not only gives me the sense of a like-minded being but also makes me aware of what "I" am outwardly like myself.[23]

No subject, in other words, is left unmodified by the passive movements of discord and attunement that Michael Theunissen will call "Veranderung," when it comes to the particular sort of "alteration" (*Veränderung*) that proceeds from the "other" (*Andere*) to the "self" and thus permits something like "self"-definition.[24] Even "I" am negotiable, and in a manner that is not merely a matter of affective dynamics, as Theunissen suggests, but that is before all else indexical, gestural, and vocal—and therefore linguistic—rendering the phenomenological process of "Veranderung" an instance of philological "Veranderung" along the lines that Werner Hamacher would describe, when he addresses the ways in which language "gives itself over" to an "a priori self-distancing [apriorischen Selbst-Entfernung] and immediate self-othering [immediaten Selbst-Veranderung]."[25] In all of these ways and more, the constitution of objects and (other) subjects alike thus appears to trace back not to any certain foundations but to an otherwise ungrounded flux of appeals, where, as Augustine had reiterated: "Abyss invokes abyss."[26]

The various modulations of resonance and dissonance that should subtend perception, memory, doxic modality, and intersubjectivity thus also show the mind to be open to debate among competing instances of "speech" before anyone could tell what to think—and thus, before the "Logos" of "unifying sense" that otherwise guides phenomenological analysis[27]—and they show the subject to be involved in an ambivalent and polyvocal "dialogue" with alterity before any apparition of ego or alter ego. To at least the same extent, then, that Husserl's descriptions of passive synthesis expose the most radically reduced, primordial consciousness to be, as Natalie Depraz has written, "inhabited by alterity,"[28] his rhetoric implies that this alterity would have to be thought as the alterity of language, as many readers have indicated, with different accentuations. Echoing Husserl's analyses of passivity, it was language that Maurice Merleau-Ponty would emphasize when he rearticulated the structure of sensation as a dialogue with the world in which "a sensible that is about to be sensed poses to my body a sort of confused problem," whose "solicitation" prompts the embodied subject to seek "the response" in turn.[29] With a lesser emphasis upon embodiment, Jean-Luc Marion would similarly depart from linguistic experience in order to call for another inflection of phenomenological subjectivity, according to which "I" would not originally figure as the origo of conscious acts but as the passive recipient of an appeal, where "I receive *my self* from the call that gives me to myself before giving me anything whatsoever."[30] And with a different impetus, Gilles Deleuze repeats the notion that "the world of passive syntheses" comprises a plethora of "signs," whose structure entails both "a presumption, a pretended claim [une présomption, une prétention]" with "regard" to the habitual impressions that are drawn together, as well as a "question" as to "what difference is there," each time around.[31] It was Jacques Derrida, however, who most extensively argued that "language precedes all the distinctions that Husserl makes on the basis of the reduction,"[32] especially in his introduction to *The Origin of Geometry*, where, on the one hand, the "*ability* of sense to be linguistically embodied" emerges, paradoxically, as "the only means by which sense becomes nonspatiotemporal,"[33] while on the other hand, the linguistic fixation of "sense" in spatiotemporal signs exposes each linguistic ideality to the very movements that make up passive constitution. For "linguistically embodied" signs would not only comprise *hyletic* data upon their every iteration but would also *ideally* consist in "a mobile system of relations" which permits at all times "multiple interconnections of sense."[34]

These observations suggest that both Husserl as well as those thinkers who would write in his wake cannot but speak, more or less emphatically, for a linguistic a priori that is irreducible to the objects and operations of formal logic and that also could not be dismissed as a mere metaphor,[35] as if there were a more literal alternative for articulating the movements of solicitation, consonance, and dissonance that make up the dynamic basis for every objectivity and each subjective act.[36] Where there are only appealing (or repelling) signs of sense—where sensible configurations can only appear through movements of speech—a philological movement of *Veränderung* would be constitutive for phenomenological constitution, and passive experience would consist in the linguistic "*pathos*, the *passio*—of not ever yet being already that which it could still become, and of being always more than it already is."[37] But if this *Veränderung* precedes all other matters, then the question remains as to how Husserl's texts register an experience of language in its passive character and what this passion could mean for the thought of self and others, as well as for language as we "know" it.

It is, for instance, the passive—and thus, unthought—occurrences of appeal and association that will characterize Husserl's descriptions of linguistic understanding in a manuscript on intersubjectivity from 1932, where signitive meaning is coupled not only with intentional acts but also (and more initially) with precarious and aleatory movements of interest. Whereas in the *Logical Investigations*, Husserl had primarily described signitive meanings as intentionalities that can be understood without any intuitive fulfillment,[38] in his later manuscripts, he also seeks to account for this descriptive trait of "understanding" and goes on to ascribe it to an initial coincidence of those subjects who take interest in the signs that they give and receive. In this way, both subjects thus come to be "in-one-another [*Ineinander*]" in an affective manner.[39] When "I" understand an expression, that is, "I" will have been provoked to attend to the gestures and speech of the other, who has already appealed to my interest, and whose appeal now absorbs me for however long or limited a time. "The other is experienced in such a way where I am 'sunk in him' ['*in ihm versunken*'] from whatever interest," Husserl writes, before elaborating: "When no counter-motives are in play, I perform along with him [. . .] his modes of comportment, his positionalities, his presumptions of validity, in the coincidence of my 'I' with his [*in Deckung meines Ich mit dem seinen*]."[40] Going through the motions that signify habit, thought, and value is thus what constitutes the most basic level of understanding, whether it take the form of express verbalization or gestural impulses, as when "a foreign hand moves, [and] so too does my hand itch to move, etc."[41] Communication thus turns out to be a scenario in which neither "I" nor the other "I" could be "myself"; rather, "I" pair with the other whose expressions "I" reiterate merely by hearing, seeing, sensing, or reading them: "I take over, so to speak, that which holds as valid for him as my validity, his judgments as mine."[42] And lest this talk of takeover should misleadingly imply an active judgment on "my" part, Husserl adds: "Only when, out of whatever interest, I come to loosen myself and take distance from the coincidence [*Deckung*], do I see that a proper ontic belief of my own, a proper judgment of my own has grown on me in the coincidence [*Deckung*]."[43]

Any other's words that "I" may come to have in mind—and that means any words that I may learn to understand—would therefore presuppose this passive, "most intimate coincidence [*innigste Deckung*]," which literally renders "I" a "'repetition' ['*Wiederholung*']" of another speaker, whose claims and experience "I" may otherwise never have come close to thinking or living through "myself."[44] Understanding "is not a comportment in the mode of being beside one another," Husserl insists, but one that occurs "in the mode of being inside one another on the parts of act-I and act-I [*Akt-Ich und Akt-Ich*]."[45] For this reason, moreover, a mutual penetration of actors would have to occur, even when the one or the other eventually comes to adopt a "negating, rejecting comportment [*verneinende[s], ablehnende[s] Verhalten*]"[46] toward any wishful thinking of harmony: "The wish that I direct to another has gone into him, I reach into the other I in wishing [. . .] [and] only insofar as I am already inside him with my wish, insofar as he has taken up my wish, do I experience, in him, refusal."[47] What "coincidence" or "covering" ("Deckung") signifies in such a situation is the ambivalent adoption of another's language in oneself, whose "other" language may therefore also be understood to yield an ambivalent experience of "oneself," where "the 'oneself' cannot be distributed in an unambiguous and definitive manner."[48] Listening would be like "love" in the sense that Augustine describes, when he writes: "So great is the force of love that [the mind] attracts to itself those things which it has thought for a long time with love and to which it has adhered with the glue of care [*curae glutino*], even when it returns in some way to think itself."[49] Hence, even in those dialogues where "I" would seem to play an active role, "I" do not come first and may never come into my own, nor is the role that language plays through its first-person actors initially logical in even the minimal sense of a signitive "unity,"[50] so long as such a unity is thought to be actively cognized and identified, rather than passively forged and repeated. Thus, as Husserl had written among his later annotations to the *Logical Investigations*[51]: "Just as the literal word unit is a sheer unity, a unity, which is a passive given, so to speak, so too is the confused unit of sense; this consciousness too is a passive one, with nothing of the specific activity, spontaneity of believing and connecting, of thinking in the 'proper' sense."[52]

This last remark suggests that "I" can only think and speak my mind in the "proper" sense after consciously adopting an attitude of belief, which does not exclude the alternative of leaving a notion bare of any positional character, or letting it be "merely set forth [*bloß dahingestellt*]."[53] But if belief should be what makes the difference, then it could not itself be *said* without its saying requiring another act of belief or leap of faith in order to be "thinking in the 'proper' sense." Husserl's words thus not only indicate that my apprehension of speech and sense alike would originally be improper and passive but also imply that no word of thought could ever be fully appropriated by "me," both insofar as any position of belief that I may eventually adopt would owe itself to an initial provocation, and insofar as I could never decisively know when I begin to think for myself, rather than merely allowing words to "flow through consciousness."[54] Along these lines, one could therefore not even be sure after the fact that one will have ever effectively had speech in one's power, as Husserl's close assistant Jan Patocka claims that one could eventually do when he attempts to negotiate this dilemma for himself: "So speech is an instrument which we never really have in hand, of which we never know otherwise than *ex eventu* to what extent it is within our power, an instrument which, in this respect, resembles more our natural bodily organs than it does artificial instruments."[55] Instead, Husserl's descriptions of the passive and alogical conditions for linguistic experience disclose the fundamental ambivalence that Derrida had found to be inscribed in the phenomenon of the voice, where conscious understanding coincides with mindless iteration and is therefore impossible to discern: "If one is understood / heard [*entendu*] by another, to speak is to make him *repeat immediately* in himself the understanding- / hearing-oneself-speak [*le s'entendre-parler*] in the very form in which I effectuated it."[56]

There could be no telling the source and direction of speech in any given situation, then, and it could bring one no further to appeal to the reflective distance that may eventually be taken from one "I" to another "I." For although Husserl does not directly say so himself, the initially passive experience of language that he describes would also imply that any separation that could set "me" apart from another speaker would depend not (or not only) upon "me" but upon further and other linguistic occurrences. Besides the fact that every single "act" would pass without a trace if it were not for those linguistic formulations "I" owe to others, there could hardly be any alternative but alterity, if it is only from "out of [some] interest [*aus welchem Interesse immer*]" that I can recognize the judgments that will have "grown" upon me,[57] and if "interest" cannot be awakened without the call of an appeal. Because and not despite of the arguments that Husserl, among others, would *repeat* to the contrary, it would not possible to determine, strictly speaking, whether and to what extent any act of critical reflection on the part of a first-person subject would not itself reiterate in yet another way the discursive performances of those "others" who, as Bernhard Waldenfels has written, "speak from out of me whenever I speak with them."[58] The problem of external attractions and confusions that Augustine had addressed, when he explicated the need for admonitions such as "Know thyself" to call oneself to mind, thus receives its most radical articulation in Husserl's phenomenological considerations of linguistic comprehension, where every subject and word of admonition would belong among the attractions that complicate any sense of "self" that one could form. Only our divergent interests and callings—and that means: our other "others"—are what would open the interval that separates "me" from any other "me," rather than merely disposing "me" to follow "your" every word.[59] This is not to say, however, that singular instances of subjectivity play no part in what is said and done among us but that no participants in such transactions could ever be determined, assured, or known unto themselves. Because and not despite of the fact that "I" could only hear, read, and understand what "I" intend to—or what "I" intend, too—there could be no way of telling what comes from "you" or "me," but for the shifting interests whose pursuit allows for the bifurcation of our respective trajectories. Or, as one lover will say in *Gravity's Rainbow*: "You go from dream to dream inside me. You have passage to my last shabby corner, and there, among the debris, you've found life. I'm no longer sure which of all the words, images, dreams, or ghosts are 'yours' and which are 'mine.' It's past sorting out."[60] The irreducible intertwinement of passivity and activity that readers of Husserl have increasingly emphasized in their commentaries signifies in this linguistic context: one is always and never quite thinking, always and never quite speaking for oneself.[61]

It could, of course, be argued that all of these meditations would presuppose the "apperception of the other" that constitutes "the other person [. . .] as an expressive phenomenon," as Patocka would insist,[62] echoing Husserl's remarks on the "original genesis of th[e] act" of "communication": "It has its presupposition [. . .] in reciprocal empathy, in the modus of reciprocally, actually perceiving [subjects], in which the one enters into the subjective being of the other and the one understands the other in this regard."[63] Nor is there a lack of further commentaries by and on Husserl which would repeat that the phenomenological genealogy of communicative speech leads back to a prelinguistic mode of perception that yields the pronominal relations of "I" and "you": as if, when "I turn myself toward the other," the "other" thereby turns without a word into a "you": "the other 'I,' [. . .] becomes a 'you' for me."[64] But insofar the passive constitution of an alter ego is itself a linguistic occurrence, the model for his explications turns out to be none other than the experience of registering the words and appeals of an "I" who is and is not "I,"[65] and who therefore renders "my" proper being a possible fiction that "I" will have to live with.

As Husserl would write in the *Cartesian Meditations*, his most widely known treatment of the subject, others "announce [*bekunde[n]*]" themselves through gestures that recall "my" embodied "behaviors,"[66] which he exemplifies in his manuscripts by citing "my retreat before a thing that incites fear in me, [or] [. . .] attraction to a piece of food."[67] These examples, in turn, recall Augustine's understanding of "the natural words of all peoples": namely, the "movements" of bodily members "indicating the affection of the soul concerning those things that they sought, wished to hold on to, rejected or shunned altogether."[68] And it was with an eye to similar passages that Derrida would underscore: "The lived experience of another is made known to me only insofar as it is mediately indicated by signs."[69] But differently than Augustine, Husserl gives no sign that such "announcements" of subjective suffering and desire could be heard or read as such at the passive level of experience, whose synthetic formations are what first provoke conscious attention and therefore take place themselves "without a mediating act of thinking," as Theunissen has emphasized.[70] Instead, the signs that proceed from what Husserl will call the "original interpretation-substrate [*originale Interpretationssubstrat*]"[71] of others' bodies—in distinction to the "original" givenness of one's own subjective life—are undergone through what he calls "pairing." This process takes place, according to Husserl, whenever "two data are given intuitionally, and with prominence, in the unity of a consciousness"—that is, within a stretch of streaming, temporal experience—"and on these grounds, essentially, already in pure passivity, and thus regardless of whether they are noticed or not," these "differently appearing" data "phenomenologically ground a unity of similarity, and are thus steadily constituted as a pair."[72] As previously discussed, this pairing involves indices, gestures, and appeals that are passively transmitted without a clear instance of source or address. In the particular pairing that involves "me" with some body or other, the "prominent" data of my own "live-body [*Leibkörper*]" pair of their own accord with the hyletic data that "I" receive whenever another "body [*Körper*]" that "is 'similar' " to mine "steps forth into prominence within my primordial sphere."[73] Far from indicating features of resemblance that "I" could consciously recognize, these data could not be distinguished by any specific quality, since, on the one hand, the active objectification of qualitative differences would have to follow from this passive synthesis of hyletic data; and since, on the other hand, "I" have no sense of my body or the limits of my "sphere" until my encounter with the other.[74] As Theunissen succinctly writes: the other affects me "as the embodiment of my body [*Verkörperung meines Leibes*]."[75] Hence, although Husserl considers "similarity" at the level of perceived body parts in one of his manuscripts from the 1920s, where he speaks of the other having "a hand-analogue, analogues of feet, a head-analogue, etc.,"[76] he will later specify that it is not sufficient to appeal to the appearance of bodily "members [*Gliedern*]," nor even to their "outer behavior [*äußeren Gehaben*]."[77] Instead, any "similarity" or "analogy" that may obtain between live bodies would have to be founded solely in kinaesthetic trajectories and gestural associations that differ from the causally determined movements of inanimate matters. The "announcements" of other minds, that is, belong to a body-language that is given forth before anybody knows it, before I know myself to have a body of my own, and before any subject of speech could be so much as pronominally distinguished.

This is why the "similarities" that Husserl evokes will come down to those semblances of motivated pursuit and flight, which will have marked the conception of language since Aristotle. Unlike Aristotle or Augustine's understanding of those "symbols of the affections in the soul,"[78] however, the passive comprehension through "pairing" that Husserl describes could only take the form of simulation, either insofar as "my" body goes through the motions of the other, as with the "foreign hand" that enters into one of Husserl's remarks cited above—"If I see a foreign hand," writes Husserl, "so too do I feel my hand; if a foreign hand moves, so too does my hand itch to move, etc."[79]—or insofar as the performance of the other "reminds" me of the movements I would perform in similar circumstances, by bringing my inner (hypothetical) "memories" to outer life: "That of which I am reminded [*erinnert*] just as soon *steps forth* [*eintritt*] into exteriority [*Äusserlichkeit*]."[80] Yet whether I am moved to stir my limbs or whether I see my "memories" acted out in a quasi–motion picture, "I" comprehend the analogous "other" insofar as my lived present and past lifetime alike are themselves initially comprehended and reiterated in the other's movements. What takes place in the analogical transfer, that is to say, is a virtual and anachronistic coincidence not unlike the "most intimate coincidence [*innigste Deckung*]," which occurs when "I" apprehend another's words by repeating after him, or: by repeating after "me."[81]

What makes this coincidence particularly strange, however, is that the excitation of movements or memories need not be motivated by anything that "I" would otherwise have "sought, wished to hold on to, rejected or shunned altogether,"[82] since it would be provoked primarily by the performance of such movements or memories. In other words, it would not be appealing or repelling matters, but the sheer appeal of (another's) being appealed or repelled that moves me. The striking character of this passion, irrespective of the presence or absence of any object of affection, makes up yet another reason for why pairing can be said to take place abruptly—"in one stroke [*in einem Schlage*]"—like the self-knowledge that, according to Augustine, should arrive in the "same stroke [*eo ictu*]" as one hears and understands the dictum, "Know thyself"[83]: "The pairing of association," writes Husserl, "is reciprocal 'overlapping,' and should each of the pairing-ones have, in his way, presumptive validities with concomitant possibilities in themselves, this translates over from the one to the other—passively, without further ado, in one stroke [*in einem Schlage*]."[84] But this time, it is not "my" immemorial presence of mind that is awakened by this syncopation of experience. Instead, "my" past and present desires are opened to foreign articulation and variation, exposing "my" experience to interventions that cut into my very body and mind, and that may thereby render the most moving and memorable occurrences in my life anachronisms or simulacra that could never have been proper to "me" alone. The passive transference that Husserl describes indicates not only that "I" am originally porous but also that it would be as indeterminate in embodied experience as it is in first-person speech who is meant, exactly, when "my" "live-body [*Leib*]" is felt to be the sole object "*in* which I immediately *steer and wield*."[85] Every action or speech act that I may perform—and these alternatives would ultimately signify the same, once embodied experience is itself thought to be structured like language—could at all times have been provoked or echoed by any number of others, rendering "my" voice plurivocal and passive *ab initio*.

Hence, although Husserl will say that the other body receives "for its part, the character of being *mine* [*Character* mein], through the initiating and contrasting pairing that now necessarily takes place,"[86] the pair that is formed through "our" association would initially have to be understood as a parity without the "with" or the "cum" that would connect separate partners and allow for their comparison. All subjects involved would be more and less than one to begin with; no one would be without the other; and each would thus be constitutively exposed to "the *pathos*, the *passio*—of not ever yet being already that which [one] could still become, and of being always more than [one] already is."[87] It is this indefinite character that yields the confused melding or "Verschmelzung"—the smelting (*Schmelzen*) gone awry (*ver-*)—toward which "every overlapping at a distance that grows through associative pairing" would tend according to Husserl.[88] Thus, Depraz translates "Paarung" with "co-union," arguing that alternatives such as "accouplement" "let the *terms* of the 'couple' or 'pair' appear in too much of a static manner."[89] But if pairing is, as Depraz argues, "a unity that lets difference be," then the differentiations that it permits would have to be in flux as well, in such a way where there are no two clear-cut "terms."[90] Husserl suggests as much, when he describes the situation between "us" as one in which the sense of what is "mine" does not precede but rather follows the sense of what is "other," which arrives solely when certain "demand[s]" prove themselves to be impossible to fulfill: "The live-body that is seen demands the present of sensory fields," Husserl writes, but this "present" is "not an experiential present as with my live-body. Lived experiences are co-posited here apprehensively, which are not my lived experiences."[91] The contingency of this "qualitative experiential difference between what is and is not *mine*," however, speaks in yet another way against drawing any definitive boundaries between subjects,⁹² and it is testimony to the rigor of Husserl's descriptive rhetoric that the "demands" that he evokes are ascribed neither to "me" nor to anybody else but to the "live-body [*Leibkörper*]" that is not yet possessed.

It is only through this simultaneous experience of demand and refusal that "contrasting" could begin as soon as the other gets under "my" skin and that "my" assimilation of the other could be impeded sufficiently to let us at least partially separate.⁹³ Without any prior foundation or criterion for our respective limits, however, the results of this process cannot but remain contestable, while the contingent character of "contrasting pairing" cannot but entail the possibility that it may also always occur otherwise than in such a way where "I" and "you" emerge as the recognizably separate selves we may take ourselves to be at any given time. These alternatives remain largely implicit, if not suppressed in Husserl's analyses, but they are not beyond all description, and in this regard the fictive scenarios of other writers such as Maurice Blanchot may be read to complement the exemplary fictions of phenomenological investigation. In one episode from Blanchot's novel *Aminadab*, for example, the protagonist Thomas collapses together with Dom, a figure to whom he has, for the most part, been chained since his arrival at the boarding house where the narrative takes place. The process of collapse begins as Dom supports Thomas in ascending a staircase, only for the relation of support to give way to a movement of oppositional overlapping⁹⁴: although he had at first seemed too weak to stand, Thomas soon finds that he is "gluing himself [*se collant*]" to Dom's body with a force that shows his strength (and stature) to equal those of his companion cum "adversary [*adversaire*]."⁹⁵ Remote as Blanchot's vocabulary may be from the technical terms of Husserl's phenomenology, the coincidence or "Deckung" that plays out in Thomas and Dom's fall-in incorporates the movement that Husserl would call "initiating and contrasting pairing," as one body matches itself against the other, compelling a comparison that is passively suffered more than it is actively drawn, despite the mutual show of strength.⁹⁶ For although Thomas will try to "examine his former companion" while they are entangled, the analogical relation that he undergoes in pressing his partner surpasses his capacity to observe it, to the point where Thomas gets carried away by the resemblance and ceases to hold his own entirely:

> In the course of this struggle, he examined his former companion at leisure; he wanted to fashion for himself an idea of the resemblance that could exist between them; if this resemblance

> existed, it was not striking; his eyes had perhaps the same
> color, and the cut of his face might well be identical; there
> were small spots here and there on his skin that rendered the
> confusion impossible. He was discouraged nonetheless by the
> analogy between certain traits, and ceasing his resistance, he
> let himself be carried away by the young man, who stretched
> him out on the bed immediately.[97]

Conscious acts of comparison are thus undercut and overcome through passive coincidences, which issue into an abandonment of "resistance," nor does this abandonment arrive without signs of self-abandonment as well. For the lines that follow the announcement of Thomas's intention to form "an idea of the resemblance that could exist between" Dom and himself break down into a series of paratactic, tentative remarks in which "he" drops out of the picture as a subject of perception. The observations that ensue instead seem to be related in "free indirect discourse," but if this mode of narration should approximate Thomas's perspective, it also frees the description from being attached unequivocally to any single figure's point of view, with the consequence that "his" or "his" distinguishing features can no longer be told apart. Far from the passive analogizing that, according to Husserl, should issue into the constitution of the alter ego and confirm the continuity of subjective experience proper, the "analogy between certain traits" that is drawn in the face-off between Thomas and Dom lets scattered marks of difference surface and sort themselves out—"there were small spots here and there on his skin that rendered the confusion impossible'—but it does not let them be ascribed to either member of the pair. It is therefore in keeping with the character of this experience that both Thomas and Dom are reduced to placeholders for a subject in its wake: Thomas will be "stretched out" on a bed, physically posturing as the *subjectum* or ὑποκείμενον, while Dom assumes the role of the one who sees and speaks: " 'Now,' this one said to him, 'rest peacefully. I will keep watch in your place, and I will inform you as soon as something important will have arrived.'"[98]

As Nicolas Abraham would likewise observe, the "paradigm of 'association,' of 'passive synthesis,' is the liaison that establishes itself between a locus and a conflict," rather than figuring as anything that "I" could own or know.[99] But if no singularly plural instances of subjectivity should ever be alike, then neither would the divisions that render them separate,[100] which emerge through linguistic movements and counter-movements that remain themselves negotiable, not unlike the altercations that Husserl locates within the singularly plural world of the senses: "The senses conflict with one another, but this conflict can be decided in view of the fact that precisely afterwards an organ must be cut off as anomalous; all the other senses together yield a world that sets itself forth univocally [*einstimmig*], while the cut-off sense does not concord [*zusammenstimm[en]*] with the course of prior experience."[101] Because it would be not an inalienable essence, moreover, but an unconscious desire for univocity which drives the scission and decision in both cases, Husserl's language for passive pairing does not confirm an epistemological premise, so much as it reiterates—most likely despite his intentions—the alterable character of the "boundaries of the ego and the external world" that Sigmund Freud would speak of in, among others, *Civilization and Its Discontents*.[102] The figures of literary fiction and the claims of psychoanalysis can complement phenomenological reflection in all of these ways and more, however, because subjectivity is itself a function of appeals, demands, and refusals, which speak before conscious awareness and testify to the uncontainable character of linguistic experience. As Husserl would write in one of his manuscripts on passive synthesis: "My passivity stands in connection with the passivity of all others."[103]

Husserl's genetic analyses of embodiment and intersubjectivity may thus be read as a philological meditation on the linguistic passions of experience, where fundamental notions such as identity and difference are first provoked, but where the appeals and protests that prompt them also contest them in the same stroke. The operations that configure embodiment and subjectivity are those of language, which "on the one hand thematizes, objectifies, and defines, and on the other hand is emancipated as an unthematizable, objectless, and addresseeless movement of alteration [*Veranderung*] into another language and perhaps into something other than language."[104] Retracing the philological character of phenomenological passivity may displace the role of consciousness in the constitution of what is called our world; it may decenter the "center of affectivities and activities" that "I" am supposed to be;[105] and it may deviate radically from the methodological approach that Husserl intends by way of the phenomenological reduction.[106] But it also allows other pathbreaking traits of Husserl's writing to emerge than those that could be made evident within the more restrictive framework or fiction of intuitive givenness, which all descriptions of passivity would necessarily exceed on the strictest phenomenological grounds. Husserl's phenomenological descriptions of passive synthesis may thus say more about the movements of language that shape our overlapping and contested lives than they do about the logos of subjective experience, as they disclose language not only to be at the unthought core of what is called conscious subjectivity but also to be other than one ever could have thought.

Precisely insofar as Husserl seeks to provide expression for those operations and matters that would precede the activity of the *cogito*—and that could not therefore be given or spoken of in terms of objects or propositional grammar—this other and prior language may be further traced through a closer analysis of the ways in which his formulations trouble apparent lexical unities and do not assume logically coherent syntactic forms. Exemplary in this regard are Husserl's explications of the "overlapping [*Überschiebung*]" that characterizes the radically non-conceptual, if not inconceivable dynamic that first renders two bodies alive to one another.[107] In the *Cartesian Meditations*, Husserl describes the "overlapping" of embodied subjects as a "living, reciprocal awakening-of-one-another; a reciprocal, overlapping overlaying-upon-one-another according to their objectival sense [*ein lebendiges, wechselseitiges Sich-Wecken, ein wechselseitiges, überschiebendes Sich-Überdecken nach dem gegenständlichen Sinn*]."[108] This repetitive formulation not only indicates a thoroughgoing movement of "mutuality," "coincidence," and "crossing,"[109] as Depraz has emphasized in her attentive reading of Husserl's rhetoric but also stresses a change (*Wechsel*) of sides (*Seiten*) that is at once amplified *and* crossed through with the hyperbolic "overlaying" that is itself "overlapping." This restless movement of crossover lets no term be settled in the first place,[110] yielding instead a thoroughly perplexing—an over-, or *hyper*-plexing—dynamic that not only cannot come to an end (because its aim is overshooting) but that also can originate from no single, recognizable "side" because each is "over" with the other to begin with. Along the crossing lines that Husserl retraces, what lives and awakens with "reciprocal awakening [*Sich-Wecken*]" is no one and nothing, other than a movement of alteration (*Wechsel*), which the alternating resonance of *Wecken* and *Wechsel* itself makes pronounced. Whatever else may associate my body with another, that is to say, it is before all else an awakening change or change of awakening that lets each "Ich" ("I") oscillate with the "sich" ("self") of the intersecting itself, before any body could know where either one will have begun or left off.[111]

This articulation of "overlapping" is impossible to parse without provisionally positing the very subjects and objects whose formation remains outstanding and whose future status is already overpassed and crossed through. But what this passage also exposes is how that which is unthinkable and the impossible may ever yet be registered in language, through formulations that depart from the forms of predicative syntax, or through fictive narrations such as the one from *Aminadab* previously cited. Nor is this articulation of overlapping from the *Cartesian Meditations* an exception within Husserl's oeuvre: should one read further, the cognitive dissonance that Husserl's description yields is not resolved but rather amplified when he claims elsewhere that the confusing tendencies of "overlapping" are also canceled out in no time: it would have to be "immediately cancelled out [*sofort aufgehoben*]," he writes in one manuscript, since any carryover from one self to another would immediately "overshoot its 'justified' limits [*über ihre 'rechtmässigen' Grenzen hinausschiess[en]*]."[112] For if the occurrence of "overlapping" can be characterized without contradiction by *both* a movement of overshooting *and* the immediate annulment of said movement, then this aporetic stretch is also nothing that could be gotten past, despite Husserl's suggestions to the contrary.[113] Thus, this aporia will be reiterated in the passage concerning "the initiating and contrasting pairing that now necessarily takes place" between me and my alter ego,[114] where the "now" signals the coincidence of inchoate coupling and immediate contrast one more time.

Husserl's articulations of "overlapping" turn out, then, not only to override the notion of subjective identity and the principle of non-contradiction but also the experiential and empirical order of temporal succession. In these respects, the descriptions cited above are radically counter-intuitive, like the fictive scenarios Husserl entertains in his manuscripts on intersubjectivity, from his early consideration of how "I, the living, embodied I, would look, if I could shift 'myself,' my live body, from here and shove it over there [*dorthin schieben*],"[115] to the question of a more radical displacement that he raises in his manuscripts from the early 1930s: "But can my live body take off and another live body be surreptitiously slipped on me [*mir unterschoben werden*], or can it be cut off or amputated away, and the participation in some other one be given in return for it?"[116] These phantasmatic formulations for pairing are at least as inconceivable from the point of view of the cogito as the one that Georges Bataille sketches, when he asks his readers to consider the implications of scissiparity for all cells or selves involved:

I suggest that you imagine arbitrarily the passage from the state you are in to one in which your person is completely doubled, which you could not survive, since the doubles issued from you would differ from you in an essential manner. Each of these doubles is necessarily distinct from you as you are now. To be the same as you, one of the doubles would have to be actually continuous with the other, and not opposed to it, as it has become. There is a bizarrerie there that the imagination can hardly follow.[117]

But whereas all of these fictions depart from "me," "I" am no longer or not yet "myself" in the experience of overlapping that Husserl traces in the *Cartesian Meditations*, whose syntax of participles, adverbs, reflexive pronouns, and nominalized infinitives effectively place every single subject out of action and leave time impossible to tell.

Pairing renders the subjective and temporal conditions of possible experience out of joint from the outset. Nor could the radical foreignness of Husserl's rhetoric to the life as we know it be reduced by appealing, say, to the coincidence of every "now" with a retentional "not-now" that Husserl elaborates in his analyses of internal time consciousness.[118] For if, on the one hand, it is this temporal differential that could permit the "coincidence" of "overlapping" and "contrast"—if retention opens time for at least two mutually exclusive occurrences to be held in mind "at once"— then it is also this alterity internal to time that will have "destroy[ed] any possibility of a simple self-identity" in advance.[119] And if, on the other hand, counter-arguments could be made in order to minimize the "nonpresence and otherness" that is thereby admitted into "presence"—such as Husserl's claim that each "now" would be structured as a continuum of retentional modifications,[120] making it absurd to compare, let alone contrast, a "now" with the modifications that make it up every time[121]—these arguments could no longer hold when it comes to the contrasting movements that coincide in the "now" of "overlapping." Far from cohering into an ordered continuum of lived experience, the "now" of intersubjective "overlapping" is itself divided between simultaneous movements of coupling and scission that assimilate and dissimulate the very subject of experience, that announce or "demand [*fordert*]" a sensory "present [*Gegenwart*]" whose promise can never be fulfilled,[122] and that make virtual reminiscences "immediately *step forth* into exteriority [*alsbald in der Äusserlichkeit eintr[eten]*]."[123] Since, moreover, Husserl will maintain that subjectivity can only hold its own through its continuous stream of consciousness—it is in the "streaming of the present" that "I am subject of affections and actions," he writes, before continuing: "This present is the sole vitality [*einzige Lebendigkeit*], one ur-present [*Urgegenwart*], one stream"[124]—the coincidence or "Deckung" of one embodied "consciousness" with another suggests that consciousness itself becomes duplicitous and two-timing per se whenever it decks itself out in this manner. Overlapping, that is, yields the dilemma of a lifetime for all those involved, and through his rhetorical performance, Husserl also "says" that this dilemma is what consciousness would have to live with for all the time that others are involved in "my" life. For if the overlapping of similar data would do as he says, then my own "originary" givenness—and that means: my givenness "incarnate," "in the flesh," "leibhaft da"—would always be incorporated with that of others who give a semblance of "myself."[125]

There is, in other words, no way out of the complications that passive syntheses entail for the coherence and activity of the *cogito*, which Husserl's writing attests every time that the voice of the phenomenologist gives way to utterances that speak otherwise than any coherent subject could intuit, that speak for the improper and inappropriable "inter-" of intersubjectivity, and that thus speak beyond all recognition. These underlying tendencies from within the logos of phenomenology only become more legible, should one leave the scene where the "alter ego" is said to make its entrance and attend more closely to the ways in which Husserl traces the tension between overlapping and contrasting in general. Since this tension would precede both identity and identifiable differences, cohesion is initially characterized as being founded in that which is alogical and anonymous—"the irrational that makes rationality possible,"[126] as Husserl puts it in one manuscript—while subsequent disruptions will be said to owe themselves not to avoidable anomalies but to upsurging protests that object to the assimilative tendency of passive synthesis and thus advocate for alterity per se. The rigor of Husserl's reduction of experience to the passive sphere leads to these chaotic consequences, and as a further consequence of the passive conditions for conscious activity, all cohesive and unequivocal intentionalities would have to entail the possibility of being illusory and repressive, without any guarantee that one would ever tell the difference. In the last analysis, then, subjective and objective coherence would be structurally contentious, as Husserl suggests when he formalizes the "ABCs"[127] of assimilation among disparate reproductive memories: "The constituent parts, a and b, are, now as before, pieces of intentional wholes; they have repressed supplementary pieces, which protest from underground against the demands directed in the illusory image from a to b and vice versa, and they protest before all else against their reciprocal fulfillments, although the protests are too weak, too little audible to lead to a clear doubt or a negation"[128] (Die Bestandstücke a und b sind nach wie vor Stücke von intentionalen Ganzen, sie haben verdrängte Ergänzungsstücke, welche gegen die im Scheinbild von a auf b und umgekehrt gerichteten Forderungen und vor allem gegen ihre wechselseitigen Erfüllungen vom Untergrund her protestieren, obschon die Proteste zu schwach sind, zu wenig hörbar um zu einem klaren Zweifel und einer Negation zu führen).[129]

Whether or not Husserl's initial privileging of assimilation over differentiation in this passage is founded—elsewhere, difference will be said to come first: only an "interruption [. . .] of 'absolutely smooth' streaming, fusing," Husserl writes, "makes affection possible and, with it, turns of attention and [conscious] activity"[130]—his insistence that evidence for dissimilarity would be contingent upon the strength of the "protests" launched by diverse factions or factors of experience implies that dissent is less likely to be "heard" than agreement.[131] On these terms, the first refusal that announces alterity could therefore never have been the first, nor could the absence of all audible protest ever be conclusive. Since these are the tentative and contentious conditions for passive synthesis, moreover, every synthetic formation would be open to further determination, deformation, and disintegration, not unlike Husserl's syntagm, where internal discrepancies quietly disintegrate the whole. From the outset, his initial proposition ("The constituent parts, a and b, are before as after pieces of intentional wholes") is unsettled with an apposition ("they have repressed supplementary pieces"); then, the *ultimate* failure for demands to be fulfilled is said to contest those demands *before all else* ("which protest [. . .] against the demands [. . .] and before all else against their reciprocal fulfillments"); and ultimately, this contestation is again diminished with the subordinate clause that arrives in the end and renders the very premise of conflict itself contestable, if not negligible and moot ("although the protests are too weak, too little audible to lead to a clear doubt or a negation").

In other words, the logical formalization that Husserl would seem to trace in this passage on the overlap and contrast between "a" and "b" not only speaks against the possibility of any but a contestable "intentional whole"; it also speaks against its own speaking, to the point where even the "illusory image [*Scheinbild*]" that Husserl posits would have to be a mere semblance of a semblance as well. Strictly speaking, it would be more plausible that nothing would appear to be *illusory* in the situation that Husserl describes, where protests pass unnoticed, and in a situation of amplified protest, it would not be the protests, but rather *nothing* that appears, since no tendencies toward assimilation could gain hold against what speaks against them. Hence, as Husserl begins to attend more closely to the barely audible protests that he invokes—as if making them louder, so to speak—he will soon retract the image quality of any "image-to-be-divided-up-among-different-memories [*ein auf verschiedene Wiedererinnerungen aufzuteilendes Bild*]," using a nominal phrase that is itself stretched nearly to the breaking point and that thus supports his further clarification that no such apparition could be "completely clear."[132] If Husserl stops short of describing a situation where appearance and experience would default entirely, moreover, the withdrawal of sense over the course of his passage lets such a default be felt, not in the modality of the "not" that Husserl had elaborated in the *Logical Investigations*, where the disappointment of expectations or empty intentions is intuited through the alternative fulfillments that arrive in their place,[133] but in a sheer refusal for an appearance or intention to take shape. This default would, in other words, be more like the "affection of the soul" that Augustine evokes to explicate "nothing" in *De magistro*, "when [the soul] does not see a thing and further finds or imputes itself to find it not to be."[134] And just as this explication shows that "nothing" should not be dismissed, despite Augustine's protests to the contrary, Husserl's formulations speak against dismissing those passages like the one previously cited that undo themselves and thus verge upon saying nothing in the propositional or logical sense of the word. To the contrary, both his express affirmations of dissonance as well as the dissonance of his expressions let language itself emerge as unheard of.

What is at stake in drawing out this trait of Husserl's prose is not the exposition of curious idiosyncrasies within the corpus of phenomenology, or the provision of evidence against self-sovereign expression, but the amplification of those barely audible strains of protest that challenge the harmony that forms the irrational basis or bias of rational thought. Because and not despite the fact that we may, for all our passive absorption in our (several) selves, be inclined to ignore dissonance and even amputate that which cannot be assimilated to common sense, it is all the more critical to let dissent come across and trouble thought, lest we suppress the alterity that belongs to the truth of experience. Nor does Husserl only occasionally suggest the correlation between suppressed dissonance and harmonious verification. In fact, "repression" will be paired with "overlapping" in his discussions of passive association, and it will be articulated in ways that contaminate the semblances of truth that association should deliver. Just after introducing the "overlapping" that may take place among only partially similar data, Husserl writes: "Repression signifies that the one covers over the other, that the covered tends towards discovery, then breaking through covers the previously discovered thing, and so forth. [*Das Verdrängen besagt, daß eins das andere verdeckt, daß das Verdeckte zur Aufdeckung tendiert, durchbrechend dann das vordem Aufgedeckte verdeckt usw.*]."[135] With this formulation, Husserl not only reiterates the tendency of overlapping to cover over difference but also renders the similar tendencies toward "covering" (*Verdecken*) and "discovering" (*Aufdecken*) through the apposition of clauses "that" (*daß*) indicate simultaneity, and "then" (*dann*) alternation, marking a disturbance within the articulation of time that indicates a similar turbulence within the flow of experience.[136] At the same time, moreover, the alternation between past and present participles ("the covered [*das Verdeckte*]," "breaking through [*durchbrechend*]," "the previously discovered [*das vordem Aufgedeckte*]") suggests that this movement would at all times be completed and ongoing, past and present—and therefore thoroughly aporetic, through to its open-ended conclusion: "and so forth."

There would seem to be no end, then, to the crisis that overlapping and repression create and therefore no univocal basis for the formation of phenomenal unities and relations. On the contrary, the crisis is redoubled and complicated further by the fact that the permutations of "*deck-*" throughout Husserl's description of repression also persistently recall the word for "coincidence" (*Deckung*), which figures not only in Husserl's definition of overlapping[137] but also in his definition of evidence: namely, "a synthesis in which what was meant coincides and agrees with what is itself given [*Synthesis der stimmenden Deckung*]."[138] Husserl's formulations for the dissonance of repression not only trouble the semblance of consonant appearances, then, but also resonate with the rhetoric of evidence itself; and in so doing, they contest of their own accord those univocal claims that may be made on the basis of "coincidence." But beyond this more negative effect of Husserl's rhetoric, is also in this oblique way that his writing on repression may be seen to advocate for those differences that evident agreement otherwise tends to keep under cover. One could even venture to say that the "true" sense of "coincidence" (*Deckung*) itself opens "up" (*auf*) with "das *Auf*-gedeckte" and veers "awry" (*ver-*) with "das *Ver*-deckte," and thereby already testifies to its association with those other voices and figures whose possibility Husserl would affirm elsewhere: "Various figures could have been formed from out of the chaos and could still be formed."[139] Whatever may be said in favor of harmonious coincidence, its coincidence with repression also says that it could never be the same and that the truth could always be different.

The more dissonant traits of Husserl's phenomenological descriptions bear testimony for the sake of others without speaking over or in lieu of them, and they therefore speak for alterity without assimilating alterity into any epistemological notions of the same. They speak "for" others, that is to say, in the manner that philology speaks " 'for' a language that does not only register and communicate what is at hand but rather, open to alterity and history, still remains turned toward a word—even one within language—that can be grasped in no word of no language."[140] The "other" trajectories that traverse his writing become most pronounced, however, when Husserl turns to those passive voices that appeal and protest "from the underground [*vom Untergrund*]" of experience and thought,[141] whose foundation is not originally constituted from the "first-person perspective"[142] but turns out to be made up of those inconstant, anonymous instances of speech that intersect as "abyss invokes abyss."[143] This abyssal underground of experience is repressed by those approaches to Husserl that aim to discover a univocal sense in his corpus and thus reduce the discursive disparities and complexities that mark his thinking: but it is not repressed within his manuscripts, which demand to be read with philological as well as philosophical rigor. As Rodolphe Gasché has argued, Husserl's writing solicits a reading that would account "for what Husserl *does* in his texts, in contradistinction to what he *says*."[144] For what Husserl's extensive descriptions of similarity, alterity, association, overlapping, and repression offer before all else is an experimental language of experience that never fully accords with any logical principle of unity or aesthetic principle of harmony but traces out shifting structures that subvert the very sequential acts and objective formations that they are supposed to subtend.[145] And ultimately, Husserl's writings therefore offer a language that fundamentally unsettles even the metaphysical presuppositions that enter into his more explicit considerations of words along the lines of body and soul, exterior expression, and interior meaning.[146] For the linguistic character of those appeals that provoke our interest and protest our assimilation, as well as those traits of body language and spoken understanding that make "my" every thought and move an ambivalent "repetition," also show how linguistic structures enter into the very tissue of every "body"—before any *ego* or *logos*—and beyond this, they show how speech structurally escapes the wishes, claims, and grasp of every subject.[147]

That is to say: language never could have just been between subjects like "you" and "me," and not because, ideally, "words bear the stamp of 'everyone'" *ab initio*,[148] but because other speaking instances and figures of speech will have always come before and cut across each apparent speaker or outspoken claim. In a sense that Husserl may or may not ever have intended when he wrote of it: "*Expressive* speech goes so far beyond the intuitive data necessary for the actual appropriateness of the expression of acquaintance."[149] Yet as it fails to fulfill our intentions, language also surpasses every expectation and allows us to go on speaking, among others, with *and* without "ourselves."

Chapter 3

Parsing Pairing

George Bataille and the Scripts of Subjectivity

The words that let "you" and "me" come alive to one another, the speech that gives word of "lived experience," and the language that will have formed "our" lifelines both before and beyond our lifetimes: these are the relations that intimately concern, trouble, and surpass the subject of Husserl's phenomenology as well as Augustine's theology. But whereas Augustine appeals to the authority of scripture despite the fundamentally unknown character of language, and whereas Husserl more obliquely contests the irreducibility of language to the intentions of conscious life through his writings on passive synthesis, both Georges Bataille's *Summa Atheologica* and his literary oeuvre draw out those traits of language and experience that exceed the subject, by testing, contesting, and crossing the limits of the doctrinal, logical, and existential notions that would otherwise provide a basis for our beliefs and even ourselves. Early in his "Sketch of an Introduction to *Inner Experience*," Bataille parts ways with both "philosophical" and "religious" approaches to experience, whose pursuit of "knowledge" and presumption of "authorities," respectively, impose restrictions that prevent them from "proceeding to the end": namely, to "the extreme limit of the possible" that "experience" may attain.[1] Without authoritative *arché* and beyond every epistemological *telos*, the extremes of experience are instead to be broached, Bataille contends, through the movements of "contestation" that make up experience itself: "Experience, its authority, its method, do not distinguish themselves from the contestation"; "the foundation for all 'spiritual' life can only [. . .] be contestation of itself and non-knowledge."[2]

And insofar as he finds these movements to be unthinkable apart from "the work of discourse in us,"³ Bataille also proceeds to "link [*lier*] contestation to the *liberation* [libération] *of the power of words*,"⁴ through a manner of speaking that should also liberate language *from* the power of words to "direct[] attention towards what [they] grasp[],"⁵ or to issue directives in the name of "salvation" and "domination."⁶

Remote from devotional confession as well as phenomenological intuition, experience thus becomes an issue of speaking with and against the means and meanings of speech that will have made of language a "law,"⁷ yielding a thoroughgoing contra- and contestation where "the difference between inner experience and philosophy resides principally in this: that in experience, what is stated is nothing [*l'énoncé n'est rien*], if not a means [*moyen*] and even, as much as a means, an obstacle [*obstacle*]; what counts is no longer the statement of wind, but the wind."⁸ And should this coincidence of "means" and "obstacle" still recall the language of certain philosophical predecessors such as Hegel, for whom "terminology" was similarly thought to "arrest thought," Bataille's emphasis upon "nothing" but the "wind" sets the drift of experience apart from the spirit of knowledge that animates Hegel's turn to the "terms of living language," whose "different significations, invite[] thought not to become fixed, but rather [. . .] to discover the internal relations among things [. . .]; to discover—or find again—[. . .] the living identity of the concrete."⁹ The philosophical terms, statements, and concepts of not only Hegel but also Augustine, Heidegger, Kierkegaard, and Nietzsche, among others, may resonate in *Inner Experience*,¹⁰ but their signifying intentions are no longer "what counts," so much as the verbal encounters that are thereby staged, so as to expose words to be means and obstacles to experience. Experience cannot, in other words, be claimed or explicated, but only registered as words interrupt themselves and slip toward silence, like "the word *silence*" itself, which already marks "the abolition of the sound that the word is."¹¹ And beyond this express example for what Bataille calls a "'slipping' word [mot *glissant*]"¹²—as well as beyond any dialectic of speech and silence—word of experience may also slip out along the lines of Bataille's "linking" (*l-i-e-r*) of "contestation" with "liberation" (*l-i-b-é-r-ation*), which itself spells the possibility of "reading" (*l-i-r-e*) differently the "liaison" that forms the root of all binding ligations—religious and otherwise—while freeing both "linking" and "liberation" from signifying any single thing or even signaling opposites. More pronouncedly than with "silence," the "contestation" in and of (linguistic) experience in such passages as these would be neither reductive, positional, nor oppositional, and even its legibility would be tested, as the liberties internal to speech play out, affecting all projections of identity, intentionality, and mastery, including those of Bataille and his readers.

The introductory premises that Bataille sketches for *Inner Experience* would therefore not only be impossible according to any doctrines that would aim to maintain the power of a transcendent god or a transcendental subject of cognition—to say nothing of Hegel's notion of "absolute knowledge," whose analysis dissolves into "anguish" and "abandon" for Bataille.[13] For these premises would also render Bataille's project impossible as such. Yet unlike the projects of writers such as Augustine and Husserl, the condition of possibility for Bataille's writing is its impossibility, since it could not expose the atheological and aphenomenological traits of experience that it addresses without exposing the powerlessness of its language to do so. Hence, Bataille goes on to describe "inner experience" as a project that would abolish itself as a "project," and he suggests that this abolition would be carried out through the very same words that make up the terms of its design.[14] "Nevertheless inner experience is project, no matter what," he writes, before continuing: "It is such—man being entirely so through language which, in essence, with the exception of its poetic perversion, is project. But project is no longer in this case that, positive, of salvation, but that, negative, of abolishing the power of words, hence of project."[15] What this passage says is that words would remain in *Inner Experience* but solely duplicitously: as signifiers that abolish their power to signify and as remnants of this abolition, which itself takes place through the undecidability between significance and insignificance that Bataille bespeaks.

If these words on words indicate the slippage that any range of terms may undergo, however, the movements that Bataille traces also affect the subjects of *Inner Experience*—that is, "you" and "me"—whose emergence depends upon "paths" of communication that also cross through and efface them. "Now to live," as Bataille writes at one point,

> signifies for you not only the flux and the fleeting play of light which are united in you, but the passage of warmth or of light from one being to another, from you to your fellow being or from your fellow being to you (even at the moment when you read in me the contagion of my fever which reaches you): words, books, monuments, symbols, laughter are only

so many paths of this contagion, of this passage. Individual beings matter little and enclose points of view which cannot be acknowledged, if one considers what is animated, passing from one to the other in love, in tragic scenes, in movements of fervor. Thus we are nothing, neither you nor I [*ni toi ni moi*], beside burning words [*paroles brûlantes*] which could [*pourraient*] pass from me to you, imprinted on a page [*imprimées sur un feuillet*]: for I would only have lived in order to write them, and, if it is true that they are addressed to you [*et s'il est vrai qu'elles s'adressent à toi*], you will live from having had the strength to hear them.[16]

With these words, Bataille announces an experience of reading that could only be projected in the conditional, since no "I" lives before or apart from "your" reading in order to prepare, let alone assure, its occurrence, and since "you" have no say concerning the words that you will have not only "had the strength to hear" but that will also have already spoken for "you." Whatever experience may be addressed to the reader therefore could not be bound by the paradigm of religious confession: it is rather a matter of "experience laid bare, free of ties, even of an origin, of any confession whatever."[17] Nor could it be described according to "the sole philosophy" that Bataille claims to be "living": namely, the phenomenological philosophy "of the German school,"[18] which most likely refers not only to the pages of Hegelian thinkers such as Alexandre Kojève, Alexandre Koyré, and Jean Wahl but also to the writings of Martin Heidegger and Karl Jaspers, who had taken inspiration from Husserl's phenomenology.[19] The "contagion" of which Bataille speaks here is not the "contagion" or "Ansteckung" that Hegel had ascribed to the "I," as an expression of subjectivity that spreads to all who may hear, making up both its universal and "proper knowledge of itself,"[20] nor are the "burning words" in Bataille's book "manifestations of [the] philosophical energy," which, according to Jaspers, "makes me strive to arrange all questions, thoughts, and views so that through them the spark of self-being will be kindled in one who thinks along with me."[21] Instead, "you" and "I" neither transcend nor constitute the sense of Bataille's utterances, but are contingent upon passing encounters and paths of contagion that precede and exceed "us."[22] It is not that "you" or "I" are given so that words may be "given" to us, or so that "we" may give words to one another; instead, each word of "you" and "I," among others, is given over to movements that may or may not bring "us" to be (in touch) and that no one and no word could know to ignite in advance. At the same time, however, if Bataille's suggestion of a mutual surrender of "I" and "you" may distantly recall the ardent gestures of sacrifice in Augustine—from the praise that he offers God in the *Confessions* ("I sing a hymn and offer sacrifice of praise to you who sanctify me"[23]) to the sermons that he delivers to his congregation, where the love of the Holy Spirit is said to ignite the bread, bodies, hearts, and tongues of those who take the Eucharist, rendering the sacrament a burnt offering of the Church itself[24]—there is no source and destination beyond Bataille's page for the agent and patient of "burning words." All speakable subjects would instead be subject to the sheer passion of expenditure that "burning words" bespeaks, offering one among many indications of what would have to be undergone in the language of *Inner Experience* for those whose very lives would depend on it.

The "life" that is at stake in Bataille's text would thus no more signify the "wakeful being-I in affection and action [*Leben : waches Ichsein in Affektion und Aktion*]" that characterizes the Husserlian *cogito*,[25] than it would signify the subject of "possible existence" in Jaspers's *Philosophy*,[26] or the Christ to whom Augustine will ultimately trace the life of the mind, upon the authority of Scripture: "for 'that which was made' was already 'life in him.'"[27] Instead, life would belong to the "warmth," "light," or "burning" that words may bear, which is also why it is only in the wake of this passage that "I" will have "lived" to write the words you read, and that "you will live from having had the strength to hear them." With such words as these, Bataille's text says not only that "my" life and speech depend upon another, which had already been said with the biblical verses that Augustine repeats in order to establish the very fact of "my" speaking as an effect of being heard: "I have cried out, *since you heard me, God* [*Ego clamaui, quoniam exaudisti me Deus*]."[28] For the passage from *Inner Experience* also says that we would have to miss this chance of communication whenever it should happen to occur, since the language that lends "us" our lives and ourselves would exceed "my" lifetime and precede the living that "you" begin to do after having heard from me. If "we" should ever live to become involved with one another, then we could do so only through a writing that brings the two of "us" to a life we will never live to see ourselves.

Previously, Bataille had similarly spoken to this point: "Life is never situated at a particular point: it passes rapidly from one point to another (or from multiple points to other points), like [*comme*] a current or like [*comme*] a sort of electric flow."²⁹ Insofar as "life" takes place as passage, it could not endure for any subject whom one could call "living"; still less could it be fixed and identified as an object for consciousness; and in the last analysis, it could not even be known by name, if names are thought to serve as "instruments of useful acts" for knowing subjects, as Bataille later suggests,³⁰ echoing Husserl's association of names with cognition, and cognition with possession: "in naming [*im Nennen*]," as he writes in the *Logical Investigations*, one "knows *Hans* as *Hans*, *Berlin* as *Berlin*,"³¹ which knowledge will translate to what Husserl elsewhere calls an "abiding acquisition or possession" on the part of the concrete ego.³² Both when Bataille evokes "life" in his lines on "burning words" and when he speaks of the movements of "life" itself, what the term could designate is instead left fundamentally indeterminate, rendering it a name for nothing known and itself an unknown name. On the one hand, the vital transfusion of words from "me" to "you" is never posited as an actuality but only evoked as a virtual possibility with Bataille's conditional verb ("could [*pourraient*] pass") and conditional clause ("if it is true that they are addressed to you [*et s'il est vrai qu'elles s'adressent à toi*]").³³ And on the other hand, the shifting metaphors that make up Bataille's description of life's "electric flow [*ruissellement électrique*]" emphasize its metaphoric character, where the "like's" of it ("like [*comme*] a current or like [*comme*] a sort of electric flow") further suggest that the communication of vitality so radically escapes grasp, it could only ever give a passing semblance of itself. As Rodolphe Gasché has observed in a related context, "with the *comme*, [. . .] the rampant production of images gets underway and the images begin to follow each other in a series in which every image aspires to explicate and supplement the previous one," without "ever catching up with" anything like an original.³⁴ Hence, when it comes to "our" lives in *Inner Experience*, *comme* accents the fleeting, irreal character of *comm*unication still more than the *community* of the living that it should make possible.

In all of these respects, however, what is called our "life" also turns out to be another word for language, not in the narrow sense of any known tongues but in the sense of their condition of possibility, which entails those movements that exceed every instrumental and nominal function, as well as those prior moments of passage that overdetermine every term, passing "from multiple points to other points" at every point in time,³⁵ and thus linking indefinitely many instances of speech each time that a word happens to reach anyone. "In that which touches humans," as Bataille later writes, "their existence is linked to language [*se lie au langage*]. Each person imagines, and therefore knows of his existence with the help of words. Words come to [one] in [one's] head loaded [*chargés*] with the multitude of human—or non-human—existences with respect to which [one's] private existence exists."[36] Before and beyond all talk of "you" and me," that is, any notions that may occur to us would already be "loaded" with the existence of unidentifiable, anonymous multitudes—whose "charge" may bear the sense of a dead weight or the sense of energy, electricity, and life—placing the manifold acts of discursive consciousness on an ambivalent form of life support that infinitely surpasses its operations, renders its "knowledge" passive, and draws it toward the verge of annihilation so long as it "lives." There is only living on this edge, where the "help of words" also always approaches "sacrifice,"[37] and where the links that they forge may be delirium. Hence, even the slightest reflection upon the multitude of linguistic existences that may make up "my" mind—as well as the multitude of alternatives which would virtually annul "my" current existence—really renders "my" being a "crazed" or "mad" ("folle") "improbability."[38] Once language is in "us" and once "we" live on it, Bataille suggests, we are also carried away, contaminated by others, and dispossessed of every vital claim that could be "yours" or "mine."[39]

It was in light of such passages as these that Jacques Derrida would speak of Bataille's writing as a suspension or "*epoché*" of "the epoch of sense," which is irreducible to a subject and, unlike the phenomenological "epoché," no longer "conducts itself *in the name and in view of sense*."[40] It could hardly be otherwise, once not only the givens but also the transcendental subject—as well as transsubjective life—are shown to be linguistic effects that precede and therefore surpass the scope of subjective intuition and intentionality.[41] As Benjamin Noys similarly observes: "It is language which discloses the impossibility of an autonomous being, and it is language which places us in an impossible *relation* that we can never master."[42] For the same reason, however, this "epoché" is not and could not be enacted by any writing, reading, or thinking subject, and it is certainly no "*matter of our complete freedom* [Sache unserer vollkommenen Freiheit]," as Husserl had claimed the phenomenological reduction to be.[43] The "epoché" that Derrida addresses is instead undergone passively through the words that one may live to write, read, speak, or think: the suspension of sense is the passion of language that charges each subject with the lives of indefinitely many others; that subjects all involved to an alterity that is other than any thinking "I"; and that thereby consumes and decomposes the very "subjects" whose lives it sustains. This passivity is suggested already with the "burning" that Bataille ascribes to words, which not only implies that words would be suffered—"being-burned [καίεται]" being *the* example, besides "being-cut [τέμνεται]," of "suffering [πάσχειν]" in Aristotle's treatise on the *Categories*[44]—but that also associates words with the invisible heat of fire, whose destructive potential for phenomenality and phenomenal matters alike had troubled those heretics who, according to Augustine, "wish to see, but not to burn."[45] The "burning" force of words thus speaks to the aphenomenonal character of language, which ultimately entails that even Bataille's word of "burning" would have to suffer a withdrawal from phenomenality as well. This withdrawal takes place as the over-determination of "burning words" through the words of Aristotle, among others, issues into their indetermination, as "burning" remains recognizable as a "word" and thereby fails to do as it says, and as these internal contradictions void the signifying power of the phrase, leaving "burning" unsaid even as it appears to stand written. If "we are nothing [. . .] beside burning words [*paroles brûlantes*] which could [*pourraient*] pass from me to you," then we may also be "nothing" to speak of; and either way, the transmission of "burning words" from "me to you" would itself have to go without a word, as a vital or lethal occurrence which could neither be guaranteed nor realized by virtue of being "imprinted on a page" in Bataille's text.[46]

To at least the same degree that word of burning withdraws, however, traces of burning also remain legible through the asignificant traits that cross through the words before "our" eyes. In particular, the alternating plosives (*p, b*) and liquids (*r, l*) of the "*paroles brûlantes*" literally bring the words for "words" ("paroles") and "burning" ("brûlantes") to meld together "upon a page [*feuillet*]," which would itself be set on "fire" (*feu*), if that possibility were not also written off by the spread of this "feu" to the "leaf" (*feuillet*). It is perhaps in this way that the "liberation" from "the power of words" could occur;[47] that an "epoché" of the "epoch of sense" takes place in Bataille's book; and that the language of *Inner Experience* could be "read," without reducing it to the very sort of sense that it contests. Because, moreover, such traces do not belong to the order of the signifier or the proposition—and therefore could not be confirmed as meaning or saying anything—they may register an experience of language that eludes subjective apprehension and undermines in advance any attempt to take words for a given in the first place. At this elemental level of analysis and decomposition, there would be no telling whether "burning" and "words" in fact burn into one another in a way for which there is no word; nor would there be any way to tell whether the "fire" (*feu*) of the "page" (*feuillet*) should be read into the latter. And finally, there would be no telling what sort of relation, if any, could obtain among those residual indications of intersubjectivity—perhaps an intersubjectivity of "the non-subject"[48]—that are marked and crossed off in the name of "me," "you," or "us." Instead, these words or particles, among others, both break down and survive in ways that render them different from one another and from "themselves," as the traits of Bataille's writing cut or burn through their distinctions as units, suspending any decision over and between them, yet without ending in indifference or blending out the differential "aspects" that they so flagrantly display.[49]

To be sure, similar movements had figured in Husserl's studies of intersubjectivity, where the passive process of pairing that should found the apperception of alterity was described through a rhetoric of "overlapping" that renders the identities of all participants, elements, and givens anything but clear-cut.[50] As discussed in the previous chapter, when Husserl writes of a "living, reciprocal awakening-of-one-another; a reciprocal, overlapping overlaying-upon-one-another according to their objectival sense [*ein lebendiges, wechselseitiges Sich-Wecken, ein wechselseitiges, überschiebendes Sich-Überdecken nach dem gegenständlichen Sinn*],"[51] the alternation and alliteration between "reciprocal [*wechselseitig*]" and "awakening [*Wecken*]" subjects the awakening itself to change (*Wechsel*), while the alterity signaled by the reflexive pronoun, "**Sich** [*one another*]" alters, echoes, and displaces the "**Ich** [*I*]" that most often names the wakeful subject of conscious life: "Life: wakeful being-I [*Leben : waches Ichsein*]."[52] But whereas Husserl more vocally insists upon the notion of a living consciousness endowed with a proper sphere of givens, the contingencies of language that contest the unity of subjective life in his descriptions become the point of departure for the "exscriptions" of Bataille.[53] Alone, the passage from *Inner Experience* that has been analyzed most extensively so far marks a pairing where "you [*toi*]" and "I [*moi*]" graphically and phonically cut into each other ("*toi* [. . .] *moi*"), where each word of "us" follows an index of negation from the outset ("ni [. . .] ni"), and where "we" both remain exposed to the alterity of all other words that may pass between us "besides": "Thus we are nothing, neither you nor I [*ni toi ni moi*], beside burning words [*paroles brûlantes*] which could [*pourraient*] pass from me to you."[54] Nor are "you" and "I" the sole or primary vehicle for those inter- and alter-subjective lifelines that let us burn with fervor and pass away as we speak. For beside these figures of speech from *Inner Experience*, the passions of linguistic experience, as well as their implications for life and death, logic and sense, testimony and address, will be still more drastically exposed in Bataille's various writings on "scissiparity," which provide the cutting complement to the suffering that was conveyed with "burning words": the "being-cut [τέμνεται]" that complements the "being-burned [καίεται]" in language.[55]

At least as emphatically as "experience," "scissiparity" recurs through Bataille's oeuvre, where the term that more often designates the asexual reproduction of unicellular organisms is invoked to describe the dynamics of scission, alteration, and replication that modify all modes of being. If scissiparity may thus seem to designate a dialectical movement of continuity and rupture in the Hegelian spirit, however, the linkage of existence with language in Bataille also renders the sense of "scissiparity" inseparable from its textual occurrences, whose sheer variety renders this word, name, or figure none that could be reduced to a dialectical concept or "living identity"[56] but one whose plural articulations, like Bataille's "burning words," solicit meticulous readings to the letter. From the critical moment when the growth of a cell, human, estate, or society abruptly cuts off and gives way to expenditure and loss within what Bataille calls the "general economy" of life,[57] to the alphabetic characters "Alpha, Bêta" in his narrative, *La Scissiparité*, whose fictive and ad hoc "proper" names only barely draw the semblance of a distinction between two twins:[58] "scissiparity" marks various sexual, economic, existential, and fictional experiences, without congealing into a fixed notion. Bataille's proliferating appeals to "scissiparity" thus bifurcate throughout his oeuvre in ways that testify themselves to the contagious yet discontinuous character of (linguistic) life.

Hence, even "inner experience" will be marked by "scissiparity" when Bataille returns to it in writings such as "Eroticism, or the Placing in Question of Being" (1956) and *Eroticism* (1957),[59] where the incongruous pairing of microbiology and intimacy cuts to the core of that which was in question in his earlier approaches to the language of experience. As Bataille writes in *Eroticism*, if inner experience "did not have the universal," and thus scientific "character of an object to which its return is linked [*le caractère universel de l'objet auquel se lie son retour*], we could not speak of it" at all;[60] and conversely, we could speak of no objects "without the private experience" that first moves us to do so, and that as such remains unbound to the terms of objectivity.[61] On the one hand, then, "inner experience is never given independently of objective views,"[62] and on the other hand, every single course of objective research could only have begun from out of inner experience, which is not itself determined by knowledge, and thus exposes "scientific" terminology to slippages that betray its unscientific provenance: "But inner experience within me precedes objective reflection, [. . .] most often, the memory of some state or other was the origin of boring researches (would I have reflected on scissiparity if I had not initially lived the gliding that I consider?)."[63] At the same time, moreover, a plethora of past experiences would affect our thought before we know it, insofar as the "aspects" or "forms" of all perceptible things are "only given to us [*nous sont données*] from the perspective where the aspect or form historically took its sense. We cannot entirely separate the experience that we have of them [. . .] from their historical appearance."[64] On these terms, the language for experience could only ever be borderline crazed, integrating elements that also threaten to disintegrate it, not unlike "the plethora that initiates the glide towards the division of the organism" in scissiparity, where the decisive moment of splitting is still only slipping and therefore decidedly ambiguous: "It divides at the very moment, the moment of the glide, the critical moment when these two beings about to become separate [or: opposed] at any minute are still not yet so [*ne s'opposent pas encore*]"[65] As Dennis Hollier has likewise observed: "Scissiparity torments vocabulary by multiplying meanings beyond the possibilities of any totalizing project [. . .]. Everything divides in two. Meaning moves through cleavage."[66] If it is at all paradoxical that the language of inner experience and the language of objective science intersect and cut into one another, then, this paradox would be founded in the very process of scissiparity that objective discourse describes; it would therefore be no paradox beside any orthodox understanding but the sole, double, and self-divided truth—or a scissiparadox.

It is in remaining true to these traits of inner life and outer objectivity that Bataille broaches "inner experience" from outside the bounds of experience as we "know" it in passages such as the following:

> In order, then, to get at the inner experience, we shall now discuss physical conditions. In the fields of objective reality life always brings into play, except when there is impotence, an excess of energy which must be expended [*il faut se dépenser*], and this super-abundance is in fact either expended in the growth of the unity envisaged or in a pure and simple loss [*une perte pure et simple*]. [. . .] To have a clear picture of this process we must base ourselves on scissiparity [*il faut nous fonder sur la scissiparité*], the simplest mode of reproduction.

> The scissiparous organism does grow, but once it has grown the single organism will one day or another split into two [*un jour ou l'autre, cet organisme unique en forme deux*]. Let it be that the infusorium *a* is becoming *a'* + *a"* [*Soit l'infusoire* a *devenant* a' + a"]; then the passage [*passage*] from the first state to the second is not independent of the growth of *a*, as *a'* + *a"*, compared with the earlier state represented by *a*, represents the growth of the latter.
>
> What must be noted is that *a'*, although other than *a"*, is not, any more than the latter, other than *a*. Something of *a* subsists [*subsiste*] in *a'*, something of *a* subsists [*subsiste*] in *a"*. I shall return to the disconcerting character of a growth that calls the unity of the growing organism into question [*met en cause l'unité de l'organisme qui croît*].[67]

Here, Bataille's proposal to access "inner experience" through "physical conditions" turns the issue inside out from the very first word. But this turn is no simple inversion that would allow for a return to any supposed distinction between inside and outside, or metaphor and authentic speech; rather, the ensuing description of "physical conditions" troubles the integrity of every term and blurs the boundaries that would determine their limits. The over-determined motif of "life"—which had been invoked as indubitable evidence for the actuality of the mind in Augustine and redefined to signify the actuosity of the *cogito* in Husserl—turns out to signify a growth that expends and dispenses with itself, not by virtue of its autotelic activity but by default, as signaled in the phrase: "It *must* be expended [*il faut se dépenser*]." This paradoxically passive mobilization of "excess [. . .] energy" thus cannot but give way to the scissiparous "passage" that rends life apart and renders it different from itself, whether the process yields reduplication or "pure and simple loss." With this movement, moreover, it is not only the *bios*- but also the -*logos* of bio-logy that breaks down, as the straightforward formula, "the single organism will one day or another split into two," shows one to equal zero and two, and two to equal one, in the same stroke. For the scission that Bataille traces is one in which the initial *a* at once goes utterly lost and doubly survives itself, fundamentally troubling the apparent sameness that had allowed *a* to be identified in the first place: as Bataille emphatically notes, "*a'*, although other than *a"*, is not, any more than the latter, other than *a* [a' *étant autre que* a" *n'est, pas plus que n'est ce dernier, autre que* a]."[68]

The duplicates are and are not other than one another; their prototype does and does not subsist within them, and for the one (or the ones) that would undergo this process, there could therefore also be no consistent substrate upon which their differentiation or identification could be based. Far from providing a "simple" and solid basis for "us" to "have a clear picture" of anything, then, scissiparity thus cuts to the abyssal ground of thinking, living, and being. More radical than even the "logical impossibility" that Jaspers locates in reflexive consciousness and illustrates in similarly formulaic terms—"The reality of a being is thus defined as a logical impossibility," he writes, "as 'I' being one which is two, or two which are one"—Bataille's formulations presuppose no self-consistency that would allow for the cells or selves to "conceive" themselves both "as being one, and as being two."[69] With the most basic form of life, increase instead culminates with decease, and the most elementary entity turns out to be at odds with the elementary form of identity ("a = a"), exposing alterity, disequilibrium, and incoherence at the core of existence. The *a*sexual reproduction of "a"—where the prefix, in this context, may not simply signify a privation of sexual difference, but the dissecting movement of "a"—annihilates the integrity of "a," at the same time that it exposes the baselessness of all onto-logical notions that could have ever let "a" "be." If we should nonetheless "base ourselves on scissiparity," then, this would entail supposing every subject to be more, other, and less than one—at once inter-, alter- and "a"-subjective—and in a manner that breaks with the very lexical and alphabetical units whose "universal character" first makes it recognizable. Hence, Bataille calls the inner experience of scissiparous reproduction the "crisis of being [*crise de l'être*]," which nearly spells the "crisis of letter" (*crise de lettre*), and in any case signals a crisis in language, insofar as all figures involved escape the minimal identification that speech-recognition would require. What Bataille's articulation of "physical conditions" indicates concerning all speakable experience is that "one" can only cut one's losses—already with *alpha*, all bets are off.

This is not to say, however, that scissiparity—and all that may be "based" on it—could not be addressed. Its description marks nothing less than Bataille's approach to the question of being. The aim that he announces at the outset of *Eroticism*—namely, to "see" eroticism "as the disequilibrium in which the being consciously calls his own existence into question"[70]—lets the eros of desire (ἔρος) and questioning (ἐρῶν) echo the scissiparous "growth that calls the unity of the growing organism into question,"[71] while giving a new turn to the "question of the meaning of being [*Sinn von Sein*]" that inaugurates Martin Heidegger's *Being and Time*,⁷² as well as the self-questioning that motivates Augustine's *Confessions*: "I have been made a question for myself [*mihi quaestio factus sum*]."⁷³ But the disequilibrium of Bataille's subject—from "*a*" to "be"—means that his inquiry could only play out through an experimental mode of writing that is not predicated upon the "identifying unions [*identifizierende[n] Einigungen*]" which found phenomenological and scientific knowledge.⁷⁴

When it comes to scissiparity and eroticism, no "one" could survive the experiences in question to tell of them, and there would be no truth to tell that would not be undercut by the very passion and parting that it "is." Yet what is impossible to undergo or know oneself is not impossible to register in language, which is unbeholden to the principles of positive evidence and logical noncontradiction; disperses itself through echoes, repetitions, and ruptures; calls "itself" into question; and is thus structurally disposed to "be" itself erotic, self-divided, and fictive.⁷⁵ The passages from Bataille's oeuvre that describe the alogical movements of asexual reproduction or that reduce "you" and "me" to the imparting of "burning words" are themselves erotic fictions, and within his study of *Eroticism*, Bataille explicitly takes recourse to a fictive scenario in order to clarify the "changes" undergone by scissiparous beings, which again implicates "you" in the process:

> To clarify these changes, which may seem insignificant, but which are the basis for all forms of life, I suggest that you imagine arbitrarily the passage from the state you are in to one in which your person is completely doubled, which you could not survive, since the doubles issued from you would differ from you in an essential manner. Each of these doubles is necessarily distinct from you as you are now. To be the same as you, one of the doubles would have to be actually continuous with the other, and not opposed to it, as it has become. There is a bizarrerie there that the imagination can hardly follow.⁷⁶

> Pour éclairer ces changements, qui peuvent sembler insignifiants, mais qui sont la base de toutes les formes de vie, je vous suggère d'imaginer arbitrairement le passage de l'état où vous êtes à un parfait dédoublement de votre personne, auquel vous ne pourriez survivre, puisque les doubles issus de vous différeraient de vous d'une manière essentielle. Nécessairement,

chacun de ces doubles ne serait pas le même que celui que vous êtes maintenant. Pour être le même que vous, l'un des doubles devrait en effet être continu avec l'autre et non opposé comme il est devenu. Il y a là une bizarrerie que l'imagination a peine à suivre.⁷⁷

"You" could not imaginatively vary yourself in the way that Bataille solicits, since "your" reduplication would effectively discontinue your ability to bear witness to your selves. It is in exposing this unthinkable scenario as unthinkable, however, that the thought-experiment Bataille describes approaches the "experience" of scissiparity more closely than his discussions of "physical conditions" had done.⁷⁸ And when Bataille broaches this experience again in his fictional narratives, where "you" and "I" are no longer directly addressed and where all pretense to an "objective" view is abandoned, he approximates it further, while exposing the complications that eroticism and scissiparity would entail when one departs not from a single life but from a multitude of testimonies.

Among those narratives, Bataille's novel from 1950, *L'Abbé C.*, is exemplary. Simply put, *L'Abbé C.* traces the trajectories of two twins in occupied France, one of whom pursues the career of a priest but comes to consort with prostitutes before dying at the hands of the Gestapo, while the other pursues a libertine lifestyle but briefly attempts to seek God and survives liberation only long enough to attempt to edit his dead brother's papers, before losing faith, handing off the task to another, and committing suicide himself. The similarities between these seemingly opposite yet identical twins may suggest a dialectical movement, or they may recall the will to sovereignty that Bataille had already described in *Inner Experience*, when he wrote that between "the rich debauchee and the devout individual, snug in the anticipation of salvation, there were as well many affinities, even the possibility of being united in a single person."⁷⁹ But the language of the novel is also irreducible to any such paradigm: for *L'Abbé C.* registers, before all else, an erotic, scissiparous movement that solicits attention to the letter, as the ABCs of Bataille's title suggests, and that attests to the cutting and burning passions of linguistic experience in ways which no dialectical or narratological approach could conceive. Whether one zeroes in upon the pairing and parting of Bataille's twin protagonists, Charles C. and Robert C.—the one seeing the other "as another me-myself [*autre moi-même*]"⁸⁰ and therefore also as his own "negation"⁸¹—or whether one tracks the ways in which the distinctive traits of both characters divide and multiply through the other figures with whom they come to cross—be it a question of their respective desires, sentiments, vestments, or voices[82]—or whether one teases out the threads that allow *L'Abbé C.* to be drawn into connection with other texts, such as the Marquis de Sade's diptych, *Juliette* and *Justine*[83] and James Hogg's more obscure novel about a religious fanatic and his diabolical doppelgänger, *Confessions of a Justified Sinner*[84]—as well as less likely literary predecessors, such as Emily Brontë's *Wuthering Heights*[85]—the figures and language of *L'Abbé C.* are thoroughly marked by the splitting and splicing dynamic that Bataille would describe elsewhere as "scissiparity."[86] This is not to say, however, that the novel offers a more comprehensible picture of the scenario that Bataille had asked the reader of *Eroticism* to imagine. Because, on the one hand, *L'Abbé C.* bifurcates in multiple ways, no description could be given of it that would not at the same time betray other traits of the text that diverge from said description. Yet on the other hand—and for the same reason—it is also the case that no description could be given of the text that would not replicate the dynamics of semblance, divergence, and betrayal that are traced within it. *L'Abbé C.* exceeds the "givens," in the manner that Bataille had elsewhere claimed all "communication" to do, rendering each experience of his novel both partial and shattering.[87] Hence, various commentators have reiterated the resistance of *L'Abbé C.* to interpretation, writing that "the *dicendum*, the thing-that-must-be-said, is essentially silent, so that to approach it is to increase the distance from it,"[88] or insisting that "the reader is plunged into the heart of a crisis that he must reconstitute in departing from heterogeneous, fragmentary narratives of unequal length, incomplete ones, which, however, intersect on what concerns the essential and all pertain to the fiction."[89] But even before all such critical commentary, the fragmentary and fictive notes of the eponymous abbot,[90] as well as the prefaces upon prefaces that precede them and make up the greater part of the text, already indicate that each attempt to write on *L'Abbé C.* could only be another duplicitous and doubtful fiction that breaks from it and writes it further.[91]

It is because and not despite of the fact that each critical response to *L'Abbé C* would be contested by the movements of language traced within it, however, that this fiction radically exposes the questions and passions of linguistic experience, which never could have been proper to any subject or related in words of one's own. Throughout the novel, at least four divergent voices alternate, intersect, and part ways in testifying to the final days of the twins' life trajectories, as the manuscripts of Charles C.

and Robert C. are supplemented with the written and oral reports of an anonymous friend of Charles and a former cellmate of Robert, respectively. According to Charles C.'s first-person account of his last encounters with Robert, which makes up most of the text, the eponymous "abbé," Robert C., had returned to his hometown of "R." upon the death of their parents during the Second World War, where he was "to replace for two months [*deux mois*] the recently deceased parish priest."[92] Once Robert takes up his new position, his former lover, the prostitute named Éponine, seeks to seduce him with the help of Charles, who had replaced his brother as her "most diligent lover" almost as soon as he returned to "R." himself, after a period of childhood illness spent in Savoie.[93] Robert assumes his new role in his old habitat until his own apparently moribund condition compels him to abandon his service—until he becomes too much of a stand-in for the "dead priest"[94]—at which point he takes up residence roughly ten kilometers from R. with two prostitutes, Rosie and Raymonde, who also happen to be friends of Éponine. He dies several weeks later when he is arrested, imprisoned, and tortured by the Gestapo, during which time he betrays his brother and Éponine but not his fellow members of the Resistance, as his former cellmate reports to Charles years later.[95] It cannot be decided whether this last act of Robert's lifetime is the extreme betrayal of the religious principles that he had pretended to preach,[96] or whether it is the truest that he will have ever been to God, whose "religion" had revealed to him that, above all, "*God betrays us!*"[97] Either way, however, Charles escapes arrest under undisclosed circumstances, and only Éponine is captured and killed, while Robert's remains are reduced to the "heap of small leaves [*amas de petits feuillets*]" that he had "cover[ed] with illegible writing."[98]

For his part, Charles C. survives Robert by two years, two months, and two days,[99] leaving him just enough time to forge a text out of his brother's dispersed and illegible papers, and to preface it with a first-person narrative, before handing the entire manuscript over to a friend to edit and publish, in a transfer and betrayal of his own. The distinction between Robert's and Charles's roles in the text, however, collapses already with the preface, which is presented by the (fictive) editor as the "Narrative of Charles C. [*Récit de Charles C.*]," but will be introduced by Charles as "a narrative of the death of Robert [*un récit de la mort de Robert*]."[100] From the "first" words of "Charles," that is to say, a certain indecision emerges as to whether the narrative that he passes on is a story of his own, a story of Robert, or a story of death, which may all say the same thing if it is true, as Charles admits, that he is unable to write about one or the other without doubling and thereby effacing the life in question. "I should have spoken only of my brother," he confesses in the wake of a "fever" near the end,[101] "but I couldn't properly [*à sa mesure*] speak of him without speaking of myself."[102] Charles's "ardent"[103] yet failed attempt to speak as he "should have" done thus not only says that he will have foregrounded his experience at Robert's expense but also that he could not speak of his life, either, since any talk of the one would implicate the other. But the implications of this double default are not merely negative; for just as Charles's writing conflates and confutes both self and (br)other, it also testifies to the passion of which Bataille had spoken, when he wrote: "Thus we are nothing, neither you nor I, beside burning words which could pass from me to you, imprinted on a page: for I would only have lived in order to write them, and, if it is true that they are addressed to you, you will live from having had the strength to hear them."[104] And similarly, when Charles names the impossible conditions for speaking "properly" or "according to the measure [*à sa mesure*]" of his brother, this coincidence of duplicity and erasure nonetheless measures up to the incommensurable equivalence of two and zero that Bataille had traced in his writings on scissiparity, where the splitting of "a" annihilates "a," but leaves a' and a" in its wake.[105] When the burning of words and the cutting of life translate to biographical and autobiographical narrative, they may render every claim a death sentence and every first-person utterance suicidal, but in so doing, they expose the life of every "one" or "two" to have been fictive in the first place. At once inter-, alter- and a-subjective, the duplicitous textual figures of the narrative of Charles C. or the narrative of the death of Robert proliferate and perish in ways that cannot be contained by the notion of any biological being or biographical personage.

Hence, the intersections and reduplications that affect these figures play out primarily at the level of circumstantial and linguistic details that could hardly belong to any "proper" sphere of life or lived experience. With the specification that only *two* years, *two* months, and *two* days intervene between Charles's suicide and his brother's passing, for instance, it is as if this period of bereavement were a countdown to Charles's death, whose length is determined by the "twofold" life that he and Robert shared; and at the same time, it is as if Robert's death did not terminate the duality that structures Charles's life, since last "two months [*deux mois*]" itself reiterates the "two me's [*deux moi*]" that they once were. Besides those coincidences that could still be loosely related to the figures of the twins, moreover, the report of Robert's betrayal of Charles that is related by Robert's former prison-mate also replicates the dilemma that Charles speaks of in speaking of "himself," as this anonymous witness carries on the voice of the dead, repeats his message of death, and visibly resembles a corpse—"he was so thin that it made you feel as if you were talking to someone more dead than alive [*un être plus proche des morts que des vivants*]."[106] All of these features render Robert's "cellmate [*compagnon de cellule*]" the split image of the dead man that Robert is and the dead man that Charles would have been had Robert's betrayal succeeded, while parodically repeating or metonymically recalling the cell division from which the two twins had initially been born.[107]

The instances of pairing and fission in Bataille's novel thus open the narrative and its various personae to movements that exceed each simple binary, cross through every discursive order, contest all personal accounts, and thereby communicate the passivity of every voice. Not even the apparent integrity of the simplest constative utterances can withstand the erotic and divisive passions of language, as when Charles states: "During the summer of 1942 [*l'été de 1942*], Robert, Eponine, and I [*l'abbé, Éponine et moi*] found ourselves, for various reasons, reunited [*réunis*] in the small town where we were born."[108] Here, the initial naming of "l'**ábbé**, Éponine, **et moi**" recalls to the letter the introduction of "**Alpha**, **Be**ta, [. . .] Mme. **E** . . . **and me**" [*Alpha, Bêta, [. . .] Mme E . . . et moi*]" in Bataille's earlier narrative, "La Scissiparité,"[109] rendering the phrase an echo that breaks the narrative frame. At the same time, the words for the recurrent season and the singular reunion themselves split and spill over into recalling what had "been" (*été*) between the protagonists—"summer" (*été*) and "been" (*été*) being homonyms—while spelling out the "ruin" (*r-u-i-n-é-s*) of the "reunited" (*r-é-u-n-i-s*). This anagrammatical index points, in turn, to the ruinous reunions that will draw Robert, Éponine, and Charles to fall apart together, as well as the more intimate collapse of Robert and Charles's outwardly opposite lives, which comes to pass at the level of what could be called "inner experience."

None of these "reunions," moreover, leads to a seamless fusion or indicates a process that could reverse the scissiparous divisions and duplications that cut through all elements of the novel. Hence, if the growing resemblance between the twins disintegrates their semblance of ever being separate members of a pair, it also opens both to a plethora of further differences that are unique to neither but belong to an experience that traverses them, marks their words, and renders their voices passive vehicles for communications that escape them. On the one hand, the closer that the brothers come, the less they find themselves able to speak "to each other" and perhaps even as the "inverse of each other"—"l'un envers l'autre"[110]—since their words seem to underscore the alignment that leaves them each with no one to address. Already "at the point where [Charles's] account begins," Robert recites the English advertising slogan, "*Say it with flowers!*" to exemplify the blasphemy that should be "saved" for the "love of God," coupling love and commerce, vulgar talk and pious silence, in a manner that dissolves the distinction between the religious and dissolute behaviors that had seemed to set the brothers apart.[111] Yet on the other hand, precisely as Robert suggests that only "vulgar [*vulgaire*] slogan[s]" such as this one could maintain "almost imperceptibly [. . .] a sealed silence [*un silence fermé*],"[112] he also speaks in a way that Charles fails to comprehend: "To this day," Charles confesses, "I have no idea what he was getting at."[113] This lapse in understanding is the secret of communication that makes all the difference and marks the separation that first allows for speech, but it is also not something that Robert keeps to himself or even clearly knows. It is instead an occurrence of silence that could not be assured even if it were intended, for what is withheld from comprehension with so minimal a phrase as "Say it with flowers" also could not be restricted to the intention of its speaker(s). Besides the profane and ineffable senses that Robert invokes, for instance, it also resonates beyond the narrative, recalling *the* exemplary "Language of Flowers" that Bataille had cited in an earlier essay of that name, in order to illustrate the filth at the root of "ideal beauty": "While the visible parts are nobly elevated, the ignoble and sticky roots wallow in the ground, loving rottenness just as leaves love light."[114]

Both outspoken opposition and verbal consensus between the brothers could therefore always be other than either knows himself to say, which becomes perhaps most pronounced when Charles says at one point, "Between us, each phrase is necessarily false [*Entre nous, chaque phrase est nécessairement fausse*],"[115] and when Robert reiterates the same assertion differently: "If I were to speak right now, I would be speaking without saying anything."[116] Much as this latter remark would seem to verify Charles's "false" claim—this conditional statement, like Charles's affirmation, could not be asserted without falsifying itself—its self-negating character also means that it truly says nothing and thus breaks off speaking as it speaks. Even and especially when the brothers reach an accord in refusing to speak, that is to say, there is no telling whether they are in agreement or not. To the contrary, the coincidence of truth and falsehood and speech and silence in the brothers' words render their rhetoric self-differentiating in ways that surpass their respective claims and thus let them speak—in the passive voice—for a sort of speaking that would differ from the opposition of truth and lie, "accord" and "rupture."[117] Hence, when Robert blesses the decision that they make to break off communication with the words, "It's better this way" or "It is good this way" ("C'est bien ainsi"),[118] these parting words mark the point of departure for another, still stranger conversation. No sooner does Charles leave his brother than he finds himself carried away: "I [. . .] couldn't help repeating with a sort of lamentable gaiety: 'It's better this way [*C'est bien ainsi*]: the moment has come, and it's time for everything to go!' "[119] Nor does repeating after Robert in "this way" merely let Charles continue speaking with his brother in now-familiar terms, for beside the fact that Robert's blessing may itself be only a play on his common name ("**abbé C.**" / "**C'**est **b**ien **a**insi") rather than the affirmation it is taken to be, its affective force also discontinues Charles's ability to speak, insofar as he could not have chosen what he "couldn't help repeating." What Charles says is beyond him, which is also registered in the logical incoherence of his gloss on Robert's utterance, as it summons and defers the decisive "moment" that should have already "come" and that is itself divided between coming and going ("it's time for everything to go!"). "Robert's" words thus spread like an impersonal and irrational contagion, and it is also in keeping with this trait of their communication that Charles soon feels compelled to surround himself with "books" that "would bring [him] closer to [his] brother" and thereby break "the perfect silence [Robert] had put up."[120] Without any say of their own, the mute and remote voices of other "others," such as "Saint Theresa," promise to draw Robert "closer," if not on the basis of any inner religiosity that Robert and Saint Theresa might have shared, then on the basis of those citations that had made up Robert's outward performance as a priest, or on the basis of the *imitatio* that will have long been cited to define authentic Christian life.[121]

It is in the same spirit of imitation or contagion, moreover, that Charles then "ironically" resolves to "seek the solitude of the mountain," imagining that "after [he] had exhausted [himself] with a long walk, [he] would find it a good place 'to seek God' [*où 'chercher Dieu'*]."[122] For an *ironic* retreat from the company of books can signify neither a reduction to the *solus ipse* nor a turn to the path of saintly "solitude," while quotation marks betray from the outset the citational character of Charles's so-called resolve to "seek God," distantly recalling the famous lines from Nietzsche's *Gay Science*: "Have you not heard of that madman who lit a lantern in the bright morning hours, ran to the market place, and cried incessantly: 'I seek God! I seek God!'"[123] Once he is underway, moreover, the voices that incite him only multiply. As "the magic of panoramic landscapes" brings Charles temporarily to forget his first "decision,"[124] his new surroundings appeal to him with the "promises of a storm or the subtle variations of the light that indicate the time of day in passing from one moment to the other," rendering the mountain atmosphere a linguistic landscape. And ultimately, the volume of divergent promises and indices comes to a peak rather than a standstill when an "instant of strayed beatitude [*un instant de bonheur égaré*]" eventually occurs to Charles.[125] For no sooner does the beatific "instant" seem to evoke the *nunc stans* of eternal bliss that religious thinkers such as Augustine had long since sought in God,[126] than its "strayed" character betrays this moment of promise to be lost in advance, like the "last prospect" of Moses that Franz Kafka would address in his diaries, writing that Moses's ever-deferred glimpse of the promised land can "only have the sense of presenting how incomplete an instant human life is: incomplete, because this sort of life could endure endlessly and would again yield nothing other than an instant."[127] Unbeknownst to Charles, Robert will have nearly said the same in a diary entry of his own, which inverts the Augustinian claim that "our heart is unquiet until it rests in [God]" by insisting, "I can't even for an instant imagine a man apart from God [*en dehors de Dieu*]," and then adding: "But God doesn't leave him an instant of repose [*Mais Dieu ne lui laisse pas un instant de repose*]."[128] What these echoes expose is not, or not merely, the intertextual character of Bataille's writing, but the passive voices that disquiet every blessed instant of experience. The "instants" described by Charles and Robert speak with one another, among others, independently of any intention to broach or sever communication; and as their writings thus break apart and reunite with a plethora of other voices—which itself takes place in a loose and nonbinding manner—their proper stances are unsettled, while their words are released to go on echoing and altering indefinitely.

Such is the ruinous reunion that marks the "inner experience" of the c-h-a-r-l-a-t-a-n b-r-o-t-h-e-r-s,[129] Charles and Robert, and that sustains Bataille's erotic fiction. The true alternative to their false phrases and broken silences is the alterity to which each word and phrase opens, allowing indefinitely more than two voices to cut in. It is in this sense that the "solitude" and "silence" that Charles experiences are not mute but evocative and that they consist not in the negation but in the suspension of the spoken: "I understood then that I had been entering, that I had entered, the region that silence alone (since it is possible, in a sentence, to introduce a momentary suspension [or: suspended instant, *instant suspendu*]) has the ridiculous power to evoke."[130] Yet what these passages also indicate is that each speaking persona in the novel is reduced to "burning words which could pass from me to you,"[131] while at the same time each personal testimony splits off as with the "perfect duplication of your person, which you could not survive, since the doubles issued from you would differ from you in an essential manner."[132] Once being, speaking, and inner experience are reduced in this way, moreover, "speech and language categories don't settle anything [*ne règlent rien*],"[133] giving way to the unruly play that also permits Bataille's narrative to go on replicating and dividing beyond the life and death of the two twins in any number of telling and untold ways.[134]

This radical permission is made explicit when Charles hands his and his brother's manuscripts over to an anonymous friend, with the express request that the latter add a preface and edit the papers. This friend, who recounts only his first encounter with Robert,[135] and who claims to have entertained merely loose relations with Charles,[136] describes the transfer in his preface as follows:

> With a gesture that expressed at once both lassitude and insistence and which left me with an impression of resolute despondency, he asked me to write the preface of this book: he wouldn't read it and left me the task of editing the text.
>
> He was apprehensive because he had introduced thinly-drawn characters who moved about in a demented world and could never be convincing. The first thing I was supposed to do was to save Robert from caricature, without which the book wouldn't make any sense but which made of it a 'vague provocation.' He also found his portrait of himself unacceptable: it lacked vulgarity, and thereby falsified the meaning of the book [*par là faussait l'intention du livre*].[137]

The transfer is made with "lassitude" and "insistence": it marks at once an abandonment of the text and an urgent demand for further and other writing, while leaving utterly open what remains to be said. This openness is not restricted, moreover, when Charles requests that his hitherto distant friend emend the caricatures he and his brother had made of themselves.[138] For by asking a near-stranger to correct his text, Charles makes plain that the more accurate version he envisions could in no way be grounded in truth: the editorial interventions that he solicits could only part ways from the truth in other ways than he had already done and multiply the alterations that he and his brother will have already made to their textual alter egos. On these premises, the "falsified" character of his and his brother's testimonies is irremediable, which is also to say that, in truth, Charles calls for supplemental fictions, while his lassitude casts them in advance as gratuitous and inconsequential. This consequence of sheer inconsequentiality is what Brian T. Fitch likewise emphasizes when he insists that all of the "manuscripts" of the novel "share the same attribute: that of being unfinished, and that by this alone, they reprise and repeat one another."[139] There could be no final word to Charles's self-proclaimed "incomplete account,"[140] and no end to the "liberation" of and from "the power of words" that this fiction of "inner experience" delivers.[141]

Like Robert, the editor-narrator can therefore only betray his subject, and like Charles, he becomes the latest survivor to resume, extend, and intervene in the bifurcating biographies of the brothers, both inscribing and effacing himself in his rendition of their libidinal, morbid, and scriptural trajectories. Even his initial words on his background sound more like echoes owed to the brothers than confessions of his own: "I should have avoided talking about myself," he admits, "but before presenting the book formed by Charles's narrative and Robert's notes, I wanted to give an account of what I remember about the two brothers,"[142] distantly recalling or anticipating Charles's confession: "I should have spoken only of my brother, but I couldn't properly [*à sa mesure*] speak of him without speaking of myself."[143] But since these words from Charles's narrative will have first passed through the editor's hands, there could also be no telling whether this editor is echoing the "original" text, or whether the resemblance between the respective passages of his preface and Charles's testimony is the result of his in(ter)ventions. The possibilities of duplicity and betrayal become infinite and untraceable from the moment Charles abandons his papers to his friend so completely that he neither wishes to read his friend's work, nor survives the transfer longer than two months. And since this editor can likewise only abandon the text himself—"editing" says precisely this: "to give" (*dare*) "out" (*e-*, *ex*)—the book does not cease to pass over into others' hands and to remain exposed to other interventions.

There would be no end to the passages that testify to the suicidal self-abandon and double-crossing that are perpetrated and perpetuated throughout *L'Abbé C*. But the instances of testimony cited in these pages already expose how the novel registers the implications of scissiparity for biography, where the original vanishes as it splits and replicates—"it leaves no trace."[144]—where one gives life by losing the very possibility to have it—"for the individual making it, the gift [*le don*] is the loss of his having [*la perte de son avoir*]"[145]—and where the products of multiplication exceed all imagination: "There is a bizarrerie there that the imagination can hardly follow."[146] What remains and proliferates instead of "Charles" and "Robert"—as well as their editor and reader—is none, other than the abyssal and "impersonal plethora [*pléthore*] of life itself" to which they will have owed their semblance of existence and fictions of self-consciousness.[147] Yet insofar as Bataille's fiction exposes those fictions, the experiences of language he traces in his novel also approach the "abysses" and "conjunctions" that he will elsewhere call the "truth": "Only these abysses, these conjunctions, can give us the truth."[148] Because this "truth" escapes conscious knowledge, neither the rigorous science of Husserl's phenomenology nor the confessional theology of Augustine could contain it: they could only let it speak despite themselves, through those passages where they break character and contest their proper premises—as when Augustine fictionalizes the immemorial and speechless life of infantile existence, or when Husserl lets conscious life go lost in the "overlap" of intersubjective pairing. In multiplying such moments, which betray another sort of experience than any that could be claimed, Bataille's erotic fiction offers a more sustained response to what Charles calls, echoing countless philosophers and theologians, the "classic 'ultimate questions.'"[149] For the "truth" in question is none that could be found or taken for a foundation; ever uncertain and inconclusive, it names the exposure to those "abysses" and "conjunctions" which are broached in Bataille's oeuvre and spelled out in *L'Abbé C.* through the scissiparous passions of language.

Chapter 4

Writing Out of Sight

On the Papers and Traces of Kafka

Toward the end of Bataille's *L'Abbé C.*, Charles C. delivers prefatory remarks upon the version of his dead brother's papers that he had deciphered, transcribed, and edited, and that are reproduced in the penultimate section of the text. The fictive commentary titled "Foreword by Charles C." introduces the papers thus:

> These notes (having become those of a dead man—which would henceforth betray the one who wrote them—since they give limits to one who either did not have them, or who had others), annoyed me for a long time. Not solely for my brother, but also for myself, I had a feeling of failure. Rereading them, I no longer saw in Robert anything but the "fraud" that he had tried to be at the time when he was striving to be pious.
>
> Death, which makes all traits definitive, was, in my eyes, condemning him, without appeal, to be a show-off [*le malin*]. These papers, henceforth, could no longer be burned, and, supposing that he had made a blaze of them himself, he would have written them again [or: still, *encore*]! I would have ignored by error the limit he had admitted; my error would not have been able to change it.[1]
>
> Ces notes (devenues celles d'un mort—qui, désormais, devaient trahir celui qui les écrivit,—car elles donnent des limites à

celui qui, ou n'en eut pas, ou en eut d'autres) m'énervèrent longtemps. Je n'avais pas seulement pour mon frère, mais pour moi, le sentiment d'un échec. À les relire, je ne voyais plus en Robert que le "faiseur" qu'il voulait être, au temps où il s'efforçait à la piété.

La mort, qui rend les traits définitifs, à mes yeux le condamnait à faire le malin sans recours. Ces papiers, désormais, ne pouvaient plus être brûlés, et, à supposer qu'il en eût fait lui-même une flambée, il les aurait encore écrits! J'aurais par erreur ignoré la limite qu'il admit, mon erreur n'aurait pu la changer.[2]

This brief narrative concerning the reading and burning of a legacy reiterates the duplicitous splitting and splicing that characterize the novel's multiple speakers or figures—its multiple figures of speech—whose trajectories bifurcate and cross with one another, among other others, over the course of the text, exemplifying the more than biological notion of scissiparity that cuts through Bataille's oeuvre. Now that Charles's twin is dead, it is up to him to reread and edit his sibling's remains: that is, to think and write "I" on the part of his alter ego or other half, whose personal notes do not reveal so much as they mask a persona who had failed to appear "authentically" already during his lifetime, and whose last traces of being a "show-off," "fraud," "clever one," or "evil one" (*malin*) now appear impossible to remove or destroy. The effects of scissiparity, which makes up Bataille's answer to the phenomenological notion of pairing in his theoretical essays and erotic fiction, are thus registered once more in *L'Abbé C.* through a departed "I," whose words remain in the absence of any conscious actor, and whose speech does not cease to dissimulate. Once subjectivity is reduced to such posthumous traces, however, any "I" who would write in the wake of the "I" would likewise be exposed to breaches in coherence and unforeseeable coincidences that no one could intend or know to suffer. It is this passivity beyond all possible experience that the "Foreword by Charles C." bears out, as "I" and "I" vanish with each trace, and as the fictions of subjectivity and intersubjectivity are broken through the same figures of speech that had sustained them.

From the first, the passage cited above implies that no subject could give the semblance of speaking without being crossed and betrayed in the same stroke. If the writings of Robert must "betray the one who wrote them," then this "one" cannot but refer to at least two, from the second that

Charles takes up the task of transcribing and editing—and thus, rewriting—Robert's notes. Nor could the betrayal that is described here remain between the two brothers alone, since it would have to extend to anyone who should open this book and write on it, like the anonymous friend to whom Charles eventually hands over his and Robert's papers, in turn. Yet at the same time, no one could be the origin for these betrayals either if it is also true that they are an effect of writing, as "Charles's" writing suggests: for the fact that Robert's papers are what expose this erstwhile priest to have been a "fraud" or *faiseur* for all his pious life entails that the counterfeit-effect begins postmortem and postscriptum, rather than owing to any thought or action of his "own." And beyond Charles's words on the papers, his professed adherence to the "definitive" traits of Robert's legacy soon plays out with a forced and false piety that is perhaps still more radical than one he ascribes to his brother, as he admits that the pains he took in deciphering his brother's writing gave way, first, to "a great malaise [*un grand malaise*]"; and ultimately, they provoke a desire on his part to alter those words, which he claims "sounded false to [his] ears."[3] He strains to be faithful to the letter, yet the letter itself rings untrue; he wishes to do something about it, yet he pretends to do nothing but record "the final text of these notes"[4]—all of which issues into an edition whose language could only be forced, false, and inconclusive, whether Charles had forged corrections, as he admits he would have wished to do,[5] or whether he faithfully reproduced the original falsifications of his brother as he suggests he has done.[6]

There is no having done with the dilemmas that are inscribed in this text, and there also is no writing them off, as Charles goes on to indicate when he considers the impossibility of burning the manuscripts he has taken into his hands. Instead, what is at stake when he claims that "these papers, henceforth, could no longer be burned" are effects of death and writing that trouble affirmative gestures of acceptance, as well as negative acts of refusal, and that even exceed conscious awareness. For no sooner does Charles evoke the burning of his brother's notes (in the passive voice) than a slippage occurs from his description of what would have happened if *Robert* had burned his own papers—"*he* would have written them again [or: still, *encore*]"—to Charles's further description of what *he* would have thereby achieved—"*I* would have ignored by error the limit he had admitted." This slippage may indicate, on the one hand, that the burning that Charles imagines his brother performing is a fiction and projection of his own, since "Robert" neither did it nor lives to be capable of doing any such thing. On the other hand, even if burning the papers were a real possibility for Charles, they could not eliminate Robert's failure or refusal "to atone" for what he calls "the sin of writing" by "annihilat[ing] what is written" himself, nor could the destruction of Robert's "ingenuous documents" erase the remaining fact of loss itself: the silent testimony that the subject of testimony will have already escaped beyond recall.[7] Nothing vital could be changed, in other words, if the papers were burned, such that this as-if scenario is "as if" to say that it would be as impossible for the "living" as it is for the "dead" to destroy those false traces left by Robert—which, moreover, themselves never appear apart from the edited version that Charles gives forth in their place.

The manuscripts cannot be destroyed, then, because they already bear the marks of erasure: the "false" traits that they display show nothing verifiable concerning the "proper" traits which Robert may have borne, rendering their pretention "to strip bare" ("dénuder") his "tortured soul" a cliché citation and sheer cover-up that cannot "conceal" or "rob" ("dérober") the fabricated character of his disclosure.[8] Robert's signature only lies, that is, in these indelible marks of his "fraudulence," and thus, of his de-negation ("de-Robert"); and similarly, the "definitive" character that death assigns to his writings delimits them in a manner that eliminates any alternative limits or absence of limits that Robert may otherwise have "had." To destroy the papers of Robert could therefore not undo the erasure, effacement, and elimination that they attest *ab initio*, but could only repeat those gestures and leave yet another misleading trace of his missing person. It is for this reason that Charles can state without contradiction, "Destruction leaves that which is essential intact,"[9] and that this statement could be said of both burning and writing, suspending the distinction between affirmation and negation, productive operations and the ruinous work of time: "I can," writes Charles, "tie negation so closely to affirmation that my pen gradually effaces what it has written. In so doing it accomplishes, in a word, what is generally accomplished by 'time'—which, from among its multifarious edifices, allows only traces of death to subsist."[10] Just as each passing moment is, as Hegel had written, nothing other than "its coming-to-nothing and, again, the continuous coming-to-nothing of this vanishing,"[11] so too should inscription and effacement vanish into one another with each stroke of the pen but with the difference that no universal category such as "now" results. Rather, "only traces of death [. . .] subsist," which remain heterogeneous to the acts and insights of those subjects who produced them. Hence, the analogy to "time" is placed in quotation marks that mark it off as an improper analogue, while at the same time, what Charles claims he "can" do in writing also turns out to be nothing that he can prevent, which also means that it is nothing that "can" ever properly lie in his or anyone's power. The destruction of writing takes place instead in a manner that comes closer to what Bataille describes as "alteration" in an earlier essay on "Primitive Art," where he aligns the impulse to leave marks not with a will to self-expression or annihilation, but with the "decomposition that is partially analogous to that of cadavers and at the same time the passage to a perfectly heterogeneous state which corresponds to what [Rudolf] Otto calls the *entirely other* [*tout autre*], that is, the sacred."[12] Drawing upon the example of children who "set fiercely to covering blank paper" with "scrawl [*griffonages*],"[13] Bataille suggests that "alteration" not only works destruction upon its material "support," but may also be repeated to alter any iterable, representational figures that may result from scrawling, subjecting each "new object itself' to "a series of deformations."[14] Every line that may appear to mark a limit, that is, is always already itself an alteration and remains exposed to alteration without limit.

It is this structural feature of writing that allows a signature to emerge through the incapacity of Robert's notes to "conceal [*dérober*]" their altered and citational texture—a passive signature, which identifies nothing and no one but Robert's disidentification ("de-Robert"). But it is also what lends truth to Charles's apparently paradoxical assertion that if Robert had burned his papers, he "still" would have written them, or he would have written them "again": "Il les aurait encore écrits!" And it is similarly through alteration that Robert's passing away can also give admission to his mortal limits in a manner that can neither be ascribed to him nor simply spoken away but that takes place as a silent occurrence that exceeds his written words and proper capacities. Insofar as this unspoken "admission" crosses the limits of Robert's presence and utterance, moreover, it also grants unrestricted admission to further iterations and alterations of his writing in absentia. Its open-ended character was the condition of possibility for Charles's commentary in the first place, but even the words that name Robert's "admission" are themselves altered through an anagrammatical permutation of the "limit" itself: "la *limite* qu'*il* ad-*mit*" ("the li*mit* he had ad*mit*ted").

This paradoxical admission is not founded in any subjective consciousness and therefore remains beyond the opposition of sincerity and fraudulence that Charles otherwise emphasizes in his "foreword." There is no telling the damage that will have been done in writing and no measuring the allowances that writing gives: writing crosses writer and reader alike; it translates talk of "time" to an improper inscription; and in the end, it transgresses the apparent finality of death as well, since each text would have been a "death" writ upon being committed to paper, *and* since each such death would always be subject to further alteration. Bataille's text does not describe, however, "the death of the author" avant la lettre;[15] nor do the excesses to which it opens repeat the critique of the phenomenological approach to communication that Bataille had formulated with an appeal to "lived states" in his draft materials for *Guilty*: "In all of the movements that I have described, the lived states transcend in some way the givens. It is this way in every veritable 'communication,' just as there is no phenomenology of 'communcation': that is impossible."[16] For rather than recurring to a notion of life or making a decisive theoretical claim—and thereby preserving, however provisionally, the thought of a (theoretical) subject—Charles's first-person narrative and commentary; the version of Robert's papers that he offers; as well as the less visible interventions of the anonymous friend to whom Charles had given the task of finishing his editorial work, all place first-person speech at stake and let the telling effects of its inscription cross through all conclusive limits that may be drawn.

Writing is itself the admission of an alterable limit, which, as such, exceeds the terms of truth, will, time, and death. But if this trait should render it a passive operation, it is also what permits writing to mark the end of ends and to give the ultra-ultimate allowance: as words are delivered from the intentions, actions, aims, and person of any author, they are left at liberty to haunt, provoke, and derange what Bataille describes in *Literature and Evil* as the "eloquent" or "disserted world [*monde disert*],"[17] where "logic reduces each thing to a certain order" of discourse.[18] In short, they wreak evil (*le mal*), which is what speaks through Charles's confession of "malaise" upon reading the notes of his brother,[19] just as it is what condemns Robert "to be a show-off [*à faire le malin*]" for all his afterlife;[20] and it is also what allows the other *mal-propos* characteristics of Charles's *avant-propos* to be broached, including the fact that the very thought of burning Robert's notes, which would seem to presuppose a prior wish on the part of either Robert or Charles, has no trace of a precedent within the narrative of Robert's last days that precedes these meditations on his legacy.

Strictly speaking, there is no telling where "fire" came from when it comes up in Bataille's novel. Nor could its provenance be traced back in any definitive way to other lines from Bataille's corpus, such as the passage from *Inner Experience*: "Thus we are nothing, neither you nor I, beside burning words which could pass from me to you, imprinted on a page."[21] Since writing ruins and razes as it leaves its mark; since each line, at its initial and utmost limit, would be barely distinguishable from the blank that it covers, in that both grant space for other and further writing: since, in short, these are the impossible terms that writers at once do admit and cannot admit themselves, an apparent absence of traces could give no evidence against them, and no phenomenological principle of intuitive givenness could offer a criterion to track the unprincipled movement of inscription.[22] This is the "essential" trait that destruction leaves "intact,"[23] with the consequence that it would essentially have to be as undeniable as it must remain uncertain that some prior talk of burning may have been scratched from the record, only to flare up again, as if sui generis here in Bataille's text. But since, along the same lines, writing dispossesses writers of both their speech and act of inscription—since writers allow, in writing, the limit of their death, and thus admit what none can claim—it is also as undeniable as it must remain uncertain that other voices and texts may be operative in the work that appears under "Bataille's" name, none of which could be owned once and for all. Beyond the rhetoric of fire that traverses Bataille's oeuvre, then, the evocation of fire in this passage may be none that pertains "properly" to his work, but one that, at the limit, opens the bounds of his book to admit other words on burning, such as those that will have marked Franz Kafka's legacy, ever since Max Brod transcribed, edited, and published his friend's posthumous papers (perhaps against his will). This coincidence would appear all the more plausible, should one consider that *L'Abbé C.* falls within the same period as the essay on Franz Kafka that Bataille would rework for his manuscript on *Sovereignty* and eventually publish in *Literature and Evil*—namely, "Franz Kafka before Communist Critique" ("Franz Kafka devant la critique communiste")—where the focal point is none other than Kafka's gesture of consigning his oeuvre to flames, while leaving it intact.[24] And although Bataille's words of fire may provoke other associations—which could not be restricted by dates or givens—pursuing this one offers a chance to broach further ways in which language crosses the limits of subjectivity and phenomenality; to trace how this crossing exposes the fraud of authority; and, perhaps most importantly, to enter further into what it could mean to speak openly on such terms.

Among the papers of Kafka that were to be burned were, namely, two unsent letters addressed to Brod in which Kafka had framed requests for Brod to burn all that he wrote, "preferably unread [*am liebsten ungelesen*],"[25] which requests Brod does not fulfill, but reproduces in full and comments upon at length in his "afterword" to *The Trial*, as if to defend his decision and extend Kafka's legal fiction. Simply given the fact that Brod must have already failed Kafka's requests, in order to read of them in the first place (though there are other reasons, too[26]), the internally incoherent complex of texts comprising Kafka's letters and Brod's afterword renders Kafka's written demands impossible and draws their divergent stipulations into an epochal suspension that, unlike the phenomenological reduction, includes all writing, reading, wishing, and acting subjects in what is set "out of action," "switched off," and "enclosed in parentheses."[27] It was precisely this nexus of texts that Bataille had drawn upon when he opened his Kafka essay with a characterization of Kafka as an "author, who lived, or at any rate died, tormented by the desire to burn his books."[28] But it is likewise to the issue of final words—an issue that Brod's and Kafka's texts leave open—that Bataille's Charles C. would seem to respond, when he evokes and suspends the question of burning his brother's papers. As Bataille describes them, moreover, the flames that appear in Kafka's pages—"leaves [*feuillets*]" themselves composed of "fire [*feu*]"—would have to bear the potential to spread to Brod's afterword, as well as the foreword of Charles C., in the nearly imperceptible manner that they appear to do, since the phantasmic character of this irreal phenomenon would also at all times preclude both its extinction and its verification and thus allow it to recur indefinitely, without ever being realized: "Those imaginary flames," Bataille writes in his Kafka essay, "even contribute to the understanding of his books: they are books for the fire [*livres pour le feu*], objects which miss the truth of being on fire [*des objets auxquels il manque à la vérité d'être en feu*]; they are there, but they are there in order to disappear, as though they have already been annihilated."[29] And it is also most likely with an eye to this most volatile trait of Kafka's writing that Bataille goes on to call Kafka, like Robert C., "malin," in an exclamation that no sooner explodes than it trails off with an ellipsis and thus leaves off from any claim: "Of all writers Kafka was possibly the most cunning [*malin*]: he, at least, never let himself be had! . . . [*lui du moins, ne s'est pas laissé prendre! . . .*]."[30] Hence, when *L'Abbé C.* similarly reaches its virtual "burning" point—which, for lack of any prior preparation or subsequent follow-up, is also an inconsequential point: a vanishing point from no one's perspective—Bataille's novel becomes virtual as well, loses definition at this limit, and opens out to the oeuvre of Kafka that may have virtually vanished within it.

In this inconclusive manner, the intersections and divisions to which all instances of imparting are exposed in Bataille's novel offer a point of departure for approaching Kafka's writing, which probes like none other the breaches and admissions that open from within each spoken or written utterance and which thereby also parts ways with the versions of phenomenological psychology that Kafka had encountered during his years at the German Charles-Ferdinand University in Prague.[31] Alone within the diaries and notebooks that Kafka would sometimes record in the first person, words and even alphabetical characters will be said to disrupt the life of the "I" in a way that escapes both understanding and belief, as reading turns "inner" experience inside out: "I cannot understand it and cannot even believe it," Kafka writes in one entry from August 20, 1911, "I live only here and there in a small word, in whose umlaut (above 'shoves' ['*stößt*']) I, for example, lose my useless head for a moment. The first and last letter are the beginning and end of my fishlike feeling [*meines fischartigen Gefühls*]."[32] This description of "living" in a word may echo the rhetoric of "living" that appears, for example, in Husserl's descriptions of reading in the *Logical Investigations*, where he will write: "Both are 'lived through,' the presentation of the word and the sense-giving act: but, while we are living through [*erleben*] the word-presentation, we do not at all live [*leben*] in the act of presenting the word, but solely in enacting its sense, its meaning."[33] But Kafka's words situate the reader as living in the letters on the page, signaling a pronounced turn from the intentional thrust of phenomenological psychology: here, an "umlaut" or turn *in* sound occasions a turn *to* sound that marks an umlaut in the work of reading, in an otherwise unheard-of sense of the word.[34] Far from giving "sense" to what he reads, Kafka claims to have lost his "useless head," temporarily vanishing into the writing for however lengthy or limited a "moment," nor does this experience of lost experience take place in such a way where a reduced subject remains to count his losses. For despite the appearance of recalling a "moment" of reading, the words that Kafka records also drown out the subject who writes them, as his feeling is likened to that of a "fish" (*F-i-s-c-h*), whose composition subjects the "I" ("*i-c-h*") to a metamorphosis that alters its sense and renders this immersion in the (literal) elements of language both insensible and immemorial. Even before this turn or trope, moreover, the resonance between Kafka's words and the verses of Revelation, "I am the Alpha and the Omega, the first and the last, the beginning and the end" (Rev. 22: 13), not only splits and splices the "I" of Kafka's diary entry with this "I" of biblical prophecy but also suggests that the lines of Scripture may be taken literally as well. Not only the "I" inscribed in Kafka's diaries, but also the "I" of biblical scripture thus admits multiplication and division through the letters that they claim to be, which would absorb and liquidate anyone who would identify with them at least as radically as the passions of reading seem to do to Kafka "himself."

This incident in Kafka's diaries is not an isolated testimony to the illegible character of "lived" experience or the self-altering effects of language. In the later notebook entry that is often cited in studies concerning Kafka's response to the phenomenological psychology of his friend Hugo Bergmann and his former teacher Anton Marty—as well as Franz Brentano, whose works were intensively discussed during the gatherings that Kafka had attended at the Café Louvre with Max Brod—other linguistic peculiarities similarly suggest that the subject is itself a figure of speech with only an outer "interior" to observe, and thus one with none but slipping, metaphorical "limits." "How lamentable [*kläglich*] is my self-knowledge," Kafka writes, "compared, for instance, with my knowledge of my room [*meines Zimmers*]. (Evening.) Why? There is no observation of the inner world [*der innern Welt*], as there is of the outer [one]. Psychology is most likely in its entirety an anthropomorphism, a [gnawing] at the limits [*ein [Annagen] der Grenzen*]."[35] Peter Neesen has read this passage as an indication of Kafka's observation that the "area of inner perception" that descriptive psychology was designed to disclose cannot but be addressed "with the help of generally used language" for other, outer things, rendering it impossible to "penetrate to the kernel of the inner world."[36] With a different emphasis, Arnold Heidsieck has interpreted the same words to suggest that Kafka "insists that consciousness—along with its linguistic expression—has no choice but to aim at and grasp an objective world instead of an elusive self."[37] Stephen Dowden has observed that Kafka's acknowledgment of the "problem of representing inner life" nonetheless implies "that some very tentative gesturing at the supersensible 'beyond' is possible," if only in the uncertain modus of allegorical, figurative speech.[38] Yet what is less often noticed in this passage is that "self-knowledge" is described from the start in terms of a linguistic modality that differs from the order of knowledge: namely, the "lament [*Klage*]" of the "lamentable" or "plaint-like" ("kläglich[e]") quality attributed to "self-knowledge" in a syntactic arrangement that differs from any predicative utterance that could be verified or falsified. Even Kafka's initial "how" or "wie" resounds like a plaint-like echo—perhaps unbeknownst to himself—evoking the interjection "with which the laments for the dead begin" in the Hebrew Bible, as Gershom Scholem would note around the same time.[39] With this qualification, however, Kafka does not simply suggest that a deficiency in "self-knowledge" leaves one at a "lamentable" loss. Precisely because "there is no observation of the inner world," neither "self-knowledge" ("Selbsterkenntnis") nor any other sort of inner "knowledge" could ever have been known to be had, let alone lost and mourned, leaving the word "self-knowledge" itself bereft and disposed to lamentation in a manner that must likewise lack inner certitude.

Without the certitude of inner perception that Brentano, Marty, and Bergmann had sought to affirm,[40] each claim or plaint concerning self-knowledge would be not only outwardly but also inwardly indiscernible from echoes of unknown provenance that "say" the same. Brentano himself nearly admits this dilemma when he acknowledges external testimony to be the condition for verifying inner experience, on the grounds that immediate introspection would imply the very sort of division between observer and observed that the "real unity" of psychical life excludes.[41] Due to this structural impossibility of immediate self-observation, descriptions of inner experience turn out to be reliant upon the fallible medium of personal memory, whose confirmation would rely, in turn, upon others' reports of similar experiences.[42] And if it is only this relay that establishes the "facts" of Brentano's empirical psychology, then psychological knowledge and self-knowledge alike would be functions of repeated testimonies rather than any self-evident experience, leaving all that we live through free to differ from all that we may call "reflection," "recognition," and even "human."[43] What we share and echo among ourselves is a "lamentable" or "plaintlike [*klägliche*]" self-knowledge that can itself pretend to no more than a likeness of complaint.[44]

These derivative, artificial, and mimetic traits of the psychological subject are reflected again when Kafka calls psychology "most likely in its entirety an anthropomorphism,"[45] and it is the illusory or fictive nature of "self-knowledge" that echoes in Kafka's variant of the Delphic imperative that will have resonated through Plato, Cicero, Augustine, Husserl, and beyond: "The word [know thyself] means, then: Misknow yourself! [*Das*

Wort [Erkenne Dich selbst] bedeutet also: Verkenne Dich!]."[46] Yet this is also not to say that Kafka claims to "know" better; more than through any constative statement, the deficiencies of both immanent evidence and external reflection are exposed through the modal, figural, and logical limits that his writing crosses. Thus, what distinguishes his knowledge of an outer "room" from his knowledge of "inner" life resides not in the adequacy, clarity, or certitude of the former—no evidence of such criteria is given—but in the tone of complaint or lament that characterizes his talk of the latter. And if his remarks might still seem to suppose some knowledge, to the extent that they comprise recognizable linguistic forms, Kafka's writing also breaks with those forms to allow for other permutations and it does without so much as a semblance of intentional expression. "Zimmer" ("room") and "inner-" ("inner-"), for example, not only appear in close proximity to designate two different sorts of interiors but also thereby become echo chambers for each other of their own accord. While remaining intact, the lexeme "room" thus makes room for another to resonate within it; and in this way, the resonance between the words also voids their respective proper senses, troubling the limits of both terms from within and from without. Where variations in what is called "knowledge" are marked by such linguistic modulations—and where knowledge itself, like knowledge of oneself, is fundamentally unknown—nothing could exclude such encounters between words from taking place and yielding an epoché of meaning independent of any subject. It may even be the case that the dental-fricative "z" itself marks a bite at the edges of the "Z-immer," before the word erodes further with the "-innern Welt" whose limits psychologists would seek to gnaw and know. But whether the emphasis falls upon the resonance that permits the mutual transgression between different interiors, or the gnawing that their designations render pronounced, what occurs through Kafka's passage both eludes anthropomorphism and subjects whatever one may think the words are saying to alterations that trouble any thought of inner psyches or home interiors.

In all of these ways and more, these passages seem to be there for disappearing, as Bataille had written: they retreat from the phenomenality that renders them an object for a subject; they withdraw from the very subjectivity that otherwise seems to speak through them; and they set each term and boundary under erasure. Yet precisely because these marks of erasure cannot, as such, be localized, no reading of them could be done but would have to remain itself open-ended and alterable through the further and other traces that may surface at any time. Hence, the oscillations between "inner-" and "Zimmer" resonate beyond the passage cited above in another notebook entry, where Kafka writes, "Every human bears a room in himself [*Jeder Mensch trägt ein Zimmer in sich*]," before citing the following external evidence for this inner architecture: "One can even test this fact through hearing. When one walks quickly and listens out for something, as in the night when all things around are silent, one hears, for example, the rattling of the screen or a mirror on the wall that was not sufficiently fixed [*so hört man z.B. das Scheppern eines nicht genug befestigten Wandspiegels oder der Schirm*]."[47] Since one could not enter any space that one contains without ceasing to contain and support it, disturbances from within could only be registered through those signs from without which one chances to hear, whose sources—be it a screen or a mirror—remain a matter of sheer speculation. Inner experience is thus shaken by the possibility or fiction of "sound in itself, without reference to a cause" that Kata Gellen has traced in her recent study, *Kafka and Noise*,[48] as well as the "passive" dimension of "listening" that Anthony Curtis Adler has underscored in his reading of sonic incursions in Kafka's "The Burrow."[49] With this exemplary passage in particular, however, Kafka describes a radically different sort of experiment than those observations of inner life that Brentano and Marty had recommended. For it departs from the premise that one's interior is far from immanent—it can be approached solely by way of the sounds one "listens out for"—while the experience of listening would indicate that what humans harbor is an inanimate space, whose ambiguous contents not only escape direct reflection but also threaten to shatter every reflective surface. And although Kafka does not say so directly, the signs of agitation that he cites also suggest that what shakes each inward turn and turns inner experience into a trope is language: without which there would be no room for any talk of the self, and within which there is also no limit to the repercussions. The irreducible persistence of language before both sense and self is what speaks through those moments where solitude is brought to rattle; where an umlaut "pushes [*stößt*]" the reader to lose his "head";[50] or where self-knowledge is reduced to a plaint-like (*kläglich*) tone and words become clanglike (*klanglich*) through the echoes that transpire between various terms for inner life and outer space. But it is also just such shattering repercussions for the subject of psychical acts and psychological observation that may make up what Kafka will later call the "remarkable, mysterious, perhaps perilous, perhaps absolving consolation of writing: the springing out from the series that strikes [one] dead, [comprising] deed—observation, deed—observation [*das Hinausspringen aus der Totschlägerreihe Tat–Beobachtung, Tat–Beobachtung]*,"[51] where the very connection between praxis ("deed") and theory ("observation") is itself struck through with the graphic mark that joins and separates them *eo ictu*, in the same stroke ("–").

If there were a text from Kafka's oeuvre, however, that most amplifies the incalculable effects of writing, the reduction of the subject to a vanishing trace, and the alterations that each instance of speech may undergo beyond the limits of his lifetime and his knowledge, then it would be the novel concerning the subject of letters, rumors, files, prescriptions, prohibitions, and admissions that Kafka left unfinished toward the close of his life: the inconclusive enclosure called *The Castle* (*Das Schloss*). Before the pages that open Brod's edition of the novel, the first pages of the manuscripts that comprise *The Castle* open from out of nowhere inside a village inn, where an anonymous guest is greeted and shown his room—"the Prince Room [*Das Fürstenzimmer*],"[52] as the innkeeper calls it—and where the "barmaid" or "room-maid [*Stubenmädchen*]" soon comes in, underscoring the crossings of persons and spaces that are taking place here. And just as these room assignments render the space of arrival itself a shifting matter of negotiation,[53] the anonymous guest continues to "walk back and forth, ever yet fully dressed in [his] coat, [. . .] as if it were not yet certain whether he would remain here [*als sei es noch nicht gewiss, ob er hier bleiben werde*]."[54] Kafka's private notes and diary entries had already transposed "inner" knowledge to a spatial interior, betraying the external, metaphorical, and foreign character of whatever "I" may call "myself." But the opening passage of *The Castle* unfolds the implications of this situation further, by introducing one's "own" room as a personified ("princely") space of dialogue and hospitality with a space-bound persona ("Stubenmädchen"). What makes it most troubling, however, turns out not to be its associations with other figures but rather its appearance of being meant for oneself: "The room was prepared," the guest observes, after asking: "Who indicated my arrival to you?"[55] Precisely insofar as the "Prince Room" seems to have been waiting for him, it is uncanny and estranging, for it suggests that news of his arrival will have come without him; that others will have spoken for him in advance; and that he will have thus been situated within the community before he can so much as arrive and announce himself. Haunted by the unknown versions of himself that rumors may have fashioned, the guest is out of place at his very destination, yielding a situation that cannot but void his claim that he comes with a cause of his own: "I have a difficult task before me and have dedicated my whole life to it."⁵⁶ Hence, all talk of a task will soon be given up, as the guest begins to profess his dedication to a "struggle" ("Kampf") instead, which, for lack of an opponent, sounds more like an echo of his claim to have "come" ("kam") than anything else: "I am here for a struggle [*Kampf*]," he announces.⁵⁷ Because and not despite of the fact that word of his arrival had come before him, the unaccountable coincidence between what he does and what was said renders the moment of his coming undecidable, if not embattled, and it does so without anyone's doing: "The whole village knows of your arrival," the barmaid says, "I cannot clarify it, already for weeks all people know it, it probably proceeds from the castle, more I do not know."⁵⁸ No one's word can claim priority in this discussion, where both the room and the guest mark sites of intersection for a discursive traffic that crosses the limits of both personal admissions and public knowledge.

The radically passive role that the anonymous guest seems to have already played in town life—before and beyond all experience, properly speaking—figures in advance the ways in which Kafka's more well-known protagonist K. will emerge as the key actor in others' stories throughout the more well-known portions of his novel fragment. For instance, as K.'s arrival gives the ostracized messenger, Barnabas, a destination for deliveries, K. becomes the destiny of a family and a history that is unrelated to any with which he may have been familiar. As Barnabas's sister Olga will tell him: "This turn, if it is a turn and not a deception [. . .] is in connection with your arrival here, our destiny has landed into a certain dependency upon you, perhaps these 2 letters are only the beginning and the activity of Barnabas will extend over and beyond the messenger-service concerning you—we should hope so, so long as we may—in a precursory way, however, everything is aimed solely toward you" (Diese Wendung, wenn es eine Wendung ist und keine Täuschung [. . .] ist mit Deiner Ankunft hier in Zusammenhang, unser Schicksal ist in eine gewisse Abhängigkeit von Dir geraten, vielleicht sind diese 2 Briefe nur ein Anfang und des Barnabas Tätigkeit wird sich über den Dich betreffenden Botendienst hinaus ausdehnen—das wollen wir hoffen, solange wir es dürfen—vorläufig aber zielt alles nur auf Dich ab).⁵⁹ Similarly, in one of the last segments of Kafka's manuscript, the chambermaid Pepi tells him of his role in her elevation to the rank of barmaid, which took place when K. seduced Frieda, the previous occupant of that post, on his second evening in town. Pepi's story is yet another version of his story, but now one in which K. is cast as "a hero, an emancipator of maidens [*ein Held, ein Mädchenbefreier*]," whose aim had been to free "the upward path" for her.⁶⁰ Insofar as these divergent, incompatible narratives make up who "K." is within the text, his bifurcating trajectory resembles the movements of scission, alteration, and replication that Bataille would describe as scissiparity and dramatize through the twins of *L'Abbé C*. But whereas Bataille's novel departs from the limits that seem to be drawn with the posthumous testimonies of his fictive doubles, *The Castle* exposes the fragmentary and duplicitous character of every nominal persona, whose identity, place, and cause divide and multiply through the words of others, irrespective of their apparent presence or absence.⁶¹ More radically than in Kafka's diary and notebook entries, *The Castle* exposes the consequences of being a figure of speech, starting with the room of the anonymous guest whose arrival preludes or parallels the more famous advent of K.

To be sure, it has not escaped notice that phenomenological problems are at stake in this opening scene. As Roland Reuss has written, Kafka's initial fragment reflects "a thoroughgoing critical questioning [. . .] of every usage of speech which would be steered intentionally on the part of the subject."⁶² Not even the castle, whose authority the barmaid invokes, functions as a sovereign instance of speech, insofar as the barmaid ultimately admits that what has come to be common knowledge remains of unknown provenance: "The whole village knows of your arrival [. . .] already for weeks all know it [. . .] more I do not know."⁶³ Because this minimal knowledge was without an object until the guest in fact came, moreover, it was therefore no "knowledge" at all, which leaves the village without foundation concerning not only what it "knows" of the guest, but also what it "knows" concerning itself. This last consequence of the barmaid's remark is underscored by the fact that her words on the shared anticipation of a guest also answer the guest's prior, elliptical question, "What was, then, before I came? [*Was war also, ehe ich kam?*],"⁶⁴ with the implication that rumors of his arrival were all that had been around in town before. Counterintuitive as this possibility may seem, the barmaid goes on to describe the unprecedented character of the guest in a way that suggests that the only history of this realm was the very future that he will have happened to realize: "No one comes," she relates, "it is as if the world had forgotten us."⁶⁵ Since the world's obliviousness toward the town would also entail the town's obliviousness toward itself—since the town would belong to the world that seems to have forgotten it—this obliterating logic implies that its memory and history could only have begun with the fortuitous advent of the newcomer. The encounter that takes place in the "Prince Room" allows for various personae and positions to come into the world—including the "town" and the "castle"—but it settles nothing, so much as it exposes all parties and causes to vicissitudes that render them strangers to one another and themselves. If the "aporias of communication" are at stake in this scene, as Gerhard Neumann has argued, then not even the topoi that he evokes of a self-searching "foreigner" and an expectant community can be presupposed.[66] There is only—and this is the aporia—the chances that spoken encounters admit, which exceed—and therefore also speak against—every speakable expectation. Hence, neither the guest nor the host knows to say where either is going or coming from; all is an open question; and their exchange accordingly culminates with the barmaid's imperative and promise to "speak openly": "Speak openly [*offen*] with me and I will answer you openly [*offen*]."[67]

Kafka's fragment breaks off with this sheer call for open speech, and in such a way where there is no telling whether the blank line that follows the barmaid's words marks an abrupt end, or whether the absence of any further dialogue is itself the open response she had invited. Instead of suggesting a decision either way, the paragraph that comes after this break will mark the arrival of K. and the opening of the novel according to Max Brod, who fills in the blank with the sentence, "Here begins the novel 'The Castle' M.B."[68] Yet the barmaid's last words are also not simply left behind as the questionable entrances, interiors, and inner motives that had made up Kafka's initial scene give way to the novel "proper." For the ambiguous silence that follows her utterance also says without a word that openness could be in no one's power to decide or to effect and that it would therefore also be beyond one's power to anticipate, know, or foreclose it. This impossible possibility is the limit that Kafka's manuscript admits, disclosing a passive dimension of language that is more radical than even the passivity to which the guest was subject as the talk of the town. Nor is the blank passage of Kafka's first convolute the only one where the promise and powerlessness to speak openly will resonate: in at least two later scenes from the more widely known portions of his novel fragment, the landlady and the mayor who preside, respectively, over the domestic sphere and public affairs, each promise to "tell openly [*offen erzählen*]" of various matters concerning K. and themselves,[69] and thereby come to permit more than they could know or wish. But before these more pronounced echoes of the barmaid's last words—which remain to be examined—the new scene of arrival that follows the scenario in the "Prince Room" withdraws each sign of what appears and what takes place, and therefore holds the initial space to be crossed radically open:

"It was late evening when ~~I~~ K. came. The village lay in deep snow. Of the castle mount, nothing was to be seen [.] , ~~I stayed it was~~ Fog and darkness surrounded it, ~~not once~~ not even the weakest shimmer of light hinted towards [off from] *the* great castle. Long stood ~~I~~ K. on the wooden bridge that led from the road to the village and looked up into the seemingly bare emptiness" (Es war spät abend als ~~ich~~ K. ankam. Das Dorf lag in tiefem Schnee. Vom Schlossberg war nichts zu sehn[.], ~~Ich blieb er war in~~ Nebel und Finsternis umgaben ihn, ~~nicht einmal~~ auch nicht der schwächste Lichtschein deutete [ab] *das* grosse Schloss an. Lange stand ~~ich~~ K. auf der Holzbrücke die von der Landstrasse zum Dorf führt und blickte in die scheinbare Leere empor).[70] Whatever its relation may be to the sketch that preceded it—the lowercase writing of "ab-end" indicates merely that this "evening" has broken "off" from *some* "end"—this passage broaches an exteriority that turns out to be outside any outside where a horizon of demarcation would allow for an exterior to be distinguished at all. The "village" and "castle" or "castle mount" that are foregrounded at first—and that may themselves be the leftover traces from any number of prior constructions, now barely visible[71]—are no sooner named, than they are set under erasure: the layout is buried and the surroundings, surrounded ("umgaben") by snow, fog, and darkness, whose obscurity has already reached a limit that is marked by the superlative, "not even the weakest shimmer of light [*der schwächste Lichtschein*] hinted towards [. . .] the great castle," and that is further emphasized with the alliterative "ch" and "sch" that absorb the very word of a "shimmer" into a stream of sibilants. An undecidable instance of overlapping, pairing, and scission occurs here, not between two subjects like Bataille's twins in *L'Abbé C.*, nor between two unlike phenomena, as in Husserl's manuscripts on passive synthesis but between words for appearance and absence, which trouble the very ground for any subject or object of experience.[72] The setting that initially appears to be set forth thus attains the semblance of a void (*Leere*) that is also bare of semblance (*Schein*) and stripped of sheen (*Schein*): "die schein-*bare* Leere."

It is in light of this undecidability that Joseph Vogl would write: "Between a something that does not appear and a nothing that is mere appearance, a narrative world is sketched out in which a halting start corresponds with pure semblance."[73] Besides even these apparently symmetrical alternatives, however, Kafka's writing grants admission to the limits of phenomenality and thus speaks—transitively—the opening of a space that is out of sight, unheard of, unrecognizable, beyond being, and only therefore an opening at all. Or, to put it in more phenomenological terms, the further or closer determination (*Näherbestimmung*) of each landmark does not disclose "the thing that is posited [*das gesetzte Ding*]" in its manifold aspects, while staying in tune with itself, as it should do according to the understanding of perceptual phenomena (*Erscheinungen*) that Kafka would have heard about from his teacher Marty, and that his contemporary Husserl had described. Instead, each site that is evoked literally goes under over the course of its description, which does not go anywhere or converge into a "unity of coverage [*Deckungseinheit*],"[74] so much as it appears to undergo something closer to the "corrections [*Korrekturen*]," the "alterations in apprehension [*Auffassungsänderungen*]," and the "crossing through [*Durchstreichung*]" that Husserl had admitted into the process of perception himself,[75] since, as he argues toward the end of his *Ideas Pertaining to a Pure Phenomenology*, cognition "leads through errors," and since, as he soon adds, a "phenomenology of 'void semblance' ['*nichtigen Scheins*']" is therefore "quite indispensable" for "a phenomenology of 'true actuality.'"[76] At the same time, however, neither the village nor the castle is marked by the "not" that Husserl proposed as a translation for "crossing through [*Durchstreichung*]" in his phenomenological descriptions,[77] and this is because, in Kafka's scenario, semblance and negation could themselves no more be posited than the village and castle can appear to be settled: the semblance of a void may also be none, not a *nichtiger Schein* but a *scheinbares Nichts*, whose Schein-*bar*-keit is itself ambivalent. Rather than any provisional survey of the land (*Landvermessung*), rather than any cognitive striking-through (*Durchstreichung*), and rather than any suspenseful balance between the two on the part of a character, narrator, or reader, what takes place as the initial landmarks of *The Castle* are drawn, brushed over, and stripped of their features could be called *Landstreichung* ("land-striking"), as nonword and a cover name to characterize this scripted space, whose broad strokes "neither reveal nor conceal," but extravagantly write out what can neither be known nor seen. This vanishing trace was the mark of writing that Kafka had imagined, when he wrote in his diary on November 21, 1913: "As I took the inkwell from the writing desk in order to carry it into the living room, I felt a firmness in me just as, for example, the edge of a great building appears in fog and just like that vanishes again."[78] And vanishing traces were the traits that Maurice Blanchot would emphasize as well, when he wrote of the "neutral" voice that speaks through Kafka's oeuvre: "Neutral speech neither reveals nor conceals [. . .] that is to say, it does not signify in the same way as the visible-invisible does, but rather opens another power in language, one that is alien to the power of illuminating (or obscuring), of comprehension (or misapprehension)."[79]

Where the orders or fictions of phenomenality and comprehension are crossed through in this way, the *ego cogito* to which both may be thought to correlate can hardly escape unscratched. Hence, what is literally crossed through in Kafka's text is not the "village" or the "castle," but the "I," whose effacement does not merely score yet another strike against the notion of "self-knowledge," for its remaining traces also give further indications of what a stricken subject may mean for narrated experience. The partially obliterated "I" that appears beside the "he" or the "K." who "I" will have become—beside "my" self, in all senses of the phrase—literally scratches off the possibility that "I" might speak, write, think, or see, and thereby renders all personal memory of "my" arrival, let alone any prior history, utterly beyond recall as well. With K., there is not even the semblance of a subject who could hold together, retain, or relate the first phrase on his arrival to the one beside it on the village, as the "I" might have implied, if left alone: instead, K. is said to come, and then comes word of a village whose purview he has not entered yet, and whose very mention temporarily brings him to fall out of the picture, as if disappearing upon "arrival." In this respect, what occurs when Robert and Charles write themselves to death in Bataille's *L'Abbé C.*—where writing "accomplishes, in a word, what is generally accomplished by 'time' " and "allows only traces of death to subsist"[80]—recurs when the "I" is crossed through and when "K." appears only intermittently toward the outset of *The Castle*. For the juxtaposition of I̶/ K. indicates not only that the subject of arrival is itself a leftover trace but also that this letter-variable is an evanescent placeholder that will admit permutations that need not remotely resemble the laws or functions of any continuous consciousness.

The inconsistent emergence of traces is what comes with the coming of "K.," whose temporary oblivion has next to nothing to do with someone losing grip of the past as he tries to hold his own for the present and still less to do with the self-forgetfulness that Augustine had countered by insisting upon the trinity of latent memory, knowledge, and self-presence that Marty would echo with his insistence upon our implicit, pre-reflexive "self-representation [*Selbstvorstellen*]," "self-knowledge [*Selbsterkenntnis*]," and "self-directed feeling [*auf sich selbst gerichtetes Gefühl*]" at every moment of lived experience.[81] Rather, this oblivion is one which comes to pass through the obliteration that occurs as "I" is literally written off and overwritten with a "K.," whose proximity to "I," in turn, characterizes this subject as nearly but not entirely null (*nichtig*) and not I (*nicht ich*): "I" and "K." are all "there, but they are there in order to disappear, as though they have already been annihilated."[82]

"K." is a figure of speech, whose status can no more be fixed than the initial apparition of a castle and landscape can be established, whether it is a question of personal perspective and societal role, or the various circulating stories of his "life." More radically than with the guest who appears on Kafka's first manuscript pages, this exemplary reduction of "the names of characters and places [. . .] to initials"[83] signals their irreducibility to either a first-person subject of consciousness or to an indifferent and generic "one." It is not a question of these two pronominal alternatives, as it may have been for the protagonist of Kafka's "Wedding Preparations in the Country," Eduard Raban—"as long as you say 'one' instead of 'I,'" Raban thinks to himself, "there's nothing in it and you can easily tell a story; but as soon as you admit to yourself that it is you yourself, then you feel as though transfixed and are horrified."[84] Instead, the various legends of "K.,"[85] who is seldom, if ever addressed directly by name,[86] and who only ever pretends to name himself,[87] let this letter stand for multiple narrative figures, while the figure to whom it is most often ascribed also comes to be invoked under multiple titles. Thus, "K." abbreviates no proper name that could belong as exclusive property to even a fictive biographical individual, nor do the official letters that reach K. with the greeting, "Honorable Sir,"[88] and later, "To the Land-Surveyor of the Inn at the Bridge,"[89] suggest that he will have so much as nominally been registered in the archives of the eponymous "castle." Unlike in *The Trial*, where "Josef K." will be "unequivocally" called out,[90] there is no spoken or written address that is expressly meant for "K.," who remains an aberrant, anonymous singularity throughout the text, and whose every single evocation differs from one instance to the next.[91] As Avital Ronell has elegantly written: "A mark of incompletion, the letter 'K.' anticipates interpretation while it also represents a resistance to signification [. . .], reducing thus the status of the subject from an entity to a locus," or a "typographical character."[92] Thus, in one of Kafka's many variations upon the initial scene between an anonymous guest and a barmaid, the landlady of the "inn at the bridge" will zero in upon the impossibility of discounting K. or counting him in. "You are not from the castle, you are not from the village, consequently, then, one should properly believe that You are nothing," she says, before continuing: "are Unfortunately, however, you are still something, a foreigner, one who is supernumerary [*überzählig*] [i] and overall in the way [*überall im Weg*], one on account of whom one is always in a scrape [*einer wegen dessen man immerfort Scherereien hat*]."⁹³ Because he is "supernumerary" and "foreign," K. is the near nullity that no one can suffer but who nonetheless can no more be decisively negated than could the semblance of a void that had first appeared on the textual horizon. Because he is missing a place, he is an obstacle or *skándalon* "everywhere" or "overall." Vagrant and vacant, "K." is what becomes of the subject, when the fiction of the first-person singular is abandoned in favor of a singular trace, whose persistence even under erasure is what allows him to obstruct the radically inhospitable (dis)course of town and castle life. In all of these ways and more, that is, K. also scores against the positions of those whom he encounters, not by any "struggle" or "Kampf" of his own,⁹⁴ but by withdrawing from every reckoning in the way that Werner Hamacher describes in another context: "The non-time of Kafka's narrative is that of the supernumerary, of the unutilizable leftover [. . .], it lies outside the course of history, not upon a path or even an avenue of the experience of reason."⁹⁵

This withdrawal goes not only for what others say of K. but also for what is said in the narration surrounding each dialogic exchange. By the time the landlady calls him "supernumerary," K. seems to have secured lodgings at her inn, seduced Frieda (the barmaid and former lover of the castle official, Klamm), and forged connections with the family of the castle messenger, Barnabas. As K.'s conversation with the landlady unfolds, however, her attempt to reduce his role to a negligible quantity renders uncertain every possible assessment of all that he was said to have experienced thus far. Already when he awakens from sleep and finds the landlady knitting "close by the bed," it is as if she were the main occupant of his room, and as if private "lodgings" in the world of *The Castle* did not mean what it does in more familiar parlance.⁹⁶ Similarly, when she begins their conversation with the "reproach": "I have been waiting already for a long time,"⁹⁷ she suggests that K. had been absent even as he rests in place. But the landlady's presence does not dislodge him, nor does his dormant state eliminate the fact that he leaves her waiting; rather, what the situation indicates on both counts is that trouble has been occasioned without K.'s doing for both the landlady and the apparent logic of the narrative. It is this passive production of troubling effects that the landlady emphasizes, as she goes on to tell K. that, unbeknownst to him (and the reader of *The Castle*), it was solely due to the "negligence" of her husband that he was allowed into the inn from the beginning, that Frieda was already "seduced" before any overtures on K.'s part,[98] and that the household of Barnabas, whom K. evokes as a possible refuge and resource, is a lot of "rags [*Lumpen*]" from whom Frieda will have "rescued [*gerettet*]" him.[99] (K. had been in the company of Barnabas's sister, Olga, when he first met Frieda at the bar and attached himself to her.) With her version of his story, the landlady thus implies that, far from being a protagonist, K. does not even know what has happened to him: "Wherever you may also come to be," she concludes, "remain conscious of ~~your~~ this, that you are the one who knows least of all here [*Wohin Sie auch kommen, bleiben Sie sich ~~Ihrer~~ dessen bewusst, dass Sie hier der Unwissendste sind*]."[100]

It is not anything in particular from the landlady's speech that unsettles the status of previously narrated events or contests the authority of the narrative voice. Rather, the sheer fact that previously narrated events permit such corrective or fictive variation draws out the constitutive indeterminacy of their conditions, causes, and significance—which may also be nothing but a matter of "negligence." Irrespective of whatever the "truth" could mean or be, the landlady's speech thus makes plain that "K." is not only a stranger to the town but also foreign to the very trajectory that he will have traversed and that readers will have followed. There is no authority concerning experience, in other words, and it is for this reason too that the course of events she retells would have to be foreign to the landlady as well, despite her claim to know better innately: "You are a couple of days in this place," she reproaches K., "and already you would know everything better than [I] those who are born here [*die Eingeborenen*]."[101] Her narrative exposes not the truth that only an "insider" could know, but the fundamentally unknown variables affecting all that concerns K.,[102] and in so doing, it exposes itself to be no more verifiable than any other testimony that could be given. The decisive factors that she names, moreover—such as faults of her husband, the feelings of Frieda, and social status of Barnabas's family—all rest more or less directly upon the "inner" life of strangers, which is accessible to none, including the strangers themselves: "There is no observation of the inner world [*der innern Welt*], as there is one of the outer [world]."[103]

At least as troubling as the internal faultlines of her story, however, is the external occasion of which the landlady says nothing, but without which she and K. would have had nothing to say, namely, the arrival of "K." in the first place. This conspicuous omission marks the one detail for which the landlady does not so much as try to account, namely, the "supernumerary" persistence of her interlocutor, which at once prompts her speech and betrays its contingency upon the foreign, the obstacle—the impasse—that has provoked her, among others, to occupy herself with K. The landlady's voice thus turns out to be passive to the core, affected *ab initio* by the alterity that she so vocally opposes and that structurally escapes all reckoning. What the landlady and K. thus disclose with and despite themselves is not only that no one could tell what has come to pass but also that this impossibility to tell is what occasions speaking to begin with. The consequences of this aporetic outcome, which would be characteristic of what one could also call, with Alain Badiou, an "event,"[104] may not entail the indefinitely open range of possibilities that K. evokes as his conversation with the landlady closes, and he opens the door to leave "his" room: "to the one who does not know, all seems possible—here K. already opened the door—[*dem Unwissenden scheint alles möglich—hier öffnete schon K. die Tür—*]."[105] But it does mean that each speaker cannot but remain open to the provocations of alterity that would precede every initiative, as well as the alternatives that may affect them even after the fact.

It is in this way that, for all its differences, the dialogue between K. and the landlady issues into the aporetic openness with which the exchange between guest and barmaid had culminated in Kafka's initial fragment, where neither party knew to say where either is coming from, and where other voices and arrivals were the passive premise for each question and claim. If the possibilities that "seem" to belong to "the one who does not know" are to be other than mere semblance, then this could only be possible if they are the possibilities of passivity, rather than any that could be known by a subject of volition. The passive character of "possibility" is indicated perhaps most pronouncedly, however, when K. approaches the mayor in order to learn the details concerning his actual, fictitious, or fortuitous appointment as land-surveyor.[106] It is to the mayor that K. dispatches himself when he leaves the landlady, as per the instructions of the official letter that he had received confirming his acceptance to "seignorial service."[107] The unlimited "possibilities" to which K. appeals, that is, are not without contexts or pretexts: it is this document that K. seems to follow and that relieves him of any need to know more, which may also be why, when the mayor invites K. to name his wishes—"Have a seat, have a seat, Sir Land-Surveyor [. . .] and tell me your wishes [*sagen Sie mir Ihre Wünsche*]"—K. does not say anything for himself but reads the letter aloud instead.[108] This is not to say, however, that the terms of the letter are binding; instead, it is through K.'s passive turn to the letter that the text marks a new point of departure not only for K. but also for the mayor, whose response will confirm K.'s claim that "all seems possible" to "the one who does not know," and in a manner that K. could neither have foreseen nor wished when he set out. Rather than providing K. with "all further details concerning [his] work and conditions of pay,"[109] as the letter had promised he would do, the mayor no sooner addresses his visitor, "Sir Land-Surveyor," than he takes the occasion to go off script and confront K. with "the full unpleasant truth" that the town needs no land-surveyor. The mayor then proceeds to tell K. yet another unknown story about himself, which he introduces in terms that recall the barmaid's last words from Kafka's first pages: "As to what now concerns your case," the mayor begins, "I will tell you its course openly [de[r]n Hergang offen erzählen], without keeping official secrets from you—for that I am not enough of an official, I am a peasant and it stays at that."[110] But unlike the landlady's narrative, which offers an alternative account of K.'s recent past, the mayor's narrative concerning K.'s "case" retraces a trail of paperwork that dates from so long ago, it also "could not have concerned" whomever the mayor has just greeted.[111] The mayor's disclosure, that is, opens K.'s case to "possibilities" that exceed the bounds of possibility.

What allows for this otherwise impossible link to be forged between a distant "course" of events and K.'s current trajectory is, moreover, itself nothing other a nominal coincidence that no one could have predicted, or, in a word, a passive association owed more to the vicissitudes of language than any authority: past files can be assigned relevance to K., and K. can figure in this documented history thanks to the title of "land-surveyor" that circulates between them—and that only ever named a possible, and possibly nullified position in town. During his first days in office, namely, the mayor claims to have received a writ from one department ordering the summons of a land-surveyor. Presumably for the same reasons that he had initially given for dismissing K. from work—"the limits of our small economies are staked out, all is registered in an orderly manner, change of possession hardly comes about, and we regulate small border disputes ourselves"[112]—the mayor had sent a negative reply, whose content went missing and whose envelope reached the wrong division, in turn, initiating a series of confusions, investigations, and contestations across the castle bureaucracy and village community. Far from approaching any definitive resolution, the unsurveyable range of intersecting, contradicting, and missing communications surrounding the question of a "land-surveyor" results in a situation where even the decision reached years ago to abandon the issue remains questionable. Just before recounting how one department was ultimately satisfied with his renewed assurance "that no land-surveyor is needed," the mayor confesses not to know "whether in your case such a [final] decision went through—some things speak in favor, some ~~in any case~~ against it [*manches spricht dafür, manches dagegen*]."¹¹³ Among those "things," of course, it is K.'s arrival that "speaks" most strongly against any closure in the case that would only become "his" after it had long been put to rest: "And now imagine my disillusionment, Sir Land-Surveyor, when now, after the happy ending of the whole affair [. . .] you suddenly ~~appear~~ step forth, and it receives the semblance as if the matter should begin again from the first."¹¹⁴

With these words, the mayor finally answers the request that K. had made, midstory, to hear a word about himself: "I am hearing for the first time of these supervisory offices [. . .], only I would also like to hear a word about myself."¹¹⁵ But the mayor can speak "about" K. in this context only because the channels, terms, and records of communication prevent any word "about" anyone from being unequivocal and decisive. Thus, as Henry Sussman would concisely put it, "K. is himself a remnant from a prior drama already played out,"¹¹⁶ while the "gaps, omissions, and errors generated" through the scriptural space of the castle at the same time work against its authority, allowing for an emancipatory "release" from "lived experience" in even the most supervised spheres.¹¹⁷ Yet whereas scholars such as Stanley Corngold and Benno Wagner have emphasized the connection of these effects to the crazed character of the bureaucratic apparatus—which notoriously led to cases of "files [going] missing, only to emerge on unexpected occasions years later"¹¹⁸—the mayor's rhetoric also registers numerous signs that it is also the passive conditions of speech as such which render both official and personal accounts at once possible and impossible. To begin, the mayor's very ability to welcome K. is owed not to any official duty but to the illness that renders him bedridden and keeps him from his work: "You are always welcome," the mayor says in the end, before adding: "especially now, so long as I am ill. When I can go to the writing desk again, my official work naturally takes me ~~again~~ entirely in demand."¹¹⁹ Nor is it simply the case that illness temporarily suspends the demands that would leave the mayor no time to speak; for his partial recollection of missing documents also depends upon this disruption to his "official work" at the "writing desk": "A long time ago, when I had only been mayor for several months, there came a writ, I no longer know from which division," he starts, before adding: "I would not have remembered [the initial writ] if I were not now ill and had enough time in bed to think back upon the most laughable things."[120] To at least the same extent that passivity here characterizes the occasion for speaking and remembering, moreover, it also characterizes speaking and remembering themselves: for the mayor's memory lapse concerning the source of the first "writ" testifies to the constitutive openness of his narrative to lacunae and interpolations, which may well exceed those that are noticed and noted. Both the occurrence and the content of the whole conversation, that is to say, are conditioned and crossed through by the double contingency of illness and faulty memory, and in this respect, the mayor's sick recollection of paperwork is not entirely unlike the malaise that tinges Charles C.'s attempt to read his brother's papers in *L'Abbé C.* Unlike in Bataille's novel, however, where at least the semblance of documents remains, there are no such things to be found when the mayor orders his wife to locate the file labeled "Land Surveyor,"[121] reducing the entire matter to a vanished and unverifiable trace that the mayor can only relate off the record and thus cannot guarantee.

It is precisely where personal memory and official records reach their limit, however, that the mayor's narration truly tells the case of K. "openly," albeit in a sense that the mayor could hardly have meant. So as to supplement his lack of records and limited recollection, the mayor resorts to a formal-alphabetical fiction in order to describe how his answer to the original writ "appears not to have reached the original," unknown "division [*Abteilung*]" that he proposes to name A—"ich will sie A [x]A nennen"—but instead "erroneously" reached "another division, [y]B."[122] This gesture may, to be sure, appear to be inconsequential. Yet once the substitution of false initials for proper names begins, K.'s case is reopened in a manner that not only forecloses all possible confirmation with the divisions in question—they are not to be reached under the titles "A" or "B"—but that also openly exposes the truly fictive character of remembered events and collective organizations. For in taking recourse to letter variables, Kafka's mayor echoes Marty's lecture course on descriptive psychology, where such uses of alphabetic characters were cited as exemplary for the ways in which we "represent something inauthentically" with a "surrogate," which takes place each time that "instead of really thinking this or that, I think merely of what is named this way or that [*das so oder so Genannte*], as in algebra where a particular letter is used from time to time for a certain sign."[123] Foremost among those things for which surrogates necessarily replace thinking are collectives like the "state," whose existence would essentially be fictive,[124] according to Marty's premise that only individuals can be intuited as real. But Marty also cites "foreign psychical life" as another necessary instance of fictional construction,[125] since other minds are structurally inaccessible to one another. And ultimately, one's own memories would have to be fictive in a similar manner, if it is true that, as Brentano had argued, "I" can only imagine my past experiences in analogy to the experiences of a foreign psyche:[126] "otherwise, [one] would have to err again in remembering an earlier error" or even "sin again, in remembering with regret an earlier sinful act of will."[127] Along the lines of these arguments—which Kafka may have known from his Brentanian circles—the mayor's alphabetic substitutions would not mark a departure from more proper designations, so much as his fictive variations would conspicuously underscore the way in which any "proper" remembrance and any "proper" institution would count among those figures of speech that "the usual popular language has [. . .] fashioned, [and] which function similarly to these algebraic signs."[128]

Fiction thus turns out to be the open secret of political institutions and personal biographies in (and beyond) *The Castle*. Yet whereas Marty's explication of fictive surrogates still presupposes certain laws of subjective life, no such instance of control governs the mayor's oral history, which becomes evident through the discrepancy between "A" and "B": while the mayor cannot name the forgotten division without adopting a surrogate such as "A," no such rationale is given for designating the second division "B," whose most diligent official, Sordini, the mayor still knows by name.[129] In this second instance of substitution, it is as though an arbitrary inclination for alphabetic formalization had overwritten not only the fictions that "usual popular language has [. . .] fashioned," but also the fiction that those fictions and their substitutes may be founded in rational motives. With "B," even the better known "division" or "Ab-teilung" is drawn into the mayor's alphabetical order of "inauthentic" representation, and insofar as the mayor's abbreviations thus multiply without any compelling reason—or even a claim to "name" something (as in: "ich will sie A̶ [x] A nennen")—a more radical oblivion than any lapse known to the mayor intervenes in his narration, opening his speech to permutations not unlike those that affect the figure of speech known as "K." The making of fiction thus turns out to be no supplementary speech act on the part of the mayor but another index for the passivity that speaking entails and that allows each utterance to speak otherwise than anyone may know or mean to say. Yet beyond even these indications that "A" and "B" would be irreducible to the rational function of substitutes that Marty and Brentano propose, the repetitions of "Beh" and "Ah" over the course of the mayor's story of "officials" (*Be-amten*) and "answers" (*Be-antwortungen*) also let the letters resonate like a wordless stutter throughout his more "official" pronouncements.[130] In this way, the mayor's account becomes less reminiscent of the castle bureaucracy than of the passive experience that Kafka had described, when he wrote: "I live only here and there in a small word, in whose umlaut (above 'shoves' ['*stößt*']) I, for example, lose my useless head for a moment. The first and last letter are the beginning and end of my fishlike feeling [*meines fischartigen Gefühls*]."[131]

But the ABCs of fiction writing that the mayor betrays also surpass Kafka's first-person recollection in exposing the ways in which speaking and writing cross through the bounds of empirical experience, personal claims, authorized truths, and intentional lies. Beyond and despite himself, the mayor testifies most pronouncedly to the inability to speak knowingly that traverses each voice in Kafka's novel fragment, from the preliminary scene between a guest and barmaid, to K.'s conversations with the landlady, and his encounters with Olga and Pepi toward the abortive end. But this inability to speak knowingly is also the condition of possibility for speaking openly: throughout, the letter variables and variant narratives that are repeated make room for alternatives even as they appear to draw limits, and thus trace a withdrawal both from the limits they would set and from themselves: "They are there, but they are there in order to disappear, as though they have already been annihilated."[132] It is in this way that the papers Kafka would abandon himself thereby admit what descriptive psychology and prescriptive administrations alike refuse to suffer: the patience for that which "would interrupt our reason, our speech, our experience": the patience for language.[133]

Chapter 5

Passive Voices

Echoes, Blanchot

Something other is given away with every word that may be given of oneself, according to a note that Kafka records on the likeness of confession and lie: "Confession and lie are alike. In order to be able to confess, one lies. One cannot express that which one is, for one is just that; one can only impart that which one is not, that is, a lie. A certain truth may lie only in the chorus" (Geständnis und Lüge ist das Gleiche. Um gestehen zu können, lügt man. Das was man ist kann man nicht ausdrücken, denn dieses ist man eben; mitteilen kann man nur das was man nicht ist, also die Lüge. Erst im Chor mag eine gewisse Wahrheit liegen).[1]

Even if one wanted to give a sincere confession, in other words, the difference between expression and expressed alone would render each "confession" duplicitous: being and imparting would remain apart in such way that the very intention to confess could not but be the self-deceptive effect of unknown motives. Or, as Kafka would conclude in a separate note: "The word [know thyself] means, then: Misknow thyself! [*Das Wort [Erkenne Dich selbst] bedeutet also: Verkenne Dich!*]."[2] Hence, it was in holding true to this dilemma that Kafka's diaries expressly abandon the thought of personal experience in favor of the "free area of description, which releases the foot from lived experience [*Erlebnis*]."[3] But also beyond the notes written in the first-person voice and the aphorisms offered in a gnomic tone, other voices from Kafka's oeuvre concur when it comes to the difficulties of confession. The accused protagonist of *The Trial*, Josef K., cannot so much as begin a defense writ on his own behalf,[4] while the protagonist of *The Castle* cannot speak for himself without finding himself spoken for by those members of the community who make up the stories of his life without knowing themselves any better. Throughout Kafka's oeuvre, each gesture toward confession more truly "confesses" its impossibility by default. But what these fictive situations make perhaps still clearer than Kafka's explicit note on the subject is that, once the subject of "confession" or "Geständnis" has no choice but to lie, this situation would likewise unsettle any supposition of one's "underlying" (ὑποκείμενον) being, for lack of any basis for verification beside one's word. Although Kafka asserts that "one is just" what "one is," then, this claim would have to be subject to the same duplicity as any more personal confession, implying an extreme withdrawal of truth from both subjective knowledge and substantial foundations.

Versions of this implicit thought were common in the confessional writing that Kafka would have more or less directly known. In his *Confessions*, Augustine explicitly distances himself from those audiences who might wish "to hear from my own confession what I am within, where they can direct [*intendere*] neither eye nor ear nor mind."[5] If his confessions could nevertheless be intended "to make truth [*facere [veritatem]*],"[6] then this is because the truth in question consists not in any private knowledge but in the Christian faith that Augustine aims to make pronounced through his confessional writing. It is for this reason that, as Jean-Luc Marion has argued, the last books of the *Confessions* are devoted to the exegesis of Genesis, rather than to the trajectory of Augustine per se, whose conversion will have allowed him to join the community of believers: "Starting with book X, the praise becomes definitively always plural because the *confessio* becomes communitarian, through the liturgy to be sure but also through the community of readers, as if the liturgy was extended to reading."[7] Nor is the "sense of truth [*Wahrheitssinn*]" that holds valid in the world of transcendental subjectivity any less predicated upon community than Augustine's Christian faith, since every single experience remains subject to correction, rendering the true world contingent upon the repeated "performance" of what Husserl calls "mono-subjective and intersubjective confirmation [*Bewährung*]."[8] As Hannah Arendt would write, in a continuation of Husserl's less Cartesian tendencies, "reality is guaranteed" by the fact that "members of the same species have the context in common that endows every single object with its particular meaning" and that allows them to "agree on its identity."[9] For Augustine, Husserl, and Arendt as well, a "certain truth" lies "in the chorus."

When Kafka evokes the possibility of choral truth, however, he gives no indication that this assertion rests upon the theological suppositions that underpin a project like Augustine's, nor does he suggest that it could be founded in the subjective evidence and intersubjective agreement supporting Husserl's and Arendt's respective claims.[10] Upon the minimal premises that he sets forth, the "truth" of choral speech would instead have to reside in the fact it not only says what each member is not, like every other instance of imparting, but that it also says what no members could know or say for themselves. Truth becomes speakable, that is to say, solely insofar as the multivocal utterance of a chorus emerges, which would be irreducible to the speech of those who lend it their voices and may not even be discernible to them as well. Hence, no word is given as to what, if anything, the chorus may say or sing in Kafka's fragment; and the same holds true for the "accusing chorus" that appears in Josef K.'s dreams,[11] whose accusation is left as vague and uncertain as the cause of his eponymous trial—to say nothing of the "chorus" of trumpet players in *The Man Who Disappeared*, whose "noise" renders it "difficult to make out" or "understand [*verstehen*]" anything at all.[12] Throughout these passages, both the "truth" of choral utterance and the content of said "utterance" could in no way be an object of knowledge for the very ones who speak it, just as they could neither know nor express "themselves." Hence, the "certain truth" that may lie in a "chorus" would always itself remain uncertain, as Kafka indicates in his fragment with the modal verb "mögen" ("may"), while the graphic and phonometic proximity of "liegen" ("lie") to "lügen" ("lie") suggests that his displacement of truth to a chorus may also be dissimulated.

This possible—and possibly illusory—truth is what remains, when the phenomenological subject cannot grasp itself and the supposition of transcendent foundations is suspended. But if truth would escape apprehension on both epistemological and ontological grounds, the escape of truth could nonetheless be traced through plurivocal writings whose resonances and dissonances release speech from every single source or sense and thus disclose the uncertain truth of linguistic experience in the passive voice. More than the constative rhetoric of philosophical investigations, as well as the aphoristic rhetoric of Kafka's fragment on confession, it is thus the fictive and plural language of writings such as *The Castle* that most pronouncedly let this truth escape. As the partial reading of *The Castle* offered above attests, the accounts shared among its various personae vary from encounter to encounter, yielding discordant echoes that betray the uncertain character of their every claim. Because these echoes are spoken by all and none, they exemplify the "choral" speech that Kafka evokes in his note on confession and that Maurice Blanchot would similarly emphasize in *The Writing of the Disaster*, when he describes "the exegeses that come and go in *The Castle*" as "dis-cussion: not the work of arguments bumping against other arguments, but the extreme shuddering of no thoughts, percussive stillness."[13] If there could be an approximation to choral language in descriptive propositions, it would have to resemble this one, for remote as the phrase, "percussive stillness"—or "shattered shuddering, to the point of calm [*l'ébranlement cassé jusqu'au calme*]"—may otherwise seem to be from Kafka's word of a "chorus," Blanchot's formulation suggests through both its express remarks and its internal resonance ("dis-cussion," "secousse," "cassé") the very sort of linguistic occurrence that Kafka had called by this name. Just as Kafka's choruses say nothing themselves and know not what they say, the "shuddering" that Blanchot invokes testifies to the unthought and aphenomenal dimension of language that emerges from the repercussions of speech and assumes no proper status of its own. But what Blanchot also suggests through his formulation is the linguistic character that choral speech would retain even should it approach an extreme of speechlessness, for "percussive stillness" could not take place if the shudder that is sent through all recognizable forms of speech were not borne by those very forms and if those forms did not themselves open beyond each notion that any speaker may eventually come to form of them.

In other words, the "choruses" of Kafka's prose, as well as the "exegeses" of *The Castle* and the remarks of Blanchot will have been disposed from the outset to bear another "exegetical" movement that would no longer imply clarification but rather "strike through" ("per-cuss") and "lead out" (ἐξ-ἡγεῖσθαι), if not toward a certain truth, then away from the falsehood of every story, "as though to deflect [. . .], for an instant, from the delusion into which everything goes, from which everything comes back."[14] It is in this way—beyond all claims and all common grounds—that Kafka's choral, percussive, and exegetical writing would speak in the passive voice for the absence of self and the "absence of community" that we truly share,[15] or for what Blanchot calls elsewhere the "separation" that is "presupposed" in "all true speech": "There is language because there is nothing in 'common' between those who express themselves: a separation that is presupposed—not surmounted, but confirmed—in all true speech."[16]

It is the separating and resonating traits of "true speech" that Blanchot would draw out in his essayistic and fictional oeuvre, which exposes like none other the extreme repercussions of the truth that Kafka had evoked. Hence, when Blanchot first speaks of the "We" that "oblige[s] me to hear myself in [a] chorus" in *The Last Man*[17]—a narrative that resonates with the writings of Nietzsche, Bataille, and Kafka,[18] among others—this sign of common speech does not reduce but rather discloses the separation that lets words echo, while holding speakers apart from one another and themselves: "He wasn't addressing anyone. I don't mean he wasn't speaking to me, but someone other than me was listening to him, [. . .] as though, confronting him, what had been 'I' had strangely awakened into a 'we.'"[19] If this "we" may still be described as "the presence and united force of the common spirit," as it is said to be, then what is thus made present is "my" absence—"someone other than me was listening"[20]—such that the "we" alone already says that "we are all united" solely in the "share of solitude"[21] that cuts through our common terms with a silent shudder. Our separate "solitude" is spoken, that is, in a passive, choral voice that speaks with—and at odds with—every voicing and thus remains beyond "us" all. Such is the movement that Christopher Fynsk has aptly described as the "commitment to chance and becoming" that comes with the "commitment to conversation" and may be further characterized as "a special assumption of the contingencies of life that communicates with a more profound assumption of the finitude of language itself."[22] For on the one hand, entering into "our" speech leaves "me" no say; and on the other hand, it is only the alterity and alteration that chance to come through "our" words that lets the question so much arise as to what finite "part [. . .] I have in the words that entreat me with a sweet lure to follow them."[23] And ultimately, since the words of common language include "I" as well, which comes "like a flame [. . .] to light on one or the other of us and designat[es] him to answer the general speech," the true question of speech remains—namely, "what is happening" as we speak?[24]

It is in holding true to this often unspoken question that, in *The Writing of the Disaster*, Blanchot more explicitly approaches the "passivity" that "lies, perhaps," beyond "the reach of any question" or confession. Here, he does so by questioning that which occurs in language "before anything" is known to be "spoken"[25] and thus differs from any words that could be given or received by a subject of experience known as "me"[26]: "Where might one find the language in which answer, question, affirmation, negation may well intervene, but without any effect? Where is the speaking—as distinct from anything that can be spoken—which eludes every mark, the mark of prediction and likewise of interdiction?"[27] Both this invocation of "passivity" and the question of a "speaking" that "eludes every mark" may seem at first to draw these passages in greater proximity to the writings of Emmanuel Levinas—whom Blanchot soon cites by name—than to Kafka's words of choral truth and exegetical discussion.[28] They recall the "passivity" that Levinas had traced back to the transcendence of the Other in *Otherwise Than Being*, and before this, to the temporal "lapse," which comes to pass before any "initiative of an ego," exposing the time of our lives to alterity from the outset.[29] But whereas Levinas will situate this "passivity [. . .] more passive [. . .] than any passivity that is correlative to the voluntary" in the alterity that already affects us through time, and that most urgently confronts us in the sheer "Saying" of the Other,[30] Blanchot calls both "passivity" and "saying" into question as well by asking "where" they might occur. In *The Writing of the Disaster*, linguistic "passivity" becomes a question that displaces the accent of Levinas's discussions, and in those responses that Blanchot offers—in lieu of any answer—he will emphasize not only time and the Other but also those turns that language takes through repetition and inscription, "maintaining it outside even the unity of that which is, [. . .] divert[ing] language from itself by letting it differ and defer."[31] Hence, the passive dimension of language turns out to be nowhere but elsewhere—even here and now—and it accordingly comes forth less through that which Blanchot appears to say *about* passivity than through the turns that phrases take, as *The Writing of the Disaster* repeats and alters the "passive" vocabulary of Levinas or the "dis-cussions" of Kafka, among countless named and anonymous others. Once again, a "certain truth" would lie only where the lines of Blanchot's text defer to others and alter their speech in turn or, rather, where a chorus of allusive fragments registers a "suffering" in language that no speakers induce or undergo themselves. "Without present" and "without I," this suffering would be a passion of which no one "could say that experience—a form of knowledge—would either reveal or conceal it," but which instead "draw[s] what wants to be said into a general errant drift where there is no longer any term that as meaning would belong to itself and where, for a center, each has but the possibility of being decentered: bent, inflected, exteriorized, denied, or repeated."[32] The "where" for this "certain truth" would, in other words, shift, intermittently, with the percussive "repetitiveness" that leaves "no place for distinguishing to be and not to be, truth and error, death and life"³³ and that only therefore can allow "answer, question, affirmation, negation" to "intervene, but without any effect."³⁴

Where effective speech becomes suspended, however, "the reference to the true-false dichotomy" also "no longer holds sway,"³⁵ with the further consequence that the more philosophical or theoretical passages on "passivity" in *The Writing of the Disaster* could not be privileged sites for tracing the further resonance of those passive voices that spoke through Kafka and advocated for another sort of truth than propositional forms could admit. Instead, *The Writing of the Disaster* makes explicit how each "discourse on passivity"—not unlike each "confession"—could only fail or falsify the subject in question by turning it into an object of knowledge: "The discourse on passivity necessarily betrays passivity," and thus can only "indicate certain of the traits that cause its faithlessness: not only is discourse active; it unfolds and develops according to the rules that assure it a certain coherence [. . .], a certain unity of language."³⁶ With and despite all appearance of offering coherent claims on passivity, then, *The Writing of the Disaster* makes a fiction of theory—"Here space opens to 'fictive theory,' and theory, through fiction, comes into danger of dying"³⁷—and for this reason, its "theoretical" treatment of passive voices, repetitions, and "percussive stillness" also solicits further articulations through fiction.³⁸

Especially should the passive and choral "truth" of language be approached through Blanchot's responses not only to the philosophy of Levinas but also to the fictive oeuvre of Kafka, one of its most extensive expositions may already be found in his early novel from 1942, *Aminadab*, whose resonance with Kafka's *Castle* has been recognized since, at the latest, Jean-Paul Sartre's critical review, "*Aminadab* or the Fantastic Considered as Language."³⁹ At one level, this novel appears to trace the errant trajectory of a protagonist named Thomas, who, like Kafka's K., enters into a community whose language, gestures, customs, and laws repeatedly turn out to defer and differ from any legible sense, disorienting him as he attempts to reach the upper echelons of the boarding house where the members of this community reside. Yet it would be misleading to depart from this minimal semblance of plot and character, for what is at issue in *Aminadab* is, before all else, those passive voices that make up this fictive text and unsettle the fictions of plot and character perhaps still more radically than they had done in Kafka's *Castle*, as Jeff Fort has also suggested in the introduction to his translation.⁴⁰ The setting alone says as much, for the novel takes place within a "house" or "maison" that may itself be nothing other "than an immense sonorous cage [*immense cage sonore*]."⁴¹ Not a stable edifice—and not a "house of language"⁴²—but a sonorous cage or cavity opens in Blanchot's book, whose "immense" extent gives no sign of a measure or a limit but for the phrases and echoes that sound (it) out, at a remove from any identifiable sense or source. Within this radically open framework, only a fragmentary reading that "animat[es] the multiplicity of crossing routes," rather than "reconstitut[ing] a new totality from them," could correspond to the lines that are recorded in Blanchot's text,⁴³ whose basic premise disposes speech to rebound from afar and to repeat amiss, rendering this space of resonance a space of missonance—a *maison* that rings false: one could call it a *mé-son* ("false sound") and *mensonge* ("falsehood")—which will have broken with every emission that could be ascribed to any persona—*mes sons* ("my sounds")—and delivered them void.

Hence, when Christopher Strathman reads Blanchot's novel together with Heidegger's famous characterization of language as "the house of being," he will emphasize that the experience of language traced in *Aminadab* "opens onto an abyss."⁴⁴ But this abyss is where room is made for truth of another kind. Thus, when one inhabitant speaks on behalf of the whole household, saying that "the least incident re-rings [*retentit*] *ad infinitum* over our lives,"⁴⁵ he not only affirms the passive experience of language-as-echo but also evokes a word for "reringing" (*retentir*) that itself resonates with the word for "retaining" (*retenir*), at once recalling and retracting the "retention" that would otherwise allow occurrences to be internalized, preserved, remembered, and ordered. The house is, in other words, a place where "answer, question, affirmation, negation" may ring out and "intervene, but without any effect"; a space where "speaking" may take place, "outside of anything spoken."⁴⁶ Beyond whatever this boarder may say in the form of a proposition, the resonance of "retentir" reiterates that, in lieu of retention—and beyond all intentions—the repercussions of speaking are what is amplified in this collective space: repercussions of that which will have irrevocably come to pass and yet remains unfinished—or, in a word, repercussions of the truth of language.

It would be possible to trace such repercussions through any of the "incidents" related in *Aminadab*. Soon after Thomas's entrance into the house, for instance, his movements are interrupted by a guardian, whose voice alone calls him to a halt before he hears the words that the guardian repeats: "Where are you going? Are you looking for someone? [*Où allez-vous? demandait-il. Cherchez-vous quelqu'un?*]."⁴⁷ These words first arrive as an echo—and in the wake of their arresting effect—decoupling in advance the incidence of utterance from any punctual intention to convey the meaning that Thomas gleans from the words that belatedly reach him. And even then, it remains questionable as to whether a "meaning" emerges at all, since the sole indication that Thomas has understood the guardian's utterance, which is said to leave a "painful impression" upon him, is an echo that may reflect its sheer impact at least as much as it may signal comprehension: "Indeed, where was he going?"[48] Both before it arrives as well as after the fact, then, the guardian's vocal intervention "re-rings" beyond any single moment, nor does the question of "where" he is "going" cease to haunt Thomas, both in the sense that it repeatedly returns—through to the end, where he will be told that he "chose the wrong path" and should have left the house for the "open air"[49]—and in the sense that his errant wanderings through the house do nothing if not turn the question into an ongoing quest.

Nor are these traits of the subsequent narrative the only indices that the guardian's utterance persists, for it will "re-ring" throughout the text in at least one other way, again through to the late episode where Thomas will be told that he "chose the wrong path." Since, after all, the words of the guardian resound before they are registered—and since they may have been repeated any number of times before they reach Thomas in the form that is recorded—it can only be incidental that Thomas hears, "Where are you going? Are you looking for someone? [*Où allez-vous?* [. . .] *Cherchez-vous quelqu'un?*]," rather than the equally possible alternative, "Are you looking for someone? Or are you going? [*Cherchez-vous quelqu'un? Ou allez-vous?*]," where the homophony of the words for "where" (*où*) and "or" (*ou*) lets the possibility of an exit resonate through the question of orientation. What "re-rings [. . .] *ad infinitum*" is therefore not only the questionable character of Thomas's every errant move throughout the house but also the question as to whether those movements were not themselves made in error from the outset.

The initial scene between Thomas and the guardian sets the tone for the linguistic incidents that make up the remainder of the text. The repercussions of linguistic repercussions are amplified most strongly, however, in the lengthiest episode of the novel, which begins when Thomas enters a common area that initially appears to be a café, with "numerous people [. . .] seated before drinking glasses or large white bowls"[50] but that also bears traces of other uses: there is the "platform" on the right side of the room "that could be used by a small orchestra,"[51] but that will later be said to serve as a stage for "those who have grounds for complaint [and] come to express their grievances."[52] There are "the paintings on the ceiling" that "represented in a very precise manner the room itself, such as it might appear on the day of gala ball,"[53] although it will soon be proclaimed that "dancing is no longer allowed at present."[54] This latter proclamation, moreover, is issued shortly after a vocal performance is in fact permitted to be delivered by one "member[] of the personnel."[55] Amidst all of these telling signs, then, there is no telling "where" Thomas has gone when he enters this all-purpose room, and since no framing assertions supplement the contradictory claims that various figures make concerning the main function of the room, the reader is as bereft of orientation as "Thomas" is. The divergent senses of this common space do suggest, however, that any number of scenarios and speech acts may "re-ring" within it, while its ambiguous framework would leave even the seemingly most definitive declarations indefinite and undecidable.[56] Yet also beyond these effects of those formulations that alternately accentuate the communal activities of conversing, singing, or holding a hearing—and which alternately cast their speakers and addressees as private personalities, hired personnel, legal persons, or stage personae—the acoustics of the room alone lend all that is said a choral character that resounds and sounds through (*personare*) in conflicting and converging ways at once: "The acoustics of the room were such that certain words stood out while others were muffled, which gave the impression that the same conversation was being repeated at every table and that everything they were saying was being said at the same time by the entire room."[57] The room itself yields, in a word, an "infinite conversation."

Hence, there could hardly be any difference between the "echo" that "immediately" takes "hold" of the "question" that Thomas utters to one suspect member of the personnel—namely, "Who are you exactly?"[58]—and the sonic effects of that same person's singing, where the reverberation of some notes rather than others renders his solo performance polyphonous on its own accord:

> It was a sweet and happy song whose sounds came in quick succession but did not all die away, some continuing on and, without melding with the new notes, remaining untouched by the rest of the modulation [*indifférents à la suite de la modulation*]. This singularity—which one was tempted to explain in terms of the acoustics of the room, but that Thomas attributed

to the vocal memory [*mémoire vocale*] of the singer—did not create a cacophony but finally transformed the melody entirely, a melody that was at first gracious and light but then took on a gravity and a poignant sadness. The columns of sound seemed to surround the singer and to separate him from the crowd, placing him at the center of a melancholy peristyle that he himself could not shake without danger of perishing. It soon seemed to Thomas that the man's voice had gone silent and that, overwhelmed by the sonorous monument it had constructed, it could find only in silence the expression of joy to which it had devoted itself.[59]

Both when Thomas speaks and the personnel sings, it is an issue of sounds being multiplied and altered by their echoes, without anyone's doing. Voices escape in such a way that, even should the cause for the "columns of sound" lie more with the "vocal memory of the singer" than with the "acoustics of the room," the singer reproduces the architecture that was said to affect every utterance in the space, while becoming virtually "silent" before the "sonorous monument" that his voice—but not he himself—"had constructed."

If there is a difference between these echoes of song and the prior echoes of speech that had hitherto shaped communications in this common space, then it would rest in the way in which the song's notes are released still more radically from their apparent source and sense. Whereas the question of identity that Thomas voices can still be identified—"Who are you, exactly?"—the tonalities of "joy" and "sadness" that seem to be conveyed by the song not only remain at a remove from any "expression of the natural passions" of the soul[60] but also may be mere sound effects that emerge as the singer's "solo" becomes a chorus of notes. And as this choral polyphony assumes the stature of an inanimate and static "monument," it not only becomes all the more foreign to the vocal soloist but also becomes alien to any common language: "The words were probably in a foreign language; Thomas understood so little of what they said that he thought he was hearing a melody in which music took the place of words."[61] The song thus bears no mark of the subjective interiority that would more often be associated with "musical thinking" but rather towers like the enigmatic "pyramids" of which Hegel would speak, when he wrote of those "works" that "only receive spirit into themselves as an alien, departed spirit," or "relate themselves externally to spirit as something which is there externally and not as spirit itself."[62] Nor is the foreignness of this sonic-architectonic "language" eliminated when words eventually do appear to surge up "from the confusion," "exalt[in]g the good fortune of a man who does not avoid his duty and who finds in a benevolent action the compensation for a difficult labor,"[63] for there is also no criterion for distinguishing this story of moral principles from yet another chance coincidence of consonance. Just as no principle appears to determine which notes persist, blend together, or become muffled, none could be calculated for the sake of conveying these or any other phrases, whose uncertain character is further betrayed by the fact that no exact wording is reproduced in Blanchot's text, either, but only a paraphrase of the so-called words of the song. Thomas's question, "Who are you?" may immediately resound as if it were addressed to and from "the entire room," and it will resound further throughout *Aminadab*—as it had also done in Kafka's *Castle*.[64] But while the question, "Who are you?" emphasizes the questionable character of the subject, the song that fills and reshapes the common space of Blanchot's musical interlude calls language itself into question.

Hence, if any "truth" should lie in this chorus, it would reside in the incapacity to speak that is spoken through its tonal and verbal elements, whose meaning can no longer be decided, since its signifiers may never have been meant. Instead, the terms and phrases related in the description or transcription of the song may at all times be other than any that the singer had spoken and may even be other than speech. And in this way, the song also speaks for the suspension not only of the narrative that it seems to relate but also of judgments and sentences, which becomes all the more pronounced as the "words" that it gives a semblance of imparting—and thereby exposes as sheer semblance—happen to convey a collective myth of justice, duty, and reward, recalling the connection from Greek antiquity between song (νόμος) and law (νόμος) that later writers such as Jean-Jacques Rousseau would not cease to echo.[65] With the "law" of this song, in other words, it is also said that "song" is the only law, for no law could be posited and no judgment pronounced without being similarly exposed to (and as) the lawless movements of resonance that let it be delivered. There could be none but choral "truths" and verdicts here because there is no telling truth from noise.

The indistinction of meaningful speech from murmuring noise has, to be sure, been traced throughout Blanchot's oeuvre by many readers such as Michel Foucault, who finds Blanchot's writing to be distinctly marked by perhaps nothing so much as "the repetition of what continually murmurs outside."⁶⁶ Roger Laporte echoes these remarks when he unfolds his reading of Blanchot under the sign of the "terrifyingly ancient" or "effroyablement ancien" character of speech itself, which immemorially precedes and persists through every present utterance, withdrawing our speech as we speak "into its distance" and stammering "silence."⁶⁷ More recently, Jeff Fort has read Blanchot's expositions of the "preinscribed sonorous material that necessarily precedes and structures any given act of inscription" to indicate a more "radical *indistinction*" than Blanchot explicitly acknowledges between "literary" writing and the "technical media" that make up the "contemporary conditions of mass society."⁶⁸ But the political implications of the sonic disturbances that these writers address are what the musical scene of *Aminadab* specifically exposes "in its extreme consequences,"⁶⁹ which becomes still more evident as the musical performance takes yet another turn. For no sooner does the song seem "to express the peaceful and noble happiness of life," than laughter disrupts and reverses this exaltation of "good fortune"—Thomas is "surprised to hear some of the spectators burst out laughing in mockery of the unfortunate young man"—which may have been an effect of parody all along, in the precise sense of a song that is sung "against" or "beside" (παρά) "song" (ὠιδή):

> He looked back at the audience, and seeing the open mouths and the gestures full of compunction, he saw that a large number of people in the room were singing [. . .]. He thought then that the spectators, to ridicule the singer, had taken up the melody and, instead of singing it in the order it required, sang various passages of it according to a new design with which they were familiar. [. . .] Shortly after that, everyone fell silent, and the last sounds, softly echoing, sought in vain to prolong this painful parody.⁷⁰

Although the song seems to affirm social duty and actually suspends the possibility of judgment, something about the singer's performance nonetheless seems to "attract" public blame,⁷¹ as if its choral traits came too close to the "dancing"—or: *choreia*—that is said to be "no longer allowed at present."⁷² But the closest that the collective comes to condemnation remains remote from any express and unequivocal aesthetic, moral, or legal sentence, arriving solely as the audience members themselves appear to participate in the choral song and general soundscape. And insofar as their parody, like the singer's "words," consists solely in inconsistent, "softly echoing sounds," the signs of censure that Thomas reads from the spectator's faces and gestures can still be no decisive evidence for any opinions that they may "voice," making a mockery of even their supposed mockery.

What goes for the conflicting expressions of public opinion, moreover, also goes for the expressions of the text, which opens to a plethora of further conflicting voices while holding their respective claims in abeyance. The shift from "melody" to "monument," for instance, echoes the architectural analogy that Jean-Philippe Rameau had cited in his essay, "Our Instinct for Music," where he seeks to found music upon the sheer "proportions and progressions" of harmonics, rather than any melodic trajectory.[73] Conversely, the fact that verbal melodic strains may ultimately come down to "sounds isolated and deprived of every shared effect" resonates with the critique that Rousseau had voiced in his controversy with Rameau, when he argued that the presence of a harmonic base in the absence of a melodic order accordingly fails "to form a phrase and say something."[74] At the same time, however, the tones that randomly remain in the air also recall the metaphor of "concordant" or "univocal [*einstimmige*]" experience that structures the world according to Husserl,[75] while their indifference to successive "modulation" calls Husserl's first and most often-cited example for the continuity of inner temporal consciousness into question as well. With every word—and without a word—the choral song of *Aminadab* testifies that one can no longer affirm, as Husserl had done, that "consciousness of a tonal process [. . .] exhibits a succession even as I hear it" with such evidence that "every doubt or denial appear[s] senseless."[76] And insofar as the "evidence" of tonal succession becomes doubtful, one can also no longer affirm a continuum of time and mind, whose consciousness of temporal flux is "given" solely "on the occasion of selected, simple perceptions," as Eric Voegelin had recognized.[77] The musical episode in *Aminadab* thus marks a fictive recital and refutation of these divergent contexts, at least as much as it recites and refutes an "intradiegetic" event of public performance and censure. The echoes of Rameau, Rousseau, and Husserl, among others, hover in the air,[78] as the "multiplicity of speech within the simultaneity of one language" lets theoretical debates and narrative fiction resound and intermingle indecisively,[79] exposing the passive traits of all voices involved and the dissimulated character of speech per se.

What this dissimulation means for the narrower chorus of voices in *Aminadab*, however, is far from self-evident; nor does the eventual diversion of the crowd to "drinking and singing" signify that they have abandoned their judgmental comportment in favor of a more hospitable state of nonverbal communion.[80] To the contrary, "this gaiety" will suddenly be "turned into disorder by another turn of events," when a "pair of guardians on the platform raised their pitchers, and light filled the room" with "such an intense brightness that everyone hid their faces to avoid the assault."[81] All that it takes is the slightest enigmatic gesture for celebration to turn into catastrophe, nor could this downturn be prevented or anticipated according to any measure. For even if the light were blinding, no sign indicates that the sudden illumination must have been experienced as an "assault": it was a similar "ray of light [. . .] emanating from a pitcher" that had initially attracted Thomas to the room,[82] while the sense of "assault" that it seems to provoke is almost immediately dissociated from the lighting effects: "There were some, already half drunk, who fell to the ground believing they had been struck and who cried out with all their strength, although there was no real cause for this."[83] There need be "no real cause," that is to say, for catastrophe to arrive, and since the catastrophe ultimately leaves all persons untouched, there could also be no cause to assume it had not already been taking place before any threat was felt, not unlike the "disaster" of which Blanchot would later write: "The disaster ruins everything, all the while leaving everything intact."[84]

In its radically passive character, as well as its concomitant withdrawal from "the order of lived time," "disaster" does not negate so much as it haunts the "choral" communion that is sketched in *Aminadab*, as the time of ruin that outpasses each passing moment, keeping life "on edge" with a threat that is "always already past."[85] Hence, the turn from joyful occasion to common confusion that takes place in the common room will soon be admitted to leave no verifiable trace, leaving the tragic crisis undecided and even an air of uncertainty as to whether it happened in the first place. But if these features of the text alone indicate that the musical episode in *Aminadab* is structured by the unlived temporality that Blanchot will elaborate in *The Writing of the Disaster*, these indices are more than redoubled by the way in which the lighting incident is itself an abbreviated recapitulation of the crisis into which the community had been pitched at least once before, according to the narrative that a figure named Jerome had related to Thomas earlier in the very same café, courtroom, or ballroom.[86] Although the musical performance in this common area seems to begin and break off spontaneously, in other words, the end of the music has its history, whose further examination, in turn, elucidates the disastrous "turn" that "events" will take. And at the same time, moreover, the incidents that are repeated in *Aminadab* also indicate the specific ways in which the impossible time that Blanchot will articulate in *The Writing of the Disaster* affects the unfolding of shared history and comes to be borne by those voices that carry it.

There is more than mere monotony at stake when an abridged version of Jerome's history recurs to disrupt the choral interlude in a flash: instead, the coincidence exposes not only *that* but also *how* both current and distant history could be no matter of decisive moments. If anything, both "past" and "present" would be the repercussions of the passive, untold, and disastrous share of linguistic experience to which the novel calls us to attend, if not respond. But first, a recapitulation would seem to be in order: when Thomas initially entered the room of the eventual musical performance, he had joined Jerome at one of the tables, where Jerome took the indiscernibility of domestic servants and boarders as an occasion to tell a violent history that began not with an event of conflict but with an act of service that had initially been mistaken for the work of the otherwise negligent—and possibly absent—staff of the establishment.[87] According to Jerome's story, the pivotal object was again a "pitcher" that one tenant had found "filled with hot water," but that both he and his fellow tenants came to view like a "ray of light [. . .] from above," in the shared hope that some domestic may have "disregarded years, centuries of negligence and [. . .] suddenly remembered his duty."[88] The series of associations leading from the singular discovery of a full pitcher to the general assumption of fulfilled duty nearly corresponds in reverse to the song of duty and general singing that will be disrupted with the appearance of luminous pitchers in the very room where Jerome tells his tale.

What these resemblances and reversals thereby say—again, without anyone saying so—is that no phenomenon, interpretation, or response holds a determinate meaning or even a determinate place within the historical sequence that seems to be related. Instead, events appear to be the effect of variable motifs whose sense cannot but remain undecidable even in retrospect because they are constitutively subject to further variations. This fundamental uncertainty is what renders Jerome's narrative uncontainable, allowing it to spill over into the scene of narration itself with the song that will give word of duty, and it is what would call for the impossible "patience" that, as Blanchot later writes, would let me take on "the relation to the Other of the disaster—the relation which does not allow me to assume it, or even to remain myself in order to undergo it."[89] But it is also what provokes the tenants who had at first celebrated the discovery of a full pitcher to take up the most violent measures in response. After all, they do not know, but can only "dream[] about this domestic who [. . .] had suddenly remembered his duty," which is also why they will go on "demanding explanations," rather than resting satisfied.[90] And when one tenant responds to these demands by confessing to have done the good deed himself, his utterly gratuitous act of benevolence—he merely "wanted to surprise" his "friend"[91]—does more than shake the hopes of the tenants for loyal domestic servants (rather than gracious friends). For his testimony also fails, as such, to provide any evidence for its truth, leading to an intensification of the tenants' demands for "explanations," combined now with accusations against him of "depriv[ing] the staff of praise" or plotting to "force us back into [. . .] despair": "They interrogated the accused. They made him reenact his deed in their presence. We gathered in his friend's room to watch him pour the water he had taken from the basement."[92] And since, moreover, no number of reenactments could in any but an illusory way bring the witnesses before the original event, their eventual consensus that "we had to acknowledge our illusion" would have to refer not to any dispelled belief concerning their dreams of domestic service or the testimony of the accused, but to the illusion of knowledge underlying each interrogation.[93]

To be sure, the tenants do not know this; to the contrary, their very word of "illusion" betrays their want for knowledge, which they are no more prepared to abandon than they will be to hear the truth of nonknowledge that emerges as their later song of "benevolent action"[94] hovers between meaningful speech and coincidental sound effects. But with their fraught acknowledgment, they nevertheless testify despite themselves to the truth of undecidable semblance that Kafka had similarly recognized in acknowledging that "confession and lie are alike,"[95] and that Jacques Derrida would later indicate when he wrote that testimony "always goes hand in hand with at least the *possibility* of fiction, perjury, and lie."[96] It is *this* possibility which emerges when, as Jerome reports, the tenants no longer sought to recuperate a past that had escaped all experience but instead passed over into the interminable task of exegesis, probing the "consequences [that] could be drawn from such an event," and writing "reports after reports," which establish nothing but an archive of "our lack of mutual understanding and the diversity of interpretations."[97] "Much is written here [*on écrit beaucoup ici*],"[98] as was likewise written in *The Castle* ("Much is written here [*Es wird hier viel geschrieben*]"[99]), leaving traces of incomprehension which may themselves be echoes from elsewhere. All that will have been recorded and collected concerning the pitcher "event" thus speaks *for* the interminable "passivity of a past which has never been, come back again,"[100] and in so doing, it also speaks *against* the resolution that is eventually said to approach collective agreement, when the inhabitants "almost unanimously" decide to supplement the lacking *service* of the household with anonymous acts of mutual "assistance,"[101] only to lapse into perpetuating the *lacking* service that the servants had hitherto performed, whose prior and present existence remains as doubtful as it had been before.[102] This surplus of contesting commentaries and concomitant lack of common ground are the "choral" truth that the community at once voices and fails to hear, a shared truth of divergence that could also be called "dis-cussion: not the work of arguments bumping against other arguments, but the extreme shuddering of no thoughts, percussive stillness."[103]

Such "extreme shuddering" and "percussive stillness" may be shattering for any personal claims or collective projects, yet it is not those traits of speech but rather the efforts to resist them that lead to violence. When, for instance, the tenants' belief in domestic servants gives way to the conviction "that our imaginations alone had given birth to the story of this accursed caste whom we made responsible for our ills," neither their "ills" ("maux") are assuaged nor are their latest "words" ("mots") assured in a way that could prevent the "birth" of further ill illusions.[104] Instead of holding open for the alterity that affects them—in their "ills" as in their "words"—and instead of assuming the impossible responsibility that their passions demand of them, the "we" goes on to attack those whom they call "ill" ("malades"), as if driven by the very word of "ills" ("maux") to the displace their shared malaise to another "caste" along the lines of utterly illogical—or ill-logical—associations, which only alter but do not dispel their false projections. As Jerome tells Thomas: "There were some among the sick [*malades*] whom we hated—we hated them all but those in particular with their calm and satisfied air, with the happiness they seemed to have found, these drove us mad—certain of these were beaten and tortured"—whereby it is suggested that the stillness of others is the illness that is fought.[105] Hence, torn between "want[ing] to tear from them their secret" and "desir[ing] that they too be shown the truth," the attackers of the ill expose the violence of the knowledge that they alternately seek to learn and claim to show. But insofar as violence is all that they impart, they also betray their "truth" to be lacking, whether they wish to wrest it from others or whether they cannot rest without others' recognition of the same. According to the aggressors, "being shown the truth" thus signifies nothing other than "being stripped of the consoling thoughts that were lacking to us," while "consoling thoughts" become labelled as marks of "contagion and moral uncleanliness."[106]

Such is the aggression that ensues against those who endure the "percussive stillness" of the house, turning the space of dwelling into what Blanchot elsewhere names "the sphere of violence by which [others] could be caught, grasped, snared, identified, reduced to sameness."[107] This violence is the alternative to speech that may erupt in those extreme situations where one is confronted with the "unreachableness of the Other," and where "all of a sudden you have at your disposal none of the human ways of being close and distant"; or, as Ann Smock has also written in the study of Blanchot from which these remarks are drawn: "This choice is [. . .] between power unrestrained and something else entirely, something other than power: speech."[108] But as she will also soon add, this choice is in no one's power to make—"power" may be powerless to "restrain" itself—and even when it is deliberately "chosen," as in *Aminadab*, power can only fail, because it also cannot help replicating the very frailties in language and experience that it resists.[109] Thus, the "blow and cries [*coups et cris*]" that are provoked by the tenants' acts of violence neither signify a loss of "consoling thoughts" on the part of their victims, nor do they constitute an acknowledgment of the attackers' "truth," but rather exaggerate the minimal structure of those echoes that will have made up the language of the household all along. For the same reason, moreover, the situation also suggests that no cries or blows can put an end to the ills (*maux*) or the words (*mots*) that had motivated the tenants to impose them. Instead, the sounds maintain a silence with regard to consolation and desperation alike, striking a blow to all efforts to attain a truth that could be imposed or extorted as an object of knowledge. Without reducing the unspeakable pain that it causes, violent action is thereby exposed to be fundamentally impotent and passive itself: "We tormented them in vain and could not make them understand what this gang of furious men was trying to reveal to them."[110] All that the passive-aggressive impulse can reveal is that it cannot "bring all speech down to the level of force," while at the same time, the wordless cries of the tortured nevertheless preserve their "silent presence," or "the true speech that [. . .] is the very presence of *autrui* within [themselves]."[111]

For all the injuries that may have been inflicted, then, the disaster that had already marked the discovery of a pitcher remains imminent, uncertain, and recurrent, while the tragic crisis remains undecided. It is therefore no dramatic change when Jerome goes on to relate the way in which the erstwhile torturers suddenly turn upon the entire house with the revolutionary thought to "transform the house from top to bottom."[112] The shift from authoritarian measures to revolutionary action instead reiterates the violent impulse from before, and it is equally wanting in its motives, execution, and outcome. Hence, Jerome still does not know to say "what drove us to this tragic extravagance,"[113] nor does he know what had been said of the collective plan in the first place, since all deliberations concerning the transformation of the house are themselves transformed through the house:

> Sometimes, in the far ends of the corridors, to which the echo slowly carried its sounds, we ourselves were surprised to hear our conversations repeated in indistinct rumblings that expressed their true, their repulsive nothingness. Were these even our words? And if they really were the words we had used as the instruments of our derangement, was it not permitted us to recognize them not as we believed we had spoken them but as the house had heard them in its grave and mournful solitude?[114]

These repetitive echoes give voice to nothing if not the absence of sense at the core of those arrangements that the inhabitants would overturn and remake, as well as the passive character of even the most outspoken calls for change. But even when some of Jerome's fellow tenants attempt to reclaim power in the wake of this derangement of their plans and dispossession of their speech, the "new rages and new plans for vengeance" that are inspired by the acoustic "disturbance" of their discussions in no way overcome or surpass said disturbance.[115] One contingent no sooner departs to "execut[e]" the "hateful project" than its members encounter "ideal barriers" that prove to be "insurmountable" because and not despite of the fact that their violation will have already taken place with the intention to transgress.[116] What the members of this contingent confront, in other words, is the dialectic of the limit that G. W. F. Hegel had outlined, when he wrote that the limit demarcating one thing from another necessarily "points" each one "beyond itself to its non-being and declares it to be its being, and so passes over into it."¹¹⁷ But rather than transcending their barriers along the lines that Hegel describes, the transgressors in *Aminadab* find the logic of the limit to turn upon them: the initial ideality of the "barriers" gives way instead to the "strange illusion, profound mirage" that "the entire house was forbidden to them,"¹¹⁸ while the few who do cross into hitherto "forbidden," higher floors claim after the fact that these were "comparable" or "parallel" to the parts of the building they had left: "The only thing they ever said, again and again, is that it was the same [*c'était pareil*]."¹¹⁹ On the spot, then, there is a collapse between above and below, sameness and difference, transgression and interdiction, which leaves nowhere to go and thus virtually realizes the desire of the rebels or reformers "to annihilate all, to disperse all, to kill all and to kill themselves," without really changing anything at all in a manner that could be settled.¹²⁰

This new phase of violence may be read as a reflection of "the political and literary tensions of Blanchot's situation as a writer during the Occupation," as William S. Allen has pointed out, but as Allen also argues at length, the revolution recounted in *Aminadab* marks before all else a response to the "irreducible" instability of language that troubles both the determination of limits, as well as each attempt to cross them.¹²¹ "The house is untouchable,"¹²² as Jerome will later confess, which is to say: the "sonorous cage" that houses the community cannot itself be upset or transformed because neither its limits nor anything that should occur within them could be established to begin with. Accordingly, even Jerome's narration of his peers' successive failures to bring about change and reduce indeterminacy is itself fraught with indeterminacies that undermine his efforts. As he admits, the incidents that Jerome relates escaped him at least as fundamentally as knowledge of the servants, the ill, and the house had escaped his peers: "I heard nothing, I saw nothing."¹²³ Instead of giving direct testimony, Jerome can therefore only draw upon the words of fellow witnesses to reconstruct what had occurred, or rather to construe past occurrences for the first time. But just as Jerome's ability to witness was compromised by the default of his senses—if not by a default of sensible objects as well—so too does he fail to make sense of his contemporaries' testimonies at first. For instance, he recalls hearing one man who was "invaded by a flood of words," making him a channel, if not a direct source, for oral history, but one whose outpouring as such not only renders the man's words "foreign" but also casts them as foreign to articulate forms: "The words were as foreign to me as if they had been cast out at random by a formless mouth."[124] What "invade[s]" and "flood[s]" this "formless mouth" accords instead with the carnage that inspires it, whose violence *is* the destruction of all forms of organization and thus impossible to contain in practice or even retain in memory: "Such massacre, such destruction, memory has not the power to keep its remembrance [*la mémoire n'a pas à en garder le souvenir*]."[125] But this is also to say that even testimony could yield no record.

Ungrounded in and by the events that it pretends to address, then, Jerome's narrative offers a fictive and fault-riven supplement to the history whose abyssal truth cannot be known or told but only lost with every effort to give account of it or registered through the shudder that crosses through each word thereof. The "painful sonority" of the one man's "flood of words" may have "echoed" in Jerome and "put [him] in touch with the truth," as he will also say, but it is at the same time this "truth" that Jerome "pushed away [*la vérité que je repoussais*]," both at the time and, presumably, when he collected the very different version of past events that he now relates: "Later, I collected other calmer accounts [*des confidences plus tranquilles*], and I have been able to connect some of the facts."[126] But no pushing back against "painful sonority" could prevent Jerome's from suffering: because the "calmer accounts" that he gathers must have been composed, like his "own," ex post facto—and because these "accounts" or "confidings" (*confidences*) are themselves more a matter of faith (*fides*) than of fact—Jerome instead testifies, despite his intentions, to the "fact" that there is, strictly speaking, no verifiable knowledge for the composite history he recounts, which does not therefore cohere so much as it opens, in turn, to any number of further echoes and alternatives.

In yet another way, Kafka's assertion proves true: "In order to be able to confess, one lies," but Jerome's narrative likewise suggests that a "certain truth" may yet lie "in a chorus."[127] This latter possibility is indicated less by what Jerome expressly says, however, than by the resonances between his words and other texts that his speech is powerless to exclude: for once it is an issue of adapting the others' accounts, Jerome's utterances admit their difference and distance from every original source or situation, allowing other, more remote voices to intervene as well. Hence, the "ideal barriers" that the rebels are said to encounter recall the limits that Barnabas comes across within Kafka's *Castle*. There, "barriers" similarly mark "no determinate limit," since Barnabas had already crossed several that "appear no different than the ones which he has not yet overcome."[128] The self-directed violence of the tenants, on the other hand, mirrors in reverse the defensive measures that are imagined by Kafka's burrower in "The Burrow,"[129] where the dwelling space, like the house of *Aminadab*, consists in a sonorous cage, whose tunneling structure has more than once been compared to the architecture of the ear.[130] It is not that Blanchot imitates Kafka, however, as Sartre had argued, nor are these instances of "citation" even marked as such or exclusive of other possible echoes. Instead, the unverifiable and repetitive character of events structurally disposes the versions that Jerome recollects to recall an indefinite range of voices, ensuring that none could be rendered with fidelity or definitively confirmed but that each would nonetheless confide the immemorial truth of the passive and plural experience of language. It is this speech in the passive voice that does not cease to speak against all violent efforts to suppress or destroy the alterity that escapes orders of knowledge and power.

In other words, every utterance would provoke the questions that were previously recited: "Were these even our words? And if they really were the words we had used as the instruments of our derangement, was it not permitted us to recognize them not as we believed we had spoken them but as the house had heard them in its grave and mournful solitude?"[131] These questions concerning speech are persistent and unanswerable, insofar as no response could exempt itself from them, while silence would leave the issues that those questions raise outstanding. Speech and silence alike could therefore only go on undergoing the exigence of this questioning, with a passivity that affects each passage with a "not" ("pas") that could not itself be fixed. Blanchot would decline the word "passivity" in *The Writing of the Disaster*: "Passivity, passion, past, *pas* (both negation and step—the trace or movement of an advance): this semantic play provides us with a slippage of meaning, but not with anything to which we could entrust ourselves as to a response that would content us."[132] And in *Aminadab*, Jerome's narration of narrations traces a similar decline, where what is passed on with each word is not a term but an interminable glide that gives way to a "not" and to another, rendering each at once improper, belated, and preliminary, while leaving what was and remains to be said unknown and exposed to further interferences. Such is the outspoken yet unspoken—and therefore pro-phetic—trait of language that not only lets a "flood of words" overwhelm Jerome and resound through his resistance, but that also strikes to the core of the entire community: "We were troubled by a prophecy with which our heart overwhelmed us."[133] Yet whether or not "we" are expressly "troubled," the constitutive uncertainty of "our words" would render the most emphatic constatation pro-phetic of untold alternatives, and it would unsettle both the violent efforts of the community and the more civil communications that follow in their wake.[134]

But insofar as this passivity is also what each instance of speech shares, its exposition through the acoustic space that admits, alters, and alienates various voices in *Aminadab* does not merely amplify its more troubling repercussions for knowledge, testimony, and history, for it also makes room in an uncommon way for the topos of the commonplace, whose consequences for the language of community solicit examination as well. Commonplaces mark many of the most pronounced moments and matters of contestation in the novel. Jerome will refer to a loss of "measure" and "good sense" to characterize the revolutionary plans of his housemates, as if the Delphic maxim, "nothing in excess," did not cease to haunt the house, despite the carnage and destruction that are said to have erupted.[135] But there are also less common commonplaces, such as the "sort of motto" that is embroidered on the sleeves of two men Thomas encounters early in his sojourn—namely, "*I serve alone*"—which echoes in the choral performance that he later witnesses, as well as the household history of turmoil over domestic service.[136] Because the "sonorous cage" of the boarding house opens to repetitions of all kinds, it is *the* topos for the eminently iterable topos of the commonplace, if not in the classical sense of those common relations such as "more or less" to which Aristotle says one should recur in methodical argumentation,[137] then in the sense of those common terms and phrases that had figured critically in Jean Paulhan's *The Flowers of Tarbes, or Terror in Literature*, a book that Blanchot had reviewed for the *Journal des débats* in 1941. And in Paulhan's examination of commonplaces, as well as the "terroristic" measures that various poets and critics would prescribe against them, it is again the proximity of passivity and violence that is at issue, as it is in *Aminadab*.[138] Whether the commonplace is deemed to be a symptom of inertia on the part of a writer who "contents himself with [. . .] prefabricated forms [*des formes toutes faites*],"[139] or whether its usage is supposed to carry the writer away, rendering him "prey to conventional phrases,"[140] the common critiques of commonplaces that Paulhan recites and that Blanchot reprises in his review testify to the unintentional character of common language as such,[141] which may affect speech acts to the point where it cannot be decided whether words correspond to any thought at all. Hence writers such as Saint-Beuve, Taine, Renan, Albalat, and Gourmont, among others, recommend violent measures to suppress a situation in which,[142] as Allen concisely observes, words "appear and contest that appearance in the same moment, thereby slipping between meaning and nonsense, presence and absence."[143]

But if this slippage should lead to a desire "to break with human language altogether,"[144] as the more violent moments of *Aminadab* repeatedly testify, it is precisely the ruptures and vacancies within "human" language that emerge through common words and common spaces in *Aminadab*. For the echoes of those words and spaces not only show each one to be at once plural and void—as well as subject to displacement—but also expose them to be the ever-shifting, abyssal ground for common life. A share of "fear" may thus never be far "that words, abandoned to themselves exercise a redoubtable power [*pouvoir redoutable*] upon the spirit and heart of man, out of their senses [*hors de leurs sens*],"[145] like the "prophecy with which" the inhabitants' "heart[s]" were "overwhelmed."[146] Yet since this "redoubtable power" is also a doubtable power, it is powerless to establish, let alone maintain itself, and its duplicity thus allows the most familiar "commonplace expressions, clichés and grandiose words," to "lend themselves" to at least "two opposing ways of being *understood*," yielding "a strange, almost double language, which at the same time we possess and do not possess."[147] And ultimately it is also this strangeness that speaks against the more flagrant attempts to exploit the structural ambivalence of speech, as when accusations of "murder" are dismissed as a "manner of speaking,"[148] or "attraction" is glossed as "submission to jurisdiction" in *Aminadab*.[149] For without any criterion for deciding upon one sense or another that would not be subject to the same ambivalence, no such gestures could ever hold their own.

It is by virtue of their wide-ranging usage, then, that common terms turn out not to be common any more than they can be owned,[150] and that the Aristotelian commonplace that defines man in general as the animal that "has language [λόγον ἔχον]"[151] paradoxically comes to work otherwise than Aristotle would have it. Once language is commonly held, it exceeds and estranges the intentions of its speakers so radically that its familiarity and foreignness can no more be certified than thought could be told apart from common speech.[152] These uncommon traits of "common" language are what is communicated through the stories and songs that are rendered and disrupted in the common area, café, courtroom, or ballroom. They are what speaks through the impossible questions of history and testimony that Jerome poses there, as well as the questions of personal hopes, perceptions, and memories that will be raised elsewhere—"On what do you base your hopes? The testimony of your poor, tired senses? The assurance of your perverted and troubled memory?"[153]—which questions are, appropriately, forgotten by the very same figure who raises them: "So what was I saying? [. . .] Things do not always come to pass as I explained them."[154] The common experience of language thus turns out to be one of dispossession, marking what Philippe Lacoue-Labarthe has called, in his reading of *The Instant of My Death*, Blanchot's "radical break in the name of another politics, without injustice or anything unjustifiable, whose sole object will be to loosen the grip of politics."[155]

This politics can only take place, however, so long as dispossession is not itself turned into a principle or maxim, as it seems to have been done in the wake of the violent uprising from the past, according to Jerome: "Thus, in principle, it is forbidden us to think or—but this comes to the same thing—to keep our thoughts to ourselves. We must speak or act. As soon as an idea passes through our heads, we are obliged to communicate it to a neighbor or to execute immediately the projects we have entertained for ourselves [*entretenus avec nous-mêmes*]."[156] According to this formulation, there should be no "entertainment" of ideas or private "conversation" (*entretien*) "for" or "with" ourselves (*avec nous-mêmes*) that does not take place at once for others, as if to eliminate both the silence that had provoked the inhabitants at one point to torture the ill, as well as the solitary dialogue of the soul that Plato's Socrates had once called "thinking."[157] If the structural exposure of speech to alterity appears to be affirmed with this "principle," the imperative to translate thought to word or action recalls the violent extortions that had preceded it. And insofar as it presupposes that there is something proper to transmit, the imperative also repeats the phantasy of transparency that was voiced by those "terroristic" literary critics whom Paulhan addresses in *The Flowers of Tarbes*,[158] and that Søren Kierkegaard had already pronounced in *The Concept of Anxiety*, when he described "language" and "speech" as "liberators," insofar as "the law of deliverance from the demonic is that, against [one's] will, words leave [one's] mouth [*la loi de la délivrance du démoniaque, c'est que contre son gré les mots lui sortent de la bouche*]."[159]

Unlike the revelatory communication that such principles would aim to elicit, however, both the letter and the application of the law that is rumored to rule in *Aminadab* suggest that speech and thought are always other than "proper" from the outset, leaving no way to fail or fulfill any obligation to speak one's mind or even to speak *in propria persona*. Hence, whenever a member of the house is singled out and subjected to silent treatment, what is extracted from him is no confession, but a testimony to the foreignness of his "own" words:

> He speaks passionately, but what he hears is colder and more foreign to his life than any random word spoken by another man. [. . .] When he thinks about it, and of course he can only think by speaking, he sees that the words he hears are like those of a dead man; he hears himself as if he were already deprived of consciousness; he is his own echo in a world where he is no more; he undergoes the torture of receiving from outside his existence the words that have been the soul and speech of his entire life.[160]

This "passionate" speech is none which any conscious subject intends—the speaker "hears himself as if he were already deprived of consciousness"—and it is therefore none that is properly heard, let alone uttered as an expression proper to himself. What renders speech "passionate" here is instead the impersonal and transpersonal passion of language that knows no law or rule, and that renders the common place of the "world" itself "a space-abyss of resonance and condensation."[161]

This "space-abyss of resonance and condensation" marks the placeless place—the a-topos or u-topia—where speech takes place in Blanchot's novel, and at a remove from all legal, conventional, or interpersonal relations. But the novel also indicates that it is solely in relation to this nonrelation that free relations among speakers may be entertained and that another justice may emerge than the false ones that would be predicated upon confession, violence, and evidence. For by amplifying the terrors and repercussions of these premises and by exposing their self-contradictory—and even fictive—character, the fiction of *Aminadab* speaks for the abyssal resonance that would allow others to encounter one another without reducing each other to the same, be it in the form of torture and interrogation or through the seemingly less violent histories and dialogues that cast all involved in the modus of another "I," and thus "another me-myself [*un autre moi-même*]."[162]

The monumental song that arises in the common area of the house marks one of the most hospitable passages for such encounters, as voices mingle indiscernibly, words emerge through aleatory sound effects, and notes are sustained or abandoned in the air, according to no sure principle.

All of these traits of the music yield a gaiety and choral truth that is shared by all but owed to none, and thus one that is utterly gratuitous, passive, and fragile. Hence, there is also nothing to prevent the singing from suffering a disruption, which is no consequence of any failing that could be compensated but of the weakness and groundlessness that were its strengths.[163] Although this situation not only can but also does fail to sustain itself, however, it is not the only one in which the abyssal dispossession of language allows for free encounters in *Aminadab*, nor is sound the only medium for those echoes of shared truth to occur and to "deflect [. . .], for an instant, from the delusion into which everything goes, from which everything comes back."[164]

Toward the end of the novel, at least one other scene—which at first recalls the most violent episodes of the house—turns out to trace just such a deflection. After, namely, Thomas has come to the hospital of the house and fallen ill himself, he emerges from the room that he had occupied while sick and finds a woman in the adjacent chamber, which is divided by stairs and topped with vaulted ceilings, marking the highest point that he will reach within the house.[165] At first, the young woman addresses him as a domestic servant, and he accordingly goes through the motions of cleaning even as he spreads more dirt than he removes, like those false domestics Jerome had described, who had seemed "under the pretext of giving assistance" to be "destroying the house."[166] Then after completing this performance and briefly leaving the scene, Thomas returns to the "clean" chamber, where, for lack of any other occupation, he sets to work again—this time unsolicited. The deficiency and excess of Thomas's first and second swipes at cleaning already render his labors parodic, his presence uncalled for, and his "employment" gratuitous, even before he makes the unfounded character of his behavior explicit by refusing to depart and instead "employing his last strength" to approach and nearly press himself "against the young woman," who just as soon presses upon him herself.[167] What takes place between Thomas and the woman thus recalls the pseudo-history of domestics and inhabitants that Jerome had related, from the ambivalence of Thomas's service role, through to the violence of his and the woman's eventual entanglement, which escalates as he goes on to push against "the chest of the young women with all his strength" in search of "a last explanation, a last clarification,"[168] while she "chew[s] furiously at his mouth, as though to exhaust this source of false words."[169] And as if to repeat on a smaller scale the physical destruction that had culminated Jerome's account of domestic relations, even the heaviest fixture of the room is overturned by their bodily revolutions: "Thomas heard the sound of the desk as it fell, after a shock more violent than the rest."[170]

But to whatever degree a desire for disclosure may have moved the present pair to destructive actions, as similar impulses had done for the tenants in the past, Thomas and the woman will also lose themselves in their dual movements of attraction and rejection—"attracting each other and repelling each other with moans that were only incomprehensible words, both of them lost"[171]—at which point neither has the power to seek power over the situation, and both become subject to forces that they suffer through their very exertions. Hence, it is not even "their" concerted efforts and exertions—which would remain, however minimally, graspable to them—but their "incomprehensible moans" that affect and ultimately replace them. For if Thomas and the woman truly go "lost" with their "moans" and "incomprehensible words," then the one and the other will have dissolved into a multitude of utterances that they cannot intend or understand but can only release in the passion that releases them from themselves in the same breath. All that remains of and between them, that is, are utterances issued in the passive voice that give expression to an experience of dispossession that crosses the limits of proper experience and thus escapes comprehensible grasp.[172] Unlike the pairing movements that Husserl would describe and that Maurice Merleau-Ponty would elaborate further—unlike any reciprocity, where "everything happens as if the other person's intention inhabited my body, or as if my intentions inhabited his body"[173]—the vocal pairing between Thomas and the woman so radically affects each member that they become reverberating echoes themselves, knocking every nearby surface—"knocking against the stool and then again the desk"—and rebounding senselessly: "without a hope of light, in thicker and thicker shadows, now with neither hands nor bodies to touch each other."[174] For however long or brief a span, then, Thomas and the woman will have undergone a "shattering transformation" that may, on the one hand, draw them into "a world of misfortune [*malheur*] and despair [*désespoir*],"[175] whose hopelessness surpasses even the lightless life that the tenants of Jerome's narrative had feared—the "life that no ray of light could reach from above"[176]—since no one to suffer the despair and misfortune would be left in the dark. Yet on the other hand, in delivering them from themselves, their transformation also delivers them to the "truth [*vérité*]" and "good fortune" or "happiness [*bonheur*]" of the night, which the woman will later describe precisely as an experience of nonexperience before exclaiming to Thomas: "What a shame that you cannot witness this happiness [*ce bonheur*]!"[177]

Benighted and unbeknownst to themselves, no one and nothing could be the same as it was in Jerome's history—or even in the room where Thomas and the woman first met. And for the same reason, the nocturnal truth that could have transpired between Thomas and the woman also necessarily remains impossible for them to grasp both during *and* after the fact, like the truth of a choral performance, but now in a more intimate encounter that could be called "love." Their obscure contact takes place, after all, along the lines of what Blanchot would later describe as a "sudden clandestine meeting (outside of time)" that "is never certain to be experienced by the one whom this movement consigns to the other, by depriving him of his 'self.'"[178] Yet "this movement" of self-privation for the sake of a singular other also happens to be what, according to Blanchot, lets "*loving* [. . .] *happen.*"[179] This characterization of love as an occurrence elucidates, in turn, why their "loving" is also not contradicted when both Thomas and the woman emerge from their entanglement intact,[180] and the woman goes on to speak of a future, nocturnal version of what will have just happened, as if nothing like it had yet occurred. Because "loving" entails a true dispossession, unlike any that could be sought, imposed, or claimed, it can also be in no one's power to undergo, retain, know, or remember. It leaves "little more than a fold or ripple, the eternal vibration or oscillation of an inassimilable movement of being set underway," as Christopher Fynsk has written in another context.[181] Intimacy is, in other words, also a disaster of sorts that no word or gesture could confirm or recuperate,[182] which does not negate it but rather implies the radical contingency and freedom of its passion.

Only another chance—beyond all assurance, justification, and desire— could put these erstwhile lovers (back) in touch, which happens to arrive under the least likely conditions, when the woman interprets Thomas's subsequent muteness as a way of leaving her the "initiative" and begins to draft a declaration on his behalf.[183] Once again, a state of uncertainty provokes a desire for confession; and once again, the effort to realize this desire underscores the absence of certitude that prompts it. Far from determining any past or present facts, the woman can produce only false testimony, should it be the case that "I can only testify, in the strict sense of the word, from the instant when no one can, in my place, testify to what I do."[184] Yet to the same extent that the woman replaces Thomas's voice in the first-person testimonial that she drafts, she also displaces her own through her act of impersonation, and in abandoning both him and herself to fiction, her writing abandons every pretense to subjective or objective truth in a manner that will allow them to approach again, beyond all "initiatives," the unverifiable truth of an encounter. Taking up a notebook labeled with the name "Lucie"—which may or may not be her proper name[185]—the woman writes in such a way where she seems to apply more attention "to the details of the letters" than to the "choice of words," "drawing more than writing," and thus producing a script whose design would de-sign every apparent claim in advance.[186] Along these lines, the manuscript would be beyond any distinction between truth and lie because its markings would be irreducible to any verifiable or falsifiable propositions that "Lucie" may otherwise record: "From what [Thomas] could tell" by observing her, "it was not the choice of words or the structure of sentences that preoccupied her; rather, she directed her efforts at the details of the letters, [. . .] giving full value [*donnant toute leur valeur*] to the downstrokes and the upstrokes, the punctuation signs, and all the various accents."[187] With this emphasis, whatever "speaking" the woman may initially or eventually appear to do "in [Thomas's] name" thus comes down, before all else, to a multitude of anonymous and asemantic markings, whose arrangement allows both "Thomas" and "Lucie" to lose themselves once more in an entanglement where sense becomes uncertain, in all senses of the phrase.

Like the words that had emerged from the musical performance that was delivered in the common area of the house, the "words" and "sentences" that appear on "Lucie's" page may be the unintended, coincidental effects of a calligraphic performance, at least as much as they may be meant by the woman. This resemblance between her notations and the notes of that song is further underscored by the fact that the semblances of words that emerge happen to coincide as well: one more time, the commonplaces of "good fortune," "duty," "benevolent action," and just "compensation" resurface on "Lucie's" paper,[188] as Thomas is said to have "lived modestly, simply, and correctly," while "receiv[ing]" considerable "benefits" from his "stay among [. . .] virtuous men," all of which has led him to assume "the duty [*devoir*], at a particularly important moment of my life, to thank all those who have accorded me so much favor, by communicating to them a solemn testimony of my gratitude."[189] Whether or not this confession echoes a household anthem of justice, duty, and reward, however, the fictive and aleatory character of each mark crosses through the topoi that it touches, and it thereby draws Thomas and Lucie alike into a "space-abyss of resonance and condensation,"[190] whose justice and truth lies in the suspension of all prescriptive duties, graspable favors, and verifiable claims. In lieu of void commonplaces and apart from themselves, a "conversation" opens among gestures of inscription whose "ethical impetus" is, as Fynsk has put it, "a 'good' beyond the order of the possible and any work or doing (benefaction)."[191] It is on paper that "Lucie" and "Thomas" come together again; that pairing takes place in parting from knowledge and self; and that the pair may therefore also happen to be delivered to the "union" of love "which always takes place by not taking place."[192]

All of these traits of the manuscript are further drawn out when "Lucie" asks "Thomas" to add his signature. For no sooner does he begin to commit himself in writing than his name also assumes the same calligraphic value that had already scratched out the valence of each sentence on the page. Having practiced, namely, "drawing the letters, one by one" on the scrap paper that "Lucie" lends him,[193] Thomas literally falls out of the picture as he signs: instead, the "first letter, in magnificent calligraphy, stretched to display *itself* [*sétala*] across a large portion of the rectangle" that had been set apart for his signature.[194] With his writing, too, it is less an issue of signing than of drawing, and when Thomas ceases to write beyond his first initial, this deficiency at the level of contractual obligation—which "Lucie" emphasizes: "I cannot be satisfied with this incomplete signature"[195]—is no deficiency when it comes to the connection that the document nonetheless forges. To the contrary, "Lucie" even claims that the "magnificently" engraved letter, which she can feel through the "other side of the page," makes an impression that "establishes a true point of contact between us [*C'est un vrai contact qu'elle établit entre nous*]."[196] But apart from her express feelings and her brush with the paper, this reduction of "true [. . .] contact" to crossing lines was the critical point: for she does not even know the name that "Thomas" has partially spelled out, and in whose "name" she had hitherto claimed to speak: "Your name has not come this far."[197]

It is in this nonrelation to one another and to themselves that "Thomas" and "Lucie" touch in another way that escapes all violence that could be imposed in the name of identity, power, or evidence, and that therefore remains as precarious as their prior pairing.[198] But unlike the passing "moans" or "incomprehensible words" that had once drawn them together beyond themselves,[199] the strokes of their writing remain to mark the separation that was their "true point of contact," and that

Blanchot will elsewhere call the "separation that is presupposed—not surmounted, but confirmed—in all true speech."[200] Writing is, to speak with Fynsk, a "dispossessing gift."[201] Precisely insofar as neither of them writes as or for herself[202]—insofar as both are dispossessed of the marks they make—the lines that "Thomas" and "Lucie" draw can cross beyond the marks of identity and the claims of the proper that would keep them from one another; and in this way, they will have left a singular trace of an encounter that was neither theirs nor their doing, but their passion.

What comes to pass on this page from *Aminadab* displays the passion of writing Blanchot would describe decades later in *The Writing of the Disaster*: "If there is a relation between writing and passivity, it is that both the one and the other suppose the effacement, the extenuation of the subject: suppose a change of time: suppose that, between being and not being, something which never yet takes place happens nonetheless, as having long since already happened—the unworking of the neutral, the silent rupture of the fragmentary"[203] (S'il y a rapport entre écriture et passivité, c'est que l'une et l'autre supposent l'effacement, l'exténuation du sujet: supposent un changement de temps: supposent qu'entre être et ne pas être quelque chose qui ne s'accomplit pas arrive cependant comme étant depuis toujours déjà survenu—le désoeuvrement du neutre, la rupture silencieuse du fragmentaire).[204] Nor is the resonance between these chronologically distant passages a mere coincidence: for the "unworking" of writing is repeatedly drawn out through the pages of Blanchot's oeuvre. But the fictive writing that takes place in *Aminadab* lets the commonplaces of personal confession and public community, subjectivity and communication, duty and love, all draw toward their vanishing point and disperse into echoes in a singular manner that exposes how "the effacement, the extenuation of the subject" may take place, and how passivity may give language its chances and its truth.

Augustine's confessional writing, Kafka's posthumously published notebooks and novels, Husserl's manuscripts on passive synthesis, and Bataille's erotic fiction are similarly marked by ruptures, effacements, and extenuations of the subject, which is no doubt what allows their writings to echo through the "sonorous cage" that opens within Blanchot's novel. Yet at the same time, the echoes and traces of these writings beyond the bounds of each single text are also what first allows them to say what will have been at stake within them, before and beside what any writer could have known to say. For it is through echoes and traces that all of these writers, among others, discuss one another beyond intentionality, evidence, thought, and obligation and thus come to speak in the radically passive voice that accompanies every gesture, word, mark, and silence. This "passive voice" is not a nominally or grammatically distinct form or mode, nor can it be exhausted through any one concept, however close Augustine's "confession," Husserl's "overlapping," Bataille's "scissparity," Kafka's "chorus," and Blanchot's "passivity" may have come to approaching it. It is the trait of language that crosses through all speaking, and it is what opens each subject and figure of speech for other singularities than any that could be lived, experienced, or claimed; for other others than any who could be named, addressed, or questioned; and for other points of contact than any whose touch could be established.

Postscript

There could be no end to the echoes that may be traced across the texts examined in these pages and therefore no end to the ways in which they may yet speak with one another, among others that have yet to be known or noted. Who could know the limits of such a "conversation" among writings, when the "who" of knowledge is itself unsettled through Augustine's and Husserl's iterations of the imperative, "Know thyself,"[1] Kafka's variation of the same ("Misknow thyself"),[2] and Blanchot's repetition of the question, "Who are you?"[3] There is no sure last word on the subject. Far from approaching the address they seem to intend, let alone soliciting sure answers, these variations upon the appeal to self-knowledge remove the subject ever further from the scope of cognition, not only through the turns that "you" and "know" turn out to take in each text but also through the undirected ways in which the various texts correspond with one another and thus vary themselves with each instance of resonance. Without addressing one another directly, the words of "knowing" and "you" penned by "Augustine," "Husserl," "Kafka," and "Blanchot" come to alter their sense through one another; and as they speak in these altered and unauthorized ways, *the* phenomenological question of knowing "*transcendental self-experience* with respect to its particular interwoven forms and [. . .] the universal tissue of such forms" gives way to a textual entanglement that exceeds the bounds of known "experience" and therefore remains loose both in its ties and at its ends.[4]

Hence, the nexus of texts drawn together in this book could be extended in any number of directions. Friedrich Nietzsche's opening lines from *On the Genealogy of Morality*, for instance, repeat: "We are unknown to ourselves, we knowing ones [*wir Erkennenden*], we ourselves us ourselves [*wir selbst uns selbst*]."[5] Here, Nietzsche gives word once again of the

163

ignorance among otherwise "knowledgeable" subjects which had prompted Augustine to note our need for admonitions to remind us in one stroke (*eo ictu*) of our own minds. But Nietzsche's particular formulation also suggests a possibility more radical than self-ignorance, since the repetitive insistence upon "us ourselves" (*uns selbst*) also begins to make us sound like "no selves" (*unselbst*) at all. For all we know, the striking effects of language—"which," Nietzsche writes, "construes and misconstrues all acting [*Wirken*] as conditional upon an agency [*ein Wirkendes*]"[6]—may entail that "we knowers [*wir Erkennenden*]" names nothing more than a cipher of questionable value, or even spells itself a misconstrual of misconstrued agency, *Wir. . .k. . .enden*.

"We" would then figure as a transitory sound effect, not unlike the "you" (*Du*) who will at once resound and dissipate through the "through" (*durch*) of Paul Celan's verses, "You transfathom [*Du durchklafterst*] / colorthrust, numberthrow, misknowledge [*Verkenntnis*]," whose initial invocation likewise seems to have been a mistake: "It's you, we misknow it [*du bists, wir verwissens*]."[7] Nor could it be otherwise, as if there were a better knowledge of "you" or anyone else that "we" could ever attain. For as in Nietzsche's genealogy of the "painless, timeless subject of knowledge," whose genetic constitution is wrought through "affects"[8]—and especially painful ones, from the "disgust at life" that motivates the ascetic ideals of Kantian reason to the corporeal punishments that result "in a sharpening of the intelligence, in a lengthening of the memory"[9]—the painful blows that Celan blends with sensible matters and intelligible numbers in "colorthrust, numberthrow" leave the impression that there could be no knowledge that is not stricken with something other than knowledge, and therefore itself struck through or "misknown."[10]

In both the literal dissipation of the subject "through" its invocation and the pain-laced knowledge that is enumerated thereafter, Celan's verses bear the suffering that colors Nietzsche's words of self and knowledge, as he departs from Augustine's assessment of our ignorance in all respects besides perhaps the stroke (*ictus*) that the imperative to "Know thyself" was said to deliver in *On the Trinity*. Yet beyond these intersections among Augustine, Nietzsche, and Celan—all too hastily traversed—Celan's word of "transfathoming" also gives another turn to Husserl's investigations of "transcendental self-experience," by accentuating the suffering that would be entailed with every given perceptual intuition ("colorthrust") and eidetic unity ("numberthrow"), as Celan had similarly emphasized in the "life"-line from *Threadsuns*: "colorbeleaguered, life, numberbeset

[*Farbenbelagert das Leben, zahlenbedrängt*]."[11] Along these lines, it would seem that going through the numbers and the data of experience could hardly yield reliable results but only ever throw "you" off beyond all measure, as with the strokes of the hour that Nietzsche had recounted at the outset of his *Genealogy of Morals*:

> Like somebody divinely absent-minded and sunk in his own thoughts who, the twelve strokes of midday having just boomed into his ears, wakes with a start and wonders "What hour struck?," sometimes we, too, *afterwards* rub our ears and ask, astonished, taken aback, "What did we actually experience then?" or even, "Who *are* we, in fact?" and afterwards, as I said, we count all twelve reverberating strokes of our experience, of our life, of our *being*—oh! And lose count.[12]

From Augustine and Husserl to Nietzsche and Celan, numerous textual threads converge and yield echoes emphasizing that it is not "you" or "I" who could have counted when they appeal to "us" and speak of "knowledge." Instead, what their writings address is the dimension of "experience" where "abyss invokes abyss"[13] through the unfathomable passions of language that, as Blanchot had written, let each word open onto "all the words that were in that word," as well as "those that went with it and in turn contain other words within themselves."[14]

Again, the exposition of textual entanglements such as those traced above cannot but remain open-ended and inconclusive. But each such entanglement exposes how echoes may speak across texts with one another and without subjective intention or objective guarantee. Each exposes, in a word, the passive voice that accompanies those constative, interrogative, and performative utterances that bear it out and let it strike them through. Because they are irreducible to propositional content or speech acts, the conversation threads that unravel among echoes could not be certified by any act of consciousness, and for the same reason, they could not be strung together as a dialectical exchange of question and answer, or as a dialogic performance among identifiable and self-identical subjects. Not even a dialogue in the more radical sense that Martin Buber would develop could correspond to the "intimate relations" that may be forged in the passive voice, despite the fact that "I-Thou," according to Buber, presupposes no being before the speaking of this word: "Primary words," he writes, "do not describe something that might exist independently of them, but being spoken they bring about existence."[15] For neither echoes nor traces among "words imprinted on a page"[16] could be "spoken with one's whole being,"[17] as Buber claims "I-Thou" would need to be, any more than they could be founded in an "original unity" of "lived relation,"[18] or otherwise traced back to a substance or a subject. Instead, they would figure among those figures of speech—including "you" and "me"—whose sense is subject to the vicissitudes of speaking "with the languages of others," and thus exposed to alterity from the outset.[19] All apparently recognizable traits notwithstanding, then, all that may be said among echoes would differ at bottom from anything that "we" may mean by ourselves, and this difference would be founded in no underlying common ground but would issue from the "internal resonance" of language, which invites us not "to think difference from the standpoint of a previous similitude or identity,"[20] but to "think similitude and even identity as a product of deep disparity," as Gilles Deleuze once wrote in his comparison of Plato's philosophy of the same with Nietzsche's philosophy of difference and recurrence.

Still more initially than even this thought of difference, however, the "internal resonance" of language would let each term be transfathomed, transfissured, and transformed in such a way where, as Werner Hamacher has written, speaking-"with" one another "lets this very 'with' become an *other* 'with.'"[21] Ever on the way to speaking "with" others and speaking otherwise, the terms of "our" various conversations and textual configurations would be exposed to unpredictable encounters that alter them as "we" speak and that do not cease to alter them thereafter. "Internal resonance" yields, in other words, the "plural speech" that makes up what Blanchot had called an "infinite conversation": "a speech no longer founded on equality and inequality, no longer upon predominance and subordination, nor upon a reciprocal mutuality, but upon dissymmetry and irreversibility so that, between two instances of speech, a relation of infinity would always be involved as the movement of signification itself."[22] And in this respect, Blanchot's "plural speech," as well as Hamacher's "*other* 'with'" and Deleuze's "internal resonance," also say without a word that speaking happens in the "passive voice," in the uncommon sense that has been probed throughout this book. But if the "passive voice" would thus mark one further contribution to the "infinite conversation" "'with' language" that will have entered into the "common language,"[23] then it could also only solicit others through and past the various lines of confession, narration, and description that have been traced thus far;

others that would rest upon no known terms and expose each time anew "what remains to be said."

Who knows? The "passive voice" may be another term and turn for the passion of "philology": "the passion of speaking otherwise than what it speaks to and of being spoken always otherwise than it means to speak."[24]

Notes

Introduction

1. Aristotle, *De interpretatione*, 16a, in *Aristotelis categoriae et liber de interpretatione*, ed. L. Minio-Paluello (Oxford: Clarendon, 1949). The English translation that is given here is adapted from the one offered in Matthew D. Waltz, "The Opening of 'On Interpretation': Toward a More Literal Reading," *Phronesis* 51, no. 3 (2006): 230–51, 231–32. In his essay, Waltz makes compelling arguments that Aristotle's language in this passage "is referring to the results of the soul's having been acted upon and likened to things. These affectednesses and likenednesses, moreover, are the νοήματα ('thoughts') that Aristotle begins discussing immediately after these opening lines. It is the intellect itself, then, that has been acted upon and likened to things, and this complex process is formally discussed in *De anima*, Γ.4–8, to which Aristotle alludes." Waltz, "The Opening of 'On Interpretation,'" 234.

2. Boethius, *Commentarii in librum Aristotelis ΠΕΡΙ ΕΡΜΗΝΕΙΑΣ*, ed. Charles Meiser (Leipzig: Teubner, 1877), 3, cf. 38.

3. See Thomas Aquinas, *Summa Theologiae* I, q. 79, a. 2; I, q. 84, a. 6, in Thomas Aquinas, *Summa Theologiae*, ed. Thomas Gilby et al., 61 vols. (New York: McGraw-Hill, 1964–1981)

4. Augustine, *Confessions*, IV.16.28 in Augustine, *Confessions*, ed. James J. O'Donnell, 3 vols. (Oxford: Clarendon, 1992). Henceforth, the *Confessions* will be cited by book, chapter, and section number. O'Donnell's commentary will be cited by volume and page number. Translations, unless otherwise noted, are cited and occasionally modified upon the basis of Augustine, *The Confessions*, trans. Maria Boulding (New York: New City Press, 1997). Modifications are not noted, unless commentary on my departure from the published translation furthers the argument. In his commentary on this passage, O'Donnell points to other passages from Augustine's oeuvre, which indicate that Augustine had known of arguments from *De interpretatione* as well. Augustine, *Confessions*, 2:264.

5. Augustine, *Confessions*, I.8.13; my emphasis.

6. Husserl will explicitly criticize Kant's empirical presupposition "that there are things outside of the human mind which affect it and that sensual intuitions are determined by the external things that affect [the mind]." See Edmund Husserl, *Gesammelte Werke. Husserliana* [= *Hua*], ed. Herman van Breda et al., 43 vols. (The Hague: Martinus Nijhoff, 1950–), 7:379; my translation. With such presuppositions, Husserl argues, Kant does not consider the fact that the outer world is itself an intentional object of consciousness; hence, a truly critical epistemology would need to be founded solely upon investigations of the intentional acts and objects of transcendental subjectivity.

7. Husserl, *Hua* 15:462; my translation; Husserl, *Hua* 11:199; my translation.

8. Edmund Husserl, *Ideas Pertaining to a Pure Phenomenology and to a Phenomenological Philosophy: First Book: General Introduction to a Pure Phenomenology*, trans. F. Kersten (The Hague: Nijhoff, 1982), 204–5; cf. Husserl, *Hua* 3:173. Henceforth, references to the English translation of this volume will be abbreviated *Ideas 1*.

9. Husserl, *Hua* 7:152; my translation.

10. For Husserl's tentative use of this term in his descriptions of passivity—and especially the passive self-temporalization of consciousness, see Husserl, *Hua* 15:305, 595, 598. Even in those passages that do not pivot upon the trope of personification, the "I-less" matters of hyletic data will repeatedly be drawn into connection with "I-like" operations, from Husserl's definition of the passive, associative "sphere of 'I-less-ness' [*Sphäre der 'Ichlosigkeit'*]" as the "unwakefulness of the I [*Unwachheit des Ich*]," to his explication of the "I-less streaming [*ichlosen Strömens*]" of subjective temporalization as the "pre-I-like [*Vor-Ichliche*]" condition for cognitive activity. Husserl, *Hua* 15:305, 598; my translation. The privative notion of "I-less-ness" accentuates the subjective character of these operations in a manner that a more Fichtean formulation such as "Not-I" would not do.

11. Husserl, *Ideas 1*, 44 (trans. modified); Husserl, *Hua* 3:51.

12. Augustine, *Confessions*, X.6.10.

13. Augustine, *Confessions*, X.8.12.

14. Emmanuel Levinas, "Phenomenon and Enigma," in *Collected Philosophical Papers*, trans. Alphonso Lingis (Dordrecht: Nijhoff, 1987), 61–73, 66.

15. Maurice Blanchot, *The Step Not Beyond*, trans. Lycette Nelson (Albany: State University of New York Press, 1992), 7.

16. Franz Kafka, *Das Schloss: Faksimile-Edition* (*Franz Kafka-Ausgabe. Historisch-Kritische Edition sämtlicher Handschriften, Drucke und Typoskripte*), 6 vols., ed. Roland Reuß and Peter Staengle (Frankfurt am Main: Stroemfeld, 2018), 1:121; my translation. The passage in German reads: "Und daß er Frieda manchmal rief, muß gar nicht die Bedeutung haben, die man dem gern zusprechen möchte, er rief einfach den Namen Frieda—wer kennt seine Absichten?—daß

Frieda natürlich eilends kam war ihre Sache [. . .], aber daß er sie etwa geradezu gerufen hätte, kann man nicht geradezu behaupten." Throughout, I have offered my own translations of passages that are quoted from this facsimile edition, which has not yet been reproduced in English translation.

17. For a critical survey of recent studies that suggest theories of "affect" and the intertwined "matter of bodies" may open to experiences exceeding "the reign of signification," "interpretation," and "language," see Clare Hemmings, "Invoking Affect: Cultural Theory and the Ontological Turn," *Cultural Studies* 19, no. 5 (2005): 548–67, 554. For a phenomenological appeal to the a priori pathos of subjective life as auto-affection, see Michel Henry, *Phénoménologie matérielle* (Paris: Presses Universitaires de France, 1990).

18. Jacques Derrida, *Demeure: Fiction and Testimony*, in Maurice Blanchot and Jacques Derrida, *The Instant of My Death / Demeure: Fiction and Testimony*, trans. Elizabeth Rottenberg (Stanford, CA: Stanford University Press, 2000), 29.

19. Werner Hamacher, *Pleroma—Reading in Hegel*, trans. Nicholas Walker and Simon Jarvis (Stanford, CA: Stanford University Press, 1998), 5; trans. modified.

20. Husserl, *Ideas 1*, 44 (trans. modified); cf. Husserl, *Hua* 3:51.

21. After citing Husserl's arguments for an "essential broadening" of the concept of "intuitiveness [Anschaulichkeit]" in his *Crisis of the European Sciences*, Jean-Luc Marion comments that it is "a matter of admitting that the concept affects us, and therefore that the concept is given to us, in its categorial figure." Jean-Luc Marion, *Reduction and Givenness: Investigations of Husserl, Heidegger, and Phenomenology*, trans. Thomas A. Carlson (Evanston, IL: Northwestern University Press, 1988), 12; cf. Husserl, *Hua* 6:118.

22. Martin Heidegger, *Being and Time*, trans. Joan Stambaugh (Albany: State University of New York Press, 1996), 33, 24; cf. Martin Heidegger, *Sein und Zeit* (Tübingen: Niemeyer, 2001), 37, 28. The quotation marks surrounding the words "originary" and "intuitive" indicate a certain ambivalence: although they suggest the citational character of both terms, which correspond to Husserl's formulation of the "principle of principles," the seemingly borrowed words are accompanied by no explicit reference to Husserl's *Ideen zu einer reinen Phänomenologie*, with the consequence that the quotation marks may also indicate a suspension of the usual sense of the terms, a sort of "epoché" of Husserl's terminology. For a discussion of the ways in which Husserl's thought of givenness prepares for Heidegger's reformulation of the question of being, see Marion, *Reduction and Givenness*, 40–76 and John D. Caputo, "The Question of Being and Transcendental Phenomenology: Reflections on Heidegger's Relationship to Husserl," *Research in Phenomenology* 7 (1977): 84–105.

23. Marion, *Reduction and Givenness*, 32.

24. Bernhard Waldenfels, *Phenomenology of the Alien: Basic Concepts*, trans. Alexander Korzin and Tanja Stähler (Evanston, IL: Northwestern University Press,

2011), 27 (trans. modified); cf. Bernhard Waldenfals, *Grundmotive einer Phänomenologie des Fremden* (Frankfurt am Main: Suhrkamp, 2006), 43.

25. Husserl, *Ideas 1*, 44 (trans. modified); cf. Husserl, *Hua* 3: 51.

26. Tilottama Rajan, *Deconstruction and the Remainders of Phenomenology: Sartre, Derrida, Foucault, Baudrillard* (Stanford, CA: Stanford University Press, 2002), 14.

27. Michael Marder, *Phenomena—Critique—Logos: The Project of Critical Phenomenology* (London: Rowman & Littlefield, 2014), 22.

28. Husserl, *Ideas 1*, 44–45 (trans. modified); cf. Husserl, *Hua* 3:51.

29. Husserl, *Ideas 1*, 33 (trans. modified); cf. Husserl, *Hua* 3:39.

30. This argument is the one which Eugen Fink advances in his *Sixth Cartesian Meditation*, where phenomenological communications will be characterized as the semblance of worldly objects, which phenomenology assumes for purely pedagogical purposes: "Phenomenology first becomes predicatively explicable, becomes explicating action [*Explizieren*], when through secondary enworlding it is transferred—seemingly [*scheinbar*]—into a *worldly situation for the sake of which it has to express itself*. [. . .] But we can see that the 'enworlding' of phenomenologizing, which begins with its predicative presentation, is a tendency that seems to grow out of *transcendental pedagogical impulses*: a tendency to a universal becoming-for-itself on the part of an all-inclusively communal transcendental life." Eugen Fink, *Sixth Cartesian Meditation: The Idea of a Transcendental Theory of Method*, trans. Ronald Bruzina (Bloomington: Indiana University Press, 1995), 99–100.

31. See, for example, Husserl, *Hua* 3:205, 215.

32. For this reason, the original, intuitive basis for each expression can only be supposed. It is with an eye to this problem that Jacques Derrida would write on the *"hypothesis of sight*—or the intuitive hypothesis": "One generally dissociates conjecture from perception. One even opposes hypothesis to intuition, to the immediacy of the 'I see' (*video, intueor*), 'I look at' (*aspicio*), I 'have an eye on' [*je mire*], I am astonished to see, I admire (*miror, admiror*). And so right here, and this is a paradigm, we can only *suppose* intuition." Jacques Derrida, *Memoirs of the Blind: The Self-Portrait and Other Ruins*, trans. Pascale-Anne Brault and Michael Naas (Chicago: University of Chicago Press,1993), 60; cf. Jacques Derrida, *Mémoires d'aveugle: L'autoportrait et autres ruines* (Paris: Éditions de la Réunion des musées nationaux, 1990), 64.

33. Toward the beginning of his lecture course from 1907, *Thing and Space (Ding und Raum)*, Husserl speaks to the priority of language in another way, when he introduces his phenomenological investigation of perception not with the experience of perceiving but with the word "perception": "We have, in a preliminary way, the word ['perception'], and adhering to it, [we have] a certain, vague meaning. The task will be to go back to the phenomena themselves by following the lead of this vague meaning, to study them intuitively, and then to create concepts that purely express the phenomenological givens." Edmund Hus-

serl, *Thing and Space: The Lectures of 1907*, trans. Richard Rojcewicz (Dordrecht: Springer, 1997), 7 (trans. modified); cf. Husserl, *Hua* 16:9. In yet another sense, Jean-Luc Marion writes in *Being Given* that "for every mortal, the first word was always already heard before he could utter it. To speak always and first amounts to passively hearing a word coming from the Other, a word first and always incomprehensible, which announces no meaning or signification, other than the very alterity of the initiative, by which the pure fact gives (itself) (to be thought) for the first time." Jean-Luc Marion, *Being Given: Towards a Phenomenology of Givenness*, trans. Jeffrey L. Kosky (Stanford, CA: Stanford University Press, 2002), 270. The fact that language therefore "precedes *me*" in every respect—with regard to my historical existence and to my immanent "self"-recognition—would also render its initial occurrence to "me" immemorial: before any present that I could recognize, let alone recall as lived experience. Language thus withdraws from "being given" as well. Each word would be, as Maurice Blanchot has written, "a word without presence [*une parole sans présence*]." See Blanchot, *The Step Not Beyond*, 30; Maurice Blanchot, *Le pas au-delà* (Paris: Gallimard, 1973), 46.

34. Marder, *Phenomenology—Critique—Logos*, 13.

35. Brice Parain, *Recherches sur la nature et les fonctions du langage* (Paris: Gallimard, 1942), 14; my translation. Although Parain does not explicitly address Husserl's *Logical Investigations*, both writers adopt signs as the starting point of their respective studies and address the question as to the relation between intuition and signification. But Parain's engagements with poetry, everyday speech, and mathematics, as well as the writings of Plato, Aristotle, Descartes, Leibniz, and Hegel, among others, lead to observations of linguistic phenomena that diverge from Husserl's descriptions, such as the following: "It is not the object that gives its signification to the sign, but the sign that imposes upon us the task of figuring an object of its signification [*ce n'est pas l'objet qui donne sa signification au signe, mais le signe qui nous impose de nous figurer un objet de sa signification*]." Parain, *Recherches*, 73; my translation. If this thought is teleological, like Husserl's understanding of meaning, intentionality, and intuitive fulfillment—"we do not perceive the origin of language, but we do perceive its end [*nous n'apercevons pas l'origine du langage mais nous apercevons sa fin*]," writes Parain—the "end" that language indicates is structurally open-ended and indeterminate: never a *fait accompli*, but at all times an *im-parfait*. Parain, *Recherches*, 73; my translation. See also Brice Parain, *Essai sur la misère humaine* (Paris: Grasset, 1934), 226. Other scholars who have considered Parain in the context of Husserl's oeuvre include Jean-Paul Sartre, who would criticize Parain for not maintaining 'the priority of the *cogito*, the universalizing syntheses [of transcendental subjectivity], and the immediate experience of the Other." Jean-Paul Sartre, "Aller et retour," in *Situations I* (Paris: Gallimard, 1947), 175–225, 220; my translation. Responding to both Parain's oeuvre and Sartre's critical essay, Pierre Klossowski would write: "If individual consciousness plays the role of an absolute beginning—as it does for phenome-

nology—then it is hardly capable of anything but the passive contemplation of an eternal peace: thus, says Parain, each time that peace is troubled it has the feeling of the absurd. Ultimately, inertia being the law of this consciousness, it does not know how to describe any of the events that grip us and suspend our reflection: births, deaths, acts of violence, revolts, suicides, social crises, war." Pierre Klossowski, "Language, Silence, and Communism," in *Such a Deathly Desire*, trans. Russell Ford (Albany: State University of New York Press, 2007), 71–83, 74. Before these ruptures, however, Klossowski argues that Parain exposes language to be another, still more radical rupture, which troubles conscious experience per se: "If consciousness 'were an unbroken whole [*ensemble*], it would persevere in its constitutive syntheses of objects.' 'On the contrary, the intervention of speech strips the character of finitude from every event of our existence. With language we enter, for better or worse, the order of the indefinite if not the infinite'" (74).

36. In his *Prolegomena*, Husserl indicates his proximity to Leibniz, but only to insist again that "the authority of Leibniz must, however, count even less for us than that of Kant or Herbart, since he could not give to his great intentions" of establishing a *mathesis universalis* "the weight of completed achievements," and since "authorities do not in fact carry much weight as opposed to the broad advance of a science supposedly rich and secure in its results." Edmund Husserl, *Logical Investigations*, ed. Dermot Moran, trans. J. N. Findlay, 2 vols. (London: Routledge, 2001), 1:141.

37. Early in the *Logical Investigations*, he will assert that his phenomenological approach to logic will be concerned exclusively with "experiences intuitively seizable and analysable in the pure generality of their essence." Husserl, *Logical Investigations*, 1:166.

38. Husserl, *Logical Investigations*, 2:233; 1:210 (trans. modified); cf. Husserl, *Hua* 19:607, 73. This trait is what permits signs to be used and understood as meaningful in the absence of any real or even possible intuition, as in the case of a "round square [*rundes Viereck*]." Husserl, *Logical Investigations*, 1:202; Husserl, *Hua* 19:60.

39. Husserl, *Logical Investigations*, 1:208; cf. Husserl, *Hua* 19:71.

40. Gottfried Wilhelm Leibniz, "Meditations on Knowledge, Truth, and Ideas," in *Philosophical Papers and Letters*, vol. 2, ed. L. E. Loemker (Dordrecht: Springer, 1989), 291–95, 292; cf. Gottfried Wilhelm Leibniz, "Meditationes de cognitione, veritate et ideis," in *Die philosophischen Schriften von Gottfried Wilhelm Leibniz*, ed. Carl Immanuel Gerhardt, vol. 4 (Hildesheim: Olms, 1965), 422–26, 423.

41. Sigmund Freud evokes the notion of a "screen memory" or "Deckerinnerung," first, to describe the intense memories of insignificant childhood events that displace memories of significant, yet suppressed impressions: "Instead of the mnemic image which would have been justified by the original event, another is produced which has been to some degree associatively displaced from the former one." Sigmund Freud, "Screen Memories," in *The Standard Edition of the*

Complete Psychological Works of Sigmund Freud: Volume 3 (1893–1899): Early Psychoanalytical Publications, trans. and ed. James Strachey (London: Hogarth, 1962), 298–322, 307). Further analysis of a particular patient's childhood memories allows Freud to argue, however, that a "screen memory" may also be forged by "the memory impressions and thoughts of a later date whose content is connected with its own by symbolic or similar links," again so as to suppress and "represent" significant events in the same stroke (316). In conclusion, Freud writes: "It may indeed be questioned whether we have any memories at all *from* our childhood: memories *relating to* our childhood may be all that we possess. Our childhood memories show us our earliest years not as they were but as they appeared at the later periods when the memories were aroused. In these periods of arousal, the childhood memories did not, as people are accustomed to say, *emerge*; they were *formed* at that time" (322).

42. Leibniz, "Meditations," 292; cf. Leibniz, "Meditationes," 423.

43. G. W. F. Hegel, *Enzyklopädie der philosophischen Wissenschaften im Grundrisse: Dritter Teil: Die Philosophie des Geistes*, ed. Eva Moldenhauer and Karl Markus Michel (Frankfurt am Main: Suhrkamp, 1986), §457–64. The transition from memorization to thought is said to take place in an utterly unmarked way, when signs come no longer to have "*meaning [Bedeutung]*" for the intelligence that thinks in them, since "the subjective is no longer something separate from its objectivity, just as this interiority is in itself *existent [an ihr selbst seiend ist]*" (282; my translation). For analyses of the precarity that this model for thinking entails—not least of all due to the irreducible remainder of phantasms that haunt Hegel's speculations, and to the passivity that thereby comes to be inscribed in thought—see Jacques Derrida, "The Pit and the Pyramid: Introduction to Hegel's Semiology," in *Margins of Philosophy*, trans. Alan Bass (Chicago: University of Chicago Press, 1982), 69–108; Werner Hamacher, *Pleroma*, 116–22; and David Farrell Krell, *Of Memory, Reminiscence, and Writing—On the Verge* (Bloomington: Indiana University Press, 1990), 205–39.

44. Husserl, *Hua* 6:439; my translation. Despite the preoccupation with the blind and mechanistic functions of signs that may be found in Leibniz's and Hegel's texts, Husserl's emphasis upon the unthought dimension of thought itself testifies to the distinction that Michel Foucault would draw between his approach to the *cogito* and prior philosophical considerations of the "I" that thinks. Contrasting Husserl's investigations of transcendental subjectivity with Immanuel Kant's critical philosophy in particular, he writes: "The question is no longer: How can experience of nature give rise to necessary judgments? But rather: How can man think what he does not think, inhabit as though by a mute occupation something that eludes him, animate with a kind of frozen movement that figure of himself that takes the form of a stubborn exteriority?" Michel Foucault, *The Order of Things: An Archaeology of the Human Sciences*, trans. Alan Sheridan (New York: Vintage, 1994), 323.

45. Derrida, *Memoirs of the Blind*, 47; Derrida, *Mémoires d'aveugle*, 51. See also Derrida's rigorous analysis of the role that language plays in Husserl's account of geometrical ideality: "Whether geometry can be spoken about is not [. . .] the extrinsic and accidental possibility of a fall into the body of speech or of a slip into a historical movement. Speech [. . .] constitutes the object and is a concrete juridical condition of truth. The paradox is that, without the apparent fall back into language and thereby into history, a fall which would alienate the ideal purity of sense, sense would remain an empirical formation imprisoned as fact in a psychological subjectivity—*in the inventor's head*." Jacques Derrida, *Edmund Husserl's* Origin of Geometry: *An Introduction*, trans. John P. Leavey (Lincoln: University of Nebraska Press, 1989), 77.

46. Derrida, *Edmund Husserl's* Origin of Geometry, 70.

47. Georges Bataille, *Guilty*, trans. Bruce Boone (Venice: Lapis, 1988), 29 (trans. modified); cf. Georges Bataille, *Le Coupable*, in *Oeuvres complètes* (= *OC*), 12 vols. (Paris: Gallimard, 1970–1988), 5:265–66.

48. Rodolphe Gasché, *Georges Bataille: Phenomenology and Phantasmatology*, trans. Roland Vésgö (Stanford, CA: Stanford University Press, 2012), 98.

49. There, the paternal figure is said to have had "huge, ever-gaping eyes [. . .] with a completely stupefying expression of abandon and aberration in a world that he alone could see [*de très grands yeux toujours très ouverts [. . .] avec une expression tout à fait abrutissante d'abandon et d'égarement dans un monde que lui seul pouvait voir*]." Georges Bataille, *Story of the Eye*, trans. Joachim Neugroschel (San Francisco: City Lights, 1987), 93; Bataille, *OC* 1:76.

50. Maurice Blanchot, *Thomas l'obscur: Première version, 1941* (Paris: Gallimard, 2005), 33. The English translation is based upon the one that is offered in Maurice Blanchot, *Thomas the Obscure*, trans. Robert Lamberton (New York: Station Hill, 1988), 15. The slight differences are due to the fact that Lamberton's textual basis is the revised version of the novel that Blanchot had published in 1950. Of course, Bataille not only knew of this text in its first edition but also quotes this very passage in *Inner Experience*, trans. Leslie Anne Boldt (Albany: State University of New York Press, 1988) 101–2; cf. Bataille, *OC* 5:119–20. Bataille goes on to write of the correspondence between his book and Blanchot's novel: "Outside of the notes of this volume, I only know of *Thomas the Obscure* where the questions of the new theology (which has only the unknown as object) are pressing, although they remain hidden." Bataille, *Inner Experience*, 102; cf. Bataille, *OC* 5:120. But in *Guilty*, the echo is not accompanied by an explicit reference to Blanchot, leaving it an open issue as to whether it was intended or should be noticed.

51. Augustine, *In Johannis evangelium tractatus CXXIV*, ed. D. Radbodus Willems (Turnhout: Brepols, 1954), I.19; my translation.

52. Franz Kafka, *Nachgelassene Schriften und Fragmente II*, ed. Jost Schillemeit (Frankfurt am Main: Fischer, 1992), 127; my translation. Paul North offers an elucidating commentary on this fragment, writing: "Art registers at a minimum

its withdrawal from truth. Although it has no access, either through representing truth or dialectically through failing to, art has the surprising ability to be and to show the lack of access." Paul North, *The Yield: Kafka's Atheological Reformation* (Stanford, CA: Stanford University Press, 2015), 206.

53. Husserl, *Ideas 1*, 200 (trans. modified); cf. Husserl, *Hua* 3:188.

54. Bataille explicitly refers, for example, to Augustine's *Confessions* in *Inner Experience*, and in *Guilty*, he will recur to Kafka's *The Castle*. Bataille, *Inner Experience*, 123; Bataille, *Guilty*, 54–5; Bataille, *OC* 5:143, 293.

55. Bataille, *Guilty*, 29; cf. Bataille, *OC* 5:265. Later, his "propositions" are also admitted to be unfounded, upon the premise that "nothing is founded if not upon a necessity that excludes other possibilities." Bataille, *Guilty*, 43 (trans. modified); cf. Bataille, *OC* 5:280.

56. Later Bataille will write: "What's called mind, philosophy, and religion is founded on interferences." Bataille, *Guilty*, 136; Bataille, *OC* 5:384.

57. The structure of this speaking "with" and "without" one another is elaborated extensively in Werner Hamacher, "What Remains to Be Said: Twelve and More Ways of Looking at Philology," trans. Kristina Mendicino, in *Give the Word: Responses to Werner Hamacher's 95 Theses on Philology*, ed. Gerhard Richter and Ann Smock (Lincoln: University of Nebraska Press, 2019), 217–354; cf. Werner Hamacher, "Was zu sagen bleibt: Twelve and More Ways of Looking at Philology," in *Was zu sagen bleibt* (Schupfart: Engeler, 2019), 79–202.

58. Derrida, *Memoirs of the Blind*, 4; cf. Derrida, *Mémoires d'aveugle*, 11.

59. Martin Heidegger, "Language," in *Poetry, Language, Thought*, trans Albert Hofstadter (New York: HarperCollins, 2001), 185–208, 188; cf. Martin Heidegger, *Unterwegs zur Sprache*, ed. Friedrich-Wilhelm von Herrmann (Frankfurt am Main: Klostermann, 1985), 10.

60. Derrida, *Memoirs of the Blind*, 16; cf. Derrida, *Mémoires d'aveugle*, 23.

61. This is the case, because a direct critique would implicitly or explicitly appeal to argumentative evidence that presupposes, in turn, the very notion of intuition that language can only dissimulate.

62. Derrida, *Memoirs of the Blind*, 17; cf. Derrida, *Mémoires d'aveugle*, 23.

63. Derrida, *Memoirs of the Blind*, 31; Derrida, *Mémoires d'aveugle*, 37.

64. In Derrida's *Memoirs of the Blind*, Bataille's epilogue is referred to by the italicized title, "*Réminiscences*," as it appears in the "nouvelle version" that Bataille first published in 1941; in the first published version of his novel from 1928, the section is designated "Coïncidences." Bataille, *OC* 1:73, 606. The appearance of "coincidences" and "reminiscences" as variants of one another underscores the aleatory character of memory. In his first version of the text, it is also significant that Bataille had introduced the photographs only after confessing that he had begun writing ' without precise determination, incited above all by the desire to forget, at least provisionally, that which I could be or do personally," while he claims the belief that had sustained his writing process was "that the person who

speaks in the first-person had no relation to me." Bataille, *Story of the Eye*, 89 (trans. modified); cf. Bataille, *OC* 1:73. The fact that the photographs turn out to recall a hitherto forgotten "episode" of Bataille's life—which, in turn, resembles an episode from his novel—testifies not only to the success of his intention to forget through writing but also to the obliviousness of memory itself. On the one hand, namely, Bataille's belated recollections show memory to have been operative without his knowledge; on the other hand, these recollections' contingency upon the photographs exposes them to be at least as contingent upon external "coincidence" as they are upon lived experience and entangled with mechanically reproduced images whose originals Bataille had not (yet) lived to see.

65. "But then one day I was looking through an American magazine," he writes, "and I chanced upon two astonishing photographs: [. . .] the second [was of] the nearby ruins of a medieval fortified castle on a crag in the mountain. I promptly recalled an episode in my life connected to these ruins." Bataille, *Story of the Eye*, qtd. in Derrida, *Memoirs of the Blind*, 17; cf. Bataille *Story of the Eye*, 89; Bataille, *OC* 1:73.

66. The dream reads as follows: "duel of these blind men at each other's throats, one of the old men turning away in order to come after me, to take me to task—me, poor passerby that I am. He harasses me, blackmails me, then I fall with him to the ground, and he grabs me again with such agility that I end up suspecting him of seeing with at least one eye half open and staring, like a cyclops (one-eyed or squinting, I no longer know); he restrains me with one hold after another and ends up using the weapon against which I am defenseless, a threat against my sons [*fils*]." Derrida, *Memoirs of the Blind*, 16; cf. Derrida, *Mémoires d'aveugle*, 23. A variant of this dream is also recorded in Derrida's *Circonfession*; see Geoffrey Bennington and Jacques Derrida, *Derrida* (Paris: Seuil, 2008), 60–3. For the figures from antiquity whom the dream calls up, see Derrida, *Memoirs of the Blind*, 17–26; Derrida, *Mémoires d'aveugle*, 24–33.

67. William V. Spanos, *Heidegger and Criticism: Retrieving the Cultural Politics of Destruction* (Minneapolis: University of Minnesota Press, 1993), 87. The specific context of this remark is Spanos's reading of *Of Grammatology*, yet he suggests that it would be applicable to other texts penned not only by Derrida but also by those who have taken Derrida's writing seriously, "such as Barbara Johnson, Jonathan Culler, and Christopher Norris" (100). As Rajan rightly reminds us, such comments do not "do justice to Derrida," not least because they elide the "analytic of finitude at the core of [deconstruction's] focus on language." Rajan, *Deconstruction and the Remainders of Phenomenology*, 8.

68. Derrida, *Memoirs of the Blind*, 16; cf. Derrida, *Mémoires d'aveugle*, 23.

69. Husserl, *Ideas 1*, 44 (trans. modified); Husserl, *Hua* 3:51.

70. Later, Augustine's *Confessions* will be called yet another "pre-story of the eye [*préhistoire de l'oeil*]," insofar as that text too traces a story "of vision or

of blindness [*de la vision ou de la cécité*]." Derrida, *Memoirs of the Blind*, 122; Derrida, *Mémoires d'aveugle*, 123.

71. Derrida, *Memoirs of the Blind*, 45; *Mémoires d'aveugle*, 50.

72. Derrida, *Demeure: Fiction and Testimony*, 27, 29; cf. Jacques Derrida, *Demeure: Maurice Blanchot* (Paris: Galilée, 1998), 28, 31. Without the possibilities of fiction and literature that Derrida speaks of in these passages, testimony would belong to the order of "proof, information, certainty, or archive," and it would thereby "lose its function as testimony," which rests upon the premise of singularity: "I can only testify, in the strict sense of the word, from the instant when no one can, in my place, testify to what I do." Derrida, *Demeure: Fiction and Testimony*, 29–30; cf. *Demeure: Maurice Blanchot*, 31–32. The continued relevance of Husserl to Derrida's later oeuvre has also been traced, with different accentuations in, among others, Rodolphe Gasché, *The Tain of the Mirror: Derrida and the Philosophy of Reflection* (Cambridge, MA: Harvard University Press, 1986); Leonard Lawlor, *Derrida and Husserl: The Basic Problem of Phenomenology* (Bloomington: Indiana University Press, 2002); and Detlef Thiel, "Husserls Phänomenographie." *Recherches Husserliennes* 19 (2003): 67–108.

73. In his phenomenologically inflected approach to ipseity, *Oneself as Another*, Paul Ricoeur will refer to the notion of "attestation" as one that should do justice to the alterity and passivity that affect the "self" and render it "irreducible to an instance of knowing [*irréductible à un savoir*]" in the modus of the *cogito*. Paul Ricoeur, *Oneself as Another*, trans. Kathleen Blamey (Chicago: University of Chicago Press, 1992), 350 (trans. modified); cf. Paul Ricoeur, *Soi-même comme un autre* (Paris: Seuil, 1990), 403.

74. John D. Caputo, *The Prayers and Tears of Jacques Derrida: Religion without Religion* (Bloomington: Indiana University Press, 1997), 209.

75. Jacques Derrida, *Speech and Phenomena*, in *Speech and Phenomena and Other Essays on Husserl's Theory of Signs*, trans. David B. Allison (Evanston, IL: Northwestern University Press, 1973), 1–104, 51, 56; cf. Jacques Derrida, *La voix et le phénomène: Introduction au problème du signe dans la phénoménologie de Husserl* (Paris: Presses Universitaires de France, 1967), 56, 63.

76. Derrida, *Speech and Phenomena*, 51; cf. Derrida, *La voix et le phénomène*, 56.

77. Derrida, *Speech and Phenomena*, 95; cf. Derrida, *La voix et le phénomène*, 106. Thus, Husserl's claim that the meaning of "I" might be "'realized' *by the one who is speaking*" is, strictly speaking, unverifiable. Derrida, *Speech and Phenomena*, 94; cf. Derrida, *La voix et le phénomène*, 105–6. Here, Derrida is quoting from the passage in the *Logical Investigations*, where Husserl writes: "In solitary speech the meaning of 'I' is essentially realized in the immediate idea of one's own personality, which is also the meaning of the word in communicated speech." Husserl, *Logical Investigations*, 1:219; cf. Husserl, *Hua* 19:88.

78. See Rajan, *Deconstruction and the Remainders of Phenomenology*, 1–2.
79. Derrida, *Demeure*, 26; cf. *Demeure: Maurice Blanchot*, 27. This formulation echoes remarks penned by Blanchot and Levinas, as Derrida indicates in his next sentence, where he refers explicitly to Levinas's and Blanchot's discussions of "archi-passivity."
80. For an excellent recent study that offers probing readings of "pseudo-memoirs" from a perspective inspired not only by phenomenology but also by the insight that "the idea of a life amenable to, if not made for, narration is itself a fiction," see Rochelle Tobias, *Pseudo-Memoirs: Life and Its Imitation in Modern Fiction* (Lincoln: University of Nebraska Press, 2021), 2.
81. See Steven Shaviro, *Passion & Excess: Blanchot, Bataille, and Literary Theory* (Tallahassee: Florida State University Press, 1990); Ann Smock, *What Is There to Say?: Blanchot, Melville, des Forêts, Beckett* (Lincoln: University of Nebraska Press, 2007); and Thomas C. Wall, *Radical Passivity: Levinas: Blanchot, and Agamben* (Albany: State University of New York Press, 1999). For another recent study of passivity that addresses the French phenomenological tradition but focuses primarily upon the body-soul relationship, see Christina Howells, *Mortal Subjects: Passions of the Soul in Late Twentieth-Century French Thought* (Cambridge: Polity, 2011).
82. See Martin Heidegger, *Phänomenologie des religiösen Lebens*, ed. Matthias Jung et al. (Frankfurt am Main: Klostermann, 1995); Jean-Luc Marion, *Au lieu de soi: L'approche de Saint Augustin* (Paris: Presses Universitaires de France, 2008); Jean-Louis Chrétien, *Saint Augustin et les actes de parole* (Paris: Presses Universitaires de France, 2002); and James K. A. Smith, *Speech and Theology: Language and the Logic of Incarnation* (London and New York: Routledge, 2002). These exemplary phenomenological studies of Augustine are by no means meant to be representative of the vast bibliography of literature concerning Augustine and phenomenological questions: among the thinkers who were in proximity to Heidegger alone, one would also need to cite Karl Jaspers, *Die grossen Philosophen: Erster Band* (Munich: Piper, 1957), 319–96; and Hannah Arendt, *Der Liebesbegriff bei Augustin: Versuch einer philosophischen Interpretation* (Hildesheim: Olms, 2006).
83. Augustine, *Confessions*, X.33.50. These lines echo the formulation that had already characterized Augustine's experience of radical disorientation and grief upon the death of a friend in the fourth book: "I had become a great question for myself [*factus eram ipse mihi magna quaestio*], and I interrogated my soul, demanding why it was sorrowful and why it so disquieted me, but it had no answer." Augustine, *Confessions*, IV.4.9.
84. Husserl, *Hua* 1:142; my translation.
85. Jean-François Lyotard, *Discours, figure* (Paris: Klincksieck, 1971), 56.
86. Derrida, *Edmund Husserl's* Origin of Geometry, 102.
87. Leslie Hill, *Bataille, Klossowski, Blanchot: Writing at the Limits* (Oxford: Oxford University Press, 2001), 21.

88. Michel Foucault, "La scène de la philosophie," in *Dits et écrits 1954–1988*, ed. Daniel Defert, François Ewald, and Jacques Lagrange. vol. 3 (Paris: Gallimard, 1994), 571–95, 590; qtd. in Hill, *Bataille, Klossowski, Blanchot*, 1–2.

89. Michel Foucault, *The Order of Things*, 383–4; trans. modified. My thanks to Emma Schneider for reminding me of this passage. Cf. Michel Foucault, *Les mots et les choses: Une archéologie des sciences humaines* (Paris: Gallimard, 1966), 395.

90. As Rajan observes, "These writers allow Foucault to deconstruct phenomenology—in the sense of forming an intellectual community with it." Rajan, *Deconstruction and the Remainders of Phenomenology*, 189.

91. Georges Bataille, *Literature and Evil*, trans. Alastair Hamilton (London: Marion Boyars, 2001), 152 (trans. modified); cf. Bataille, *OC* 9:271.

92. See, for example, Charles Bernheimer, *Flaubert and Kafka: Studies in Psychopoetic Structure* (New Haven, CT: Yale University Press, 1982); Stanley Corngold and Benno Wagner, *Franz Kafka: The Ghosts in the Machine* (Evanston, IL: Northwestern University Press, 2011); Henry Sussman, *Franz Kafka: Geometrician of Metaphor* (Madison: Coda, 1979); and Joseph Vogl, "Vierte Person: Kafkas Erzählstimme," *Deutsche Vierteljahrsschrift für Literaturwissenschaft und Geistesgeschichte* 68 (1994) 745–56.

93. Kafka, *Nachgelassene Schriften und Fragmente II*, 348; my translation.

94. At one point in his review, Sartre entertains the possibility that the "rigorously identical themes" to be found in Kafka and Blanchot might be attributed to the "same absurd world that they aim to depict," but he will go on to assert not only that Blanchot "stole" from Kafka but also that this gesture of theft creates a "discrepancy between sign and signified [that] makes themes lived by Kafka pass to the rank of literary conventions." Jean-Paul Sartre, "*Aminadab* ou du fantastique considéré comme un langage," in *Situations I*, 113–32, 120, 130; my translation.

95. Davies adopts the term, "*apprentissage*," in light of Blanchot's remark upon "what Kafka teaches us [*ice que Kafka nous apprend*]"; namely, that "storytelling brings the neuter into play." Maurice Blanchot, *The Infinite Conversation*, trans. Susan Hanson (Minneapolis: University of Minnesota Press, 1993), 384; Maurice Blanchot, *L'entretien infini* (Paris: Gallimard, 1969), 563. Through his readings of Kafka and Blanchot, Davies suggests that this instance of teaching (*apprendre*) signifies, before all else, an apprenticeship (*apprentissage*) in writing that knows no goal or end. Paul Davies, "Kafka's Lesson, Blanchot's Itinerary," *parallax* 12, no. 2 (2006): 23–39, 23. Hence, Davies concludes, "In addition to the statements about the neuter, about literature and language, and in addition to the development of an increasingly complex writing, there is an attentiveness to a 'project,' to the unfolding and continuing of a writing that never permits a transposition or commentary but which binds one to it interminably" (38).

96. Maurice Blanchot, *Aminadab*, trans. Jeff Fort (Lincoln: University of Nebraska Press, 2002), 174; cf. Maurice Blanchot, *Aminadab* (Paris: Gallimard,

1942), 254. Throughout, the page references to the English edition will precede those provided in the French edition.

Chapter 1

1. Edmund Husserl, *Cartesian Meditations: An Introduction to Phenomenology*, trans. Dorion Cairns (The Hague: Nijhoff, 1960), 157; trans. modified.
2. Husserl, *Hua* 1:39, 183.
3. Husserl, *Cartesian Meditations*, 83; Husserl, *Hua* 1:116.
4. Eugen Fink, *Sixth Cartesian Meditation*, 92.
5. Edmund Husserl, *The Crisis of the European Sciences and Transcendental Phenomenology*, trans. David Carr (Evanston, IL: Northwestern University Press, 1970), 71; Husserl, *Hua* 6:72–3.
6. Husserl, *Crisis*, 71; Husserl, *Hua* 6:72–3.
7. Aristotle, *The 'Art' of Rhetoric*, trans. John Henry Freese (Cambridge, MA: Harvard University Press, 1926), 285 (trans. modified); cf. Aristotle, *Aristotelis ars rhetorica*, ed. W. D. Ross (Oxford: Clarendon, 1959), 1395a.
8. Karl Marx and Friedrich Engels, *The Communist Manifesto*, in *Collected Works*, trans. Richard Dixon et al., vol. 6 (New York: International, 1976), 478–520, 519; cf. Karl Marx, *Das Manifest der kommunistischen Partei*, ed. Theo Stammen and Alexander Classen (Munich: Fink, 2009), 96.
9. See Arnold Metzger, "Die Phänomenologie der Revolution," in *Frühe Schriften*, ed. Karl Markus Michel (Frankfurt am Main: Syndikat, 1979), 13–104. In this text, which he wrote shortly before becoming an assistant to Husserl, Metzger had argued that, whereas Marxism fails to critique sufficiently the "categories of bourgeois spirit," Husserl's discovery of intentionality and eidetic analysis reawakens the "belief in the idea" that had hitherto gone lost and reconciles idea and world, rendering Husserl among the true "carriers of revolutionary movements [*Träger revolutionärer Bewegungen*]." Metzger, "Phänomenologie," 19, 85, 49; my translation. In the letter that he wrote in response to Metzger's essay, Husserl criticizes the latter for misunderstanding the "intentions" that have "determined" his "development since the *Logical Investigations*," while praising Metzger's pathos: Husserl opens his letter claiming that Metzger's prose was "music" to his and his family's ears, as his daughter read the essay aloud and allowed them to hear "a pure, indeed entirely pure tone: the tone of a truly selfless surrender to 'the ideas.'" Husserl to Arnold Metzger, September 4, 1919, in Edmund Husserl, *Briefwechsel. Band IV: Die Freiburger Schüler*, ed. Karl Schuhmann (Dordrecht: Springer, 1994), 410, 407; my translation. In the series of essays on ethics that Husserl had written for the Japanese journal, *Kaizo*, in 1923–24, Husserl echoes Metzger's basic premise that, namely, social "renewal" or "Erneuerung" depends upon the "belief" in the "idea of the human," which solely the a priori eidetic science of "transcendental

phenomenology" can prepare. Husserl, *Hua* 27:3, 6, 18–19; my translation. Of course, the total world-loss and world-gain that Husserl evokes at the close of the *Cartesian Meditations* also figures among the consequences of the absolute position of the transcendental subject: as Michael Theunissen has concisely summarized: "Because [phenomenological science] does not make subjectivity into something singular *in* the world, into the subjectivity of the world, it receives in its grasp the entire world, as the world of subjectivity." Michael Theunissen, *Der Andere: Studien zur Sozialontologie der Gegenwart*, 2nd. ed. (Berlin: de Gruyter, 1977), 24; my translation.

10. For a history of the interpretations of this oracle that would be formulated from the philosophers of antiquity through to Saint Bernard of Clairvaux, see Pierre Courcelle, *"Connais-toi toi-même," de Socrate à St. Bernard*, 3 vols. (Paris: Études augustiniennes, 1974–1975).

11. Plato, *Charmides*, trans. Rosamond Kent Sprague, in *Plato: Complete Works*, ed. John M. Cooper (Indianapolis: Hackett, 1997), 639–63, 651; cf. Plato, *Charmides* 164d–165a, in *Opera*, ed. Jonathan Burnet, 5 vols. (Oxford: Clarendon, 1900–1907).

12. Since neither phrase has been clarified when he repeats them, Critias's explication of the inscription on the Delphic temple through the notion of σωφροσύνη redoubles the uncertainty over knowledge and nonknowledge that is confronted in the dialogue. For a recent monograph on the senses of σωφροσύνη that emerge in this particular dialogue, as well as its range of uses in Ancient Greek, see Adriaan Rademaker, *Sophrosyne and the Rhetoric of Self-Restraint: Polysemy and Persuasive Use of an Ancient Greek Value-Term* (Leiden: Brill, 2005).

13. In the prologue to *De ordine*, for example, Augustine had affirmed that belief in chance and universal disorder is inspired by the "inconstancy of innumerable perturbations [*innumerabilium perturbationum inconstantia*]" affecting "human life," which should be remedied by seeking to know oneself through a withdrawal from the distractions of the senses: "The main cause of this error is that man himself is unknown to himself [*sibi ipse est incognitus*]. Yet [in] order for one to know oneself, the habit is most necessary of retreating from the senses, collecting the soul in itself, and holding oneself in oneself [*in se ipso retinendi*]." Augustine, *De ordine*, 1.1–2, in *On Order [De Ordine]*, trans. Silvano Borruso (South Bend: St. Augustine's Press, 2007), 4–5; trans. modified. For a broader discussion of Augustine's elaborations on this thought, from his earliest dialogue, *Contra Academicos*, through to his late treatise *De trinitate*, see Courcelle, *"Connais-toi toi-même,"* 1:123–63. In his erudite remarks, Courcelle also addresses the various Christian, Stoic, and Platonic sources that Augustine had drawn upon and reinterpreted in his commentaries on the Delphic inscription.

14. The necessity of "knowing oneself [*cognoscere se*]" is addressed toward the start of the tenth book. Augustine, *Confessions* X.3.3.

15. Augustine, *On the Trinity*, trans. Stephen McKenna (Washington, DC: Catholic University of America Press, 1963), 306 (trans. modified); Augustine, *De trinitate libri XV*, ed. W. J. Mountain and F. Glorie (Turnhout: Brepols, 1968), X.9.12. Henceforth, references to the Latin edition of *De trinitate* will be made by book, chapter, and section number.

16. There, he writes: "The first thinker to be deeply sensitive to the immense difficulties to be found here was Augustine, who labored almost to despair over this problem. Chapters 13–18 of Book XI of the *Confessions* must even today be thoroughly studied by everyone concerned with the problem of time. For no one in this knowledge-proud modern generation has made more masterful or significant progress in these matters than this great thinker who struggled so earnestly with the problem." Edmund Husserl, *The Phenomenology of Internal Time-Consciousness*, ed. Martin Heidegger, trans. James S. Churchill (Bloomington: Indiana University Press, 1964), 21; cf. *Hua* 10:3. As Nicolas de Warren has argued, however, Husserl's engagement with Augustine's "threefold articulation of the present" is one which "*extract[s]*" the "phenomenological core of book XI [. . .] from the complex frame in which it is situated and which it serves." Nicolas de Warren, "Augustine and Husserl on Time and Memory," *Quaestiones Disputatae* 7, no. 1 (2016): 7–46, 28–29.

17. Husserl, *Hua* 42:569; my translation. The original passage reads: "Augustin: Nur die Liebe macht sehend—für Wert und Ideal. Nemo cognoscitur nisi per amicitiam." The Latin phrase appears in *Eighty-Three Different Questions* (*De diversis quaestionibus LXXXIII*), although the well-known character of the phrase, together with Husserl's deviation from Augustine's formulation (*nemo nisi per amicitiam cognoscitur*) suggests that Husserl may have known it indirectly. Augustine, *De diversis quaestionibus*, 71.5, in *De diversis quaestionibus LXXXIII. De octo Dulcitii quaestionibus*, ed. A. Mutzenbecher (Turnhout: Brepols, 1975). Conversely, Olivier du Roy traces Augustine's conversion to the discovery of spirit and divine substance via "the return to the *intentio*, to this constituting activity of spirit [. . .] in a sense that is clearly phenomenological." Olivier du Roy, *L'intelligence de la foi en la Trinité selon Saint Augustin: Genèse de sa théologie trinitaire jusqu'en 391* (Paris: Études Augustiniennes, 1966), 57; my translation.

18. He goes on to write: "Thus [the mind] knows itself to be and to live in such a manner as intelligence is and lives [*Sic ergo se esse et uiuere scit quomodo est et uiuit intellegentia*]." Augustine, *On the Trinity*, 307 (trans. modified); Augustine, *De trinitate*, X.9.13.

19. Jean-Luc Marion, *In the Self's Place: The Approach of Saint Augustine*, trans. Jeffrey L. Kosky (Stanford, CA: Stanford University Press, 2012), 68. In the pages that precede this passage, Marion comments at length upon the way in which the immanent evidence that the mind lives leads to the "disappropriation of the *mens* to itself": the fact that "I live" means "the certainty of not having the certainty of living again, or rather of having the certainty of not living by

oneself—living gives only the certainty of dying. Only the Living par excellence lives from itself." Marion, *In the Self's Place*, 60-62. Summarizing the difference between Augustine and Descartes, he concludes: "Saint Augustine is perfectly willing to admit the argument that connects thought to being; he even inaugurates it and will impose it upon posterity (including Descartes); but he refuses to let this same argument produce and consecrate any *ego* known by itself" (63). His arguments in this study complicate the lineage from Augustine to Husserl that has been asserted on the part of thinkers such as Pierre Hadot, who opens his essay, "L'image de la Trinité dans l'âme chez Victorinus et chez saint Augustin," with the claim: "In searching for the image of the Trinity within the structure of the intellectual power of the soul, Augustine [. . .] also revealed, in a way, to all Western thought a spiritual interiority that a Descartes or a Husserl would seek to rediscover in thinking of Saint Augustine." Pierre Hadot, "L'image de la Trinité dans l'âme chez Victorinus et chez saint Augustin," in *Études de patristique et d'histoire des concepts* (Paris: Belles Lettres, 2010), 283-317, 283; my translation. Further distinctions between Augustine's notion of the mind and the modern concept of the subject are elaborated in Alain de Libera's studies of Augustine, where the emphasis falls upon Augustine's express rejection of the term "subject" to describe the consubstantial operations of memory, cognition, and will, which make up the mind and establish it as an image of the Trinity. Alain de Libera, *Naissance du sujet* (Paris: Vrin, 2007), 228-95.

20. Augustine, *On the Trinity*, 370 (trans. modified); Augustine, *De trinitate*, XIII.1.2. See also Augustine's earlier variation on these lines of scripture in *De uera religione*: "There is no life which is not of God, for God is supreme life and the fount of life. No life is evil insofar as it is life but only insofar as it verges upon death." Augustine, *Of True Religion*, in *Augustine: Earlier Writings*, ed. and trans. J. H. S. Burleigh (London: SCM, 1953), 218-83, 235 (trans. modified); cf. Augustine, *De uera religione*, XI.21, in *De doctrina Christiana. De uera religione*, ed. Joseph Martin (Turnhout: Brepols, 1962). This text will be cited in the following by chapter and section number. In the third book of the *Confessions*, Augustine will also address God as the "life" of his soul, "more intimately present to me than my innermost being, and higher than the highest peak of my spirit." Augustine, *Confessions*, III.6.10-11. Olivier du Roy traces through this passage the "double movement of interiorizing and surpassing that is, for Augustine, the threshold of the transcendent." Du Roy, *L'intelligence de la foi*, 35; my translation.

21. Marcus Tullius Cicero, *Tusculan Disputations*, trans. J. E. King (Cambridge, MA: Harvard University Press, 1927), I.22. This text will be cited in the following by book and section.

22. Cicero cites his *Consolatio*, where he speaks of the soul's "power of memory, mind, and thought [*vim memoriae, mentis, cogitationis*]," so as to illustrate that its force and life cannot be derived from those corporeal elements that make up all that comes to be and passes away. Cicero, *Tusculan Disputations*, I.27.

23. Cicero, *Tusculan Disputations*, I.22. In Latin, the passage reads: "Nam corpus quidem quasi vas est aut aliquod animi receptaculum: ab animo tuo quidquid agitur, id agitur a te." This association between the body and a vessel was itself a commonplace, as Courcelle shows, tracing the ways in which the vessel-metaphor carries over from Plato to Aristotle, and then to "the Stoics, the Epicureans, and the Christians." Courcelle, *"Connais-toi toi-même,"* 1:35–37. However, Cicero's emphasis upon the activity of the soul is notably articulated in such a way that the soul and the self are still only obliquely related to what is done (*ab animo tuo* [. . .] *a te*), while their doings are related in the passive voice (*agitur* [. . .] *agitur*).

24. These arguments for the eternal life of the soul are drawn from Plato. For a discussion of Cicero's engagement in the *Tusculan Disputations* with the *Phaedo*, see William Stull, "Reading the *Phaedo* in Cicero's *Tusculan Disputations* 1," *Classical Philology* 107, no. 1 (2012): 38–52.

25. Augustine, *On the Trinity*, 306; trans. modified.

26. Augustine, *De trinitate*, X.9.12.

27. In his *Logical Investigations*, Husserl distinguishes between "signitive" meaning and intuitive fulfillment, which are necessary to differentiate, insofar as the latter may vary or remain absent entirely, without altering the unity of meaning that a given expression signifies. "Knowledge" (*Erkenntnis*), however, is said to be attained only when signitive intentions enter into "coverage" or "coincidence" (*Deckung*) with an "intuition" (*Anschauung*). Husserl, *Logical Investigations* 2:209–10; Husserl, *Hua* 19:570–71.

28. In his *Psychology from an Empirical Standpoint*, Franz Brentano argues at length for self-consciousness as the "secondary object" of every intentional act of mental representation. Franz Brentano, *Psychologie vom empirischen Standpunkt*, ed. Oskar Kraus, 3 vols. (Hamburg: Meiner, 1971–1974), 1:181; my translation. In his *Ideas Pertaining to a Pure Phenomenology*, Husserl translates his insistence upon prereflexive self-consciousness into Kantian terms, repeating the often-cited lines from Kant's *Critique of Pure Reason*: "In Kant's words, 'The "I think" must be capable of accompanying all my presentations' ['*Das "Ich denke" muß alle meine Vorstellungen begleiten können*']." Husserl, *Ideas 1*, 133; Husserl, *Hua* 3:123. For a discussion of more recent debates on this claim, see Dan Zahavi, *Self-Awareness and Alterity: A Phenomenological Investigation* (Evanston, IL: Northwestern University Press, 1999). In this monograph, Zahavi takes recourse to the same argument that Augustine would make, when he criticizes Ernst Tugendhat's claims that "I only attain self-awareness the moment I realize that Others are able to refer to me as well," writing: "How should I know that I am the one the Other is referring to unless I am already in possession of self-awareness?" Zahavi, *Self-Awareness*, 44.

29. The premise is described by Courcelle, who writes on the tenth book of *De trinitate*: "According to Augustine, knowledge of the subject through [the subject] itself is enveloped in the act of knowing itself, and the soul cannot know

a part of itself through another part. In this way, he follows a Plotinian line of argumentation to respond to the skeptical aporia presented in Sextus Empiricus, according to which all knowledge presupposes a division between the knowing subject and the known object. The soul knows itself in its entirety intuitively." Courcelle, *"Connais-toi toi-même,"* 1:154–55; my translation.

30. Augustine, *On the Teacher*, in *Earlier Writings*, 64–101, 93; trans. modified; Augustine, *De magistro* X.33, in *Contra academicos. De beata vita. De ordine. De magistro. De libero arbitrio*, ed. K. D. Dauer and W. M. Green (Turnhout: Brepols, 1970). References to the Latin version of this text will be provided in the following by chapter and section number.

31. Phillip Cary, *Outward Signs: The Powerlessness of External Things in Augustine's Thought* (Oxford: Oxford University Press, 2008), 94.

32. Cary, *Outward Signs*, 96. C. J. Mayer similarly asserts: "The proper function of signs [*signa*] is to admonish or excite [*admonere oder excitare*]." C. J. Mayer, "Signifikationshermeneutik im Dienste der Daseinsauslegung: Die Funktion der Verweisungen in den *Confessiones* X–XIII," *Augustiniana* 24 (1974): 21–74, 22; my translation. This article builds upon Mayer's more extensive analyses of signification and signs across Augustine's oeuvre in *Die Zeichen in der geistigen Entwicklung und in der Theologie des jungen Augustinus*, 2 vols. (Würzburg: Augustinus Verlag, 1969–1974). The same premise is echoed by Klaus Kahnert, who concludes in his discussion of *De magistro*, "In its admonitory function, memory remains the sole aim of language." Klaus Kahnert, *Entmachtung der Zeichen? Augustin über Sprache* (Philadelphia: John Benjamins, 2000), 72; my translation. In his discussion of *De magistro*, Étienne Gilson compares Augustine's treatment of signs to Plato's treatment of anamnesis in *Meno*, writing: "Any meaning which words are to convey to the minds of hearers must be present in those minds beforehand; these minds clothe the words they hear in the meaning they have beforehand, and only so do the words they hear become intelligible. Then there is the classic example given by Plato in the *Meno*. Socrates questions an ignorant slave about certain problems in geometry and establishes that the slave is capable of discovering the truth for himself. Since this ignorant man can answer questions when asked, he must have been able to answer them before they were asked." Étienne Gilson, *The Christian Philosophy of Saint Augustine*, trans. L. E. M. Lynch (New York: Vintage, 1967), 69–70. Brian Stock further elaborates the philosophical parallels and theological differences between *De magistro* and *Meno* in his study, *Augustine the Reader: Meditation, Self-Knowledge, and the Ethics of Interpretation* (Cambridge, MA: Harvard University Press, 1998), 147–62. Robert A. Markus summarizes the aporetic tension thus: "In order that I may know the meaning of signs," he writes, "I have to know, in the last resort, the things they stand for. On the other hand, I have to rely on the words and signs of teachers to receive the direct experience of these things." Robert A. Markus, "St. Augustine on Signs," *Phronesis* 2, no. 1 (1957): 60–83, 69.

33. For an example of Augustine's characterization of the senses as messengers, see Augustine, *Confessions*, X.6.10.

34. Augustine, *On True Religion*, 252–53; Augustine, *De uera religione*, XXX.55–56.

35. Cary, *Outward Signs*, 98.

36. As Augustine will say in *On True Religion*, there is no external evidence for unity: "Who would venture to say, after due consideration, that any body is truly and simply one? All are changed by passing from form to form or from place to place, and consist of parts each occupying its own place and extended in space." Augustine, *On True Religion*, 253; Augustine, *De uera religione*, XXX.55. But if unity is "known" only by the mind, the mind also does not create the notion itself and cannot explain the source of the ideals by which it reasons: hence, unable to explain itself, reason leads to faith.

37. Augustine, *On the Teacher*, 100; Augustine, *De magistro*, XIV.46.

38. Jacques Lacan, *The Seminar of Jacques Lacan: Book 1: Freud's Papers on Technique 1953-1954*, ed. Jacques-Alain Miller, trans. John Forrester (New York: W.W. Norton, 1991), 260. Inspired by Augustine's characterization of "Scripture [as] 'medicine for the mind,'" Brian Stock adopts a different therapeutic perspective, arguing that, for Augustine, "one speaks or writes the self" not to impart certitudes, but "because minds are unknowable," while the value of first-person fiction lies in the ethical effects that narrative may have upon the reader *and* the writer. Stock, *Augustine the Reader*, 227, 214. Louis Mackey similarly concludes that "the sign deflects and displaces presence irrecoverably"; hence, in order "to block this regress, Augustine continually harps on the necessity for faith." Louis H. Mackey, "The Mediator Mediated: Faith and Reason in Augustine's 'De Magistro,'" *Franciscan Studies* 42 (1982): 135–55, 152.

39. See A. A. Long, "Soul and Body in Stoicism," in *Stoic Studies* (Berkeley: University of California Press, 1996), 224–49.

40. "But if [the mind] were any one of [those corporeal things]," he writes, it "would think this one in a different manner than the rest. That is to say, it would not think it through an imaginary phantasy, as absent things or something of the same kind are thought which have been touched by the sense of the body, but it would think it by a kind of inward presence not feigned but real—for there is nothing more present to it than itself; just as it thinks that it lives, and remembers, and understands, and wills." Augustine, *On the Trinity* 309–10; cf. Augustine, *De trinitate*, X.10.16. These corporeal hypotheses were also addressed in Cicero's *Tusculan Disputations*, I.17.

41. He writes: "But when the word, *caput*, was frequently repeated, observing when it was said, I discovered it was the name of a thing well known to me from my having seen it." Augustine, *On the Teacher*, 93; cf. Augustine, *De magistro*, X.33.

42. Stock, *Augustine the Reader*, 215, 222–23.

43. Augustine, *On the Trinity*, 310; cf. Augustine, *De trinitate*, X.10.16.

44. "And to no one is it doubtful that no one can understand who does not live, nor live who does not exist," Augustine writes. Augustine, *On the Trinity*, 307 (trans. modified); cf. Augustine, *De trinitate*, X.10.13.

45. As Jean-Luc Nancy observes in the context of Descartes's foundational thought, namely: "I think": "In order to feign one must think, and in order to think one must be. However, this cannot be demonstrated. It cannot be demonstrated because it is truly a matter neither of a logical consecution nor of an ontological subordination. Or rather, what can only be exposed in the form of a logical consecution ('it was necessary that . . .') is actually given through an immediate apprehension and requires no operation of thought [*se donne en réalité par une appréhension immédiate et sans aucune opération de persée*]. Being as thought is not given by a thought, but through 'that internal awareness which always precedes reflective knowledge.'" Jean-Luc Nancy, *Ego Sum · Corpus, Anima, Fabula*, trans. Marie-Eve Morin (New York: Fordham University Press, 2016), 81; Jean-Luc Nancy, *Ego sum* (Paris: Flammarion, 1979), 117.

46. When it comes to "thyself," Augustine thus adopts the modus of address which differentiates, according to Marion, his way of speaking from the metaphysical and theological gestures of "speak[ing] *of* God, *of* principles, . . . *of* the soul." Early in his study, *In the Self's Place*, Marion writes: "It could just as well be that [Augustine] does not even belong to theology, in the sense that, with the vast majority of the Greek Fathers, it tries to speak *of* God, *of* principles [. . .]. For Saint Augustine does not so much speak *of* God as he speaks *to* God. [. . .] It therefore behooves us to read him from a point of view that is at least negatively identifiable: from a nonmetaphysical point of view." Marion, *In the Self's Place*, 9. Since, moreover, "Scripture precedes my own writing," the language of praise that Augustine addresses to God in his *Confessions*—but also the language that he will elsewhere use to address the "self"—is *a priori* "citation[al]" (24).

47. Augustine, *On the Trinity*, 306 (trans. modified); cf. Augustine, *De trinitate*, X.9.12.

48. Augustine, *On the Trinity*, 301 (trans. modified); cf. Augustine, *De trinitate*, X.5.7.

49. Augustine, *On the Trinity*, 301; cf. Augustine, *De trinitate*, X.5.7.

50. Augustine, *On the Trinity*, 301; Augustine, *De trinitate*, X.5.7.

51. Marion, *In the Self's Place*, 83–84.

52. Husserl, *Crisis*, 71; cf. Husserl, *Hua* 6:73.

53. Husserl, *Crisis*, 76; cf. Husserl, *Hua* 6:77.

54. Augustine, *On the Trinity*, 310 (trans. modified); Augustine, *De trinitate*, X.10.16.

55. Augustine, *On the Trinity*, 431 (trans. modified); Augustine, *De trinitate*, XIV.10.13. The Latin passage refers to all three substantial operations of the

mind: "Never has it desisted from remembering itself, never has it desisted from understanding itself, never has it desisted from loving itself, as we have already shown [*numquam sui meminisse, numquam se intellegere, numquam se amare destiterit sicut iam ostendimus*]."

56. Augustine, *On the Trinity*, 432 (trans. modified); cf. Augustine, *De trinitate*, XIV.10.13–11.14. Similar arguments may be found in other texts penned by Augustine, such as *De libero arbitrio*, which Courcelle discusses in *"Connais-toi toi-même,"* 1:133.

57. Augustine, *On the Trinity*, 432 (trans. modified); Augustine, *De trinitate*, XIV.11.14.

58. Augustine does, however, evoke involuntary memories and sexual phantasies that arise in his dreams even after his conversion in the *Confessions*: "Yet in my memory, of which I have spoken at length, sexual images survive, because they were imprinted there by former habit. While I am awake they suggest themselves feebly enough, but in dreams with power to arouse me not only to pleasurable sensations but even to consent, to something closely akin to the act they represent." Augustine, *Confessions*, X.30.41.

59. Gilson, *The Christian Philosophy*, 75. Gilson elaborates this thought further, writing that "the term 'memory' means much more than its modern psychological connotation designates, i.e. memory of the past. In St. Augustine it is applied to everything which is present to the soul (a presence which is evidenced by efficacious action) without being explicitly known or perceived. The only modern psychological terms equivalent to Augustinian *memoria* are 'unconscious' or 'subconscious,' provided that they too are expanded [. . .] to include the metaphysical presence within the soul of a reality distinct from it and transcendent, such as God, in addition to the presence to the soul of its own unperceived states." Gilson, *The Christian Philosophy*, 299. For a critical survey of other scholars who have adopted this interpretation, see Ronald J. Teske, *Augustine of Hippo: Philosopher, Exegete, and Theologian: A Second Collection of Essays* (Milwaukee: Marquette University Press, 2009), 61–76. Although Teske questions Gilson's expansive notion of a "memory of the present," he does not challenge the observation that the "memory of the present" describes "the mind's memory of itself." Teske, *Augustine of Hippo*, 63; cf. 68, 76.

60. Augustine, *On the Trinity*, 467; cf. Augustine, *De trinitate*, XV.7.12. Augustine will elaborate the triple essence of the human mind as the "image" of the Trinity in the fourteenth book of *De trinitate*. As Marion argues, however, this distinction entails that "man does not have a proper essence but a reference to an other than himself, who, more intimate to him than himself (than his lacking essence), occupies the essential place on loan to him." Marion, *In the Self's Place*, 254–55.

61. In an earlier clarification of Father and Son as relative terms that imply no diversity in essence, Augustine glosses "pater" not only with "genitor," but also

with "principium," within the context of the first verse of the Gospel of John, "In the beginning was the Word [*In principio erat verbum*]." This relation between Father and Son will later be aligned with the relation between divine memory and the Word that it begets. Insofar as the Word cannot be absent or lacking "in" the one whose word it is—"'In the beginning was the Word,' has to be understood in the sense that the Word was in the Father [*In principio erat verbum, in pater erat verbum intellegitur*]," Augustine writes—it could not be argued that the Father first begets the wisdom of the Word, without already being this Word himself. At the same time, moreover, the fact that this Word "was" entails that the Father could not have temporal priority over the Word. See Augustine, *On the Trinity*, 201; Augustine, *De trinitate*, VI.2.3; cf. Augustine, *Tractates on the Gospel of John 1–10*, trans. John W. Rettig (Washington, DC: Catholic University of America Press, 1988), 51; Augustine, *In Johannis Evangelium*, I.12.2. Lewis Ayres traces similar basic beliefs in the earlier fathers of the church, who advocated for the Nicene creed through the "assertion of the principle of unity of substance, the use of multiple scriptural languages, the ruling out of inappropriate ways of understanding, and perhaps deployment of the language of the divine three being 'in' one another." Lewis Ayres, *Augustine and the Trinity* (Cambridge: Cambridge University Press, 2010), 51.

62. Echoing earlier passages in which it is said that all things said of God are to be taken substantially, such that "to be [*esse*]" and "to be great [*magnum esse*]" say the same thing, Augustine writes of the relation between the Father and the wisdom that he begets in the person of the Son: "But the knowledge of God is also His wisdom, and His wisdom is His essence or substance itself. Because in the marvelous simplicity of that nature, it is not one thing to be wise, and another thing to be, but to be wise is the same as to be, as we have often mentioned in the preceding books. [. . .] Wherefore, just as our knowledge is unlike that knowledge of God, so our word, which is born from our knowledge, is also unlike that Word of God which is born from the essence of the Father." Augustine, *On the Trinity*, 485; Augustine, *De trinitate*, XV.13.22; cf. Augustine, *De trinitate* V.10.11.

63. The motif of "begetting" arises earlier, as when Augustine writes of how the human mind "sees itself through thought [and] understands itself and recognizes itself; consequently, it begets this, its own understanding and its own knowledge"; and so as not to suggest that the mind "begets" its original knowledge, he clarifies further: "Yet the mind does not indeed beget its own knowledge [*istam notitiam suam*] [. . .]. But it was known to itself as things known which are contained in the memory, even though they are not thought, since we say that a man knows letters, even when he is thinking of other things and not of the letters. But these two, the begetter and the begotten, are bound together by love as a third, and this is nothing else than the will seeking for or holding on to the enjoyment of something." Augustine, *On the Trinity*, 422; Augustine, *De trinitate*, XIV.6.8. The

designation of the "known" as the "noted" (*notitia*), moreover, lends knowledge a scriptural character, which Augustine underscores in the example of "letters," and which suggests that the "memory" or "knowledge" in question is structured like a trace, whose "presence" marks an absence and pertains to no moment that will have ever been lived as "present," as David Farrell Krell has shown in his reading of memory in the *Confessions*. Krell, *Of Memory, Reminiscence, and Writing*, 53–54; see also Jacques Derrida, *Of Grammatology*, trans. Gayatri Chakravorty Spivak (Baltimore: Johns Hopkins University Press, 1997), 44–65.

64. In his sermon on the burning bush, Augustine interprets the name that God gives himself in Exodus—namely, "ego sum qui sum" (Exodus 3.14)—to signify "I am eternal [*aeternus sum*]" and "I am he who cannot change [*qui mutari non possum*]." Augustine, *Sermon 7.7*, in Augustine, *Sermons, (1–19) on the Old Testament. Volume III/1*, ed. John E. Rotelle, trans. Edmund Hill (New York: New City, 1990), 237; cf. Augustine, *Sermones de vetere testamento (1–50)*, ed. C. Lambot (Turnhout: Brepols, 1961). See also Augustine, *Confessions*, VII.10.16.

65. According to the scriptural premises that Augustine adopts, the "fault in the self's structure arose from the disobedience of Adam and Eve in the Garden of Eden, which introduced to mortals a type of self-knowledge that was hitherto unknown, inasmuch as it was concerned with the ineradicable potential for good and evil that is lodged in us all." Stock, *The Integrated Self*, 4; cf. Augustine, *The City of God against the Pagans*, ed. and trans. R. W. Dyson (Cambridge: Cambridge University Press, 1998), 555; Augustine, *De Civitate Dei*, ed. B. Dombart and A. Kalb, 2 vols. (Turnhout: Brepols, 1955), XIII.13. References to the Latin edition of this text will be made in the following by book and chapter number.

66. Augustine, *On the Trinity*, 306 (trans. modified); Augustine, *De trinitate*, X.9.12.

67. Nancy, *Ego Sum*, 88; cf. Nancy, *Ego sum*, 135.

68. Nancy, *Ego Sum*, 97; cf. Nancy, *Ego sum*, 143.

69. This contingency is implicit as well in the lacuna that du Roy locates in his meticulous study of Augustine's articulation of the trinitarian structure of the mind in *De trinitate*, when he writes: "How this presence of the inalienable image [of God] renders the soul capable of remembering God, Augustine does not say." Du Roy, *L'intelligence de la foi*, 445; my translation.

70. In his erudite study of the ways in which Augustine develops a notion of an "integrated" self against the background of monastic ascetic practices designed to train body, soul, and mind towards God, Stock describes these efforts as modes of resistance to the "natural tendency of the soul towards directionless wandering." Stock, *The Integrated Self*, 44. It is, in a sense, an artificial "memory" that fashions "stability" for the "soul," and that renders "self-realization" synonymous with "self-transformation." Stock, *The Integrated Self*, 44, 46. Thus, Stock will later write of the "artificial memory of writing," with reference to "the Augustinian interpretation of the idea of anamnesis, [where] the soul is replaced by the text

and the notion of transmigration by that of commemorative reflections in the mind of the reader." Stock, *The Integrated Self*, 150. Whether this citational procedure can yield a "single integrated piece of writing," however, is not certain, not least because the citational character of memory leaves the act of mind which integration would require structurally unascertainable (152).

71. Many other readers have recognized this point and drawn various conclusions from it. O'Donnell notes that "speech and memory enter together" in his commentary on the *Confessions*. Augustine, *Confessions*, 2:56. Stock interprets the "absence of memory" which characterizes Augustine's discussions of infancy to signal that "the soul's education depend[s] on the infant's acquisition of speech." Stock, *Augustine the Reader*, 24. Jean-François Lyotard speaks of the unspeakably lost time of infancy—which Augustine nonetheless "confesses"—as "the sin of time, delay. The encounter with the act is missed from the beginning. The event comes before writing bears witness, and writing sets down once the event has passed. Confession reiterates this condition of childhood measured against the scale of full presence: I will have always been small with regard to your greatness." Jean-François Lyotard, *The Confession of Augustine*, trans. Richard Beardsworth (Stanford, CA: Stanford University Press, 2000), 27.

72. Augustine, *On the Trinity*, 420; cf. Augustine, *De trinitate*, XIV.5.7.

73. Augustine, *On the Trinity*, 337 (trans. modified); cf. Augustine, *De trinitate*, XI.8.15.

74. The imaginary quality of memories of sensible objects, which traces back to Platonic and Aristotelian thinking on the soul, is described in Augustine, *On the Trinity*, 333–40; cf. Augustine, *De trinitate*, XI.8.13–XI.10.17.

75. David Tell, "Beyond Mnemotechnics: Confession and Memory in Augustine," *Philosophy & Rhetoric* 39, no. 3 (2006): 233–53, 242.

76. Augustine, *On the Trinity*, 344 (trans. modified); Augustine, *De trinitate*, XII.2.2.

77. See Krell, *Of Memory, Reminiscence, and Writing*, 53–54. The critical role of language in memory has also been acknowledged by scholars such as Calvin L. Troup, who writes that "signs animate our memory and are prerequisite to epistemology. Access and use, even of intelligible things which reside in memory a priori, demand sensible discourse." Calvin L. Troup, *Temporality, Eternity, and Wisdom: The Rhetoric of Augustine's Confessions* (Columbia: University of South Carolina Press, 1999), 108.

78. Augustine, *On the Trinity*, 420; Augustine, *De trinitate*, XIV.5.8.

79. Giorgio Agamben, *Infancy and History: The Destruction of Experience*, trans. Liz Heron (London: Verso, 1993), 53. For a further discussion of Agamben's study, see Christopher Fynsk, *Infant Figures: The Death of the 'Infans' and Other Scenes of Origin* (Stanford, CA: Stanford University Press, 2000), 94–96.

80. Augustine, *On the Trinity*, 419 (trans. modified); Augustine, *De trinitate*, XIV.5.7.

81. The light that attracts the infant also resonates with the visible light which the Manicheans deified, and of which Augustine speaks critically already in his early dialogue, *De beata uita;* for a discussion of the relevant passages from the latter work, see du Roy, *L'intelligence de la foi*, 32. Insofar as infants are drawn to a false light, rather than the invisible light of God which is addressed in the prologue to the Gospel of John, the condition that Augustine describes here would continue until conversion. This implication is further suggested by the way in which Augustine recurs to "infancy" in his "Sermones ad Infantes," where, as Brian Stock has written, "infants refers to catechumens who have completed a programme of basic instruction and are to be taken before their bishop for baptism." Stock, *Augustine the Reader*, 24.

82. Blanchot, *Thomas the Obscure*, 15 (trans. modified); cf. Blanchot, *Thomas l'obscur*, 33. This translation is modified according to the way in which the passage appears in the first French version of Blanchot's text. It remains to be seen whether the sentences that immediately follow suggest that conscious perception remains operative in this vision: "Not only did this eye which saw nothing apprehend something [*quelque chose*], it apprehended the cause [*cause*] of its vision. It saw as object that which prevented it from seeing." Blanchot, *Thomas the Obscure*, 15; *Thomas l'obscur*, 33. While the conventional grammar relating a subject and object of apprehension appears recognizable in this passage, the apprehension of the "thing [*chose*]" or the "cause [*cause*]" of vision—which etymologically say the same "thing"—may also signify that the eye takes (*prendre*) itself toward (*ad*) nothing other than the sightless opening for vision, and thus takes itself toward the voiding of itself, along with the possibility of having an eye for anything else. It is for the same reason, moreover, that the phrase, "it saw as object," implies not only that the eye saw what "prevented it from seeing," but also that the eye saw in the manner of an object, that is, as that which does not see in being seen. The passage as a whole presents, moreover, an inversion of the model of luminosity that Plotinus had described in his *Enneads*, where the subject and object of vision coincide in the self-illumination of the intellect's proper, luminous cause: "There [in the intellect], it is not through another, but through itself" that light is seen, "for there is no outside. Another light sees in another light, not through another. For the one light sees another light; for light sees itself [ἐκεῖ δὲ οὐ δι'ἑτέρου, ἀλλὰ δι'αὐτῆς, ὅτι μηδὲ ἔξω. Ἄλλωι οὖν φωτὶ ἄλλο φῶς ὁρᾶι, οὐ δι'ἄλλου. Φῶς ἄρα φῶς ἄλλο ὁρᾶι αὐτὸ ἄρα αὐτὸ ὁρᾶι]." Plotinus, *Enneads*, V.3.8; my translation; in Plotinus, *Ennéades*, ed. Émile Bréhier, vol. 5 (Paris: Belles Lettres, 1931), 59. Augustine's knowledge and allusions to this Neoplatonic source is discussed in du Roy, *L'intelligence de la foi*, 145. For an excellent discussion of this passage from Blanchot in its (a)theological contexts, see Kevin Hart, *The Dark Gaze: Maurice Blanchot and the Sacred* (Chicago: University of Chicago Press, 2004), 26–27. William S. Allen also discusses the echoes between Plotinus's words on luminosity and Blanchot's description of "an eye that sees without seeing anything"

in his study, *Aesthetics of Negativity: Blanchot, Adorno, and Autonomy* (New York: Fordham University Press, 2016), 156–58.

83. Augustine, *On the Trinity*, 263 (trans. modified); cf. Augustine, *De trinitate*, VIII.8.12. In the fifteenth book of *De trinitate*, Augustine argues that the "will" or "voluntas" of God is properly said of the Holy Spirit, which he immediately glosses as "love"—"caritas"—before posing the rhetorical question that implies their identity: "For what else is love [*caritas*] than will [*voluntas*]?" Augustine, *On the Trinity*, 505; Augustine, *De trinitate*, XV.20.38. For an elucidating discussion of the evolution of Augustine's thought on the relation between love and will, see Hannah Arendt, *The Life of the Mind*, 2 vols. (New York: Harcourt, 1978), 2:84–104.

84. Miles Burnyeat will claim in his discussion of the first book of the *Confessions* that "the divine presence" is what "explains" Augustine's exceptional first memory of learning to speak, as well as the transition from infancy to speaking subjectivity. Miles Burnyeat, "The Inaugural Address: Wittgenstein and Augustine, De Magistro," *Proceedings of the Aristotelian Society* 61 (1987): 1–26, 4.

85. Augustine, *On the Trinity*, 306.

86. Fynsk also writes of infancy as "an opening *of language* that cannot be brought to speech and yet attends every speech event like the trace of a primal scene." Fynsk, *Infant Figures*, 178.

87. The phrase "eo ictu" is drawn from Augustine's discussion of the precept, "Know thyself." Augustine, *On the Trinity*, 306 (trans. modified); Augustine, *De trinitate*, X.9.12.

88. Agamben, *Infancy and History*, 7.

89. Blanchot, *The Infinite Conversation*, 55; cf. Blanchot, *L'entretien infini*, 79.

90. Many of these features of infantile experience will return at the critical limits of Husserl's thinking as well. In his posthumously published manuscripts on the "lifeworld," Husserl speaks of the anonymous, necessarily unexperienced onset of subjective, temporal experience as "a μὴ ὄν; it is not nothing, but the 'presupposition' of being from out of a forgotten temporalization, which is not yet the temporalization of an ὄν [*ein μὴ ὄν, es ist nicht nichts, sondern 'Voraussetzung' des Seins aus einer vergessenen Zeitigung, die noch nicht Zeitigung eines ὄν ist*]." Husserl, *Hua* 39:471; my translation. The point of departure for Husserl's remarks, however, remains the subject of "I am [*Ich bin*]" and "I think [*ich denke*]," which the child will have become. Husserl, *Hua* 39:471; my translation; cf. Husserl, *Hua* 39:479. In his late manuscripts on intersubjectivity, where children likewise appear among the foreign and forgotten subjectivities whose understanding he seeks to reconstruct, Husserl also insists upon departing from the familiar rather than the foreign, insofar as the inquiring phenomenological subject *is* an adult consciousness: "Every man—my semblable. Each an 'other,' each will be experienced in understanding as a modification of myself [*Jeder Mensch—meinesgleichen. Jeder ein 'Anderer,' jeder verstehend erfahren als Abwandlung meiner selbst*]." Husserl, *Hua* 15:622; my translation.

91. Augustine, *Confessions*, I.8.13.

92. Lyotard, *The Confession of Augustine*, 27. As Augustine writes in his *Confessions*, "so I have been told [*hoc enim de mihi indicatum est*]" (I.6.8). In his commentary, O'Donnell notes that "indicatum est" is a "favoured verb (28 X) in *conf.*," but he does not comment further upon how this designation of adult testimony as "indicated" may also index its tentative character, insofar as it does not signify something that can be known, properly speaking, but rather marks the interpretive gestures which others make towards an experience that had irrevocably escaped the very person who lived through it. O'Donnell, *Confessions*, 2:37.

93. Burnyeat likewise recognizes the exceptionality of this memory, which he contrasts with the accounts of infancy that Augustine had previously related as hearsay. Noting that Augustine's account of learning language does not "rest on testimony or inference from observation," he claims that "*Post adverti* ('I have since realized') is stronger than and different from *credidi* ('I believed') and *conieci* ('I conjectured')." Burnyeat, "The Inaugural Address," 4.

94. Augustine, *Confessions*, I.8.13.

95. Agamben, *Infancy and History*, 48.

96. Boulding's translation is more frequently modified in this quotation than elsewhere in this chapter, for even if Augustine's enunciation could also be rendered in a way that supplies referents for his pronouns, as Boulding does in her rendition of the passage: "I was unable to express the thoughts of my heart by cries and inarticulate sounds and gestures in such a way as to gain what I wanted or make my entire meaning clear to everyone as I wished," such choices obscure how the indetermination of Augustine's rhetoric exposes the infant's original ignorance of signs to entail an equally radical indeterminacy of will, which renders all volition necessarily ineffective, which is also to say—: what Augustine calls infantile "will" will have been destined to fail itself. Augustine, *Confessions*, I.8.13. Philip Burton points to the "infinite regress" that the will to will implies in this passage—whereby "wishing," as Burton also argues, is indistinguishable from "meaning"—but he does not comment further upon the self-cancelling implications of the radical absence of an object or an addressee for this "meaning." Philip Burton, *Language in the* Confessions *of Augustine* (Oxford: Oxford University Press, 2007), 174.

97. Fynsk, *Infant Figures*, 77.

98. Augustine, *On the Teacher*, 71 (trans. modified); cf. Augustine, *De magistro*, II.3. Because there is nothing more to know or say of this affection of privation, he immediately goes on to state: "But let us go on [. . .], lest something most absurd [*res absurdissima*] befall us." Augustine, *On the Teacher*, 71 (trans. modified); cf. Augustine, *De magistro*, II.3. The strictly unknowable character of privation is elaborated at greater length when Augustine addresses evil as a "deficient cause" in, among others, the twelfth book of *The City of God*. Augustine, *The City of God*, 507–8; cf. Augustine, *De Civitate Dei*, XII.7.

99. Augustine, *Confessions*, I.6.7. Boulding's translation is more frequently modified in this quotation than elsewhere in this chapter, since the version that Boulding offers does not reflect the insistent repetition of "dare" or "to give," which organizes the entire description of the relationship between the infant and his nurses as one that depends upon a divine grace that exceeds them. Boulding renders the passage thus: "You restrained me from craving more than you provided, and inspired in those who nurtured me the will to give me what you were giving them."

100. Augustine, *Confessions*, I.8.13.

101. The fact that Augustine does not cross this phenomenological limit of givenness but rather exposes its structure to differ from Husserl's later descriptions, emerges from the way in which Augustine elaborates the givenness of self through his experience of emerging from infancy, whereas Husserl evokes "self-givenness" or "Selbstgebung" as the limiting principle that would preclude a "psychology of early childhood [*Psychologie der Frühkindheit*]": "Do I not have [. . .] the task of making the bundled infant understandable to myself in his inner life [. . .]? 'Psychology of early childhood.' [. . .] In a certain sense, that is correct. And yet there is precisely a radical and essential cut here [*ein radikaler und wesensmässiger Schnitt*]. The world as the world of real and possible experience reaches only so far as experience in the proper sense of self-givenness [*Selbstgebung*], self-demonstration [*Selbstausweisung*] reaches." Husserl, *Hua* 15:620; my translation.

102. Augustine, *Confessions*, I.8.13.

103. Augustine, *Confessions*, I.8.13. This undecidable trait of "memory" speaks against Algis Mickunas's insistence "that the self is memory, that the self finds itself in memory," whose atemporality guarantees "the soul's continuous identity with itself." Algis Mickunas, "Self-Identity and Time," in *Augustine for the Philosophers: The Rhetor of Hippo, the* Confessions, *and the Continentals*, ed. Calvin L. Troup (Waco: Baylor University Press, 2014), 107–25, 115–16. The original alterity of memorial traces would confirm, however, the conclusion Mickunas draws from Husserl's further elaborations of the problems that Augustine had exposed in his writings on memory, self-identity, and time: "If the self is an anonymous life, then it cannot have the slightest power of disposal over itself. In this context, it is difficult to say which activities are of the self and which belong to an ego as distancing from the self, as the sense of otherness." Mickunas, "Self-Identity and Time," 124.

104. Augustine, *On the Teacher*, 74 (trans. modified); Augustine, *De magistro* III.6. The passage reads in full: "A special case would arise if, while I was speaking, someone asked me what 'speaking' was. In order to let him know I must speak, whatever I actually may say. And I shall continue to show him until I make plain to him what he wants to know, not departing from the actual thing which he wished to have demonstrated to him, and yet not seeking signs apart from the thing itself wherewith to demonstrate it."

105. Augustine, *Teaching Christianity*, trans. Edmund Hill (New York: New City, 1996), 135 (trans. modified); Augustine, *De doctrina christiana*, II.9.14. The practice that Augustine recommends may also be read in the context of the Christian ascetic reading practices that Stock describes, where words of prayer were to be "ceaselessly meditated upon" in the "heart," until their sense was assumed by the soul, to the exclusion of extraneous thoughts. But Stock does not comment further in this context upon the possibilities of void meaning that such iteration structurally could not exclude. Stock, *The Integrated Self*, 28–29.

106. Jacques Derrida, "Circumfession: Fifty-Nine Periods and Periphrases, Written in a Sort of Internal Margin, between Geoffrey Bennington's Book and Work in Preparation (January 1989–April 1990)," trans. Geoffrey Bennington, in *Jacques Derrida*, by Geoffrey Bennington and Jacques Derrida (Chicago: University of Chicago Press, 1993), 87.

107. Augustine, *Confessions*, I.8.13.

108. Aristotle, *De interpretatione*, 16a. Again, the English translation that is offered here is adapted from the one which is offered in Waltz, "The Opening of 'On Interpretation,'" 231–32. For a discussion of Augustine's likely knowledge of this Aristotelian text, see "Introduction," 1.

109. In a discussion of the finitude of the human mind, in distinction to the infinite mind of God, Augustine writes: "We do not conjecture the past from the future, but the future from the past, yet not with a sure knowledge. [. . .] This can be proved by those sayings and hymns which we render from memory in the proper sequence. For unless we foresaw in our thought what follows, we certainly could not utter them. And yet it is memory, not foresight, that enables us to foresee them [. . .]. We do not say that we sing or speak from foresight, but from memory [*non dicimur prouidenter sed memoriter canere uel dicere*]." Augustine, *On the Trinity*, 468; Augustine, *De trinitate*, XV.7.13.

110. Augustine, *Confessions*, III.4.8. Boulding's rendition of the passage, "How ardently I longed," conveys the same sense, but the fire of Augustine's outspoken fervor is less pronounced.

111. Lyotard, *The Confessions*, 29. With an accent upon different texts and contexts, David J. Depew arrives at a similar observation through a genealogy of linguistic thought from Augustine to Lyotard and Derrida: "Language (*langue*) endlessly repeats and circulates these signs. Yet there is no speech occasion or speech act (*parole*) in which the very same thing is or can be repeated. There is always a difference, even in the 'I.' There is always a new event that happens. In this way, indeterminacy worms its way into the system of language itself, and the evental quality of predication—the fact that it happens out of nowhere, which Aristotle both recognized and attempted to subvert by subsuming language under general terms—is liberated from its grammatical tomb to make possible Events with a capital 'E.' Derrida's playfulness with language enacts a serious philosophical claim." David J. Depew, "Lyotard's Augustine," in *Augustine for the Philosophers:*

The Rhetor of Hippo, the Confessions, and the Continentals, ed. Calvin L. Troup (Waco: Baylor University Press, 2014), 59–76, 69–70. Yet what this reading of Augustine draws out is that the "Event" of difference is itself undecidable, as Derrida's writings would also reiterate.

112. Bataille, *Inner Experience*, 94; Bataille, *OC* 5:111–12.

113. Augustine, *Confessions*, I.8.13.

114. Augustine, *On the Trinity*, 420 (trans. modified); Augustine, *De trinitate*, XIV.5.7.

115. Lacan, *The Seminar of Jacques Lacan: Book 1*, 260.

116. Husserl, *Cartesian Meditations*, 157; trans. modified.

117. Just before the passage quoted below, Augustine speaks of created life as one that is "alive even in its own dark turbulence [*vivit etiam fluitans in obscuritate sua*]." Augustine, *Confessions*, XIII.4.5.

118. Augustine, *Confessions*, XIII.7.8.

119. Augustine, *Enarrationes in Psalmos I-L*, ed. E. Dekkers and J. Fraipont (Turnhout: Brepols, 1956), XLI.12. Throughout, references to this text will be provided by psalm and section number; all translations, unless otherwise noted, are mine.

120. Augustine, *Enarrationes in Psalmos*, XLI.13.

121. For a survey and bibliography of prior, allegorical interpretations of the "abyss," see I. Bochet's introductory notes in Augustine of Hippo, *Les commentaires des Psaumes: Enarrationes in Psalmos, Ps. 37–44*, ed. M. Dulaey et al. (Paris: Institut d'Études Augustiniennes, 2017), 358–59.

122. Augustine, *Enarrationes in Psalmos*, XLI.13.

123. Augustine, *Enarrationes in Psalmos*, XLI.13. After defining an abyss as a profundity, in the precise sense of that "which cannot be penetrated down to a fundament [*quae penetrari usque ad fundum non potest*]," Augustine explicitly points to the connection between this notion and the human heart: "If an abyss is a profundity, do we not repute the human heart to be an abyss? What, then, is more profound than this abyss? [*Si profunditas est abyssus, putamus non cor hominis abyssus est? Quid enim est profundius hac abysso?*]." Augustine, *Enarrationes in Psalmos*, XLI.13.

124. Augustine, *Confessions*, I.8.13.

125. Smith, *Speech and Theology*, 135. Smith develops careful arguments for "an absence at the core of the self" in Augustine, and he locates language "in a space construed as a *rift*, an abyss between interiorities." Smith, *Speech and Theology*, 135–37. But one could add that the "self," as Augustine addresses it, would also be cut through with a multiplicity of voices, which turns inner life inside out *ab initio*. It is in unfolding these latter implications of Augustine's writing on language that the readings offered in this chapter differ from Smith's elucidating interpretation, as well as from the one offered by Courcelle, who cites Augustine's assertions that "man [. . .] does not know what takes place within

him [*ce qui se passe en lui*]," but who insists nonetheless upon a self, whom God "makes us know" by "speaking to us and illuminating us." Courcelle, *"Connais-toi toi-même,"* 1:134, 137; my translation.

126. This line appears in the sixteenth Psalm. In *The City of God*, Augustine comments upon the seemingly counterintuitive claim that "I" cried because God heard me: "When, namely, the psalmist "said: 'I cried out,' then, as if someone had asked him to prove that he had cried, he uses the effect—that is, God's answering his cry—to prove his own act. It is as if he had said, The proof that I have cried out is that Thou hast heard me" [*Sed cum dixisset: Ego clamavi, tamquam ab eo quaereretur, unde se clamasse monstraret, ab effectu exauditionis Dei clamoris sui ostendit affectum; tamquam diceret: Hinc ostendo clamasse me, quoniam exaudisti me*]." Augustine, *The City of God*, 468–69 (trans. modified); Augustine, *De Civitate Dei*, XI.14.

127. Jacques Derrida, "Composing Circumfession," in *Augustine and Postmodernism: Confessions and Circumfession*, ed. John D. Caputo and Michael J. Scanlon (Bloomington: Indiana University Press, 2005), 19–27, 25.

128. Kafka, *Nachgelassene Schriften und Fragmente II*, 348; my translation.

129. Stock, *The Integrated Self*, 3. Among the many passages in which Augustine speaks to the radical precarity of belief, his commentary on the "abyssus" of Psalm 41 includes a discussion of Peter's betrayal of Christ, despite his outspoken assurances of fidelity: "What profundity of infirmity was hidden latent in Peter, when he did not know what was at work within himself and promised with temerity to die with the Lord or for the sake of the Lord!" Augustine, *Enarrationes in Psalmos*, XLI.13. This radical precarity is emphasized in Marion, *In the Self's Place*, as well as in Martin Heidegger's early lecture courses on Augustine and the factical traits of religious experience in Martin Heidegger, *Phenomenology of Religious Life*, trans. Matthias Fritsch and Jennifer Anna Gosetti-Ferencei (Bloomington: Indiana University Press, 2004); cf. Martin Heidegger, *Phänomenologie des religiösen Lebens*.

130. Augustine, *Enarrationes in Psalmos*, XLI.13.

131. Augustine, *Enarrationes in Psalmos*, XLI.13. This remark implies not only that teaching could take place only surreptitiously, but also that wisdom and faith would be untraceable for the very ones who may come to receive it.

132. Husserl, *Cartesian Meditations*, 83; cf. Husserl, *Hua* 1:116; Husserl, *Crisis*, 71.

Chapter 2

1. Edmund Husserl, *Analyses Concerning Passive and Active Synthesis: Lectures on Transcendental Logic*, trans. Anthony J. Steinbock (Dordrecht: Kluwer, 2001), 41; Husserl, *Hua* 11:5. In one of his later manuscripts on inner time

consciousness from the early 1930s, Husserl adopts a similarly dramatic rhetoric to describe the gradual constitution of the intentional object: "In the explication of an object, there come ever new moments that begin pressing to get into words and get a hearing [*die sich zunächst aufdrängen, zu Wort und Gehör*]." Edmund Husserl, *Späte Texte über Zeitkonstitution (1929–1934): Die C-Manuskripte*, ed. Dieter Lohmar (Dordrecht: Springer, 2006), 192; my translation.

2. Husserl, *Hua* 15:462; my translation.

3. Husserl, *Analyses*, 166; cf. Husserl, *Hua* 11:121.

4. Husserl, *Analyses*, 224; cf. Husserrl, *Hua* 11:175.

5. As he speaks of the "most primitive" state of affections, Husserl writes in one manuscript on passive synthesis: "Already prior to every turning toward, the particular elements [of sensible groups] have a community exercising affection in their particularity: they stand in a relationship of 'resonance' ['*Resonanz*'], one promotes the other, that is, the affective allure on the ego by the one promotes the affective allure of the other, and vice versa, but in such a way that these affective allures do not remain separated, but rather go together to form the unity of one multi-radiating affective allure [*mehrstrahligen affektiven Reizes*] in which the augmented affective allures are unified, and in this unification, each one bears the character of reciprocally furthering and resonating with one another ('recalling' each other)." Husserl, *Analyses*, 521–22; Husserl, *Hua* 11:418. The same rhetoric marks Husserl's description of association in *Experience and Judgment*, where he writes: "Association comes into question in this context exclusively as the *purely immanent connection of 'this recalls that'* ['*etwas erinnert an etwas*'], 'one calls attention to the other' ['*eines weist auf das andere hin*']." Edmund Husserl, *Experience and Judgment: Investigations in a Genealogy of Logic*, trans. James S. Churchill and Karl Ameriks (London: Routledge, 1973), 75; Edmund Husserl, *Erfahrung und Urteil: Untersuchungen zur Genealogie der Logik*, ed. Ludwig Landgrebe (Prague: Academia Verlagsbuchhandlung, 1939), 78.

6. Husserl, *Analyses*, 224; Husserl, *Hua* 11:175.

7. Husserl, *Späte Texte*, 192; my translation.

8. Dastur, *Questions of Phenomenology*, 36.

9. Bruce Bégout, *La généalogie de la logique: Husserl, l'antéprédicatif et le catégorial* (Paris: Vrin, 2000), 109; my translation. This dissimulation of an origin recapitulates precisely the feature of subreption that Sng underscores when he speaks of this structure in his reading of Kant's philosophy as a reflexive, specular dynamic "that reverses origin and goal." Zachary Sng, *The Rhetoric of Error from Locke to Kleist* (Stanford, CA: Stanford University Press, 2010), 101.

10. As Klaus Held also observes in his study of the auto-temporalization of transcendental subjectivity: "It leaves the realm of reflexive graspability, intuitiveness, demonstrability; it entertains the possibility that there are not only *riddles* to which possible solutions belong, but also questions which cannot be answered with reference to an originarily giving, objective 'presence in person.'" See Klaus

Held, *Lebendige Gegenwart: Die Frage nach der Seinsweise des transzendentalen Ich bei Edmund Husserl entwickelt am Leitfaden der Zeitproblematik* (The Hague: Nijhoff, 1966), 145; my translation. In other words, the questions of genetic phenomenology themselves lead back past the principle of intuitive givenness that Husserl insists upon elsewhere.

    11. Husserl, *Experience and Judgment*, 95 (trans. modified); Husserl, *Erfahrung und Urteil*, 103–4.

    12. Husserl, *Hua* 39:454; my translation.

    13. Bégout, *La généalogie*, 137, 139; my translation.

    14. Anne Montavont, *De la passivité dans la phénoménologie de Husserl* (Paris: Presses Universitaires de France, 1999), 244; my translation.

    15. Already as Husserl approaches knowledge in his *Logical Investigations*, he writes: "A class of acts—those known as 'objectifying'—are in fact marked off from all others, in that the fulfilment-syntheses appropriate to their sphere have the character of *knowings*, of *identifications*, of a 'setting-into-one' of that which is 'consonant' ['*Übereinstimmendem*'], while their syntheses of disappointment, accordingly, have the correlative character of the 'separation' of that which 'conflicts' ['*Widerstreitendem*']." Husserl, *Logical Investigations*, 2:184 (trans. modified); cf. Husserl, *Hua* 19.1:539. In a study from the 1920s, Husserl will repeat still more categorically: "In every case, the production of univocity, and ultimately, the perduring univocity of the sum total of experience is possible, and solely in it [univocity], as is self-evident, is thorough and consistently doubtless cognizance taken of the existing world." Husserl, *Hua* 7:244–45; my translation. For all the differences between the *Logical Investigations* and Husserl's later writings, the rhetoric of univocity and consonance is maintained, as when he contrasts less complete experiences of evidence with the ideal completion of evidential experience in the *Cartesian Meditations*: the latter, he writes, unfolds "as a synthetic course of further univocal / harmonious [*einstimmiger*] experiences in which these attendant meanings become fulfilled in actual experience." Husserl, *Cartesian Meditations*, 15 (trans. modified); Husserl, *Hua* 1:55. Husserl also emphasizes the relationship between univocity and the structure of the world as such in, among others, the second volume of his *Ideas Pertaining to a Pure Phenomenology*, where the norm for perceptual experience is determined by correlative appearances "that coalesce into a unity of univocal / concordant [*einstimmigen*] experience." Edmund Husserl, *IdeasIzed Pertaining to a Pure Phenomenology and to a Phenomenological Philosophy: Second Book: Studies in the Phenomenology of Constitution*, trans. Richard Rojcewicz and André Schuwer (Dordrecht: Kluwer, 1989), 71 (trans. modified); cf. Husserl, *Hua* 4:66. In the following, the title of this volume will be abbreviated, *Ideas 2*. Natalie Depraz has drawn attention to the harmonizing thrust of Husserl's thought, which she reads as an indication of the originally nonvisual and nonstatic structure of passive formations. Commenting on Husserl's characterization of passive association as resonance, Depraz observes: "A contrast is necessary with

association by resemblance, which permits awakening, then resonance. The appeal to terms with musical connotation testifies to an apprehension of the phenomenon that is essentially sonorous, pre-logical, but also pre-visual." Natalie Depraz, *Transcendence et incarnation: Le status de l'intersubjectivité comme altérité à soi chez Husserl* (Paris: Vrin, 1995), 129; my translation.

16. Husserl, *Hua* 9:396; my translation. The constitutive ideality and alterity of language, which expose "inner" monologue to iteration and to the words of others, respectively, is discussed at length in Derrida, *Speech and Phenomena*, 72–87. For another analysis of the intersubjectivity that intervenes in monologic discourse, see Bernhard Waldenfels, *Das Zwischenreich des Dialogs: Sozialphilosophische Untersuchungen im Anschluss an Edmund Husserl* (The Hague: Nijhoff, 1971), 164.

17. Husserl, *Experience and Judgment*, 95 (trans. modified); cf. Husserl, *Erfahrung und Urteil*, 103–4.

18. Husserl, *Analyses*, 250; cf. Husserl, *Hua* 11:199.

19. In the fourth of his meditations, Husserl writes: "The *universal principle of passive genesis*, for the constitution of all objectivities given completely prior to the products of activity, bears the title *association*." Husserl, *Cartesian Meditations*, 80; cf. Husserl, *Hua* 1:113.

20. Husserl, *Späte Texte*, 191; my translation. The linguistic character of this "dispute [*Streit*]" is emphasized in a similar passage from Husserl's manuscripts that Bégout cites: "Various affections can meet in the ego, loose and intensive ones, different affections, [and] such [affections] of different 'objects,' 'sense,' 'sentences,' inhibit one another, disturb one another, stand in affective counterstrife [*Es können mancherlei Affektionen im Ich zusammentreffen, schlaffe und intensive, verschiedene Affektionen, solche verschiedener 'Gegenstände,' 'Sinn,' 'Sätze,' hemmen sich, stören sich, stehen in affektivem Widerstreit*]." Quoted in Bégout, *La généalogie*, 186; my translation.

21. Husserl, *Cartesian Meditations*, 114 (trans. modified) cf. Husserl, *Hua* 1:144.

22. Husserl, *Cartesian Meditations*, 114; cf. Husserl, *Hua* 1:144.

23. For a discussion of "tuning in" to a musical performance as a model of intersubjective experience, see Alfred Schütz, "Making Music Together: A Study in Social Relationship,' *Social Research* 18, no. 1 (1951): 76–97. The distinguishing feature of music, according to Schütz, should stem from the fact that its structure as a temporal object lends itself to bringing disparate, singular streams of "inner" time consciousness to coincide.

24. Summarizing the passive transfers that Husserl traces between the ego and the alter ego, Theunissen writes: "I become a real, objective I, as whom I find myself in the natural attitude. As an objective I, I am a human and as a human, I am, on the one hand, a human among inhuman worldly objects, and on the other hand, a human among humans. [. . .] The fact that I am a human worldly object

among inhuman worldly objects follows from out of the unification of my "I" with my body that was carried out by the foreign-I [. . .], as my body appears to the foreign-I as a localized, spatiotemporal worldly object among other worldly objects. [. . .] Insofar as it makes me a thing, the alteration that I suffer through the other is [. . .] an instance of *becoming-something-other*. By contrast, I also become *an* other thanks to my being inserted in the community of humans. [. . .] We shall terminologically bring the becoming-*an*-other and the becoming-*something*-other under a common denominator, in that we designate the alteration which I [. . .] suffer through the other as '*Veränderung.*'" Theunissen, *Der Andere*, 84; my translation. The passage in German reads: "Durch den Anderen werde ich zum objektiven, realen Ich, als das ich mich in der natürlichen Einstellung vorfinde. Als objektives Ich bin ich Mensch und als Mensch bin ich einerseits Mensch unter nichtmenschlichen Weltobjekten, andererseits Mensch unter Menschen. [. . .] Daß ich als Mensch Weltobjekt unter nichtmenschlichen Weltobjekten bin, folgt aus der vom Fremdich unter der Voraussetzung der objektiven Welt vollzogenen Vereinigung meines Ich mit meinem Körper, der dem Fremdich eben als ein raumzeitlich lokalisiertes Weltobjekt unter anderen Weltobjekten erscheint. [. . .] Als Verdinglichung genommen, ist aber die Veränderung, die ich durch den Anderen erleide, nach allem, was wir hier angeführt haben, ein *Zu-etwas-Anderem-werden*. Demgegenüber werde ich dank meiner Einordnung in den Menschheitsverband zu *einem* Anderen. [. . .] Das Zu-*einem*-Anderen- und das Zu-*etwas*-Anderem-werden bringen wir terminologisch auf einen gemeinsamen Nenner, indem wir die Veränderung, die ich hier wie dort durch den Anderen erleide, als '*Veränderung*' bezeichnen."

25. Hamacher, "What Remains to Be Said," 255; cf. Hamacher, "Was zu sagen bleibt," 117.

26. Augustine, *Enarrationes in Psalmos*, XLI.13.

27. Paul Ricoeur, "A Study of Husserl's *Cartesian Meditations* I–IV," in *Husserl: An Analysis of His Phenomenology*, trans. Edward G. Ballard and Lester E. Embree (Evanston, IL: Northwestern University Press, 1967), 82–114, 99; cf. Paul Ricoeur, "Étude sur les 'Méditations Cartésiennes' de Husserl," in *À l'école de la phénoménologie* (Paris: Vrin, 1986), 161–95, 179. Bégout insists that because passive syntheses found the logical operations of consciousness—and because they are nothing if not *for* transcendental consciousness—"inferior passivity contains nothing in itself that is *refractory* to predicative grasp." Bégout, *La généalogie*, 224; my translation. Later, however, he will argue that "it is because the *one* pre-constitutes itself in passive multiplicity that the highest logical acts can be reduced to this pre-logification of objectal affections into a unity of sense," without entering further into the implications of the ways in which passive tendencies may also *not* coalesce. Bégout, *La généalogie*, 308; my translation. The constitution or preconstitution of associatives unities may itself be an effect of repression, which will be discussed in the last pages of this chapter.

28. Depraz, *Transcendance et incarnation*, 119; my translation. Later, Depraz will return to the alterity that is already "at work" in the passivity of "the flesh" as that which prepares for the experience of intersubjectivity, with reference to similar arguments on the part of Paul Ricoeur, who speaks of passivity as "*the attestation of alterity [l'attestation même de l'altérité]*" at the core of the self. Depraz, *Transcendance et incarnation*, 273; my translation; Ricoeur, *Oneself as Another*, 318; Ricoeur *Soi-même comme un autre*, 368.

29. Maurice Merleau-Ponty, *The Phenomenology of Perception*, trans. Donald A. Landes (London and New York: Routledge, 2012), 222; cf. Maurice Merleau-Ponty, *La phénoménologie de la perception*, in *Oeuvres*, ed. Claude Lefort (Paris: Gallimard, 2010), 655–1167, 904.

30. Marion, *Being Given*, 269.

31. Gilles Deleuze, *Difference and Repetition*, trans. Paul Patton (New York: Columbia University Press, 1994), 72–73, 78–79 (trans. modified); Gilles Deleuze, *Différence et répétition* (Paris: Presses Universitaires de France, 1968), 99–100, 106–7.

32. Lawlor, *Derrida and Husserl: The Basic Problem of Phenomenology* (Bloomington: Indiana University Press, 2002), 22.

33. Derrida, *Edmund Husserl's* Origin of Geometry, 90. Derrida's description in this text of the paradoxical contingency of ideality upon the historical facticity of linguistic "embodiment" is anticipated, however, in the paradoxes that Derrida had traced in his earlier study, *The Problem of Genesis in Husserl's Philosophy*, where his analysis of the passive genesis of temporality suggests the need to replace "the pure 'ego' [. .] by a subject producing itself in a history which, passively received by the subject in its intentional moment, can no longer be individual and monadic." Jacques Derrida, *The Problem of Genesis in Husserl's Philosophy*, trans. Marian Hobson (Chicago: University of Chicago Press, 2003), 93.

34. Derrida, *Edmund Husserl's* Origin of Geometry, 104.

35. The recurrence of this motif across very different readers of Husserl, from Merleau-Ponty to Deleuze, is meant to suggest the passive character that this recognition may take and thus to offer a supplement to those excellent studies of Derrida and Husserl such as Lawlor's and Dastur's, which emphasize the "neutralizing facticity" of language that opens the possibility of both transcendental philosophy and "history itself." Françoise Dastur, "Finitude and Repetition in Derrida and Husserl," *Southern Journal of Philosophy* 32, no. 5 (1993): 113–30, 122.

36. For an excellent description of the metaphorical slippage that, in turn, shapes Husserl's descriptions of the relation between meaning and expression, "sedimentation" and sense, see Jacques Derrida, "La forme et le vouloir-dire: Note sur la phénoménologie du langage," *Revue internationale de philosophie* 21, no. 81 (1967): 277–99. Derrida will more subtly emphasize the role of "transfer" in Husserl's descriptions of passive, prepredicative modalization in *The Problem of Genesis in Husserl's Philosophy*, albeit without explicit reference to its metaphoric implications. Derrida, *The Problem of Genesis*, 117.

37. Werner Hamacher, "For—Philology," trans. Jason Groves, in *Minima Philologica* (New York: Fordham University Press, 2015), 107–56, 122–23; cf. Werner Hamacher, "*Für*—Die Philologie," in *Was zu sagen bleibt*, 7–49, 20.

38. See especially the chapter devoted to "The Phenomenology of the Levels of Knowledge [*Zur Phänomenologie der Erkenntnisstufen*]," in Husserl, *Logical Investigations*, 2:226–49; cf. Husserl, *Hua* 19.1:596–631.

39. Husserl, *Hua* 15:477; my translation.

40. Husserl, *Hua* 15:462–63; my translation.

41. Husserl, *Hua* 13:311; my translation. In the same manuscript, Husserl describes the impossible promise of alterity—namely, that "something psychical must now step forth in original experience"—in the language of a "demand": "The live body that is seen demands [*fordert*] the present of sensory fields. The present is, however, not an experiential present as with my live body. Lived experiences are co-posited here apprehensively, which are not my lived experiences." Husserl, *Hua* 13:310; my translation; cf. Husserl, *Cartesian Meditations*, 114 (trans. modified); Husserl, *Hua* 1:144. These passages support Theunissen's arguments that, before the other subject can be apperceived, a "body-pairing" takes place where the body of the other appears, like "my" body parts, as a "determining piece of myself [*Bestimmungsstück meiner selbst*]." Theunissen, *Der Andere*, 64; my translation. Yet as the impossibility of embodied perception from the other body's perspective is experienced, it will appear that, "at the same time, the other indirectly affects me already." Theunissen, *Der Andere*, 65; my translation.

42. Husserl, *Hua* 15:463; my translation.

43. Husserl, *Hua* 15:463; my translation.

44. Husserl, *Hua* 15:489; my translation. The placement of "repetition" in quotation marks recalls the way in which this "mode of 'remembrance' ['*Erinnerungs'modus*]" traces back to no experience that will have ever been immediately "present" for me. Improper "remembrance" of this kind includes not only the way in which the body of the other " 'reminds' ['*erinnert*'] me of my own" through those gestures that announce subjective motivation but also through language, whose tradition and sedimentation yield impressions of self-evidence that are "in truth no self-givenness [*keine Selbstgebung*]." Husserl, *Hua* 15:489; my translation; Husserl, *Hua* 39:542; my translation. This is why, as Husserl had already written in the first volume of his *Ideas Pertaining to a Pure Phenomenology*, confusion is frequently found even in the clearest instance of linguistic understanding: "A distinct understanding of word and sentence (or a distinct, articulated effectuation of the act of stating) is compatible with the *confusion belonging to the substrata* [*Verworrenheit der Unterlagen*]. [. . .] The substratum can be a confused unitary something (and often is [*und ist es zumeist*]), which does not actually include in itself its articulation, but instead it owes <its articulation> to mere adaptation to the stratum of the logical expression actually articulated and effected in original actuality [*der bloßen Anpassung der wirklich artikuliert und in*

ursprünglicher Aktualität vollzogenen Schicht des logischen Ausdruckes]." Husserl, *Ideas 1*, 298; Husserl, *Hua* 3:289.

45. Husserl, *Hua* 15:477; my translation

46. Husserl, *Hua* 15:489; my translation.

47. The passage in German reads in full: "Aber auch das Gegeneinander, das verneinende, ablehnende Verhalten ist ein Verhalten nicht im Nebeneinander, sondern im Ineinander von Akt-Ich und Akt-Ich. Der Wunsch, den ich an den Anderen richte, ist in ihn eingegangen, ich reiche wünschend in das andere Ich hinein, als es motivierend, aber nur sofern ich schon in ihm mit meinem Wunsch bin, er meinen Wunsch aufgenommen hat, erfahre ich, in ihm, Ablehnung." Husserl, *Hua* 15:477.

48. Bernhard Waldenfels, "Hearing Oneself Speak: Derrida's Recording of the Phenomenological Voice," *Southern Journal of Philosophy* 32, no. 5 (1993): 65–77, 72. The radical consequence of this argument, however, would be that no one, properly speaking, could ever be in a position to draw the distinction between "the own and the alien." Waldenfels, "Hearing Oneself Speak," 72.

49. Augustine, *On the Trinity*, 301; Augustine, *De trinitate*, X.5.7.

50. In *Formal and Transcendental Logic*, Husserl speaks of "the *unity of the locution* [Einheit der Rede]" as a minimal logical unit, but only after excluding cases that deviate from "normally functioning and actual speech [*normal fungierende und überhaupt wirkliche Rede*]." Edmund Husserl, *Formal and Transcendental Logic*, trans. Dorion Cairns (The Hague: Nijhoff, 1969), 22; Husserl, *Hua* 17:26. Thus, "a parrot does not actually speak." Husserl, *Formal and Transcendental Logic*, 22; Husserl, *Hua* 17:26. Address itself, however, would also not fall under the auspices of what Husserl calls "normative" speech, "in so far as the character of speaking-to [*Anrede*] is not expressed in the speech," nor would passively "functioning associations" be significant factors, when it comes to those logical operations which "bestow a sense." Husserl, *Formal and Transcendental Logic*, 23, 26 (trans. modified); Husserl, *Hua* 17:27, 29. Any positing of a stable distinction between the signitive meaning of an expression and the initial, passive experiences involved in receiving it would have to be questionable, however, insofar as the comprehension of the former would be contingent upon (and contemporaneous with) the latter, strictly speaking. The overlapping between parroting and understanding would rather render any decision as to where logical operations begin structurally impossible.

51. The annotations and insertions that are reprinted in the critical edition of Husserl's text are not precisely dated by the editors but ascribed to a period ranging from 1901 to approximately 1911. Husserl, *Hua* 19:923.

52. The passage in German reads: "*So wie die Wortlauteinheit eine schlichte Einheit ist, eine Einheit, die sozusagen ein passiv Gegebenes ist, so auch die verworrene Sinneseinheit; auch dieses Bewußtsein ist ein passives, nichts von der spezifischen Aktivität, Spontaneität des glaubenden und verknüpfenden Denkens, des 'eigentlichen'*

Denkens in sich schließend." Husserl, *Hua* 19:869–70. The English version of this passage previously offered is my translation.

53. In his fifth investigation on "Intentional Experiences and Their 'Contents,'" Husserl uses this phrase, which elsewhere characterizes what he will call the "neutrality"-modification, through which the doxic character of the noema, or intentional correlate of conscious acts, would be neither positive nor negative but the "counterpart [*Gegenstück*]" of all such pros and contras, namely, their "Neutralisierung." Husserl, *Ideas 1*, 258; Husserl, *Hua* 3:248. In particular, Husserl evokes neutralization *avant la lettre* when he describes the moments involved in an act of assent, writing: "to *judge concordantly*, simply to accept a communication [*eine Mitteilung einfach übernehmen*], is not to assent to it. Assent rather involves an original understanding of a statement that we do not ourselves judge true: what is said is "merely set forth" [*'bloß dahingestellt'*] in consciousness, is *pondered* and *considered*. Plainly all these acts are involved in the mere presentation, to which assent is added. We enter more deeply, considering what the other means [*Wir vertiefen uns nachsinnend in das, was der andere meint*]; what is initially merely set forth for us should not remain merely set forth [*was uns zuerst bloß dahingestellt ist, soll nicht dahingestellt bleiben*]; we place it in question, we intend a decision. And then the decision, the affirmative determination steps in by itself [*tritt* [. . .] *selbst ein*], we judge now for ourselves [*wir urteilen nun selbst*] and concordantly with the other person [*gleichstimmig mit dem andern*]." Husserl, *Logical Investigations*, 2:141 (trans. modified); Husserl, *Hua* 19:464. Husserl's parallel construction, where the automatic entrance of assent—"then the decision [. . .] steps in by *itself* "—is juxtaposed with the autonomous act of judgment—"we judge now for *ourselves*"—suggests that the "self" that is at work in this process, as well as the timing of one's "proper" judgment, would be most uncertain. In this respect, Husserl's description of assent parallels the description of speech that is offered above, where there would appear to be no decisive way to tell whether or when I begin to think the words that come to mind.

54. Husserl, *Hua* 19:870; my translation.

55. Jan Patocka, *The Natural World as a Philosophical Problem*, ed. Ivan Chvatík and Lubica Ucník, trans. Erika Abrams (Evanston, IL: Northwestern University Press, 2016), 90.

56. Derrida, *Speech and Phenomena*, 80 (trans. modified); Derrida, *La voix et le phénomène*, 89. The implicit undecidability between intention and iteration that Derrida will go on to unfold is already indicated not only through the emphasis that Derrida places upon the paradoxical notion of "immediate" repetition but also through the ambivalence of the verb "entendre," which may signify both the conscious act of understanding and the more passive experience of hearing. "Entendre" is a double entendre, so to speak.

57. Husserl, *Hua* 15:463; my translation.

58. Waldenfels, *Das Zwischenreich*, 184. Here, Waldenfels insists on the possibility of an "act of reason [*Vernunftakt*]," which would free the subject from

absorption in others' trajectories of speech and thought, just as Husserl repeatedly recommends "self-reflection [*Selbstbesinnung*]" as a method for gaining insight into the sedimented heritage of terms and concepts that make up both the philosophical tradition and everyday language (see chapter 1). Ricoeur seeks to reconcile the effects of sedimentation with the "life of intentional consciousness" by developing a notion of ispeity where alterity and passivity are considered to be integral to the self, which comes to fruition through the attestations that one gives "through the objectifying mediations of language, action, narrative, and the ethical and moral predicates of action." Ricoeur, *Oneself as Another*, 301–02; cf. Ricoeur, *Soi-même comme un autre*, 330. This concept allows for those cases of indeterminacy in which, for example, the "motif and cause" of an act "are indiscernible." Ricoeur, *Oneself as Another*, 77; cf. Ricoeur, *Soi-même comme un autre*, 97.

59. In this respect, "inter-est" describes precisely the unsituatable character of affection that Dastur emphasizes, when she writes on Husserl's descriptions of passivity in *Experience and Judgment*: "Can we really 'situate' the affecting? Is it in the object or in consciousness? The origin cannot in fact be identified because it depends on the preliminary capacity to be affected, which Husserl calls 'receptivity,' and which is neither 'in' the subject (because it comes in some way 'prior to' the subject) nor 'in' the object (since the encounter with the object presupposes it). As neither in the subject nor in the object, it can only be 'between' them." Françoise Dastur, *Questions of Phenomenology: Language, Alterity, Temporality, Finitude*, trans. Robert Vallier (New York: Fordham University Press, 2017), 39.

60. Thomas Pynchon, *Gravity's Rainbow* (New York: Penguin, 1973), 180.

61. The nonopposition between passive operations of consciousness and the acts of the cogito that are founded in them is emphasized not only in the studies of Depraz and Bégout cited toward the beginning of this chapter but also in Dan Zahavi's study "Self-Awareness and Affection," where he argues on the basis of a broad range of Husserl's manuscripts that the hyletic data of the passive sphere constitute an "immanent type of alterity which manifests itself directly in subjectivity, which belongs intrinsically to subjectivity, and which subjectivity cannot do without. Both are, as Husserl says, inseparable, both are irreducible structural moments in the process of constitution, in the process of bringing to appearance." Dan Zahavi, "Self-Awareness and Affection," in *Alterity and Facticity: New Perspectives on Husserl*, ed. Natalie Depraz and Dan Zahavi (Dordrecht: Springer, 1998), 205–28, 217; cf. Depraz, *Transcendence et incarnation*, 235–36; Bégout, *La généalogie*, 78–79. Dastur similarly insists in her reading of *Experience and Judgment* that "Husserl recognizes the existence of a passivity in activity itself, a passivity built on the very activity of apprehension. There is thus an entangling of activity and passivity such that one cannot factually distinguish them." Dastur, *Questions of Phenomenology*, 31.

62. Patocka, *The Natural World as a Philosophical Problem*, 94.

63. Husserl, *Hua* 15:473, my translation.

64. Husserl, *Hua* 15:473, my translation.

65. This paradoxical formulation is inspired by Husserl's manuscripts, where he will speak of the other as "the Not-I that is itself I [*das Nicht-Ich, das selbst Ich ist*]." Husserl, *Hua* 15:366; my translation.

66. Husserl, *Cartesian Meditations*, 114; trans. modified. The passage from Husserl's German version reads in full: "Als andeutender Leitfaden für die zugehörige Klärung kann der Satz genügen: Der erfahrene fremde Leib bekundet sich fortgesetzt wirklich als Leib nur in seinem wechselnden, aber immerfort zusammenstimmenden 'Gebaren,' derart, daß dieses seine physische Seite hat, die Psychisches appräsentierend indiziert, das nun in originaler Erfahrung erfüllend auftreten muß." Husserl, *Hua* 1:144.

67. This passage, drawn from a manuscript on intersubjectivity dating from 1922, reads in full: "Indem nun im fremden Leib das äussere Gehaben durch seine Analogie an ein inneres Gehaben, an eine Subjektivität, die in diesem Leib ihr Organ hat, 'erinnert,' ist nun das Wesentliche dies, eben dass nicht eine blosse starre ruhende Dingähnlichkeit da ist, auch nicht eine blosse Ähnlichkeit des Gehabens von Dingen, denen ich bloss zusehe, also nach Seiten ihres Sich-veränderns und der Kausalität ihrer Veränderungen. Sondern eine Ähnlichkeit eines 'Gehabens' mit meinem leiblichen Gehaben als leiblichem, wobei ein Vorgang erinnert als Analogon an mein Zurückweichen vor einem mir Furcht erregenden Ding, an ein Ausweichen oder an ein Angezogenwerden von einer Speise, sie Ergreifen, Essen etc. Aber nicht nur erinnert das daran, sondern im Ablauf des Vorgangs ist es so, 'wie wenn' ich, nachdem ich das getan, einem solchen Ding gegenüber, und nachdem ich es ergriffen, nun so tue, esse, und jede der neuen Erinnerungen ist durch die vorangegangene motiviert und zugleich bestätigt sie sich durch das, was in der für mich äusserlich erfahrenen Gegenständlichkeit eben äusserlich <sich> zeigt, sofern das, woran ich erinnert werde, alsbald in der Äusserlichkeit eintritt." Husserl, *Hua* 14:284.

68. Augustine, *Confessions*, I.8.13.

69. Derrida, *Speech and Phenomena*, 39.

70. Theunissen, *Der Andere*, 60; my translation. Husserl's repeated insistence upon the immediate character of an analogical transfer between "me" and "you"—rather than any "analogical deduction [*Analogieschluss*]"—are what also distinguish his rhetoric of "announcement [*Kundgabe*]" from Theodor Lipps's use of the same term, when he sought to derive intersubjective empathy from a "drive toward 'expressions of life' or the announcement [*Kundgabe*] of inner processes through corporeal processes." Husserl, *Hua* 15:14; Husserl, *Hua* 13:72. The latter quotation is Husserl's paraphrase of one of Lipps's hypotheses, which he formulates amidst passages cited verbatim from Lipps's *Leitfaden der Psychologie* in a manuscript on empathy dating from around 1913.

71. Husserl, *Hua* 9:393; my translation. He glosses this phrase later in the same manuscript as "a secondary form of originality" (9:395; my translation).

72. Husserl, *Cartesian Meditations*, 112; trans. modified. The passage reads in full: "In einer paarenden Assoziation ist das Charakteristische, daß im prim-

itivsten Falle zwei Daten in der Einheit eines Bewußtseins in Abgehobenheit anschaulich gegeben sind und auf Grund dessen wesensmäßig schon in purer Passivität, also gleichgültig ob beachtet oder nicht, als unterschieden Erscheinende phänomenologisch eine Einheit der Ähnlichkeit begründen, also eben stets als Paar konstituiert sind." Husserl, *Hua* 1:142.

73. Husserl, *Cartesian Meditations*, 113 (trans. modified); cf. Husserl, *Hua* 1:143.

74. As Husserl had written in a manuscript on intersubjectivity dating from 1922, which generally concerns the structural correlation of transcendental subjectivity with others (as objects of conscious): "In this entire process of the progressive formation of sense, it is the hyletic data that function as the original kernel, and not as elements from which the world to be constituted constitutes itself through composition in the literal sense. Rather, it constitutes itself, in the sense that the hyletic data exercise an adumbrating function through the donations of sense which emerge from the apprehensions and intentional unities that form out of them as the intentional counter-poles to the subject-pole." Husserl, *Hua* 14:245; my translation.

75. Theunissen, *Der Andere*, 65; my translation.

76. Husserl, *Hua* 14:240; my translation.

77. Husserl, *Hua* 14:284; my translation.

78. Aristotle, *De interpretatione*, 16a.

79. Husserl, *Hua* 13:311; my translation. Merleau-Ponty will "cite" the mimicry of infantile gestures as testimony to the passive, preverbal communication that Husserl exemplifies with hand gesticulations: "A fifteen-month-old baby opens his mouth when I playfully take one of his fingers in my mouth and pretend to bite it. And yet, he has hardly even seen his face in a mirror and his teeth do not resemble mine. His own mouth and teeth such as he senses them from within are immediately for him the instruments for biting, and my jaw such as he sees it from the outside is for him immediately capable of the same intentions. 'Biting' immediately has an intersubjective signification for him. He perceives his intentions in his body, perceives my body with his own, and thereby perceives my intentions in his body." Merleau-Ponty, *Phenomenology of Perception*, 368; cf. Merleau-Ponty, *La phénoménologie de la perception*, 1052.

80. Husserl, *Hua* 14:284; my translation. The passage is cited in full in note 67.

81. Husserl, *Hua* 15 489.

82. Augustine, *Confessions*, I.8.13.

83. Augustine, *On the Trinity*, 306 (trans. modified); Augustine, *De trinitate*, X.9.12.

84. In German, this passage dating from August 1931 reads: "Die Paarung der Assoziation ist wechselseitige 'Überschiebung,' und haben die sich Paarenden jedes in seiner Weise in sich präsumptive Geltungen mit zugehörigen Vermöglichkeiten, so überträgt sich das wechselseitig von dem einen auf das andere—passiv, ohne weiteres, in einem Schlage." Husserl, *Hua* 15:252.

85. Husserl, *Hua* 1:128; my translation. In Cairns's published English translation, the passage reads, "in which I '*rule and govern*' *immediately.*" Husserl, *Cartesian Meditations*, 97.

86. Husserl, *Cartesian Meditations*, 115 (trans. modified); Husserl, *Hua* 1:144.

87. Hamacher, "For—Philology," 122–23; cf. Hamacher, "Für—Die Philologie," 20.

88. Husserl, *Cartesian Meditations*, 118 (trans. modified); Husserl, *Hua* 1:147. This is why, as Theunissen has argued, I receive a sense of "myself" only after I encounter the impossibility of embodied perception from the (other) body's perspective: only with this sense of the other's alterity may I recognize our separate human existences. Thus, "the other indirectly affects me already," in the sense of effectively giving "me" myself, which again means that "I" am subject to alterity, or what Theunissen calls "Veranderung," on which see Theunissen, *Der Andere*, 65, 84. For a helpful discussion of Husserl's notion of "fusion [*Verschmelzung*]" in the context of the psychological studies of Carl Stumpf, among others, where the term signifies the tendency of qualitive contents to fuse into a perceptual whole, see Elmar Holenstein, *Phänomenologie der Assoziation: Zu Struktur und Funktion eines Grundprinzips der passiven Genesis bei E. Husserl* (The Hague: Nijhoff, 1972), 118–31.

89. Depraz, *Transcendance et incarnation*, 144; my translation.

90. Depraz, *Transcendance et incarnation*, 144; my translation.

91. The passage in German reads: "Der gesehene Leibkörper fordert Gegenwart der Empfindungsfelder. Die Gegenwart ist aber nicht Erlebnisgegenwart wie bei meinem Leibkörper. Erlebnisse werden hier apprehensiv mitgesetzt, die nicht meine Erlebnisse sind." Husserl, *Hua* 13:310.

92. Joone Taipale, *Husserl and the Constitution of Subjectivity* (Evanston, IL: Northwestern University Press, 2014), 81.

93. Husserl, *Cartesian Meditations*, 115 (trans. modified); Husserl, *Hua* 1:144.

94. This oppositional overlapping was already implicit in their initial posture, "shoulder against [*contre*] shoulder." Blanchot, *Aminadab*, 183 (trans. modified); cf. Blanchot, *Aminadab*, 267.

95. Blanchot, *Aminadab*, 183; cf. Blanchot, *Aminadab*, 267.

96. The passage on "coincidence" to which I allude reads: "Im Vergleichen findet eine Art Überschiebung des einen Bewußtseins über das andere statt, durch Übergehen erhält sich das eine Bewußtsein, trotz der Modifikation, die es durchmacht, als Bewußtsein vom selben ersten Gegenstand und kommt mit dem zweiten Bewußtsein, dem von dem zweiten Gegenstand, zu einer Deckung." Husserl, *Hua* 11:130; cf. Edmund Husserl, *Analyses Concerning Passive and Active Synthesis*, 176.

97. Blanchot, *Aminadab*, 183 (trans. modified); cf. Blanchot, *Aminadab*, 267.

98. Blanchot, *Aminadab*, 183 (trans. modified); cf. Blanchot, *Aminadab*, 267.

99. Nicolas Abraham, "Le symbole ou l'au-delà du phénomène," in L'écorce et le noyau, ed. Nicolas Abraham and Maria Torok (Paris: Flammarion, 1987), 25–76, 59; my translation. The linguistic a priori explored throughout this chapter owes much to Abraham's interpretation of life, consciousness, temporality, and intersubjectivity along the lines of symbolic formations in this essay. Abraham's study yields different insights and conclusions, however, not only due to the psychoanalytic inspirations for his arguments but also due to the fact that he does not primarily derive his claims from analyses of the specific passages of Husserl that are examined here.

100. The notion of singularly plural instances of subjectivity refers implicitly throughout to Maurice Blanchot's writings on "plural speech" in *The Infinite Conversation*, as well as Jean-Luc Nancy's *Being Singular Plural*. Blanchot, *The Infinite Conversation*, 3–82; Blanchot, *L'entretien infini*, 1–116; and Jean-Luc Nancy, *Being Singular Plural*, trans. Robert D. Richardson and Anne F. O'Byrne (Stanford, CA: Stanford University Press, 2000); Jean-Luc Nancy, *L'être singulier pluriel* (Paris: Galilée, 1996) In his brilliant discussion of the presuppositions that insinuate themselves into Husserl's descriptions of perception in *Ideas Pertaining to a Pure Phenomenology*, Gérard Granel likewise insists: "Thus, what comes first is henceforth the 'plural.' But this 'plural' does not have the sense of a plurality which gathers unities." Gérard Granel, *Le sens du temps et de la perception chez Husserl*, 2nd. ed. (Paris: Éditions T.E.R., 2012), 235; my translation. In taking further Husserl's insistence upon the "adumbrations" ("Abschattungen")—or, as Granel translates, the "sketches" ("esquisses")—through which each perceptual phenomenon is given, Granel suggests that intentionality would ultimately have to signify that the things that appear would be "like the nodes of a wave from the great nexus that radiates from the bottom of infinity [*comme des noeuds d'onde du grand réseau qui rayonne du fond de l'infini*]," whereby, in this context, the "nexus" or "réseau" also lets itself be heard as the liquidation ("eau," "water") of the "things" ("res") themselves (Granel, *Le sens du temps*, 235; my translation).

101. Husserl, *Ideas 2*, 78; trans. modified. In German, the passage reads: "Die Sinne streiten miteinander: dann wird der Streit dadurch entschieden werden können, daß eben nachträglich ein Glied als anomal ausgeschieden werden muß; alle übrigen Sinne zusammen geben eine einstimmig sich fortsetzende Welt, während der ausgeschiedene Sinn mit dem Gang der früheren Erfahrung nicht zusammenstimmt." Husserl, *Hua* 4:73.

102. Sigmund Freud, *Civilization and Its Discontents*, ed. and trans. James Strachey (New York: Norton, 1961), 13; cf. Sigmund Freud, *Das Unbehagen in der Kultur*, in *Gesammelte Werke: Vierzehnter Band: Werke aus den Jahren 1925–1931*, ed. Anna Freud et al. (London: Imago, 1948), 419–506, 423. With respect to the hyletic data that enter into a relation of resemblance, Bégout also acknowledges that passive association "cannot be an entirely valid criterion for the foundation

of the identity of an objectivity. Resemblance remains a relation and, as such, it is subjected to a permanent variation of its parameters." Bégout, *La généalogie*, 161; my translation.

103. Husserl, *Analyses*, 632; cf. Husserl, *Hua* 11:343.

104. Hamacher, "For—Philology," 122; cf. Hamacher, "*Für*—Die Philologie," 20.

105. The centrality of the ego is a topos that recurs throughout Husserl's writings, from his hesitant characterization of the "I" as the "necessary centre of relations [*notwendige Beziehungszentrum*]" for all intentional acts and correlative objects in the *Logical Investigations*, to his more affirmative characterization of the "I" in a manuscript from May 1933 "as the center of my affections and activities [*als Zentrum meiner Affektivitäten und Aktivitäten*]." Husserl, *Logical Investigations*, 2:92; Husserl, *Hua* 19:374; Husserl, *Hua* 15:574, 576; my translation.

106. Acknowledging a certain similarity between Husserl's formulations for passive association and the Freudian notions of "condensation [*Verdichtung*]" and "displacement [*Verschiebung*]"—as well as the rhetorical figures of "metaphor" and "metonymy"—Holenstein argues that Husserl's phenomenological explication of "associative achievements [*assoziativen Leistungen*]" differs, insofar as it exposes the transcendental "presupposition for the unity and richness of the (un-) conscious and its nexuses of sense [*Sinnzusammenhänge*]." Holenstein, *Phänomenologie der Assoziation*, 328; my translation. Yet what this argument does not account for is the way in which associative nexuses are already structured linguistically in Husserl, as well as the way in which both language and (its) associations trouble the very unities that they found and thereby preclude every constitutive "achievement" from being definitive.

107. It is "inconceivable" in the strict sense, because it is "no syllogism, no act of thinking [*kein Schluss, kein Denkakt*]." Husserl, *Hua* 15:14; my translation. However, as Bégout points out, Husserl also appeals to "Überschiebung" or "overlapping" as a method that should guide the description of "the first laws that enter onto the scene among the hyletic saliences which lift into relief upon the field of passive pre-donation," upon the assumption that this "imaginary operation" would "correspond to the real operation." Bégout, *La généalogie*, 115–16; my translation. The arguments offered in this chapter should, however, suggest that the shifts that "overlapping" undergoes in Husserl's writing deviate from any consistent methodological trajectory, be it straightforward or "zig-zagged" (as Husserl would often describe the way of phenomenological investigation).

108. Husserl, *Hua* 1:142; my translation. Cairns's English translation smooths over the unusual features of Husserl's formulation, which do not accord with the logic of transitivity that Cairns maintains in writing of "a living mutual awakening and an overlaying of each with the objective sense of the other." Husserl, *Cartesian Meditations*, 113. In his lectures on passive synthesis, Husserl evokes the data that enter into the process of pairing with relatively familiar terms, such as "red" and

"blue," but he also makes explicit that the passive syntheses of similar data are what first constitute whatever may be named and known as a unified qualitative phenomenon like color. He writes, for example: "Several discrete color-data in the visual field are grouped together; they are especially united by virtue of their similarity; [and they are united in] different ways as well. This kinship has its degrees and according to them it unites them now more strongly, now more weakly." Husserl, *Analyses*, 175; cf. Husserl, *Hua* 11:129. Shortly thereafter, he adds: "All of this takes place, however, prior to the occurrences of the higher lying activities of cognitively fixing the common element as something concretely general or as a generic generality proper to a higher level.' Husserl, *Analyses*, 177; cf. Husserl, *Hua* 11:131.

109. Depraz, *Transcendence et incarnation*, 141–42; my translation. Here, she insists that the "passage of one element into another" that is signaled by the "recurrence of the prefix 'über' " does not suggest "confusion." But it could be argued that the "overlapping" of "overlaying" also outstrips and crosses through any possible discretion as well.

110. As Claudia Brodksy has observed in her reading of related passages, Husserl does not draw phenomenological conclusions "by prioritizing any single 'side' of this always recognizably subdividing, intentionally multiplying 'collective' " that constitutes the "life of the analyzing subject." Claudia Brodksy, " 'A Now Not *toto caelo* a Not-Now': The 'Origin' of Difference in Husserl, from Number to Literature," in *Phenomenology to the Letter: Husserl and Literature*, ed. Philippe P. Haensler, Kristina Mendicino, and Rochelle Tobias (Berlin: de Gruyter, 2021), 283–307, 294.

111. As Bégout observes on Husserl's notion of association, it is nothing at all, if not dynamic: "There cannot be, then, a static association; this is a contradiction in terms Association is genetic, or it does not exist [*L'association est génétique ou n'est pas*]." Bégout, *La généalogie*, 140; my translation.

112. Husserl, *Hua* 15:254, 252; my translation.

113. This suspension within the occurrence of pairing speaks against a generalizing description of the phenomenon on the basis of its supposed results (e.g., the separate egos that become conscious for "me" when I become cognizant of another). Thus, when Bégout describes pairing as a dynamic in which "there is no fusion, properly speaking but just a *tendency toward fusion*, a fusion at a distance that is restrained by the dissension of different elements," it is not necessarily the case that the elements involved "coexist solely separately in a pair" during the process of pair-formation itself. Bégout, *La généalogie*, 151; my translation.

114. Husserl, *Cartesian Meditations*, 115 (trans. modified); Husserl, *Hua* 1:144.

115. Husserl, *Hua* 13:274; my translation. In German, the passage reads: "er sieht so aus, wie mein Leib, wie ich, das leibliche Ich, aussehen würde, wenn ich 'mich,' meinen Leib, vom Hier fortrücken und dorthin schieben könnte." This text is dated from 1914 or 1915, according to Iso Kern. Husserl, *Hua* 13:270.

116. Husserl, *Hua* 15:251; my translation. In German, the passage reads: "Aber kann mein Leib fortrücken, und ein anderer Leib mir unterschoben werden, oder abgeschnitten werden, mir wegamputiert werden, und dafür mir irgendein anderer zuteil werden?"

117. Georges Bataille, *Eroticism: Death and Sensuality*, trans. Mary Dalwood (San Francisco: City Lights, 1986), 14; trans. modified.

118. Husserl writes "that this ideal now is not something *toto coelo* different from the not-now, but is continually mediated through it [*daß auch dieses ideale Jetzt nicht etwas* toto coelo *Verschiedenes ist vom Nicht-Jetzt, sondern kontinuierlich sich damit vermittelt*]." Husserl, *The Phenomenology of Internal Time-Consciousness*, 63 (trans. modified); Husserl, *Hua* 10:44. He will later speak of temporalization in terms of infinitesimal differentials, claiming that "whereas with other continua the talk of generation was only figurative, what we have here is proper speech [*eigentliche Rede*]. The temporally constitutive continuum is a flux of continuous generation of modifications of modifications." Husserl, *The Phenomenology of Internal Time-Consciousness*, 130 (trans. modified); Husserl, *Hua* 10:100.

119. Derrida, *Speech and Phenomena*, 65–66.

120. The example of melody is cited just before Husserl speaks of the continuous mediation of the "now" with the "not-now." Husserl, *The Phenomenology of Internal Time-Consciousness*, 60–61; cf. Husserl, *Hua* 10:39–40.

121. Husserl, *The Phenomenology of Internal Time-Consciousness*, 56; cf. Husserl, *Hua* 10:34.

122. Husserl, *Hua* 13:310; my translation. For a discussion of this rhetoric of "demand," see above, n. 41.

123. Husserl, *Hua* 14:284; my translation. The full passage is reproduced above, n. 67.

124. Husserl, *Hua* 15:348–49; my translation.

125. This formulation is the one Husserl repeatedly uses in order to describe intuitive evidence, as when he argues in *Ideas Pertaining to a Pure Phenomenology* for the intuitive evidence of essences, whose vision entails "seeing in the pregnant sense and not a mere and perhaps vague making present; the seeing is an originarily giving intuition [*originär gebende Anschauung*], seizing upon the essence in its 'incarnate' ['*leibhaften*'] selfhood," or when he defines the principle of principles for knowledge as "originarily [*originär*] giving intuition," which offers itself, "so to speak, in its incarnate reality [*leibhaften Wirklichkeit*]." Husserl, *Ideas 1*, 10, 44 (trans. modified); Husserl, *Hua* 3:15, 51. For an extensive analysis of this emphasis on incarnation, see Didier Franck, *Flesh and the Body: On the Phenomenology of Husserl*, trans. Joseph Rivera and Scott Davidson (London: Bloomsbury, 2014). Franck's reading also implies, through different arguments than those offered here, that "the other ego is what originally affects me," and that the very "form" of passive synthesis "evokes alterity." Franck, *Flesh and the Body*, 68, 109.

126. Husserl, *Hua* 42:116; my translation.

127. Suspended between graphology and formalization, a new beginning of philosophy would, as Husserl writes elsewhere, consist of the "ABCs" that are to be derived from "a systematic and purely immanent analysis of consciousness." Husserl, *Hua* 7:125; my translation. Whether this recurrent alphabetical analogy in his writings could serve as "the invention or generation of an order, a system of rules for decipherment," however, is questionable, as Detlef Thiel points out in his excellent study, "Husserls Phänomenographie," *Recherches Husserliennes* 19 (2003): 67–108, 95; my translation.

128. Husserl, *Analyses*, 250; trans. modified.

129. Husserl, *Hua* 11:199.

130. Husserl, *Hua* 42:26; my translation. The passage in German reads in full: "Nur 'Abhebung' als Unterbrechung <des Strömens> in der Form des 'absolut glatten' Strömens, Verschmelzens ermöglicht eigentliche Affektion und damit Zuwendung und Aktivität, Beschäftigung damit." Shortly before, Husserl had written on the same page: "If a sensory field has the mode of a fully smooth, streaming fusional unity, as is normally, for example, the haptic field of the inner eye socket, it makes no special affection possible, no mode of attentiveness to singularity, and thus no course of objectivation in which the field would be apperceivable as a spatial field of 'things.'" Husserl, *Hua* 42:26; my translation. The relation between salient differences and memory is drawn within the same constellation of manuscripts on "limit-problems [*Grenzprobleme*]" of phenomenology, when Husserl writes of how an "affection that awakens the I" is the condition of possibility for "the movements of association" to be set in "play," which include those of memory. Husserl, *Hua* 42:15; my translation.

131. Bégout also emphasizes how Husserl's descriptions "suppose from the temporal point of view that fusion via resemblance is more immediate than contrast via dissemblance, given that the latter cannot appear as such, except in relation to the existence that is already constituted by the former process as a point of reference." Bégout, *La généalogie*, 153 (my translation); cf. Bégout, *La généalogie*, 156–59. The dynamics of contestation and protest that Husserl evokes in the passages discussed in this chapter, however, speak against Bégout's subsequent assertion that, while similarity admits degrees, "the detachment of a datum effectuates itself in a non-intensive manner, in one stroke [*en un coup d'oeil*]." Bégout, *La généalogie*, 164; my translation. It was with an eye to a similar problem that Jan Patocka would assert that "qualitative scales would have to be analyzed, too, as facts of significance for lifestyle. Where dark colors are not differentiated, for example, we would have to inquire into the interest which inhibits differentiation." Patocka, *The Natural World as a Philosophical Problem*, 102. The notion that an interest can "inhibit differentiation" testifies to the passive intentionalities that not only facilitate but also filter the sensory data that give themselves to be seen. Later, Patocka will derive the ideal character of the

phoneme from a similar "nonobservation of disagreements." Patocka, *The Natural World as a Philosophical Problem*, 104.

132. Husserl, *Analyses*, 251 (trans. modified); Husserl, *Hua* 11:200. When Husserl addresses the "affections" that may solicit divergent, incompatible apprehensions of the "same" perceptual object in *Experience and Judgment*, he explicitly states of the two overlapping and contrasting alternatives: "In truth, neither of the two stands there" in the manner that anything may have stood "before the onset of doubt." Husserl, *Experience and Judgment*, 93 (trans. modified); Husserl, *Erfahrung und Urteil*, 101. Instead, "the unidirectional consciousness [*das einsinnige Bewußtsein*]" itself "falls apart [. . .] into a multi-directional one [*zerfällt* [. . .] *in ein mehrsinniges*]," and at the limit, the appearance-in-the-making suffers a breach or explodes. Husserl, *Experience and Judgment*, 94 (trans. modified); Husserl, *Erfahrung und Urteil*, 102. Husserl explicitly speaks of "exploding" with respect to similar disruptions of "univocity" or "Einstimmigkeit" in *Ideas Pertaining to a Pure Phenomenology*, whereas the term that he uses in *Experience and Judgment* is "breach" or "rupture" ("Abbruch"). Husserl, *Ideas 1*, 364; Husserl, *Hua* 3:353; Husserl, *Erfahrung und Urteil*, 111–12.

133. Hence, if the signitive intention "green house" were to be disappointed in the intuitive experience of a red house, the negative modification of that initial intention would coincide with a positive intuitive fulfillment. Husserl, *Logical Investigations*, 2:248–49; cf. Husserl, *Hua* 19:630. In the descriptions of this process in the *Logical Investigations*, however, Husserl derives the very notion of a "not" from experiences that presuppose the intentionality of the *cogito*, which would not be operative at the passive level. At the passive level, Husserl therefore speaks of "disappointment" not as a categorial intuition of "negation" but as a vague feeling that something is missing: "Let us note, moreover, that when in place of an expected 'a' only a partial 'α' steps forth, the supplementary part 'ß' is now 'missing,' it is 'lacking.' Indeed, proper to expectation is a certain coinciding between the present and the associatively awakened remembered past, the retentional past and potentially the remote past; and the surplus of fulfillment as the surplus of a coinciding, the surplus of too much and too little, becomes prominent within the coinciding; what has not stepped forth stands there in the consciousness of 'lack.'" Husserl, *Analyses*, 239 (trans. modified); cf. Husserl, *Hua* 11:189. But this feeling depends upon the affective "force [*Kraft*]" of the remembered expectations and the present givens, which depend themselves upon the affective dispositions, interests, and habits that make up the subject's "motivational situation [*Motivationslage*]" at the time. Husserl, *Analyses*, 239; Husserl, *Hua* 11:188–89. These forces thus also fluctuate blindly and can therefore, theoretically, yield no decisive sum of force, be it positive or negative: "In the empty sphere of retentions," Husserl continues, "the forces sum and inhibit one another [*summieren und hemmen sich*], and with them also the forces of expectation, blind like any drive." Husserl, *Analyses*, 240 (trans. modified); Husserl, *Hua* 11:189. This is why the emergence of any con-

figuration from out of affect is utterly contingent, as Husserl's next conditional protasis suggests: "*If* one configuration has formed a prominent, specially bound unity through the affective forces governing it [. . .]" Husserl, *Analyses*, 240 (my emphasis); cf. Husserl, *Hua* 11:189.

134. Augustine, *On the Teacher*, 71 (trans. modified); cf. Augustine, *De magistro*, II.3.

135. Husserl, *Hua* 11:131; my translation. Steinbock's English version of the passage reads as follows: "Repressing means that the one conceals the other, that the concealed element tends toward unconcealment, then breaking through conceals the previously unconcealed element, etc." Husserl, *Analyses*, 176. The translation offered above is meant to give a closer approximation to the permutations of "decken" that bring this formulation to resonate with Husserl's technical term, "Deckung" ("coincidence").

136. And even if this disturbance could not affect the immanent time of consciousness itself, as Husserl insists when he returns to the dynamics of repression, overlapping, discord, and doubt in his Bernau manuscripts on time consciousness, the rapid alternation between alternatives—such that there are neither two nor one—would thoroughly impair the formation of a concrete unity from the phases of appearing objects, literally de-con-structing the "concrete construction [*Aufbau*] of the living present" that should coincide with "the construction [*Aufbau*] of the singular concretions arising from constitutive elements [*dem Aufbau der einzelnen Konkretionen selbst aus konstitutiven Elementen*]." Husserl, *Hua* 33:551–52; Husserl, *Analyses*, 214 (trans. modified); Husserl, *Hua* 11:165. These conclusions converge with those that Granel derives from his exquisite reading of Husserl's lectures on inner-time consciousness, where the difference that Husserl insists upon between hyletic data and their intentional formation entails that there would be "no possible perception as 'concording' unity of the *hyle* and the *morphe*. Such a concord conceals the most profound discord, the derision of understanding by and before itself" Granel, *Le sens du temps*, 72; my translation.

137. Husserl, *Hua* 1:142; my translation.

138. Husserl, *Cartesian Meditations*, 11; Husserl, *Hua* 1:51; cf. Husserl, *Hua* 19:567–68.

139. Husserl, *Analyses*, 241; cf. Husserl, *Hua* 11:191.

140. Hamacher, "For—Philology," 150; cf. Hamacher, "Für—Die Philologie," 43.

141. Husserl, *Hua* 11:199; my translation.

142. This phrase is drawn from Anthony Steinbock's recent study, *Limit-Phenomena and Phenomenology in Husserl*, where he recapitulates Husserl's descriptions of the "alter ego": "When Husserl begins to explicate the meaning of the alien, the radically other person, he does not assert 'what' it is—as if to begin in a natural attitude description of the 'Other' or the 'alien.' Rather, as a phenomenologist, he inquires into *how* the other is given to me from a first-

person perspective." Anthony Steinbock, *Limit-Phenomena and Phenomenology in Husserl* (Lanham, MD: Rowman & Littlefield, 2017), 17. After recognizing the abyssal "underground" of conscious life—albeit through a very different line of argumentation, which emphasizes the irreducible facticity of subjective life—Montavont similarly insists upon the first-person singular subject, describing the main achievement of Husserl's investigations of passivity as the disclosure of "a mode of being of the subject that is more originary than the reflective mode." Montavont, *De la passivité*, 199, 280; my translation. The linguistic and plural character of the "I"—as well as "my" body—that have been traced throughout this chapter would render any "I" equivocal in a manner that cannot be reduced to a single, self-identical subject, not even one whose passive life, as Montavont elucidates, precedes its self-reflection and thus remains "beyond that which is mine, that which pertains to me." Montavont, *De la passivité*, 136; my translation.

143. Augustine, *Enarrationes in Psalmos*, XLI.13. Through his reading of the differential adumbrations or "esquisses" through which phenomenal unities show themselves, Granel likewise speaks of the "abyssal character [*abyssalité*]" of the phenomenological "fundament," which "refuses to exhibit the unity indicated by the adumbrations." Granel, *Le sens du temps*, 162; my translation.

144. Rodolphe Gasché, "On Re-presentation, or Zigzagging with Husserl and Derrida," *Southern Journal of Philosophy* 32, no. 5 (1993): 1–16, 5–6. Granel likewise offers minute and precise analyses of the unthematic discrepancies and traditional presuppositions that language inscribes into Husserl's phenomenological investigations (see, e.g., Granel, *Le sens du temps*, 219–25). Further recent, exemplary studies that indicate the need to take the differential, figural, citational, and critical traits of Husserl's writing seriously include Thiel, "Husserls Phänomenographie"; Brodsky, "'A Now Not *toto caelo* a Not-Now'"; and Philippe P. Haensler, "Fort. The Germangled Words of Edmund Husserl and Walter Benjamin," in *Phenomenology to the Letter: Husserl and Literature*, ed. Philippe P. Haensler, Kristina Mendicino, and Rochelle Tobias (Berlin: de Gruyter, 2021), 85–112. In particular, Brodsky exposes the plurality of the singular that has been emphasized in this chapter, but she traces it through readings of different textual complexes: "The necessity of the perception of a collectivity to perceiving any individual identity, already stated in its 'purest' (and thus most heterodox) mathematical form in the early *Philosophie der Arithmetik*, and developed in the opposite objective orientation to abstract number in the discussion of the 'Leiblichkeit' 'fungierendes Organ' [. . .] is perhaps most effectively stated in the *Logische Untersuchungen*," where Husserl "describes not the objects themselves but their 'relational' 'acting in place of' [. . .] a composite 'Sachlage.'" Brodsky, "'A Now Not *toto caelo* a Not-Now,'" 291. She will later read Husserl's writing as "the material occasion for the internal production of temporality that they themselves describe, enacting, so to speak, what they say." Brodsky, "'A Now Not *toto caelo* a Not-Now,'" 302.

145. This conclusion echoes Theil's provocative comment on Husserl's descriptive method in general: "Does Husserl, in writing, carry out anything other than the infinite, virtuosic probing of horizons, rhetorical styles, literary techniques; the testing out of grammatical and semantic fields?" Theil, "Husserls Phänomenographie," 80; my translation. Later, Theil elaborates the "auto-affective function" of writing for the phenomenological subject as well, which in turn exposes the "autos" or "self" to the alterity of language, that is, to "the possibility of a certain passivity, anonymity, even intransitivity of the act of writing." Theil, "Husserls Phänomenographie," 93; my translation.

146. As is well known, Husserl will often compare the comprehension of another embodied subject with the comprehension of a speech whose "animating sense" should have "its support, or better, its Corporeality in verbal substrata [*ihre Leiblichkeit in Wortunterlagen*]." The "whole of a speech," he writes, should thus be "through and through a unity of Body and spirit [*durch und durch eine Einheit von Leib und Geist*]." Husserl, *Ideas 2*, 253; Husserl, *Hua* 4:241. Jacques Derrida points to the metaphysical prejudice implicit in such formulations in *Speech and Phenomena*, 35.

147. It is a similar movement of escape and deferral that Haensler traces through his stunning reading of Husserl, via Derrida and Walter Benjamin, among others, which culminates in the suggestion that "the deeper 'Sinn' of Husserl's phenomenology" may yet have been a "certain (Benjaminian) stage in phenomenology: to conceive of a kind of 'Sinn' that *needs* to be 'fort' (as one might also 'translate' the observation [. . .] of the 'Beilage III,' 'est fehlt ihr Immerfortsein') from the original 'Wort-Leib': a kind of 'Sinn,' in other words, *in* other words, a kind of 'Sinn,' that, by (infinite) extension, is (not yet) what it is in the mode of the *new*." Haensler, "Fort," 109.

148. Dan Zahavi, *Husserl and Transcendental Intersubjectivity: A Response to the Linguistic-Pragmatic Critique*, trans. Elizabeth A. Behnke (Athens: Ohio University Press, 2001), 96.

149. Husserl, *Logical Investigations*, 2:223; cf. Husserl, *Hua* 19:593. The full passage from Husserl's *Logical Investigations* reads in German: "Damit hängt auch zusammen, daß das ausdrückende Sprechen so weit über das hinausgeht, was zum Zwecke wirklicher Angemessenheit des erkennenden Ausdrucks anschaulich gegeben sein müßte. Daß dies zum Teil einen entgegengesetzten Grund hat in der besonderen Leichtigkeit, mit der sich die Wortbilder durch die gegebenen Anschauungen reproduzieren lassen, um dann ihrerseits die symbolischen Gedanken, aber nicht die diesen entsprechenden Anschauungen, herbeizuziehen, wird niemand bezweifeln. Es ist aber auch umgekehrt zu beobachten, wie die Reproduktion der Wortbilder hinter den durch die jeweilige Anschauung reproduktiv erregten Gedankenreihen oft recht weit zurückbleibt. In der einen und anderen Art kommen die unzähligen inadäquaten Ausdrücke zustande, welche sich den

aktuell vorhandenen primären Anschauungen und den auf sie wirklich gebauten synthetischen Formungen nicht in schlichter Weise anmessen, sondern über das so Gegebene weit hinausgehen."

Chapter 3

1. Bataille, *Inner Experience*, 8–9; cf. Bataille, *OC* 5:20–21.
2. Bataille, *Inner Experience*, 12, 102; cf. Bataille, *OC* 5:24, 120.
3. Bataille, *Inner Experience*, 13; cf. Bataille, *OC* 5:25.
4. Bataille, *Inner Experience*, 15; cf. Bataille, *OC* 5:28.
5. Bataille, *Inner Experience*, 14; cf. Bataille, *OC* 5:27.
6. Bataille, *Inner Experience*, 22, 29; cf. Bataille, *OC* 5:35, 41.
7. Bataille, *Inner Experience*, 13; cf. Bataille, *OC* 5:27.
8. Bataille, *Inner Experience*, 13; Bataille, *OC* 5:25.
9. This description of Hegel's thinking on terminology is drawn from Alexandre Koyré's essay, "Notes sur la langue et la terminologie hégeliennes," in *Études d'histoire de la pensée philosophique* (Paris: Gallimard, 1961) 175–204, 179–80; my translation. Bataille had reviewed this essay for *La critique sociale* shortly after it appeared in the *Revue philosophique* in 1931. Bataille, *OC* 1:300–301.
10. Exemplary readings of Bataille's "attempt to reach the beyond of the restricted logic of the dialectic" may be found in Gasché, *Georges Bataille*, 238–76, 245. By shifting focus away from Hegel, however, the observations offered in the following pages should complement those studies that emphasize Hegel as a "decisive[] reference point for Bataille's philosophical development." Christopher M. Gemerchak, *The Sunday of the Negative: Reading Bataille Reading Hegel* (Albany: State University of New York Press, 2003), 12.
11. Bataille, *Inner Experience*, 16; cf. Bataille, *OC* 5:28.
12. Bataille, *Inner Experience*, 16; cf. Bataille, *OC* 5:28.
13. Bataille, *Inner Experience*, 53; cf. Bataille, *OC* 5:67–68. It may also have led to anguish for Hegel as well, if it is true that "at the moment when the system closed, [he] believed himself for two years to be going mad." Bataille, *Inner Experience*, 110; cf. Bataille, *OC* 5:128.
14. The project thus signifies a paradoxical situation in which existence does not and cannot yet exist, precisely because it is "put off" for "later" ("à plus tard") in this way. See Bataille, *Inner Experience*, 46 (trans. modified); Bataille, *OC* 5:59.
15. Bataille, *Inner Experience*, 22; cf. Bataille, *OC* 5:35.
16. Bataille, *Inner Experience*, 94; Bataille, *OC* 5:111–12.
17. Bataille, *Inner Experience*, 3; cf. Bataille, *OC* 5:15.
18. Bataille, *Inner Experience*, 8; cf. Bataille, *OC* 5:20.

19. After all, Bataille refers to "phenomenologists" in the plural on the same page, excluding exclusive reference to "Hegel." Bataille, *Inner Experience*, 8; cf. Bataille, *OC* 5:20. He refers explicitly to Heidegger shortly before in his introductory "Sketch" (Bataille, *Inner Experience*, 7; cf. Bataille, *OC* 5:19), and his emphasis upon "communication" in and beyond *Inner Experience* resonates closely with Karl Jaspers's thought, who would elaborate "communication" as a critical existential notion in his three-volume magnum opus, which Bataille had borrowed from *La bibliothèque nationale* in September 1941 and returned in 1943—that is, precisely during the period when he prepared *Inner Experience* for publication. See Bataille, *OC* 12:617. Throughout Jaspers's study, "communication" is approached along the lines of an ever-singular "potential for appeal [*Möglichkeit des Appells*]," which is irreducible to any "objective *formulation*" that may "be taken for *knowledge*." Karl Jaspers, *Philosophy: Volume 2*, trans. E. B. Ashton (Chicago: University of Chicago Press, 1970), 96 (trans. modified); cf. Karl Jaspers, *Philosophie: Zweiter Band* (Berlin: Springer, 1932), 108. Insofar as the appeal of communication is thought to elicit and assure the singular possibility of one's own existence, however, Jaspers does not draw the radical consequences that Bataille will pursue: "In this communication," Jasper writes, "which is absolutely historical and unrecognizable from outside, lies the assurance of selfhood." Jaspers, *Philosophy* 54; cf. Jaspers, *Philosophie*, 58. Bataille will likewise emphasize that "historical [. . .] conditions," rather than "formal bonds" are what first permit "the communication of a given 'Dasein,'" but the movement of communication, in the extreme, also dissolves those discrete existences that enter into it: 'There is passage, communication, but not from one to the other: *the one and the other* have lost their separate existence [. . .] the subject is no longer there." Bataille, *Inner Experience*, 24, 59; cf. Bataille, *OC* 5:37, 74. Hence, when Bataille returns to "communication" with explicit reference to Jaspers in the paralipomena to *Guilty*, he writes: "There is no phenomenology of communication: that is impossible. Under this name Jaspers speaks of relations that are directly graspable, relations entertained each day among humans." Bataille, *OC* 5:541–42; my translation. Finally, the likelihood of an allusion to Jaspers in Bataille's remark on the "sole philosophy" that is "living" may be strengthened by the similar words that were used in the context of a review of Jaspers's Nietzsche monograph that had appeared in *Acéphale*: "The work of Jaspers [. . .] adds [. . .] all the interest that touches upon the personality of Jaspers, one of those who give life today to the great [tradition of] German philosophy [*l'un de ceux qui rendent vie aujourd'hui à la grande philosophie allemande*]." Bataille, *OC* 1:474; my translation.

20. This passage from Hegel's *Phenomenology of Spirit* is quoted in both French and German in Koyré, "Notes sur la langue et la terminologie hégeliennes," 185. "Contagion" is also the word in French that Koyré uses to render "Ansteckung."

21. Jaspers, *Philosophy*, 11; cf. Jaspers, *Philosophie*, 10–11.

22. Earlier writers' indications of the unsettling implications of contagion and contingency for "us" are elaborated in David Farrell Krell's excellent study, *Contagion: Sexuality, Disease, and Death in German Idealism and Romanticism* (Bloomington: Indiana University Press, 1998).

23. Augustine, *Confessions*, X.34.53.

24. In one relatively late sermon delivered on Easter morning to the new initiates of the Church, Augustine had said: "Turn your attention and see the way in which the Holy Spirit is to come on Pentecost. And it comes thus: in tongues of flame it shows itself. Thus it inspires the love with which we may burn for God and condemn the world and burn off our dross and purify our heart like gold. Thus the Holy Spirit accedes; after the water [comes] the fire, and we are made the bread that is the body of Christ. And that is how, in a way, the unity [of the Church] is signified." [*Adtendite ergo et uidete qua uenturus est pentecoste spiritus sanctus. Et sic ueniat: in linguis igneis se ostendit. Inspirat enim caritatem qua ardeamus in deum et mundam contemnamus et foenum nostrum exuratur et cor quasi aurum purgetur. Accedit ergo spiritus sanctus, post aquam ignis et efficimini panis quod est corpus Christi. Et ideo unitas quodam modo significatur.*] Augustine, *Augustin d'Hippone: Sermons pour la Pâque*, ed. Suzanne Poque (Paris: Cerf, 2003), 238; my translation.

25. Husserl, *Hua* 42:221; my translation.

26. Insofar as singular, historical existence is precisely that which cannot be fixed according to the criteria of objective knowledge or within the framework of subjective categories, "Existenz" for Jaspers is always "possible Existenz": "Existenz must be present as a possibility if general thoughts are to have the transcending significance of existential elucidation." Jaspers, *Philosophy*, 11; cf. Jaspers, *Philosophie*, 10.

27. Augustine, *On the Trinity*, 132; cf. Augustine, *De trinitate*, IV.1.3. It is in light of these lines that Augustine's later words on the mind would need to be interpreted: "And no one doubts that no one understands who does not live, and that no one lives who is not" [*Et nulli est dubium nec quemquam intellegere qui non uiuat, nec quemquam uiuere qui non sit*]. Augustine, *On the Trinity*, 307; cf. Augustine, *De trinitate*, X.10.13. As Rodolphe Gasché points out, however, Bataille's use of over-determined words such as "life" may also "be borrowed" from the "vocabularies" of the "irrationalist individual philosophies and philosophies of life" of the nineteenth and twentieth centuries as well. Gasché, *Georges Bataille*, 86.

28. Augustine, *The City of God*, 468 (trans. modified); Augustine, *De Civitate Dei*, XI.14. Upon citing these verses from Psalm 17, Augustine writes: "When he had said: 'I cried out,' then, as if someone had asked him to prove that he had cried, he uses the effect—that is, God's answering his cry—to prove his own act. It is as if he had said, The proof that I have cried out is that Thou hast heard me." [*Sed cum dixisset: Ego clamavi, tamquam ab eo quaereretur, unde se clamasse*

monstraret, ab effectu exauditionis Dei clamoris sui ostendit affectum; tamquam diceret: Hinc ostendo clamasse me, quoniam exaudisti me]. Augustine, *The City of God*, 468–69 (trans. modified); Augustine, *De Civitate Dei*, XI.14.

29. Bataille, *Inner Experience*, 94; Bataille, *OC* 5:111.

30. Bataille, *Inner Experience*, 135; cf. Bataille, *OC* 5:156.

31. Husserl, *Logical Investigations*, 2:199 (trans. modified); Husserl, *Hua* 19/1:565.

32. Husserl emphasizes the acquisitive character of iterable knowledge in, among others, his *Cartesian Meditations*: "By virtue of this freedom to reactualize such a truth, with consciousness of it as one and the same, it is an abiding acquisition or possession and, as such, is called a cognition." [*Vermöge dieser Freiheit der Wiederverwirklichung der dabei als die eine und selbe bewußten Wahrheit ist sie ein bleibender Erwerb oder Besitz und heißt als das eine Erkenntnis.*] Husserl, *Cartesian Meditations*, 10 (trans. modified); Husserl, *Hua* 1:51.

33. Bataille, *Inner Experience*, 94; cf. Bataille, *OC* 5:111–12.

34. Gasché, *Georges Bataille*, 152–53. The context that he examines, however, is somewhat different: his observations are made with respect to other passages on "life" from Bataille's *Dossier of the Pineal Eye*.

35. Bataille, *Inner Experience*, 94; cf. Bataille, *OC* 5:111.

36. Bataille, *Inner Experience*, 83–84; Bataille, *OC* 5:99.

37. Bataille, *Inner Experience*, 84; cf. Bataille, *OC* 5:100.

38. Bataille, *Inner Experience*, 69 (trans. modified); Bataille, *OC* 5:83.

39. Tracing a trajectory through different passages, Jacques Derrida arrives at similar remarks: "That which *indicates* itself as interior experience is not an experience, because it is related to no presence, to no plentitude, but only to the 'impossible' it 'undergoes' in torture. This experience above all is not interior: and if it seems to be such because it is related to nothing else, to no exterior (except in the modes of nonrelation, secrecy, and rupture), it is also completely *exposed*—to torture—naked, open to the exterior, with no interior reserve or feelings, profoundly superficial." Jacques Derrida, *Writing and Difference*, trans. Alan Bass (London and New York: Routledge, 1978), 344; cf. Jacques Derrida, *L'écriture et la différence* (Paris: Seuil, 1967), 400.

40. Derrida, *Writing and Difference*, 339 (trans. modified); cf. Jacques Derrida, *L'écriture et la différence*, 393. Derrida's particular phrase, "in the name and in view of," recalls the logos and phenomenon of phenomenology, while suggesting that the "name" may come before the intuitional intentionalities in which expressive and signitive acts are supposed to be founded.

41. On this passage, Dennis Hollier has also observed: "This is the first version of the labyrinth, the one describing the nontranscendence of words as the impossibility of being cut off from words, and as the destiny of a subject who is not self-immanent." Dennis Hollier, *Against Architecture*, trans. Betsy Wing (Cambridge, MA: MIT Press, 1989), 65. He then goes on to suggest an "epoché"

of sense, when he writes that, in Bataille's oeuvre, "sense is always threatened but nonsense is never triumphant." Hollier, *Against Architecture*, 69.

42. Benjamin Noys, *Georges Bataille: A Critical Introduction* (London: Pluto, 2000), 15.

43. Husserl, *Ideas I*, 59 (trans. modified); Husserl, *Hua* 3:63. This freedom is contrasted with all other thetic "*position-takings*" that are determined by evidence and motives that we do not decide: we cannot, for example, posit the nonbeing of the world that appears with full evidence to us, even if that nonbeing remains thinkable in the modus of possibility. Husserl, *Ideas I*, 59; Husserl, *Hua* 3:63.

44. Aristotle, *Categories*, 1b 25, in Aristotle, *Categories, On Interpretation, Prior Analytics*, trans. H. P. Cooke and Hugh Tredennick (Cambridge, MA: Harvard University Press, 2002), 18–19.

45. Against those who would distinguish between light and fire along the lines of good and evil, Augustine would argue that all created beings belong to God's good order. Hence, without denying the destructive potential of fire, Augustine argues that the heat of fire is also useful "for warming, reviving, and cooking," to say nothing of those "animals" for whom it is among "the conditions appropriate to a healthy life." Augustine, *The City of God*, 503–04; cf. Augustine, *De Civitate Dei*, XII.4.

46. Bataille, *Inner Experience*, 94; Bataille, *OC* 5:111–12.

47. Bataille, *Inner Experience*, 15; cf. Bataille, *OC* 5:28.

48. In his essay on Bataille, "Outcomes of the Text," Roland Barthes writes: "Hence it is necessary—and perhaps urgent—to come out in favor of a certain subjectivity: the subjectivity of the non-subject, opposed both to the subjectivity of the subjet (impressionism) and to the non-subjectivity of the subject (objectivism)." Roland Barthes, "Outcomes of the Text," in *The Rustling of Language*, trans. Richard Howard (Berkeley: University of California Press, 1986), 238–49, 247; cf. Roland Barthes, "Les sorties du texte," in *Bataille*, ed. Philippe Sollers (Paris: Union générale d'éditions, 1973), 49–62, 59.

49. In his early essay, "The Language of Flowers," Bataille begins by speaking of the aleatory—and consequently, inexplicable—"aspect" or "appearance" that first renders a phenomenon remarkable, before distinguishing this "aspect" from its designation, which alone "allows one to consider the characteristics of things that determine a relative situation, in other words, the properties that permit an external action." Georges Bataille, "The Language of Flowers," in *Visions of Excess: Selected Writings, 1927–1939*, trans. Allan Stoekl (Minneapolis: University of Minnesota Press, 1985), 10–14, 11; cf. Bataille, *OC* 1:174. The first lines of this essay read: "It is vain to consider, in the appearance [*aspect*] of things, only the intelligible signs that allow the various elements to be distinguished from each other. What strikes human eyes determines not only the knowledge of the relations between various objects, but also a given decisive and inexplicable state of mind." Bataille, "The Language of Flowers," 10; cf. Bataille, *OC* 1:173. These

"decisive" factors, which Bataille relates to the register of values, are not the effect of conscious decisions—they expressly exceed the "knowledge" or "connaissance" of things—nor are they actively undertaken, as Bataille's insistence upon their "striking" character indicates, both in this passage and later, when he writes that "it is impossible to explain" the interpretation of roots as "ignoble and sticky" if one "does not assign moral meaning to natural phenomena, from which this value is taken, precisely because of the striking character of the *appearance* [*aspect*], the sign of the decisive movements of nature." Bataille, "The Language of Flowers," 13; cf. Bataille, *OC* 1:177–78. As Gasché has observed in his commentary on these passages, the word "aspects" in Bataille's vocabulary signifies "that through which things differentiate themselves in and among each other; the distinctive traits through which, as we will see, things can be incorporated into phantasmatic constructions." Gasché, *Georges Bataille*, 103. But beyond the visual implications of "aspects," one might also speak of those aspects of language which affect words as (well as) things, as Gasché goes on to argue, when he speaks of "word-presentations" as "signifiers" that "represent[] a *mere* differential feature, a trace, a cut, a mark." Gasché, *Georges Bataille*, 140, 141. In the relatively late essay discussed below, "Eroticism, or the Placing in Question of Being" ("L'érotisme ou la mise en question de l'être"), the linguistic character of what Bataille calls "aspects" becomes more pronounced, as he emphasizes their historicity: "These bodies, or rather their aspects, or these forms, are given to us only through the perspective where the aspect or the form have historically taken their sense [*historiquement pris leur sens*]. We cannot entirely separate the experience that we have of them from these objective forms and aspects, or from their historical appearance [*leur apparition historique*]." Bataille, *OC* 12:400–401; my translation. Here, phenomenal appearances translate to historical "apparition[s]"—with all the ambivalence of that word—which mode of spectral survival would require a concept of remains and traces, or, in a word, writing.

50. See chapter 2.
51. Husserl, *Hua* 1:142; my translation.
52. Husserl, *Hua* 42:221; my translation.
53. I borrow this word from Jean-Luc Nancy's article on Bataille, "L'excrit." In this piece, he describes Bataille's inscriptions as *exscriptions*, which point toward the exteriority of all that his texts may evoke, whereby "this 'exteriority'—entirely exscribed in the text—is the infinite retreat of sense by which each existence exists." Jean-Luc Nancy, "L'excrit," *Alea* 15.2 (2013): 312–20, 318; my translation.
54. Bataille, *Inner Experience*, 94 (trans. modified); Bataille, *OC* 5:111–12.
55. Aristotle, *Categories*, 1b 25. Hollier also suggests that scissiparity comes to figure as a "model" and a "governing fiction" in Bataille's writing, with implications not only for "eroticism" and "copulation" but also for the functions of the copula and the substantive. Hollier, *Against Architecture*, 68. Hollier does not, however, enter into detailed commentaries on the passages in which Bataille

traces the process of scissiparity, nor does he place the accent upon the question of intersubjectivity.

56. Koyré, "Notes sur la langue et la terminologie hégeliennes," 180; my translation.

57. The notion is evoked in *The Accursed Share*, where it is said that the expenditure of energy that takes place in sexual reproduction "accentuates that which scissiparity announced: the division by which the individual being foregoes growth for himself and, through the multiplication of individuals, transfers it to the impersonality of life." Georges Bataille, *The Accursed Share: An Essay on General Economy*, trans. Robert Hurley (New York: Zone Books, 1988), 35; cf. Bataille, *OC* 7:41.

58. The first-person speaker of the text introduces them "thus": "Alpha, Beta (thus we distinguish the twins issued from one reduplication) [*Alpha, Bêta (ainsi distinguons-nous les sosies issus d'un dédoublement)*]." Bataille, *OC* 3:231; my translation. The parenthetical expressly indicates the *ad hoc*—and therefore "improper"—status of these proper names, while leaving it an open issue as to which of the two twins ever responds when being called: "But who responded to you? Alpha? Beta? [*Mais qui t'a répondu? Alpha? Bêta?*]." Bataille, *OC* 3:231; my translation. (The parentheses, however, already suggest that the pretended nominal distinction is also beside [*para*] the point.)

59. The ninth chapter of *Eroticism* reproduces many of the passages that had previously appeared in Bataille's earlier essay of (nearly) the same name. Addressing the difficulties involved in describing the "inner experience" of unicellular organisms, for which scissiparity would mark a limit experience and breaking point, Bataille writes in *Eroticism*: "Even an inert particle, lower down the scale than the animalcula, seem to have this existence for-itself, though I prefer the words inside or inner experience; none of the terms used to describe it are wholly satisfactory. I cannot fail to know that this inner experience which I can neither undergo myself nor picture in my imagination implies by definition a feeling of self. [. . .] But feeling of self necessarily varies as the self concerned withdraws into its discontinuity. [. . .] Sexual activity is a critical moment in the isolation of the individual." Bataille, *Eroticism*, 99–100; cf. Bataille, *OC* 10:100–101. Although he comes to emphasize "sexual activity" in this passage, Bataille goes on to speak more generally of such experiences as the "crisis of existence" or "being" ("crise de l'être") and the "call[ing] into question" of "being" ("mise en jeu de l'être") in "the transition from continuity to discontinuity or from discontinuity to continuity." This transition, in turn, will be said to characterize scissiparity as well as sexual activity. Bataille, *Eroticism*, 101; cf. Bataille, *OC* 10:102. Hence, he will state explicitly that "the plethora of the cell [. . .] leads in these circumstances to the creation of one, of two new beings" in a manner that may be "compared with the plethora of male and female organs ending in the climax of sexual reproduction." Bataille, *Eroticism*, 97; cf. Bataille, *OC* 10:98. In this context, it is also significant

that Bataille introduces the term "plethora" as a parenthetical gloss on "croissance" or "growth," indicating that it refers neither to a unitary mass nor to a distinct multiplicity but to the internal trouble and "ambiguity" that growth occasions, where the "violent" and "turbulent agitation" that is suffered from within "calls forth the violence of separation [*appel la violence de la séparation*] from which discontinuity proceeds." Bataille, *Eroticism*, 95, 96; cf. Bataille, *OC* 10:96, 97–98. The appeal to "ambiguity" and "call[ing]" suggests, in turn, that the experience in question is (also) a linguistic one, in the broadest sense.

60. Bataille, *Eroticism*, 35 (trans. modified); cf. Bataille, *OC* 10:39. In the published translation, the quoted passage reads: "Without its universality [it] would be impossible to discuss," but this formulation does not convey the interdependence between objectivity and iterability that Bataille stresses in tying the "universal character" of objects to their "return."

61. Bataille, *Eroticism*, 35; cf. Bataille, *OC* 10:39.

62. Bataille *OC* 12:397; my translation. This passage appears in Bataille's earlier essay on "Eroticism" but resonates with the passages from his book of that name, which are cited above. In French, the lines read as follows: "Jamais l'expérience intérieure n'est donnée indépendamment de vues objectives."

63. Bataille, *OC* 12:408; my translation. Again, this passage appears in Bataille's earlier essay under the heading, "L'origine de ma méthode," and reads as follows in French: "Mais l'expérience intérieure en moi précède la réflexion objective, [. . .] le plus souvent, la mémoire d'un état quelconque était l'origine de recherches ennuyeuses (aurai-je réfléchi sur la scissiparité si je n'avais d'abord vécu le glissement que j'y considère?)."

64. Bataille, *OC* 12:400–401; my translation. The nearly equivalent passage in *Eroticism* reads: "Ces corps ne nous sont données que dans la perspective où ils ont historiquement pris leur sens (leur valeur érotique). Nous ne pouvons séparer l'expérience que nous en avons de ces formes objectives et de leur aspect du dehors, ni de leur apparition historique," which Dalwood renders as: "We cannot consider these forms except as illuminated by historical perspective with the erotic value they have acquired. We cannot separate our experience of them from their external aspect and their historical significance." Bataille, *Eroticism*, 35; cf. Bataille, *OC* 10:38. The nearly identical passages from Bataille's essay and book on eroticism draw the furthest consequences of what Husserl had called historical "sedimentation" in, among others, his *Crisis of the European Sciences*. But the possibility that "sedimented forms [. . .] can be awakened again and again and, in their new vitality [*in neuer Lebendigkeit*], be criticized" can only be maintained if universal, transcendental laws govern all subjective formations. Husserl, *Crisis*, 71; Husserl, *Hua* 6:72. Once it is possible that, as Bataille suggests, the existence and self-understanding of subjectivity is founded in the historical contingencies of language, then the extent and effects of "sedimentation" fundamentally exceed the scope of consciousness.

65. Bataille, *Eroticism*, 96; cf. Bataille, *OC* 10:97.
66. Hollier, *Against Architecture*, 77.
67. Bataille, *Eroticism*, 94–95 (trans. modified); cf. Bataille, *OC* 10:95–96. This passage repeats nearly verbatim the description of scissiparity that Bataille offers in "L'érotisme." Bataille, *OC* 12:405. The sentence on the "subsistence" of a in a' and a'' does not appear in his shorter essay, however, and the syntactic positions of "the simplest mode of reproduction" and "scissiparity" differ in the sentence that introduces the process: "Pour apercevoir le mouvement dont il s'agit, il faut nous fonder sur le mode de reproduction le plus simple, qu'est la scissiparité." Bataille, *OC* 12:405.
68. Bataille, *Eroticism*, 95 (trans. modified); Bataille, *OC* 10:96.
69. Jaspers, *Philosophy*, 14; cf. Jaspers, *Philosophie*, 14.
70. Bataille, *Eroticism*, 31; cf. Bataille, *OC* 10:35. See also Bataille, *OC* 12:397.
71. Bataille, *Eroticism*, 95; cf. Bataille, *OC* 10:96.
72. Heidegger, *Being and Time*, 1; cf. Heidegger, *Sein und Zeit*, 2.
73. Augustine, *Confessions*, X.33.50.
74. Husserl, *Ideas I*, 346; Husserl, *Hua* 3:335. At the level of even infinitesimally small waves and particles, Bataille finds that each form of unity breaks down in such a way that its very breach becomes untenable: for to the same extent that they dissolve, waves and particles suggest a greater whole, against whose cohesion their fleeting emergence will have nevertheless testified. Hence, when Bataille writes, "Waves, undulations, single particles are perhaps only the multiple movements of a homogeneous element," this element of dissolution and unity can only be suggested under the auspices of a "perhaps." Bataille, *Inner Experience*, 93; cf. Bataille, *OC* 5:110. In *Guilty*, Bataille returns to the fleeting and improbable character of unified forms, remarking upon how no whole is one, apart from the subject who construes it as such, while the same would go for the notion of a nonwhole as well: "To be considered a whole, the whole needs mind, it can exist only in the mind. Similarly a lack of the whole can appear only in someone's mind"; hence, he continues, "there are: fragments that shift and change (objective reality); a completed totality (appearance and subjectivity); a lack of totality (change when it's situated at the level of appearance but reveals reality as fragmented, changing, and incomprehensible)." Bataille, *Guilty*, 30–31; cf. Bataille, *OC* 5:266–67.
75. Bataille's writing shows scientific discourse to be marked by the eroticism of questioning, while exposing the coherence of objective terms to be fragile and fictive. Hence, the notion of "erotic fiction" would transgress the categorial notions that, as Hollier has pointed out, would entail the "loss of all value" for "erotic literature, as a genre." Hollier, *Against Architecture*, 140. Noys also argues that Bataille's articulations of scissiparity show the states of discontinuity and continuity that are at play to be themselves instable terms, with the consequence "that it becomes possible to posit the limits of continuity and discontinuity as limits that are *fictional*." Noys, *Georges Bataille*, 84.

76. Bataille, *Eroticism*, 14; trans. modified.
77. Bataille, *OC* 10:20.
78. Bataille, *Eroticism*, 94; cf. Bataille, *OC* 10:95.
79. Bataille, *Inner Experience*, 11; cf. Bataille, *OC* 5:23.
80. Georges Bataille, *L'Abbé C.*, trans. Philip A. Facey (New York: Marion Boyars, 1983), 34 (trans. modified); Bataille, *OC* 3:255.
81. Bataille, *L'Abbé C.*, 55; cf. Bataille, *OC* 3: 272.
82. For example, the figure of the "editor" who introduces the manuscripts of the two twins, Robert C. and Charles C., comes to share distinctive traits with each of them over the course of the text, which are no less remarkable for the fact that they result from circumstantial constellations and incidents. Robert, meanwhile, comes to resemble all too well the "dead priest" whose function he temporarily assumes in his hometown of R. Yet there are also countless other instances of resemblance: as the "editor" recounts his first meeting with Robert upon a visit to Charles—which most likely took place around the same time as the events of the narration, since Charles and Robert otherwise lived separately, and since the "editor" later confesses to coming from the same town as they—he compares Robert's courtesy to the comportment that generally "gives ecclesiastics a slight and deceptive resemblance to elderly ladies." Bataille, *L'Abbé C.*, 13; cf. Bataille, *OC* 3:240. This incidental remark assumes new resonance during the editor's later reunion with Charles, when an old woman passes by the place where Charles, the editor, and Charles's wife are seated. Her halting—literally, "hiccuping"—gait, combined with her clothing—she is "dressed in black," and wearing "old white canvas shoes [*des savates de toile blanches*]"—all prompt Charles's wife to speak the thought that had silently occurred to the narrator at the same time: "The ghost of Robert, cried Germaine." Bataille, *L'Abbé C.*, 19; Bataille, *OC* 3:244. Later, the manuscript of Charles reveals that he had once visited the abbot and found him "dressed in a pair of white cotton trousers [*un pantalon de toile blanche*] and a black woolen undershirt." Bataille, *L'Abbé C.*, 47; Bataille, *OC* 3:266. These threads of the text—and the textiles—thus tie Robert together with an old woman whose age and gender render her an otherwise unlikely "twin." In another context, Andrée Douchin-Shahin also briefly notes this resemblance between Robert and the old woman. See Andrée Douchin-Shahin, "Pardoxalement parlant: quelques réflexions sur *L'Abbé C.* de Georges Bataille," *Romantic Review* 78, no. 3 (1987): 368–82, 376.
83. Noys notices the parallel between the brothers of Bataille's narrative and the eponymous heroines of Sade's novels, where "Justine demonstrates the misfortunes of virtue and Juliette the profits of vice," before adding that "Bataille is not as schematic as Sade is," since "his novel is organised around the fact that 'this absolute contrast was tantamount to a perfect identity.'" Noys, *Georges Bataille*, 90.
84. The connection between Bataille's *L'Abbé C.* and this novel by James Hogg, *Confessions of a Justified Sinner*, has been emphasized in a number of scholarly discussions. Francis Marmande suggests that access to Bataille's convoluted novel

could best be attained in following the "play of returns and differences, equivalencies and ruptures, the infinite differentiation of the same" that unfolds between Bataille's narrative and Hogg's novel. Francis Marmande, "L'incitation ou l'oeil de l'histoire," in *Georges Bataille et la fiction*, ed. Henk Hillenaar and Jan Versteeg (Amsterdam: Rodopi, 1992), 49–57, 54. More recently, Jean-Louis Cornille has argued for reading Hogg's novel "as a sort of twin text" to *L'Abbé C.* Jean-Louis Cornille, "Georges Bataille: un rat dans la bibliothèque," *Revue de littérature comparée* 313 (2005): 35–50, 47; my translation. But Cornille importantly adds that the structural openness of *L'Abbé C.* to other texts also invites a reading of the ways in which it furthers—and further complicates—other literary projects that Bataille had undertaken during the same period, such as *La Scissiparité* and *La Haine de la poésie*, which are themselves crossed through with other intertextual strands. Hence, he argues, "The oeuvre constitutes itself to the degree that [Bataille's] readings encase one another." Cornille, "Georges Bataille," 50; my translation. Cornille considers, moreover, scissiparity to be a model to describe the intertextual relations that he traces.

85. Toward the end of the portion of the narrative that is presented as the "Story of Charles C. [*Récit de Charles C.*]," the prostitute Éponine, who is Robert's former lover and the current lover of Charles—among countless unnamed others—is said to be "the same thing as Robert [*la même chose que Robert*]," to which she assents: "Yes, she said. I am happy." Bataille, *L'Abbé C.*, 114 (trans. modified); Bataille, *OC* 3:321. In Robert's edited notes offered later, he appears to have parenthetically written the same, namely: "Eponine also: the same thing as Chianine [*Eponine aussi*: la même chose *que Chianine*]." Bataille, *L'Abbé C.*, 139; Bataille, *OC* 3:347; emphasis in original. ("Chianine" is the name Robert will have adopted for himself in his notes.) The first verbalization of Éponine and Robert's identity echoes the "decisive phrase" from *Wuthering Heights* that Bataille emphasizes in his essay on Brontë's novel, where Catherine proclaims her identity with Heathcliff: "Catherine Earnshaw is herself absolutely moral. She is so moral that she dies of not being able to detach herself from the man she loved when she was a child. But although she knows that Evil is deep within him, she loves him to the point of saying the decisive phrase [*la phrase decisive*]: '*I am Heathcliff* (Je suis Heathcliff)." Bataille, *Literature and Evil*, trans. Alastair Hamilton (London: Marion Boyars, 1973), 21 (trans. modified); Bataille, *OC* 9:179. Gilles Ernst notes parallels at a moral level between the evil that Bataille finds in Brontë and the "'hypermorality' of pure Evil" that would appear to be at work in the suicide of Charles C. Gilles Ernst, *Georges Bataille: Analyse du récit de mort* (Paris: Presses Universitaires de France, 1993), 98; my translation.

86. This argument is also made by Cornille, but the passages and contexts that he addresses differ from those discussed here, as does his emphasis, which rests upon an understanding of "intertextuality" that not only exemplifies a movement of transgression—"literary transgressivity," as he puts it—but also serves as

"a powerful agent of conservation" of tradition. Cornille, "Georges Bataille," 50; my translation. Bataille's writing exposes, however, that nothing could be less certain than the integrity of a textual object, which not only conservation but also transgression would presuppose. Without explicit reference to scissiparity, Douchin-Shahin speaks of the text as demonstrating "the irremediable fracture of being, a fracture which neither the reading of psychoanalysis, nor the world of religion [. . .], nor sexual expenditure, nor idealist systems can obviate." Douchin-Shahin, "Paradoxalement parlant," 381; my translation.

87. Among the papers surrounding *Guilty*, Bataille had drafted notes that set his thinking on communication apart from that of Jaspers, whereby the difference would lie primarily in the fact that Bataille concerns himself with "lived states which in some way transcend the givens [*les états vécus [qui] transcendent en quelque sorte les données*]." Bataille, *OC* 5:541.

88. Tommaso Giartosio, "'La vérité du bonheur': The Legitimation of Literature in Georges Bataille's *L'Abbé C.*," *Qui parle* 5, no. 2 (1992): 21–47, 40. Noys also indicates the elusive-recursive character of the text by speaking of the "shifts in identities of the two brothers," which "unfolds in the exchange of narrators throughout the novel, where the shifting viewpoints of the writing reflect the shifting of identity." Noys, *Georges Bataille*, 91.

89. Douchin-Shahin, "Pardoxalement parlant," 371; my translation.

90. As Brian T. Fitch has said of the segment titled "Notes de l'Abbé C."—which at first promises to offer the most direct insight into Robert C.'s thought and experience—"at its center, the narrator whom one expected to find beneath the lines of Robert effaces itself before the fictive being Chianine, born under the pen of Robert whose imagination is solely responsible for it." Brian T. Fitch, "L'Énigme faite texte: *L'Abbé C.* de Georges Bataille," *Ecrivains de la modernité* (Paris: Minard, 1981), 43–64, 54; my translation.

91. Other readers such as Noys have drawn attention to this feature of the text: "*L'Abbe C.* is literature in a state of collapse," he succinctly states, "and this is the effect of the impulse of transgression that runs through the text and leaves it open." Noys, *Georges Bataille*, 94. Douchin-Shahin especially emphasizes how the editor figures within the text as a "first reader" and thus as a model for the other "eventual readers of the book." Douchin-Shahin, "Paradoxalement parlant," 371; my translation.

92. Bataille, *L'Abbé C.*, 50; Bataille, *OC* 3:268.

93. Bataille, *L'Abbé C.*, 50, cf. Bataille, *OC* 3:268. It is perhaps a noteworthy coincidence that the proper name of the town to which Charles had temporarily removed himself also happens to break down into "his way" (*sa voie*).

94. After Robert affirms in a private conversation with Charles that he was "seriously ill," Charles goes on to indicate "that he couldn't stay up on his feet. He had called the bishop's residence and had reluctantly promised to say Mass the following Sunday; that would undoubtedly be the final act of his life

as a priest." Bataille, *L'Abbé C.*, 59; Bataille, *OC* 3:275–76. Robert's subsequent collapse at the altar during the mass dramatizes or inspires Charles's retrospective claim that "he couldn't stay up," while his dead appearance in that place not only makes his replacement of the dead priest appear to be all too real but also assumes the semblance of a supernatural, legendary scene: "The divine light of grace was shining rather faintly on my brother's face, and there was something supernatural about his deathly palor; it made him look like one of the figures in a stained-glass window [or: stained-glass depiction of legend, *vitrail de légende*]." Bataille, *L'Abbé C.*, 78; Bataille, *OC* 3:292.

95. Bataille, *OC* 3:327–29. The story of Robert's temporary "idyll" with the prostitutes, whom he chances upon as he leaves the parish, is related in the manuscript composed by his brother, Charles. The testimony of Robert's torture, however, is given by his former cellmate, who survives internment and deportation, and who seeks out Charles after the war in the hopes that "he would be rid" of the "obsession" that "was haunting him." Bataille, *L'Abbé C.*, 157, 153; cf. Bataille, *OC* 3:365, 362. But the testimony of this messenger is related only orally by Charles to the friend who ultimately edits and publishes his and Robert's manuscripts, leading the narrator to surmise that Charles "had finished the manuscript he had given me before the young deportee had come to see him"—that is, before the story was complete. Bataille, *L'Abbé C.*, 158; cf. Bataille, *OC* 3:365. The fact that Charles's completed manuscript can be complemented after the fact betrays the constitutive incompletion of every seemingly definitive narrative in the novel, including the one that his friend edits and publishes.

96. Robert's betrayal may also be the fulfillment of the future that Charles claims once to have "seen" from out of nowhere: as Charles slips on a ladder at one point in the text, and Robert grabs hold of him, his suspension on the verge of an abyssal fall gives way to a vision of his "brother in agony, surrounded by torturers in uniforms." Bataille, *L'Abbé C.*, 36; cf. Bataille, *OC* 3:257.

97. Bataille, *L'Abbé C.*, 140; cf. Bataille, *OC* 3:347.

98. Bataille, *L'Abbé C.*, 123 (trans. modified); Bataille, *OC* 3:328.

99. When Charles approaches the friend who will edit his and Robert's manuscripts, Robert is said to have been "dead for two years." Bataille, *L'Abbé C.*, 19; cf. Bataille, *OC* 3:245. Two months and two days after handing the manuscripts over, Charles commits suicide. Bataille, *L'Abbé C.*, 28; cf. Bataille, *OC* 3:250.

100. Bataille, *L'Abbé C.*, 16 (trans. modified); Bataille, *OC* 3:242.

101. Bataille, *L'Abbé C.*, 119; cf. Bataille, *OC* 3:325.

102. Bataille, *L'Abbé C.*, 122; Bataille, *OC* 3:327.

103. Bataille, *L'Abbé C.*, 121; Bataille, *OC* 3:327. It is also not insignificant that Charles's confession of his failure to speak truly of Robert is preceded by his confession of an "ardent desire to faithfully communicate the truth about my fever." Bataille, *L'Abbé C.*, 121–22; cf. Bataille, *OC* 3:327. He also claims to have "sought the truth about [his] brother in [his] fever," upon the premise that

"God can't be separated from the devotion he inspires, or a woman loved from the passion she has aroused." Bataille, *L'Abbé C.*, 121–22; cf. Bataille, *OC* 3:327.

104. Bataille, *Inner Experience*, 94; Bataille, *OC* 5:111–12.
105. Bataille, *Eroticism*, 95 (trans. modified); Bataille, *OC* 10:96.
106. Bataille, *L'Abbé C.*, 153; Bataille, *OC* 3:362.
107. Bataille, *L'Abbé C.*, 153; cf. Bataille, *OC* 3:362.
108. Bataille, *L'Abbé C.*, 34; Bataille, *OC* 3:256.
109. Bataille, *OC* 3:231.
110. Bataille, *L'Abbé C.*, 60 (trans. modified); Bataille, *OC* 3:276.
111. Bataille, *L'Abbé C.*, 33; cf. Bataille, *OC* 3:255.
112. Bataille, *L'Abbé C.*, 33 (trans. modified); Bataille, *OC* 3:255.
113. Bataille, *L'Abbé C.*, 33; cf. Bataille, *OC* 3:255.
114. Bataille, "The Language of Flowers," 12–13; cf. Bataille, *OC* 1:175, 177–78.
115. Bataille, *OC* 3:276; my translation. In his translation, Facey writes: "Everything we say to each other is necessarily false," which shifts the emphasis away from the interval "between" (*entre*) the brothers, as well as the false character of "each phrase" (*chaque phrase*), which suggests a falsification of language itself. Bataille, *L'Abbé C.*, 59.
116. Bataille, *L'Abbé C.*, 61; cf. Bataille, *OC* 3:278.
117. Bataille, *OC* 3:286; my translation. The sentence (attributed to Charles) reads in full: "Ne pouvais-je, je ne dis pas en un violent movement, mais par la rigueur de l'indifférence, trouver dans le coeur de la solitude la verité que j'avais entrevue, furtivement, dans mon accord et dans ma rupture avec mon frère?" (3:285–86), which Facey renders: "Couldn't I, I won't say 'in a violent manner,' but by the rigor of my indifference, find in the heart of solitude the truth I had furtively glimpsed in the deterioration of my harmonious relationship with my brother?" Bataille, *L'Abbé C.*, 71. The formulation, "deterioration of my harmonious relationship," however, introduces an temporal order and qualitative distinction that is not conveyed by the juxtaposition or apposition of accord and rupture in the phrase, "dans mon accord et dans ma rupture."
118. Bataille, *L'Abbé C.*, 62; Bataille, *OC* 3:278.
119. Bataille, *L'Abbé C.*, 63; Bataille, *OC* 3:279.
120. Bataille, *L'Abbé C.*, 69; cf. Bataille, *OC* 3:284.
121. Bataille, *L'Abbé C.*, 69; cf. Bataille, *OC* 3:284. It may be with reference to the traditional topos of the *imitatio Christi* that Robert's priestly conduct becomes cast as a theatrical performance: "You're not surprised to see that I've finally come to the point where I can't go on with my masquerade," he confesses to Charles, "But that doesn't mean I have to tell you what is happening to me today. It's enough for you that I've stopped pretending [*Il te suffit que j'aie cessé une comédie*]." Bataille, *L'Abbé C.*, 61–62; Bataille, *OC* 3:278. The word "comédie" also occurs when Charles later reflects upon the way in which Robert had (perhaps) faked a collapse during the last Mass he delivers: "He had acted out so

many different parts [*Tant de comédie*]—from the jovial priest to the tragic hero dying in the church." Bataille, *L'Abbé C.*, 87; Bataille, *OC* 3:300. Yet it is also to the extent that Robert's suffering escapes knowledge that he could approach the "imitation de Jésus" that Bataille had addressed in *Inner Experience* as "the moment of 'non-knowledge' of the '*lamma sabachthani.*'" Bataille, *Inner Experience*, 47; Bataille, *OC* 5:61. For the same reason, moreover, Bataille implies that no genuine imitation of Christ could know itself as such, however closely or remotely it may resemble the scripts offered by religious authorities, such as Saint John of the Cross and Thomas à Kempis.

122. Bataille, *L'Abbé C.*, 70 (trans. modified); Bataille, *OC* 3:284.

123. These lines open the section titled, "Der tolle Mensch" ("The Madman"), which famously announces the death of God as well. Friedrich Nietzsche, *The Gay Science*, trans. Walter Kaufmann (New York: Vintage, 1974), 181.

124. Bataille, *L'Abbé C.*, 70; cf. Bataille, *OC* 3:285.

125. Bataille, *L'Abbé C.*, 70 (trans. modified); cf. Bataille, *L'Abbé C.*, 285.

126. See Augustine, *Confessions* XI. The reflections of Charles that immediately follow upon the invocation of "beatitude" speak still more directly to the futility of bliss as a goal, and ultimately of goals as such: "The pleasure of living, in fact, pertained to the world that had rejected me: that was the world of those who are, by incessant change, alternately united and disjoined, separated and brought together again, in a process by which despair itself leads back at once to hope. [. . .] It wouldn't do any good, under those conditions, to continue along a path that had only one meaning / direction [*un chemin qui n'avait qu'un sens*]." Bataille, *L'Abbé C.*, 70 (trans. modified); Bataille, *OC* 3:285.

127. Franz Kafka, *Tagebücher: Kritische Ausgabe*, ed. Hans-Gerd Koch, Michael Müller, and Malcolm Pasley (Frankfurt am Main: Fischer, 1990), 867; my translation. In German, the passage reads: "Diese letzte Aussicht kann nur den Sinn haben, darzustellen, ein wie unvollkommener Augenblick das menschliche Leben ist, unvollkommen, weil diese Art des Lebens endlos dauern könnte und doch wieder nichts anderes sich ergeben würde als ein Augenblick." In *Literature and Evil*, Bataille quotes and unfolds the implications of Kafka's emphasis on instantaneity ("Augenblick" is translated in the French version that Bataille cites with "instant"), writing: "This is no longer a mere denunciation of the vanity of one 'aspect of life,' but of the vanity of all endeavours, which are equally senseless: an endeavour is always as hopeless in time as a fish in water. It is a mere point in the movement of the universe, for we are dealing with a human life." Bataille, *Literature and Evil*, 152; cf. Bataille, *OC* 9:272. Bataille does, however, offer meditations on "the instant, wherein the object of our thought is no longer reducible to discourse" in, among others, his essay, "Nonknowledge." Bataille, "Nonknowledge," in *The Unfinished System of Nonknowledge*, trans. Michelle Kendall and Stuart Kendall (Minneapolis: University of Minnesota Press, 2001), 196–205, 201; cf.

Bataille, *OC* 12:277–88, 284. This text, which concerns the experience of divinity without God, especially invites a reading in the context of *L'Abbé C.*, not least because Bataille repeats in it the (already citational) phrase that will be ascribed to Robert: "*Deus sum, nil a me divini alienum puto.*" Bataille, "Nonknowledge," 197; cf. Bataille, *OC* 12:279; Bataille, *OC* 3:345.

128. Augustine, *Confessions*, I.1.1; Bataille, *L'Abbé C.*, 137 (trans. modified); Bataille, *OC* 3:345. The likelihood that Robert's denial of repose should evoke the opening lines of Augustine's *Confessions* is underscored by Bataille's explicit commentary on those "often-cited" words in *Inner Experience*: "What is presumptuous in the little sentence, often cited, of Saint Augustine, is not the first affirmation: 'our heart is uneasy [*inquiet*],' but the second: 'until the moment when it rests [*repose*] in Thee.' For there is deep down [*au fond*] in a man's heart so much uneasiness [*inquiétude*] that it is not in the power of any God—nor of any woman—to allay it [*de l'apaiser*]." Bataille, *Inner Experience*, 123; Bataille, *OC* 5:143.

129. If the anagrammatic proximity of "Robert" to "b-r-o-t-h-e-r" would seem to be noticeable only in English, but not in Bataille's French idiom, the language of Robert invites such an association, since one of his first lines is the English advertising slogan, "*Say it with flowers.*" Bataille, *L'Abbé C.*, 33; Bataille, *OC* 3:255. Anagrams also feature in Éponine's designation of Robert as an "*ercu*," and in employing this (non-)word of French slang in lieu of "curé" ("parish priest"), she literally exposes both her speech and Robert's appellation to be perverted. Bataille, *OC* 3:279. The fact that this perversion is performed by a prostitute, whose speech is also generally characterized as strange—"she fooled around [*s'amusait*] with words that, in her mouth [*dans sa bouche*], sounded utterly bizarre"—makes Éponine an exemplary mouthpiece for the commercial-blasphemous language that Robert had imagined to be appropriate for speaking of God. Bataille, *L'Abbé C.*, 108 (trans. modified); Bataille, *OC* 3:317.

130. Bataille, *L'Abbé C.*, 71; Bataille, *OC* 3:286.

131. Bataille, *Inner Experience*, 94; cf. Bataille, *OC* 5:111.

132. Bataille, *Eroticism*, 14 (trans. modified); cf. Bataille, *OC* 10:20.

133. Bataille, *Guilty*, 55 (trans. modified); Bataille, *OC* 5:293.

134. While readers of Bataille repeatedly emphasize how "the linguistic translation of desire in [his] texts is always viewed as a distortion of what silence alone can adequately render," this structural trait is less often discussed as an effect of the scissiparous mode of (non-)being that Bataille interweaves into his discussions of eroticism and desire. Leslie Boldt-Irons, "Irony/Humor in the Fast Lane: The Route to Desire in *L'Abbé C.*," *Romantic Review* 85, no. 2 (1994): 271–90; 283).

135. His preface opens with the remarks: "I remember it precisely: the first time I saw Robert C. [. . .], I was in a painful state of anguish." Bataille, *L'Abbé C.*, 11; cf. Bataille, *OC* 3:239.

136. Bataille, *OC* 3:241.

137. Bataille, L'Abbé C., 16; trans. modified; Bataille, OC 3:242.

138. The distortions that Charles names are also themselves ambivalent: for example, his words on a lack of "vulgarity" either misrepresent the vulgarity that in fact appears to characterize his self-presentation throughout, or they indicate an initial lacuna in the text that his editor and friend will have emended by changing the "Narrative of Charles C." himself. Since the editor is the author who reports Charles's criticism of the manuscript, moreover, there is also no telling whether he has distorted Charles's admission of distortion in the first place, thanks to a personal interest or unintentional lapse of his own.

139. Fitch, "L'Enigme faite texte," 62; my translation.

140. Bataille, L'Abbé C., 132; cf. Bataille, OC 3:339.

141. Bataille, Inner Experience, 15; cf. Bataille, OC 5:28.

142. Bataille, L'Abbé C., 14; cf. Bataille, OC 3:241. It is for this reason that the concept of the textual "architecture" that Ernst adopts—"It is necessary, then, to conceive of the architecture of this novel as a series of three concentric circles"— would also disintegrate, and it would do so all the more radically because and not despite of the fact that the interventions of each speaker in the manuscripts remain unmarked. Ernst, Georges Bataille, 139–40; my translation.

143. Bataille, L'Abbé C., 122; Bataille, OC 3:327.

144. Bataille, Eroticism, 97; cf. Bataille, OC 10:98.

145. Bataille, Eroticism, 96 (trans. modified); Bataille, OC 10:97.

146. Bataille, Eroticism, 14 (trans. modified); cf. Bataille, OC 10:20.

147. Bataille, Eroticism, 91 (trans. modified); Bataille, OC 10:92.

148. Bataille, Literature and Evil, 183; cf. Bataille, OC 9:296.

149. Bataille, L'Abbé C., 133; cf. Bataille, OC 3:340.

Chapter 4

1. Bataille, L'Abbé C., 127; trans. modified.

2. Bataille, OC 3:335.

3. He writes, "Struggling to decipher his words, I at once began to feel a great malaise [un grande malaise], so much so that from time to time I would blush: these outbursts from the pen of the libertine sounded just as false to my ears [sonnaient faux à mes oreilles] and embarrassed me just as much as the malicious statements made before by the priest." Bataille, L'Abbé C., 128 (trans. modified); cf. Bataille, OC 3:336.

4. Bataille, L'Abbé C., 131; cf. Bataille, OC 3:338.

5. He claims within the context of his foreword: "The affection that bound me, that still binds me to my brother was so strong, so thoroughly based on a feeling of identity that I wished I could change his words as if I had written them myself. It seemed to me that he would have changed them himself: every naïve

audacity eventually creates a need for sleep and the recognition of an error without which we wouldn't have had it." Bataille, L'Abbé C., 128; Bataille, OC 3:336.

6. Bataille, OC 3:336.

7. Bataille, L'Abbé C., 128; cf. Bataille, OC 3:336.

8. Bataille, L'Abbé C., 127; Bataille, OC 3:335. Although "dérober" would, according to common usage, signify "conceal," its occurrence in a passage that emphasizes a performance of denuding ("denuder") and later, of fraudulent "immodesty" ("impudeur"), allows the etymological derivation of the verb from "rauben" or "rob" to resonate as further variations of Robert's stripping, whose exhibition is literally a cover, insofar as it appears solely through the written marks that cover the sheets he leaves behind. The further association between "Robert" and the predicate, "dérober," in the phrase "whose fraudulence can't be concealed by any artifice or ruse [*dont l'artifice et la ruse ne peuvent dérober la tricherie*]" also suggests that Robert's signature lies in the indelible traces of his fraudulence, and thus also in his de-negation (de-Robert)

9. Bataille, L'Abbé C., 128; cf. Bataille, OC 3:336.

10. Bataille, L'Abbé C., 128; cf. Bataille, OC 3:336.

11. G. W. F. Hegel, *The Science of Logic*, trans. George di Giovanni (Cambridge: Cambridge University Press, 2010), 156.

12. Bataille, OC 1:251; my translation.

13. Bataille, OC 1:248; my translation.

14. Bataille, OC 1:252–53; my translation.

15. See Roland Barthes, "The Death of the Author," trans. Stephen Heath, in *Image, Music, Text* (New York: Hill & Wang, 1977), 142–48.

16. Bataille, OC 5:541; my translation. For a further discussion of this passage on "communication," see chapter 3.

17. This adjective for talkativeness—namely, "disert"—comes from the Latin *disserere*, the frequentative verb composed of *dis-* and *serere* ("to chain"), marking a *dis*crepancy from within its own binding terms, while resonating with the "desert" that would follow from the reduction Bataille describes. This latter topos is never far when it comes to Bataille's meditations on literature, experience, evil, and mortality, as when he writes in a passage from *Guilty*: "The way goes through a deserted region, which is, however, one of apparitions (of delights and frights) [*région toutefois d'apparitions (de délices ou d'effrois)*]. Beyond: are a blind man's motions, eyes wide open, arms stretching out, staring at the sun, and inside he's turning to light." Georges Bataille, *Guilty*, 29 (trans. modified); Bataille, OC 5:265. The traversal of phenomenal appearances—which Bataille, like Augustine, sees not through a neutral lens of perception but through desire (hence the parenthetical "delights and frights")—thus issues into a lucidity that is blind and deserted by both subject and object. For another discussion of this passage, see "Introduction."

18. Bataille, *Literature and Evil*, 96 (trans. modified); cf. Bataille, OC 9:237.

19. Bataille, *L'Abbé C.*, 128 (trans. modified); cf. Bataille, *OC* 3:336.
20. Bataille, *L'Abbé C.*, 127; Bataille, *OC* 3:335.
21. Bataille, *Inner Experience*, 94; cf. Bataille, *OC* 5:111.
22. See Husserl, *Ideas 1*, 44; cf. Husserl, *Hua* 3:51. For a more extensive elaboration of the structure that has been described, through analyses of other texts and contexts, see Werner Hamacher's discussions of *Ammarkierung* in "Bogengebeten," in *Aufmerksamkeit*, ed. Norbert Haas, Rainer Nägele, and Hans-Jörg Rheinberger (Eggingen: Isele, 1998), 11–43, which he explicates further with relation to the zero sign of Roman Jakobson in "What Remains to Be Said," 239–43.
23. Bataille, *L'Abbé C.*, 128; cf. Bataille, *OC* 3:336.
24. For a brief summary of the publication history of this essay, see Bataille, *OC* 9:466. The following considerations, however, only offer one among other possible ways to respond to structural openness of Bataille's text(s).
25. Max Brod, afterword to Franz Kafka, *Der Prozess*, ed. Max Brod (Munich: Deutscher Taschenbuch Verlag, 1997), 279–90, 282.
26. There are also important discrepancies between the two undated letters, which entail that the adherence to the letter of either "testament" would necessarily entail the transgression of the other, and vice versa. The first letter specifies that all of Kafka's writings and drawings—or rather, "all that is written or drawn [*alles Geschriebene oder Gezeichnete*]"—should be burned "unread, without rest or remainder": "restlos und ungelesen." Brod, afterword, 281; my translation. In the second letter, however, Kafka asserts that "only the following books are valid: *The Judgment, The Stoker, The Metamorphosis, In the Penal Colony, A Country Doctor*, and the story: *A Hunger Artist*," before going on to write: "By contrast, all writings of mine that otherwise exist (printed in journals, in manuscripts, or in letters), without exception, as far as it is attainable or to be received by petitioning the addressees (you know, after all, most of the addressees [. . .])—all of this is, without exception, and preferably unread (though I do not forbid you from looking into [the papers], it would be preferable to me if you would not do it [. . .])—all of this is to be burned without exception" (281–82). Between the two letters, a double bind is made pronounced, which Brod could not have escaped, had he sought to follow Kafka's instructions either way. Yet besides these complications, Brod also recalls in his afterword an oral conversation with Kafka, in which Kafka had predicted what his testament would say—"My testament will be completely simple: the plea to you to burn everything [*Mein Testament wird ganz einfach sein—die Bitte an dich, alles zu verbrennen*]"—at which point Brod claims to have responded: "In case you would seriously demand such a thing of me, I tell you already now that I will not fulfill your plea [*Falls du mir im Ernste so etwas zumuten solltest, so sage ich dir schon jetzt, daß ich deine Bitte nicht erfüllen werde*]" (283). Hence, Brod draws the conclusion that Kafka would have had to designate "another executor of his will [*einen andern Testamentsexekutor*],"

if he had been serious about his supposed request (283). Whether or not one should accept Brod's counter-factual deduction, however, one could also say that Kafka's oral testimony, insofar as it was purportedly uttered in the future tense, does not yet stipulate his will even then. For a further analysis of the intricacies of Kafka's "testament," as well as the debates that have ensued in its wake through to the twenty-first century, see Judith Butler, "Who Owns Kafka?" *London Review of Books* 33, no. 5 (2011): https://www.lrb.co.uk/the-paper/v33/n05/judith-butler/who-owns-kafka (accessed December 21, 2020). For an excellent study of the paradoxes of inheritance, see Gerhard Richter, *Verwaiste Hinterlassenschaften: Formen gespenstischen Erbens* (Berlin: Matthes & Seitz, 2016).

27. In *Ideas Pertaining to a Pure Phenomenology*, Husserl describes the modification that the phenomenological reduction yields as follows: "*We do not give up the positing we effected, we do not in any respect alter our conviction* which remains in itself as it is as long as we do not introduce new judgment-motives: precisely this is what we do not do. Nevertheless the positing undergoes a modification: while it in itself remains what it is, *we, so to speak, 'put it out of action'* ['außer Aktion'], *we 'exclude it'* [or: 'switch it off', 'schalten sie aus'], *we 'parenthesize it'* [or: 'enclose it in parentheses,' 'klammern sie ein'] [. . .] We can also say: The positing is a mental process, *but we make 'no use of it'* [wir machen von ihr aber 'keinen Gebrauch']." Husserl, *Ideas 1*, 58–59; Husserl, *Hua* 3:63. Derrida's analyses in *Speech and Phenomena* unfold the implications of writing for phenomenology in ways that have inspired the readings of Bataille and Kafka that are offered in this chapter, as well as the previous one. Both chapters may also be read as further pursuits of Derrida's suggestive remark that Bataille's writings mark an "*epoché*" of "the epoch of sense," which appears in his essay on Bataille from *Writing and Difference*. Derrida, *Writing and Difference*, 339; cf. Derrida, *L'écriture et la différence*, 393.

28. Bataille, *Literature and Evil*, 151; cf. Bataille OC 9:271.

29. Bataille, *Literature and Evil*, 152 (trans. modified); Bataille, OC 9:271. In the English version, no translation is offered for the phrase "des objets auxquels il manque à la vérité d'être en feu."

30. Bataille, *Literature and Evil*, 152 (trans. modified); Bataille, OC 9:272. In the English version, the ellipses that follow Bataille's exclamation mark are left out.

31. For a thorough documentation of not only those sources on psychology and phenomenology that Kafka would have encountered during his university studies but also during his high school years, as well as his involvement with the philosophical circle known as the "Louvre Circle," see Arnold Heidsieck, *The Intellectual Contexts of Kafka's Fictions: Philosophy, Law, Religion* (Columbus: Camden House. 1994), esp. 5–12, 15–18, 22–44, 53–54.

32. Kafka, *Tagebücher*, 38. There, the passage reads: "Ich kann es nicht verstehn und nicht einmal glauben. Ich lebe nur hie und da in einem kleinen

Wort, in dessen Umlaut (oben 'stößt') ich z.B. auf einen Augenblick meinen unnützen Kopf verliere. Erster und letzter Buchstabe sind Anfang und Ende meines fischartigen Gefühls."

33. Husserl, *Logical Investigations,* 1:193; trans. modified. In German, the passage reads: "Erlebt ist beides, Wortvorstellung und sinngebender Akt; aber während wir die Wortvorstellung erleben, leben wir doch ganz und gar nicht im Vorstellen des Wortes, sondern ausschließlich im Vollziehen seines Sinnes, seines Bedeutens." Husserl, *Hua* 19/1:46.

34. For an excellent discussion of the umlaut in another context, which has inspired the reading of Kafka's diary entry that is offered here, see Anna Henke, "Sound and Unsound Advice: Unveiling Walter Benjamin's Umlaut," in *Playing False: Representations of Betrayal,* ed. Kristina Mendicino and Betiel Wasihun (Oxford: Peter Lang, 2013), 229–60.

35. Franz Kafka, *Nachgelassene Schriften und Fragmente II,* 31–32; my translation. The slanted brackets surrounding "Annagen" ("gnawing") indicate, according to the editor, that the decipherment of Kafka's handwriting is uncertain. Kafka, *Nachgelassene Schriften II,* 684.

36. Neesen writes: "What Kafka calls an inner world is the area of inner perception. There is no adequate language for it. Whatever is nevertheless brought from this inner world to the surface and thus into the outer world with the help of commonly used language is no more than that which is experienced in 'gnawing at the limits' of the whole. Since descriptive psychology takes recourse to the procedure of describing inner perceptions, which are imparted through a language that is, in itself, unsuitable, it cannot penetrate to the kernel of the inner world. It gnaws at authentic human life only along its limits [*Sie nagt das eigentliche menschliche Leben nur in seinen Grenzen an*]." Peter Neesen, *Vom Louvrezirkel zum Prozess: Franz Kafka und die Psychologie Franz Brentanos* (Göppingen: Kümmerle, 1972), 149; my translation.

37. Arnold Heidsieck, "Physiological, Phenomenological, and Linguistic Psychology in Kafka's Early Works," *German Quarterly* 62, no. 4 (1989): 489–500, 496. Heidsieck sees this resignation to be an affirmation of Edmund Husserl's notion that "sensation and intentional grasping are by nature conscious in the sense of being 'in consciousness' but are not necessarily conscious in the Brentanoan sense of being the evident object of or being known by inner perception." Heidsieck, "Physiological," 495. Johann Christian Marek and Barry Smith have cited Kafka's note as evidence for the fact that he shares Brentano's and Marty's recognition that direct "self observation" is an "impossibility," though without indicating Kafka's position on these thinkers' insistence upon the evidence of "inner perception." Johann Christian Marek and Barry Smith, "Einleitung zu Anton Martys Elemente der deskriptiven Psychologie," *Conceptus* 21, no. 53/54 (1987): 33–47, 36–37. In a separate and more extensive study on "Kafka and Brentano," however, Smith argues that the "outward descriptions" that enter into

Kafka's fiction expose something like an "inner world" whenever they register "some contrast with an expected or somehow typical order in external reality." Smith, "Kafka and Brentano," in *Structure and Gestalt: Philosophy and Literature in Austria-Hungary and Her Successor States*, ed. Barry Smith (Amsterdam: John Benjamins, 1981), 113–59, 128. In this oblique way, the 'associated psychical phenomena can show themselves," and in "this sense," Smith concludes, "Kafka can be said to have developed a characteristically Brentanian mode of representation of the self." Smith, "Brentano and Kafka," 128.

38. Stephen Dowden, *Kafka's Castle and the Critical Imagination* (Columbia: Camden House, 1995), 83–34.

39. Scholem writes in his essay from 1917, "Über Klage und Klagelied": "The infinite tension that ignites with every word in lamentation and, so to speak, makes it weep—hardly is there a word in human languages that weeps and falls silent more than the Hebrew word 'how' [*das hebräische Wort* איכה *[ekha]* ('Wie')], with which the lamentations for the dead begin." Gershom Scholem, "Über Klage und Klagelied," in *Tagebücher nebst Aufsätzen und Entwürfen bis 1923: 2. Halbband 1917–1923*, ed. Karlfried Gründer et al. (Frankfurt am Main: Jüdischer Verlag, 2000), 128–33, 132; my translation.

40. This inner evidence is what Brentano would call the "fixed point [*festen Punkt*]" upon which "knowledge [*Erkenntnis*]" should be based." Franz Brentano, *Psychologie vom empirischen Standpunkt*, ed. Oskar Kraus, 3 vols. (Hamburg: Meiner, 1971–74), 1:14; my translation. Similarly, Anton Marty would say in the lecture course on descriptive psychology that Kafka had taken, "The infallible certitude that one had noticed early on in inner perception and that, in fact, forms the foundation of all our knowledge of experience is possible through that inner relation which subsists between the perceived phenomenon and the perception directed toward it." Anton Marty, *Deskriptive Psychologie*, ed. Mauro Antonelli and Johann Christian Marek (Würzburg: Königshausen & Neumann, 2011), 29; my translation. In the doctoral thesis that he wrote under Marty's guidance, *Untersuchungen zum Problem der Evidenz der inneren Wahrnehmung*, Bergmann similarly wrote: "Now for inner perception, we stake our claims on *evidence*. [. . .] One has for a long time sought the grounds for the fact of evidence in the particular intimacy with which perceiving and the perceived are here united in a single reality [*in einer Realität vereint sind*]." Hugo Bergmann, *Untersuchungen zum Problem der Evidenz der inneren Wahrnehmung* (Halle: Niemeyer, 1908), 11; my translation.

41. The notion of "real" unity was critical for establishing the certitude of inner perception because any other relation between a perceiving consciousness and its conscious perception would imply their possible separation and thus introduce the possibility for error. Marty argues: "If the psychic act were merely the effective cause of the perception of it, then it could very well happen that a deception intervenes, since different causes can have the same effect." Marty,

Deskriptive Psychologie, 29; my translation. See also Marty, *Deskriptive Psychologie*, 34–35. Bergmann speaks of this "real unity" in *Untersuchungen*, 12; my translation.

42. On the impossibility of inner observation, Brentano cites the English psychologist Henry Maudsley, who had insisted that the "thinking individual cannot divide itself into two, from which the one thinks back, while the other sees it thinking back." Brentano, *Psychologie* 1:45; my translation. Brentano then cites memory as a solution to this dilemma: "This has often been made valid as the most preeminent means to obtain knowledge of psychical facts, and thinkers of entirely different directions are in accord on this point" (1:48; my translation). The citational character of Brentano's writing in this passage also anticipates his subsequent argument that others' testimonies may compensate for the self-deception to which memory exposes each thinker (1:49–50): through language, namely, there "accrues to us the possibility to bind whatever another has observed in himself with our proper inner experiences and to test our proper experiences [. . .] against foreign ones, wherever observations relate to similar phenomena" (1:54; my translation). For the same reason that we may deceive ourselves, moreover, it is not even what others directly "report" about themselves that will be said to offer the most telling disclosures of inner life but rather "what they involuntarily betray" against their better knowledge. Hence, Brentano recommends the "study of autobiographies for the psychologist," and approvingly paraphrases Feuchtersleben: "One should pay attention in autobiographies not so much to what they report, but to what they involuntarily betray" (1:54–55; my translation). Smith and especially Neesen emphasize the resonance of these premises in Kafka's fiction.

43. This originally inhuman character of experience is what would lead Husserl to conclude that it "is only with [. . .] the constant orientation of experiential observation onto the psychic life which is appresented along with the other's body [. . .] that the closed unity, man, is constituted, and I transfer this unity subsequently to myself." Husserl, *Ideas 2*, 175 (trans. modified); cf. Husserl, *Hua* 4:167. Before this passage, however, Husserl will insist that the "I" of transcendental subjectivity "is given in absolute selfhood and in a unity which does not present itself by way of adumbrations," as the "center whence all conscious life emits rays and receives them." Husserl, *Ideas 2*, 111–12 (trans. modified); cf. Husserl, *Hua* 4:104–5.

44. Or, as Avital Ronell has written in a most perceptive study of the modalities and implications of complaint, "complaint folds as it sounds off." Avital Ronell, *Complaint: Grievance Among Friends* (Urbana: University of Illinois Press, 2018), 3.

45. Kafka, *Nachgelassene Schriften und Fragmente II*, 31–32; my translation.

46. Kafka, *Nachgelassene Schriften und Fragmente II*, 42. Later, he will develop this thought in a commentary on the indifference of confession and lie, on which see chapter 5.

47. Franz Kafka, *Nachgelassene Schriften und Fragmente I*, ed. Malcolm Pasley (Frankfurt am Main: Fischer, 1993), 310. The fragment, which breaks off

after "screen [*Schirm*]," appears in an octavo notebook dating from 1917 according to Malcolm Pasley, which is the same year that Kafka's remarks on the limits of descriptive psychology were recorded, according to Jost Schillemeit.

48. Kata Gellen, *Kafka and Noise: The Discovery of Cinematic Sound in Literary Modernism* (Evanston, IL: Northwestern University Press, 2019), 141.

49. Anthony Curtis Adler, "The Biopolitics of Noise: Kafka's 'Der Bau,'" in *Thresholds of Listening: Sound, Technics, Space*, ed. Sander van Maas (New York: Fordham University Press, 2015), 125–42, 138.

50. Kafka, *Tagebücher*, 38.

51. Kafka, *Tagebücher*, 892. In his discussion of the passages previously cited, Heidsieck concludes that "Kafka observes that obeying the laws of writing in the act of writing may be the most effective circumvention of introspection," but in taking recourse to "laws," a restrictive approach to writing is adopted, which cannot account for those traits of Kafka's texts that cross the limits of semantics and logic. Heidsieck, *The Intellectual Contexts of Kafka's Fiction*, 64.

52. Kafka, *Das Schloss*, 1:4.

53. With respect to different aspects of these initial manuscript pages, Malte Kleinwort likewise speaks of the way in which Kafka stages an "arrival before the arrival," or a "*pre*-arrival [*Vor-Ankunft*]," before relating this dynamic of deferral to the oscillation between "self-construction and -destruction" that marks Kafka's writing practice. See Malte Kleinwort, *Der späte Kafka: Spätstil als Stilsuspension* (Munich: Fink, 2013), 109, 112; my translation.

54. Kafka, *Das Schloss*, 1:4.

55. Kafka, *Das Schloss*, 1:4, 1:7.

56. Kafka, *Das Schloss*, 1:7.

57. Kafka, *Das Schloss*, 1:8.

58. Kafka, *Das Schloss*, 1:8.

59. Kafka, *Das Schloss*, 4:195.

60. Kafka, *Das Schloss*, 6:8. Many readers have noticed the narratives that circulate within Kafka's novel and offered different interpretations of their function. Wilhelm Emrich suggests that K.'s placeless "position" in the village, where he remains "foundationless, fixated nowhere," is the "strength" that "awakens hope and fear in the village," inspiring phantasies such as Pepi's and Olga's. See Wilhelm Emrich, *Franz Kafka: A Critical Study of His Writings*, trans. Sheema Zeben Buehne (New York: Ungar, 1968), 374–75. Marthe Robert similarly suggests that the foreignness of K. is what renders him provocative to others: "He is a stranger, and consequently free of the prejudices and fears that make terror reign among the indigenous people." Marthe Robert, *L'ancien et le nouveau: De Don Quichotte à Franz Kafka* (Paris: Grasset, 1963), 207; my translation. In the essay he had initially written in response to Robert's book, Maurice Blanchot speaks of K's "peregrinations" as consisting "not in going from place to place, but from exegesis to exegesis, from commentator to commentator," placing an emphasis upon the

impotence, incompleteness, and passivity that thereby characterize each instance of interpretation. Maurice Blanchot, *De Kafka à Kafka* (Paris: Gallimard, 1981), 194; my translation. What Charles Bernheimer writes of K's role with respect to the castle also aptly describes his roles in others' narratives: "As far as the Castle is concerned, K. is actually no more than a supplementary function to its own ironic allegorical structure. K. provisionally fills in for the lack generated by the Castle's constitutive effacement of presence and origin." Charles Bernheimer, *Flaubert and Kafka: Studies in Psychopoetic Structure* (New Haven, CT: Yale University Press, 1982), 230.

61. Even as they speak, the figures of Kafka's novel thus exhibit the traits of writing that Stanley Corngold has aptly said to yield "an uncanny voice in which various voices without a specific origin mix indistinguishably." Stanley Corngold, *The Fate of the Self: German Writers and French Theory* (New York: Columbia University Press, 1986), 162. This view, exemplified by Roland Barthes, will be criticized in the course of Corngold's study, however, which concludes with the affirmation that "the life of the author—the tension between his suffering and his excessive interpretation of it—survives, for the reader, on the margin of his breaks." Corngold, *The Fate of the Self*, 177.

62. Roland Reuss, "Das Schloss: Zur Einführung," *Franz-Kafka-Heft* 9 (Frankfurt am Main/Basel: Stroemfeld/Roter Stern, 2018), 2–23, 21; my translation.

63. Kafka, *Das Schloss*, 1:8.

64. Kafka, *Das Schloss*, 1:7–8.

65. Kafka, *Das Schloss*, 1:8.

66. Gerhard Neumann, "Franz Kafka's 'Schloss'-Roman: Das parasitäre Spiel der Zeichen," in *Franz Kafka: Schriftverkehr*, ed. Wolf Kittler and Gerhard Neumann (Freiburg: Rombach, 1990), 199–221, 219; my translation. He argues that the "entire village" appears to be "at hand solely for the sake of this foreigner" and that it is defined solely by the "expectation" of the new arrival, but Neumann also claims that a process of "finding oneself" is at stake for the foreigner, which the scene does not necessarily suggest. Neumann, "Franz Kafkas 'Schloss'-Roman," 208; my translation.

67. Kafka, *Das Schloss*, 1:11.

68. Kafka, *Das Schloss*, 1:11.

69. In one early scene, the mayor of town will tell the K., "What now concerns your case, I will [. . .] tell you the course that it took openly [*Was nun Ihren Fall betrifft, so will ich Ihnen [. . .] de[r]n Hergang offen erzählen*]." Kafka, *Das Schloss*, 1:138. Shortly thereafter, the landlady of the inn where K. had first arrived concludes her narrative of her former relations with Klamm: "I have openly told openly told you my case, from which you could have learned several things [*ich habe Ihnen offen meinen Fall erzählt aus dem Sie einiges hätten lernen können offen erzählt*]" (2:60).

70. Kafka, *Das Schloss*, 1:11.

71. Kafka, *Das Schloss*, 1:27. They could recall, for example, the castle that figures in Božena Němcová's novel, *The Grandmother*, as well as her novella, *The Castle and the Village*, as readers of Kafka such as, most recently, Anne Jamison have argued. Anne Jamison, *Kafka's Other Prague: Writings from the Czechoslovak Republic* (Evanston, IL: Northwestern University Press, 2018), 91–96. However, as Robert had pointed out in her study of Kafka and Cervantes, "The real castle with which K. engages tends continually to disappear behind its literary analogues—ancient, feudal, marvelous, haunted, fairytale, invisible, mystical castles, to say nothing of those castles of Spain that are pure chimeras, as well as those of Bohemia, which were constructed by History and rewritten by legend." Robert, *L'ancien et le nouveau*, 197; my translation.

72. This trouble is perhaps still more fundamental than the one that Joseph Vogl speaks of in his exquisite commentary on the ever-altering alterity of narrative voice in Kafka's fiction, with a focus upon, among others, Kafka's shift from first- to third-person narration in his *Schloss* manuscript. For while it is true that, as Vogl argues, Kafka's writing speaks with "no unified voice, but only a system of [vocal] differences" and thus forges "no correlation between subject and world, ego and description, but only an oscillating focus," what is at stake in this passage is the possible absence of any phenomenal space for objects and subjects alike. Joseph Vogl, "Vierte Person: Kafkas Erzählstimme," *Deutsche Vierteljahrsschrift für Literaturwissenschaft und Geistesgeschichte* 68 (1994): 745–56, 756; my translation.

73. Joseph Vogl, "Am Schlossberg," in *"Schloss"-Topographien: Lektüren zu Kafkas Romanfragment*, ed. Malte Kleinwort and Joseph Vogl (Bielefeld: transcript, 2013), 23–32, 24; my translation. Similarly, the "nothing" that is to be seen of the "Schlossberg" says not only that nothing is visible of the castle "mount [*Berg*]," but also that nothing is visible of the castle's concealment, insofar as "Berg" bears with it implications of "shielding" and "concealing" (*bergen, sich verbergen*).

74. Husserl, *Hua* 19/1: 56. In the English edition, this term is translated "unity of coincidence," which is correct but also covers over the metaphor of covering that insinuates itself into Husserl's technical term, on which see chapter 2 (cf. Husserl, *Logical Investigations* 1:199).

75. These terms appear throughout Husserl's oeuvre in his discussions of those modalizations that affect the thetic character of the intentional objects of consciousness. See, for example, Husserl, *Hua* 3:97–98; Husserl, *Hua* 11:20–22, 30–33; Husserl, *Erfahrung und Urteil*, 25–26, 97–98.

76. Husserl, *Ideas 1*, 364 (trans. modified); Husserl, *Hua* 3:353.

77. See especially Husserl's lectures on *Phantasie und Bildbewußtsein* in *Hua* 23:406. In another passage from these manuscripts, he will speak of paintings and imaginative representations as already "furnished" or "versehen"—which also may imply that "seeing" (*sehen*) has gone "awry" (*ver*)—with "the character of being-struck-through, of the 'not' [*dem Charakter der Durchstreichung, des Nicht*]." Husserl, *Hua* 23:413; see also Husserl, *Hua* 19/1:579.

78. Franz Kafka, *Tagebücher*, 596; my translation. The passage in German reads: "Als ich das Tintenfaß vom Schreibtisch nahm, um es ins Wohnzimmer zu tragen, fühlte ich eine Festigkeit in mir, so wie z.B. die Kante eines großen Gebäudes im Nebel erscheint und gleich wieder verschwindet." The evocation of a barely visible "edge" or "Kante" not only marks an outer projection or transformation of "Kafka's" inner solidity but also recalls the term that Kafka had used in an early manuscript on aesthetics, where Gustav Fechner's notion of an "aesthetic threshold [*ästhetische Schwelle*]" is replaced with the notion of an "aesthetic edge [*ästhetische Kante*]." Heidsieck, *The Intellectual Contexts of Kafka's Fiction*, 28, 178. As Heidsieck has summarized, for Fechner, this threshold marks the "minimal (noticeable) intensity" that a stimulus requires in order "to enter consciousness" (28).

79. Blanchot, *The Infinite Conversation*, 386 (trans. modified); cf. Blanchot, *L'entretien infini*, 566. The phrase "neither reveals nor conceals [*ne révèle ni ne cache*]" is also an echo of one of Heraclitus's most often-cited fragments, to which Blanchot recurs throughout his oeuvre (see, e.g., Blanchot, *The Infinite Conversation*, 92; cf. Blanchot, *L'entretien infini*, 131).

80. Bataille, *L'Abbé C.*, 128; cf. Bataille, *OC* 3:336.

81. Marty, *Deskriptive Psychologie*, 30; my translation. For a discussion of Augustine's trinitarian phenomenology of mind, see chapter 1.

82. Bataille, *Literature and Evil*, 152; cf. Bataille, *OC* 9:271.

83. Henry Sussman, *Franz Kafka: Geometrician of Metaphor* (Madison: Coda, 1979), 29–30.

84. Franz Kafka, "Wedding Preparations in the Country," in *Wedding Preparations in the Country and Other Posthumous Prose Writings*, trans. Ernst Kaiser and Eithne Wilkins (London: Secker and Warburg, 1954), 7–37, 8. The German text reads: "Und solange Du 'man' sagst an Stelle von 'ich,' ist es nichts und man kann diese Geschichte aufsagen, sobald Du aber Dir eingestehst daß Du selbst es bist, dann wirst Du förmlich durchbohrt und bist entsetzt." Kafka, *Nachgelassene Schriften und Fragmente I*, 14. As Joseph Vogl has insightfully pointed out, however, even within this text, the "I" is "no self, no opposite to the anonymous 'one,' nor is 'I' its origin; it is rather first produced in the gaze of another [*im fremden Blick erst produziert*], as an 'object of the curiosity' that reads Raban's presence and body as a sign. The 'I' [. . .] is an indeterminate signifier; insofar as it is something intended, something supposed; insofar as it is the somehow significant depth of an appearance, it possesses no origin in itself, but is drawn forth through a self-interpretation that is itself aroused through interpretation, and it remains in this respect impossible." Joseph Vogl, *Ort der Gewalt: Kafkas literarische Ethik* (Zürich: diaphanes, 2010), 27; my translation.

85. Taking seriously the divergent ways in which "K." does not function as a consistent abbreviation may complicate Bernheimer's description of "K.'s" quest to resist the fragmentation to which "he" is subject: "For [K.], as for many

critics of Kafka's texts, symbolic interpretation ensures the meaningful unity of life, its comprehensibility within a totalizing system of signification. K. is a cypher searching for a name, a beginning sign questing for a nominal conclusion. That such a conclusion never comes indicates that, in the fallen world, no sign can be any more than a partial signifier. The questing interpreter, K. or his belated critic, is forever frustrated by an allegorical structure that fragments, temporalizes, and textualizes his symbolic search." Bernheimer, *Flaubert and Kafka*, 198. In attributing a "search" to K., it would have to be asked which "K." one is talking about: the "K." whom Kafka's narrator writes about, the "K." of Pepi's imagination, or the "K." whom Hans Brunswick wants to resemble when he grows up, etc., while the fact that these various "K.s" are neither entirely identical nor clearly distinct would trouble the conditions of possibility for attribution. And beyond the references to "K." that appear within *The Castle*, this variable function may just as well be read in relation to Albert Einstein's variable for various reference bodies in the popular version of his theory of relativity (i.e., "K"), as it may be read to recall Kafka's last initial. Albert Einstein, *Relativity: The Special and General Theory*, trans. Robert W. Lawson (New York: Henry Holt, 1921), 15–18.

86. Whenever it would seem that another figure speaks of K. by name, as when Hans Brunswick, whose mother K. had encountered early in the novel, says that his "his mother had also already asked about K. once [*die Mutter habe auch schon einmal nach K. gefragt*]," the passage is most often rendered in indirect discourse. Kafka, *Das Schloss*, 3:101. By contrast, when a castle official "names" K. over the telephone, it is the title "land-surveyor" that he is given: "The Castle had named [me] him land-surveyor, then [*Das Schloss hat [mich] ihn also zum Landvermesser ernannt*]" (1:19). A flagrant exception takes place when Frieda, the barmaid whom K. seduces, shouts out that she is "with K! [*bei K!*]," which Kafka crosses out and replaces with "with the land-surveyor [*beim Landvermesser*]!" (1:109). As Kleinwort shows, however, even Frieda's initial exclamation may be read otherwise, echoing as it does the Czech word for "fable," "baijka." Kleinwort, *Der späte Kafka*, 117. Whereas Kleinwort seeks to clarify the alteration by suggesting that Kafka had sought to avoid such unintentional, interlingual echoes, however, the change also allows Kafka—whether he knew it or not—to circumvent a situation where another character would refer to "K." by name and thus confirm K.'s nominal identity in a manner that the text otherwise does not support.

87. K. does call himself "Josef" while he is on the telephone with a castle official at one point, but he also calls himself the land-surveyor's "assistant [*Gehilfen*]" in the same conversation, making it doubtful that "Josef" is his "real" first name. Kafka, *Das Schloss*, 1:60. The fact that this name recalls the name of Kafka's protagonist in *The Trial*, moreover, breaks the "frame" of both fictions. As Stanley Corngold has argued, the repetition of such "allegorical fragments from the history of Kafka's writings" "throughout *Das Schloß*" turns us "back and away from the expectable progressive narrative of K.'s attempt to 'enter' the

Castle," creating a "*ritardando*" in communication, such that textual "knowledge cannot be fixed" and "produces a vertigo of indetermination." Stanley Corngold, "Ritardando in *Das Schloß*," in *From Kafka to Sebald: Modernism and Narrative Form*, ed. Sabine Wilke (London: Bloomsbury, 2012), 11–26, 12, 18.

88. Kafka, *Das Schloss*, 1:64.

89. Kafka, *Das Schloss*, 3:8.

90. In the convolute entitled "In the Cathedral [*Im Dom*]," it is said, just as a priest appears prepared to deliver a sermon, "But it was not the congregation that the priest called upon, [he] it ~~called~~ was entirely unequivocal and there were no evasions, he called: Josef K! [*Es war aber nicht die Gemeinde, die der Geistliche anrief, e[r]s ~~rief~~ war ganz eindeutig und es gab keine Ausflüchte, er rief: Josef K!*]." Franz Kafka, "Im Dom," in *Der Process: Faksimile-Edition (Franz Kafka-Ausgabe. Historisch-Kritische Edition sämtlicher Handschriften, Drucke und Typoskripte)*, ed. Roland Reuß and Peter Staengle (Frankfurt am Main/Basel: Stroemfeld/Roter Stern, 1997), 34; my translation.

91. This multiplication *and* withdrawal of "K." from spoken circulation may even disrupt the minimal continuity that Gilles Deleuze and Félix Guattari maintain, when they argue that "K." designates not "a subject" but a "*function of a polyvocal assemblage of which the solitary individual is a part.*" Gilles Deleuze and Félix Guattari, *Kafka: Towards a Minor Literature*, trans. Dana Polan (Minneapolis: University of Minnesota Press, 1986), 84–85; cf. Gilles Deleuze and Félix Guattari, *Franz Kafka: Pour une littérature mineure* (Paris: Minuit, 1975), 151–52. Of course, Deleuze and Guattari's notion of a "function" does not exclude variation and rupture; as they would write in *A Thousand Plateaus*: "A variable can be continuous over a portion of its trajectory, then leap or skip, without that affecting its continuous variation; what this does is impose an absent development as an 'alternative continuity' that is virtual yet real." Gilles Deleuze and Félix Guattari, *A Thousand Plateaus: Capitalism and Schizophrenia*, trans. Brian Massumi (Minneapolis: University of Minnesota Press, 1987), 95. The reading that is offered here nonetheless diverges from theirs, however, to the extent that it does not depart from conceptual schemes of desire, power, and collectivity but unfolds textual analyses, which expose the singular ways in which aleatory movements in language affect the subject of speech.

92. Avital Ronell, "Doing Kafka in *The Castle*: A Poetics of Desire," in *Kafka and the Contemporary Critical Performance: Centenary Readings*, ed. Alan Udoff (Bloomington: Indiana University Press, 1987), 214–35, 218.

93. Kafka, *Das Schloss*, 1:121. The assertion that K. stands in the way "overall" or "everywhere [*überall*]" says at the same time that he is scandalous, in the precise sense of a "stumbling block" or σκάνδαλον. Burkhardt Wolf also draws attention to these lines in his study of the ways in which Kafka's "statistical style [*statistische Schreibweise*]" tests the limits of the nonintuitive evidence that statistical bureaucratic institutions such as the Workmen's Accident Insurance Institute

had designs to produce. Kafka inscribes, he argues, "supernumerary and thus 'uninsurable' figures" into his narratives, who at once "stand under [. . .] the iron law of number—and undermine it nevertheless." Burckhardt Wolf, "Die Nacht des Bürokraten: Franz Kafkas statistische Schreibweise," *Deutsche Vierteljahrsschrift für Literaturwissenschaft und Geistesgeschichte* 80 (2006): 97–127, 122; my translation.

94. Kafka, *Das Schloss*, 1:8.

95. Werner Hamacher, "Ungerufen: Kommentar zu Kafkas *Prüfung*," *Die Neue Rundschau* 118, no. 2 (2007): 132–53, 141; my translation.

96. This specific discrepancy exemplifies Theodor W. Adorno's assertion that Kafka's writing exposes "the obscurity of the existent," such that "[e]ach sentence says 'interpret me,' and none will permit it." Theodor W. Adorno, "Notes on Kafka," in *Prisms*, trans. Samuel Weber and Shierry Weber (Cambridge MA: MIT Press, 1981), 243–71, 246.

97. Kafka, *Das Schloss*, 1:114.

98. The pseudo-seduction will have been accomplished, according to the landlady, from the moment that Frieda let K. look at her former lover, Klamm, through a peephole at the bar where she worked. The landlady reports, "With pain I have heard that Frieda let you look through the peephole [.], already when [S]she did that, [S]she was seduced by you [*Mit Schmerz habe ich gehört, dass Frieda Sie hat durchs Guckloch schauen lassen[.], schon als [S]sie das tat, war [S]sie von Ihnen verführt*]." Kafka, *Das Schloss*, 1:121. This allowance, however, follows no seductive gestures on K's part: rather, it is Frieda's response to the brief question that K. had addressed to her just before: "Do you know Mr. Klamm" (1:98). Only after K. looks through the peephole and resumes his conversation with her, does he mention Frieda's "tender hands," while remaining uncertain himself as to "whether I he only flattered her or was also really overcome by her [*ob ich er nur schmeichelte oder auch wirklich von ihr bezwungen war*]" (1:102). Far from a seducer, K. is not even the one who initially proposes that Frieda leave Klamm, whose lover she claims to have been up to that point. She asks K. herself, "Do you want perhaps to draw me away from Klamm? Dear God!" after which, "as if tired from so much distrust," he is reported to have said: "Exactly that is was my most secret intention. You should leave Klamm and become my lover. And now I can go" (1:102). From this context, it would seem that K's proposition is nothing but an ironic way to take leave of Frieda, which he delivers in a state of exhaustion rather than desire.

99. Kafka, *Das Schloss*, 1:126, 129.

100. Kafka, *Das Schloss*, 1:133.

101. In German, the passage reads: "Sie sind paar Tage im Ort und schon wollen Sie alles besser kennen, als [i]die Eingeborenen, besser als ich alte Frau." Kafka, *Das Schloss*, 1:125.

102. In more ways than one, her introductory words, "assurances are needed [*Sicherungen sind nötig*]," speak to the unsure character of all that concerns K.,

which extends to her concerns regarding him and Frieda as well. Kafka, *Das Schloss*, 1:117. This lack of assurance (*Sicherung*) may echo the abiding questions of insurance (*Versicherung*) that occupied Kafka in his job at the Workmen's Accident Insurance Institute, whose importance to *The Castle*, among others, has been demonstrated through studies such as Wolf's essay, "Die Nacht des Bürokraten," as well as Corngold and Wagner's *Franz Kafka: The Ghosts in the Machine*. The fact that the question of assurance first arises when K. begins to improvise a domestic arrangement with Frieda would strengthen this association: the possibility that he may be responsible for a household arguably provokes considerations of other institutional structures, among which insurance would surely figure. However, the encounter between the landlady and K. also exposes the fundamentally unassurable character of experience that Kafka had not ceased to address in the wake of his phenomenological and psychological studies.

 103. Kafka, *Nachgelassene Schriften und Fragmente II*, 31–32.

 104. The landlady's inability to discount or account for this "supernumerary" figure resonates with the structure Alain Badiou describes, when he writes of the "eventalsite" as a singular "multiple 'admitted' into the count without having to result from 'previous' counts." Alain Badiou, *Being and Event*, trans. Oliver Feltham (London: Continuum, 2007), 175.

 105. Kafka, *Das Schloss*, 1:133.

 106. Specifically, the letter states that the mayor will share "alles Nähere über Ihre Arbeit und die Lohnbedingungen." Kafka, *Das Schloss*, 1:64.

 107. Kafka, *Das Schloss*, 1:64.

 108. Kafka, *Das Schloss*, 1:137. For all his efforts to reach the upper echelons of the official hierarchy in *The Castle*, K. also displays an attraction to the alleviation that official prescriptions provide. Shortly after reading his letter to the mayor, K. is said to have felt lighter: "Once again he had the feeling of the extraordinary ease of trafficking with the authorities [*Wieder hatte er das Gefühl der ausserordentlichen Leichtigkeit des Verkehrs mit den Behörden*]" (1:137). But the "ease"—and relief from responsibility—that such traffic entails also alleviates "K." of himself, as the next sentence leaves "him" behind, recurring to the pronominal form for "one" in general: "They bore every burden; one could lay everything upon them [. . .], while remaining untouched oneself and free [*Sie trugen förmlich jede Last, alles konnte man ihnen auferlegen [.] und selbst blieb man unberührt und frei*]" (1:137).

 109. Kafka, *Das Schloss*, 1:64.

 110. The full passage reads: "Was nun Ihren Fall betrifft, so will ich Ihnen ohne Amtsgeheimnisse zu machen—dazu bin ich nicht genug Beamter, ich bin Bauer und dabei bleibt es—den Hergang offen erzählen." Kafka, *Das Schloss*, 1:138.

 111. On the writ itself, the mayor reports: "Dieser Erlass kann natürlich nicht Sie betroffen haben, denn das [vo]war vor vielen Jahren." Kafka, *Das Schloss*, 1:138.

 112. Kafka, *Das Schloss*, 1:137–38.

113. Kafka, *Das Schloss*, 2:11.
114. Kafka, *Das Schloss*, 2:12.
115. Kafka, *Das Schloss*, 1:150.
116. Sussman, *Franz Kafka*, 125.
117. Corngold and Wagner, *The Ghosts in the Machine*, 129, 124. This latter reference to "release" is drawn from a diary entry in which Kafka had written of coming into "the free arena of authentic description [. . .] that loosens one's foot from lived experience [*das Freie der eigentlichen Beschreibung [. . .], die einem den Fuß vom Erlebnis löst*]." Kafka, *Tagebücher*, 87; my translation.
118. Wagner draws from the cases described in Erich Graf Kielmannsegg's study from 1906, *Geschäftsvereinfachung und Kanzleireform*, which he finds to anticipate the scene from *Das Schloss* previously discussed. Benno Wagner, "Kafka's Office Writings: Historical Background and Institutional Setting," in *The Office Writings*, by Franz Kafka, ed. Stanley Corngold, Jack Greenberg, and Benno Wagner (Princeton, NJ: Princeton University Press, 2009), 30, cf. 27, 385.
119. In German, the passage reads: "'Sie sind immer willkommen,' sagte er [. . .], aber dann fügte er hinzu: 'Besonders jetzt solange ich krank bin. Wenn ich dann wieder zum Schreibtisch gehen kann, nimmt mich natürlich die amtliche Arbeit ~~wieder~~ ganz in Anspruch." Kafka, *Das Schloss*, 2:25.
120. Kafka, *Das Schloss*, 1:138.
121. Kafka, *Das Schloss*, 1:141.
122. Kafka, *Das Schloss*, 1:142.
123. Marty, *Deskriptive Psychologie*, 133; my translation.
124. As Marty also notes, "collective numerals [*Zahlenkollektiva*]" are "not real [*nicht real*]," which is not to say that they cannot be "authentically" represented to the mind; however, Marty will assert, following a tradition that traces back to Leibniz and Descartes, that "larger numbers are only inauthentically represented [*größere Zahlen werden nur uneigentlich vorgestellt*]." Marty, *Deskriptive Psychologie*, 113, 133; my translation.
125. Marty writes, "But we have no authentic notion of it [*Allein davon haben wir keine eigentliche Vorstellung*]," whereby his use of the first-person plural would render the supposed "authenticity" of this claim itself questionable. Marty, *Deskriptive Psychologie*, 133.
126. Brentano says, specifically, that I remember my past self "similarly to when I believe another [. . .] to be psychically active [*ähnlich wie wenn ich einen andern [. . .] psychisch tätig glaube*]. Brentano, *Psychologie*, 2:142; my translation.
127. Brentano, *Psychologie*, 2:142; my translation. The German passage reads: "es müßte doch sonst einer, der sich eines früheren Irrtums erinnert, wieder irren und einer, der eines früheren sündigen Wollens reuig gedenkt, wieder sündigen." Where Marty places one's own past thinking on a par with the thinking of another in his *Untersuchungen zur Grundlegung der allgemeinen Grammatik und Sprachphilosophie*, his arguments similarly rest upon the premise

of self-alienation: "When it is a matter of such a representational procedure for a foreign individual or in my proper past, why should it not be possible for me to be in doubt as to whether it is taking place or took place, or for me to deny it under some circumstances, and affirm it under other circumstances? [*Wenn es sich dabei um einen solchen [Vorstellungsvorgang] bei einem fremden Individuum oder in meiner eigenen Vergangenheit handelt, warum soll es nicht möglich sein, daß ich im Zweifel bin, ob er statthabe resp. stattgehabt habe und daß ich ihn unter Umständen leugne, unter anderen Umständen anerkenne?*]." Marty, *Untersuchungen*, 242; my translation.

128. Marty, *Deskriptive Psychologie*, 133; my translation.

129. Kafka, *Das Schloss*, 1:142.

130. Kafka, *Das Schloss*, 1:142. For a discussion of the ambivalence that the preposition or alphabetic sequence "ab" bears in other contexts (including Sigmund Freud's *Traumdeutung* and Johann Wolfgang von Goethe's *Wahlverwandtschaften*), see Zachary Sng, "Ablative Affinities," *Modern Language Notes* 133, no. 5 (2018): 1233–53. For a commentary on the *Abfall* that sweeps through Kakfa's writing, see Thomas Schestag, *Namenlose* (Berlin: Matthes & Seitz, 2020), 47–142.

131. Kafka, *Tagebücher*, 38.

132. Bataille, *Literature and Evil*, 152; cf. Bataille, *OC* 9:271.

133. Blanchot, *The Writing of the Disaster*, 16; cf. Blanchot, *L'écriture du désastre*, 32.

Chapter 5

1. Kafka, *Nachgelassene Schriften und Fragmente II*, 348.
2. Kafka, *Nachgelassene Schriften und Fragmente II*, 42.
3. Kafka, *Tagebücher*, 87.
4. Initially, it is said that Josef K. "wondered whether it might not be a good idea to draw up a written statement and submit it to the court. His intention was to present a brief account of his life, explaining for every event that was in any way important why he'd acted as he had, whether he now looked on his course of action with approval or disapproval, and the reasons he could adduce for either conclusion." Franz Kafka, *The Trial*, trans. Mike Mitchell (Oxford: Oxford University Press, 2009), 80. But when the task is considered again in further detail, it soon appears to be "impossible," since it would require "pass[ing] his whole life in review and describ[ing] it right down to the very last detail," which also means that it would exceed his lifetime (91). As in Kafka's note on confession, it is thus indicated that there could be no catching up with oneself in either knowledge or discourse. Instead, the project of remembering one's past could only be undertaken as a pastime, with no pretentions to accuracy, veracity, or completeness: "It was perhaps a suitable occupation for retirement, to help pass

the long days once his mind had grown senile and childish" (91). In this respect, the second thoughts that Josef K. entertains resemble those of the mayor from *The Castle*, whose illness and bedridden condition are what afford him the time to recall or fabricate the backstory of the land surveyor.

    5. Augustine, *Confessions*, X.3.4.
    6. Augustine, *Confessions*, X.1.1.
    7. Marion, *In the Self's Place*, 40.
    8. Husserl, *Hua* 9:326–27; my translation. Just after this sentence, Husserl repeats: "Scientifically valid theory is a system of intersubjective results, which bear in themselves the sense of objectivity that is constituted and enriched in subjectivity" (9:327; my translation).
    9. Hannah Arendt, *The Life of the Mind*, 50.
    10. In a letter to Felix Weltsch from November 30, 1917, Kafka had asked his friend, who had been reading Augustine at the time, about available editions of the *Confessions*. Franz Kafka, *Briefe: 1914–1917*, ed. Hans-Gerd Koch (Frankfurt am Main: Fischer, 2005), 371; cf. 773–74). As Paul North has written, Kafka would begin reading Søren Kierkegaard shortly thereafter, whose fictional and pseudonymous publications "invert[] Augustine's order of mendacity and make[] deception into a tool of revelation and a basis for faith," while at the same time remaining "thoroughly ambiguous; though published, there is little about them that is public" (126). The withdrawal that Kafka had found Kierkegaard's ambiguity to permit would correspond with the nonspeaking of truth that implicitly accompanies the false speech of confession in the passage quoted above.
    11. Kafka, *The Trial*, 183.
    12. Franz Kafka, *The Man Who Disappeared*, trans. Ritchie Robertson (Oxford: Oxford University Press, 2012), 197–98 (trans. modified); cf. Franz Kafka, *Der Verschollene*, ed. Jost Schillemeit (Frankfurt am Main: Fischer, 1983), 391, 393. The chorus of schoolchildren from "A Country Doctor" does, by contrast, sing to a "text" which reads: "Undress him, then he'll cure us, / And if he doesn't cure us, kill him! / It's only a doctor, it's only a doctor," after which the doctor is undressed and carried to the bed of his patient. Franz Kafka, "A Country Doctor," in Franz Kafka, *Selected Stories*, ed. and trans. Stanley Corngold (New York: W.W. Norton, 2007), 60–65, 64; trans. modified. If this text should seem to be more legible than the choral performances recorded elsewhere in Kafka's oeuvre, however, its truth belongs neither to the particular situation—the "text" is prescribed in advance—nor to any performative or constative utterances that it contains (only the demand to undress the doctor is met—not its consequences)—rendering the children's imperative unrealized, while the identity of the doctor that they constate becomes questionable precisely as he fails to cure or even treat his patient in any unequivocal way.
    13. Maurice Blanchot, *The Writing of the Disaster*, trans. Ann Smock (Lincoln: University of Nebraska Press, 1995), 54. In French, the fragment reads

in full: "Dans la nuit, l'insomnie est dis-cussion, non pas travail d'arguments se heurtant à des arguments, mais l'extrême secousse sans pensées, l'ébranlement cassé jusqu'au calme (les exégèses qui vont et viennent dans 'Le Château,' récit de l'insomnie)." Blanchot, *L'écriture du désastre*, 83. Although the emphasis upon shuddering ("secousse," "ébranlement") approaches the register of incoherent sound, however, the silent "shudder" that is said to traverse Kafka's novel would not be the opposite of speech but what "the exegeses that come and go" bear out, beyond any communicative function. The breach in recognizable forms of speech comes to pass through those very forms.

14. Maurice Blanchot, *The Last Man*, trans. Lydia Davis (New York: Columbia University Press, 1987), 76; cf. Maurice Blanchot, *Le Dernier homme* (Paris: Gallimard, 1957), 127.

15. These words are drawn from Blanchot's discussion of, among others, Bataille's thought of community in *The Unavowable Community*, trans. Pierre Joris (Barrytown: Station Hill, 1988), 3, 15. In the same text, Blanchot will relate the absence of community to the "impossibility" of being a self, "of subsisting as its *ipse* or, if you will, as itself as a separate individual." Blanchot, *The Unavowable Community*, 6.

16. Blanchot, *The Infinite Conversation*, 55; cf. Blanchot, *L'entretien infini*, 79.

17. Blanchot, *The Last Man*, 67; cf. Blanchot, *Le Dernier homme*, 112.

18. The title, which recites a critical phrase from Friedrich Nietzsche's *Thus Spoke Zarathustra*, also recalls Blanchot's conversations with Bataille concerning "the last man," which Bataille relates in *Inner Experience*: "Blanchot asked me: why not pursue my inner experience as if I were the *last man*," before briefly sketching how he would "imagine" the "*last one* without a chorus": "dead to himself, at the infinite twilight that he would be, [he] would sense the walls [*parois*] (even the depth) of the tomb open." Bataille, *Inner Experience*, 61; cf. Bataille, *OC* 5:76. These "walls" may resonate in the second part of Blanchot's novel, where a first-person figure—who may be dead (Blanchot, *The Last Man*, 86; cf. Blanchot, *Le Dernier homme*, 143)—speaks of how "the words that go to you go to a wall [*un mur*] that sends them back to me so that I can hear them. A wall, a real wall, four walls that form the boundaries of the place I live and make it a cell, an emptiness in the midst of everyone else." Blanchot, *The Last Man*, 72; cf. Blanchot, *Le Dernier homme*, 120. But when the question is raised as to "what would happen" if the eponymous last man "died too soon? If the suffering survived him [*lui survivait*]?" (Blanchot, *The Last Man*, 53; cf. Blanchot, *Le Dernier homme*, 90), *The Last Man* also echoes the last lines of Kafka's *The Trial*, where it is said of the dying Josef K.: "It seemed as if his shame would survive him [*e[r] s wa[s]r, als sollte die Scham ihn [ih]übe[l]rleben*]." Kafka, *The Trial*, 165 (trans. modified); cf. Kafka, "Ende," in *Der Process*, 25.

19. Blanchot, *The Last Man*, 2; cf. Blanchot, *Le Dernier homme*, 9.

20. Blanchot, *The Last Man*, 2; cf. Blanchot, *Le Dernier homme*, 9.

21. Blanchot, *The Last Man*, 69; cf. Blanchot, *Le Dernier homme*, 115.

22. Christopher Fynsk, *Last Steps: Maurice Blanchot's Exilic Writing* (New York: Fordham University Press, 2013), 83.

23. Blanchot, *The Last Man*, 76; cf. Blanchot, *Le Dernier homme*, 127.

24. Blanchot, *The Last Man*, 76–77; cf. Blanchot, *Le Dernier homme*, 127.

25. Blanchot, *The Writing of the Disaster*, 20, 24; cf. Blanchot, *L'écriture du désastre*, 37, 43.

26. Hence, Blanchot will write: "It is upon losing what we have to say that we speak—upon an imminent and immemorial disaster—just as we say nothing except insofar as we can convey in advance that we take it back, by a sort of prolepsis, not so as finally to say nothing, but so that speaking might not stop at the word—the word which is, or is to be, spoken, taken back. We speak suggesting that something not being said is speaking: the loss of what we were to say; weeping when tears have long since gone dry; the surrender which the invisible passivity of dying announces but does not accomplish—*human weakness*." Blanchot, *The Writing of the Disaster*, 21; cf. Blanchot, *L'écriture du désastre*, 39.

27. Blanchot, *The Writing of the Disaster*, 24; cf. Blanchot, *L'écriture du désastre*, 44.

28. The above-cited passages from *The Writing of the Disaster* first appeared in Blanchot's "Discourse on Patience (In the Margin of the Books of Emmanuel Lévinas)." Maurice Blanchot, "Discours sur la patience (en marge des livres d'Emmanuel Lévinas)," in *Maurice Blanchot et la philosophie*, ed. Éric Hoppenot and Alain Milon (Paris: Presses Universitaires de Paris Nanterre, 2010), 403–20. For an extensive study of Blanchot's engagement with Levinas, both here and elsewhere in his oeuvre, see Georges Hansel, "Maurice Blanchot, lecteur de Lévinas," in *Maurice Blanchot et la philosophie*, ed. Éric Hoppenot and Alain Milon (Paris: Presses Universitaires de Paris Nanterre, 2010), 315–73.

29. Emmanuel Levinas, *Otherwise Than Being, or, Beyond Essence*, trans. Alphonso Lingis (Pittsburgh: Duquesne University Press, 1998), 51; cf. Levinas, *Autrement qu'être ou au-delà de l'essence* (The Hague: Nijhoff, 1974), 66. In *Time and the Other*, Levinas had emphasized the radical difference between the recognized, recuperable time of experience, and the time of the "passage from existing to the one who exists," which "one can no longer qualify as experience." Emmanuel Levinas, *Le temps et l'autre* (Paris: fata morgana, 1979), 34; my translation. Whereas Levinas had argued in this earlier work that the identity of existence is borne out through the temporality of incarnate subjectivity, however, his later work insists upon "the gravity of having to bear the burden of alien existence," as Alphonso Lingis points out in the introduction to his translation of *Otherwise Than Being*. Levinas, *Otherwise Than Being*, xxvii; cf. Levinas, *Le temps et l'autre*, 36. In particular, the "Saying" of the other marks the situation in which "the speaking subject is exposed to the other" in a manner that "is not reducible to the objectification of a theme stated." Levinas, *Otherwise Than Being*, 84; cf. Levinas, *Autrement qu'être*, 105.

30. Levinas, *Otherwise Than Being*, 51; cf. Levinas, *Autrement qu'être*, 66.

31. Blanchot, *The Writing of the Disaster*, 34; cf. Blanchot, *L'écriture du désastre*, 60. Just before this passage, which more specifically addresses the turns that are taken through the in-between of "conversation [*entretien*]," Blanchot had associated passivity with such turns and emphasized their occurrence in writing: "The passive need not take place. Rather, implicated in the turn which deviates from the ever-turning, circuitous path and becomes in this way—with respect to the longest tour—a detour, the passive is the torment of the time which has always already passed and which comes thus as a return without any present. [. . .] This is the era destined to the intermittence of a language unburdened of words and dispossessed, the silent halt of that to which without obligation one must nonetheless answer. And such is the responsibility of writing, writing which distinguishes itself by deleting from itself all distinguishing marks, which is to say perhaps, ultimately, by effacing itself [. . .], for it seems to leave indelible or indiscernible traces." Blanchot, *The Writing of the Disaster*, 33–34; cf. Blanchot, *L'écriture du désastre*, 58. In his study, Hansel suggests that these traits of writing resonate with those that Lévinas invokes in order to characterize the relation to the Other, while underscoring the difference in vocabulary and accent between the two writers. Hansel, "Maurice Blanchot, lecteur de Lévinas."

32. Blanchot, *The Writing of the Disaster*, 15, 93; cf. Blanchot, *L'écriture du désastre*, 30, 146.

33. Blanchot, *The Writing of the Disaster*, 89 (trans. modified); cf. Blanchot, *L'écriture du désastre*, 140.

34. Blanchot, *The Writing of the Disaster*, 24; cf. Blanchot, *L'écriture du désastre*, 44.

35. Blanchot, *The Writing of the Disaster*, 43; cf. Blanchot, *L'écriture du désastre*, 73.

36. Blanchot, *The Writing of the Disaster*, 16; cf. Blanchot, *L'écriture du désastre*, 31–32.

37. Blanchot, *The Writing of the Disaster*, 43; cf. Blanchot, *L'écriture du désastre*, 73.

38. Wall speaks similarly to Blanchot's *L'arrêt de mort* in his study of *Radical Passivity*, where the *récit* exposes "an imitation of thought, a semblance of being, [. . .] written in a simulated language (i.e., a language that does not communicate, but that simultaneously reveals and conceals [. . .])." Wall, *Radical Passivity*, 87.

39. Despite the title of his essay, however, it is less a question of "language" than of knowledge and selfhood for Sartre, who will address solely the negative consequences of the ways in which Blanchot's novel articulates a world where "one is unaware of knowing what one knows; and when one knows what one knows, then one does not know," and where, as a result, "our last resource, that self-awareness in which stoicism sought refuge, escapes us and disintegrates." Jean-Paul Sartre, "*Aminadab* or the Fantastic Considered as Language," in *Literary*

and Philosophical Essays, trans. Annette Michelson (New York: Collier, 1962), 60–77, 71. Whereas Sartre insists that Kafka's K. still "struggl[es] to defend his honourable character, his life," he criticizes Blanchot for presenting a protagonist who "has no definite character" or "purpose" (76).

40. Jeff Fort, "Introduction," in Blanchot, *Aminadab*, trans. Jeff Fort (Lincoln: University of Nebraska Press, 2002), vii–xvii, xiv. In particular, Fort writes: "If there is one thing that the characters of *Aminadab* do, it is talk. Their endless commentaries, their unreliable and conflicting clarifications, their meandering stories and legends—especially the long and remarkable monologue placed near the center of the novel—open within the narrative a series of impassioned and delirious voices. I would hazard to say that with these voices, carried away by forces that far exceed the fictional situation of which they speak, this novel enters into its most singular and proper mode." However, Fort places the initial accent upon "characters" in a manner that the reading offered in this chapter does not do.

41. Blanchot, *Aminadab*, 174; Blanchot, *Aminadab*, 254.

42. Christopher A. Strathman introduces his study of *Aminadab* with remarks on Blanchot's sustained engagement with the thought of Martin Heidegger, including his "Letter on Humanism" from 1947, in which he asserts that "language is 'the house of Being,'" and thereby echoes Stéphane Mallarmé, whom Blanchot similarly claims to indicate that "language 'reveals itself as the foundation both of things and of human reality.'" Christopher A. Strathman, "*Aminadab*: Quest for the Origin of the Work of Art," in *Clandestine Encounters: Philosophy in the Narratives of Maurice Blanchot*, ed. Kevin Hart (Notre Dame, IN: Notre Dame University Press, 2010), 91–118, 93, 103.

43. Blanchot, *The Step Not Beyond*, 51; Blanchot, *Le pas au-delà*, 74.

44. Strathman, "*Aminadab*," 112.

45. Blanchot, *Aminadab*, 107; Blanchot, *Aminadab*, 160.

46. Blanchot, *The Writing of the Disaster*, 24, 71; cf. Blanchot, *L'écriture du désastre*, 44, 116.

47. Blanchot, *Aminadab*, 7; Blanchot, *Aminadab*, 18.

48. Blanchot, *Aminadab*, 7; cf. Blanchot, *Aminadab*, 18. The fact that this repetition is rendered in "free indirect discourse" also suggests that it belongs at least as much to the language of the narration as it seems to reflect Thomas's discursive thinking.

49. Blanchot, *Aminadab*, 7, 184; cf. Blanchot, *Aminadab*, 18, 268.

50. Blanchot, *Aminadab*, 68 (trans. modified); cf. Blanchot, *Aminadab*, 104.

51. Blanchot, *Aminadab*, 68; cf. Blanchot, *Aminadab*, 104.

52. Blanchot, *Aminadab*, 114; cf. Blanchot, *Aminadab*, 170. This platform is also said on the same page to be used for storing "bottles of cognac and casks of beer [. . .] beneath the planks."

53. Blanchot, *Aminadab*, 112–13; cf. Blanchot, *Aminadab*, 167.

54. Blanchot, *Aminadab*, 114; cf. Blanchot, *Aminadab*, 169.

55. Blanchot, *Aminadab*, 110 (trans. modified); cf. Blanchot, *Aminadab*, 163–64. Before his apparently condemnable performance, however, he was initially said to be "attracted" to the room "for [. . .] judgment." Blanchot, *Aminadab*, 110; cf. Blanchot, *Aminadab*, 163. The accent that is placed in this passage upon attraction to a forum for judgment also echoes the premise of Kafka's *Trial*, where it is said that "the court was attracted by guilt." Kafka, *The Trial*, 30.

56. Concerning speech acts and "speaking generally," J. L. Austin insists that "it is always necessary that the *circumstances* in which the words are uttered should be in some way, or ways, *appropriate*." J. L. Austin, *How to Do Things with Words*, ed. J. O. Urmson and Marina Shisà (Cambridge, MA: Harvard University Press, 1975), 8. If the circumstances are fundamentally unknown, however, there could be no telling what or how words may actually "perform."

57. Blanchot, *Aminadab*, 95; cf. Blanchot, *Aminadab*, 142.

58. Blanchot, *Aminadab*, 96; cf. Blanchot, *Aminadab*, 143.

59. Blanchot, *Aminadab*, 113–14 (trans. modified); cf. Blanchot, *Aminadab*, 168.

60. Jean-Jacques Rousseau, "Examination of Two Principles Advanced by M. Rameau in His Brochure Entitled: 'Errors on Music in the Encyclopedia,'" in *Essay on the Origin of Languages and Writings Related to Music*, ed. and trans. John T. Scott (Hanover: University Press of New England, 1998), 271–88, 279.

61. Blanchot, *Aminadab*, 113; cf. Blanchot, *Aminadab*, 168.

62. G. W. F. Hegel, *The Phenomenology of Spirit*, trans. Terry Pinkard (Cambridge: Cambridge University Press, 2018), 127, 401.

63. Blanchot, *Aminadab*, 114; cf. Blanchot, *Aminadab*, 168.

64. In the opening segment of *The Castle*, "Who are you?" likewise repeats like a refrain. Kafka, *Das Schloss*, 1:36, 40, 51.

65. As Rousseau asserts in "On the Principle of Melody," "Laws and songs bore the same name in those happy times" of antiquity. Jean-Jacques Rousseau, "On the Principle of Melody, or Response to the 'Errors on Music,'" in *Essay on the Origin of Languages and Writings Related to Music*, ed. and trans. John T. Scott (Hanover: University Press of New England, 1998), 260–70, 262.

66. Michel Foucault, "Maurice Blanchot: The Thought from Outside," trans. Brian Massumi, in *Foucault / Blanchot* (New York: Zone Books, 1987), 7–58, 25.

67. Roger Laporte, *Maurice Blanchot: L'ancien, l'effroyablement ancien* (Paris: Fata Morgana, 1987), 52; my translation. As Laporte notes, the phrase repeats throughout Blanchot's oeuvre in, among others, *Celui qui ne m'accompagnait pas* and *Le pas au-delà* (18).

68. Jeff Fort, "Rumors of the Outside: Blanchot's Murmurs and the Indistinction of Literature," *Angelaki: Journal of the Theoretical Humanities* 23, no. 3 (2018): 158–77, 158, 159.

69. This phrase is drawn from Fort's essay, where he writes that Blanchot

"did not want to pursue its most extreme consequences." Fort, "Rumors of the Outside," 173.

70. Blanchot, *Aminadab*, 114; cf. Blanchot, *Aminadab*, 169.

71. Blanchot, *Aminadab*, 110 (trans. modified); cf. Blanchot, *Aminadab*, 163–64.

72. Blanchot, *Aminadab*, 114; cf. Blanchot, *Aminadab*, 169.

73. Jean-Philippe Rameau, "Observations on Our Instinct for Music and on Its Principle," in *Essay on the Origin of Languages and Writings Related to Music*, ed. and trans. John T. Scott (Hanover: University Press of New England, 1998), 175–97, 177.

74. Rousseau, "Examination of Two Principles," 278.

75. In the *Cartesian Meditations*, Husserl claims that the adequacy of evidence hinges upon the "synthetic course of further harmonious experiences [*synthetische[n] Fortgang einstimmiger Erfahrungen*]." Husserl, *Cartesian Meditations*, 15; Husserl *Hua* 1:55. In the first volume of *Ideen zu einer reinen Phänomenologie*, he describes the asymmetry between the "absolute position" of immanent conscious experience and the "*presumptive reality [präsumptive[n] Wirklichkeit]*" of the world by pointing out the undeniability of the former, while demonstrating that it is "thinkable [*denkbar*]" that perceptual objects "would lack mathematical, physical determinability [*mathematischer, physikalischer Bestimmbarkeit*]," and would thus fail to provide the "experiential motives fundamental to the fashioning of the concepts and judgments of physics." Husserl, *Ideas 1*, 102, 105 (trans. modified); Husserl, *Hua* 3:98, 100. In his second volume, Husserl also argues that "dissonant phenomena [*unstimmige Erscheinungen*]" indicate bodily abnormalities, whose correction depends upon privileging those "groups" of appearances "in which, for itself, the thing already appears consonantly / univocally identical [*in denen für sich schon das Ding als einstimmig identisches erscheint*]." Husserl, *Hua* 4:66; my translation.

76. Husserl, *The Phenomenology of Internal Time-Consciousness*, 23; cf. *Hua* 10:5.

77. Eric Voegelin, *Anamnesis*, ed. and trans. Gerhart Niemeyer (Columbia: University of Missouri Press, 1978), 15. In his critical commentary on Husserl's choice to exemplify time-consciousness through the perception of a tone, Voegelin goes on to insist: "A time-consciousness without an object-consciousness can hardly be described. One is pushed to infer that that which is described on the occasion of auditory perception is not the consciousness of time but precisely the consciousness of the perception of a tone, a tone that has an objective structure determined in turn by the structure of man's faculty of perception, the noetic structure in Husserl's sense" (15).

78. To be sure, no precise citation from Enlightenment-era musical theory or twentieth-century phenomenological philosophy could be attributed on the

basis of Blanchot's text. But the explicit characterization of the house as a "sonorous cage" opens it to such instances of resonance as those traced above, whose unverifiability can no more speak against them than the integrity of the narrative voice could be maintained with any certitude.

79. Blanchot, *The Infinite Conversation*, 80.
80. Blanchot, *Aminadab*, 115; cf. Blanchot, *Aminadab*, 170.
81. Blanchot, *Aminadab*, 116; cf. Blanchot, *Aminadab*, 172.
82. Blanchot, *Aminadab*, 66; cf. Blanchot, *Aminadab*, 102.
83. Blanchot, *Aminadab*, 116; cf. Blanchot, *Aminadab*, 172.
84. Blanchot, *The Writing of the Disaster*, 1.
85. Blanchot, *The Writing of the Disaster*, 1.
86. Whereas the song and its disruption are narrated over the course of several pages, Jerome's narration extends for nearly sixty pages of the French edition of *Aminadab*. Blanchot, *Aminadab*, 106–62. In the English translation, the corresponding segment can be found on pp. 69–109.
87. As Jerome describes the negligence of the personnel, he admits early on: "We never see them, ever, not even from a distance; we do not even know what the word see could mean when it comes to them, nor if there is a word to express their absence, nor even if the thought of this absence is not a supreme and pitiful resource to make us hope for their coming." Blanchot, *Aminadab*, 75; cf. Blanchot, *Aminadab*, 114.
88. Blanchot, *Aminadab*, 76; cf. Blanchot, *Aminadab*, 114–15.
89. Blanchot, *The Writing of the Disaster*, 14; cf. Blanchot, *L'écriture du désastre*, 29.
90. Blanchot, *Aminadab*, 76; cf. Blanchot, *Aminadab*, 115.
91. Blanchot, *Aminadab*, 76; cf. Blanchot, *Aminadab*, 115.
92. Blanchot, *Aminadab*, 76; cf. Blanchot, *Aminadab*, 115–16.
93. Blanchot, *Aminadab*, 77; cf. Blanchot, *Aminadab*, 116.
94. These were the words ascribed to the "song." Blanchot, *Aminadab*, 114; cf. Blanchot, *Aminadab*, 168.
95. Kafka, *Nachgelassene Schriften und Fragmente II*, 348.
96. Derrida, *Demeure: Fiction and Testimony*, 27; cf. Derrida, *Demeure: Maurice Blanchot*, 31.
97. Blanchot, *Aminadab*, 77; cf. Blanchot, *Aminadab*, 117.
98. Blanchot, *Aminadab*, 77; cf. Blanchot, *Aminadab*, 117.
99. Kafka, *Das Schloss*, 2:142.
100. Blanchot, *The Writing of the Disaster*, 17; cf. Blanchot, *L'écriture du désastre*, 34.
101. Blanchot, *Aminadab*, 80; cf. Blanchot, *Aminadab*, 120.
102. Blanchot, *Aminadab*, 77–80; cf. Blanchot, *Aminadab*, 117–21.
103. Blanchot, *The Writing of the Disaster*, 49; cf. Blanchot, *L'écriture du désastre*, 83.

104. Blanchot, *Aminadab*, 81; cf. Blanchot, *Aminadab*, 122.
105. Blanchot, *Aminadab*, 81; cf. Blanchot, *Aminadab*, 122–23.
106. Blanchot, *Aminadab*, 81; cf. Blanchot, *Aminadab*, 123.
107. Blanchot, *The Writing of the Disaster*, 54; cf. Blanchot, *L'écriture du désastre*, 90.
108. Smock, *What Is There to Say?*, viii, 46–47.
109. Smock, *What Is There to Say?*, 48, 60. See also her discussion of the impotent violence of "the torture session" to "prove much of anything" in Marguerite Duras's "Albert of the Capitals" (71).
110. Blanchot, *Aminadab*, 81; cf. Blanchot, *Aminadab*, 123.
111. Blanchot, *The Infinite Conversation*, 132.
112. Blanchot, *Aminadab*, 82; cf. Blanchot, *Aminadab*, 123.
113. Blanchot, *Aminadab*, 83; cf. Blanchot, *Aminadab*, 123.
114. Blanchot, *Aminadab*, 85–86; cf. Blanchot, *Aminadab*, 128–29.
115. Blanchot, *Aminadab*, 86; cf. Blanchot, *Aminadab*, 129.
116. Blanchot, *Aminadab*, 87, 89 (trans. modified); cf. Blanchot, *Aminadab*, 130, 134.
117. Hegel, *The Science of Logic*, 99–100.
118. Blanchot, *Aminadab*, 89; cf. Blanchot, *Aminadab*, 134.
119. Blanchot, *Aminadab*, 90; cf. Blanchot, *Aminadab*, 134.
120. Blanchot, *Aminadab*, 89; cf. Blanchot, *Aminadab*, 134.
121. Allen, *Aesthetics of Negativity*, 150–51.
122. Blanchot, *Aminadab*, 94; cf. Blanchot, *Aminadab*, 140–41.
123. Blanchot, *Aminadab*, 89; cf. Blanchot, *Aminadab*, 133.
124. Blanchot, *Aminadab*, 88–89; trans. modified; cf. Blanchot, *Aminadab*, 133.
125. Blanchot, *Aminadab*, 89 (trans. modified); cf. Blanchot, *Aminadab*,134.
126. Blanchot, *Aminadab*, 89; cf. Blanchot, *Aminadab*, 133.
127. Kafka, *Nachgelassene Schriften und Fragmente II*, 348.
128. Kafka, *Das Schloss*, 3:190, 195.
129. The very thought of another penetrating the burrower's entranceway is accompanied by phantasies of violence: he anticipates, namely, the moment when he "could finally, in a fury [. . .] and free from all second-thoughts, spring upon [the enemy], bite him to pieces, flay his flesh, tear him to shreds, and drink him out [*endlich in einem Rasen [. . .], frei von allen Bedenken ihn anspringen könnte, ihn zerbeißen, zerfleischen, zerreißen und austrinken*]." Kafka, *Nachgelassene Schriften und Fragmente II*, 596; my translation. The main threat that is addressed in *The Burrow*, however, is signaled by a dubious acoustic disturbance, on which see Adler, "The Biopolitics of Noise" and Gellen, *Kafka and Noise*, as well as Mladen Dolar's essay, "The Burrow of Sound," *differences* 22, no. 2/3 (2011): 112–39. Further reverberations of that disturbance will resound when the subterranean areas below the house of *Aminadab* are described. The description culminates,

namely, with a moment where "you" are said to "ask yourself if you may not have heard, through the silence of the underground spaces, a message or at least the echo of a message." Blanchot, *Aminadab*, 189; cf. Blanchot, *Aminadab*, 275. Alexandre Vialette's French translation of "Der Bau" ("Le terrier") had appeared in 1933 in *La Nouvelle Revue Française*, the journal to which Blanchot would frequently contribute.

130. For a recent study of this resemblance in the context of contemporary scientific discourse, along with a bibliography detailing other readings that similarly trace the auricular anatomy of the burrower's cavity, see Tyler Whitney, "Inside the Ear: Silence, Self-Observation, and Embodied Spaces in Kafka's 'Der Bau,'" *Germanic Review* 92, no. 3 (2017): 301–19. Dolar aptly speaks of the inner space of the burrow as well as the channels of hearing as an "orifice of being." Dolar, "The Burrow of Sound," 135.

131. Blanchot, *Aminadab*, 85–86; cf. Blanchot, *Aminadab*, 128–29.

132. Blanchot, *The Writing of the Disaster*, 16–17 (trans. modified); cf. Blanchot, *L'écriture du désastre*, 33.

133. Blanchot, *Aminadab*, 86; cf. Blanchot, *Aminadab*, 129. As Blanchot would write elsewhere: "When speech becomes prophetic, it is not the future that is given; it is the present that is withdrawn, and with it any possibility of a firm, stable, and lasting presence." Maurice Blanchot, "Prophetic Speech," in *The Book to Come*, trans. Charlotte Mandell (Stanford, CA: Stanford University Press, 2003), 79–85, 80 (trans. modified); Maurice Blanchot, "La parole prophétique," in *Le livre à venir* (Paris: Gallimard, 1959), 109–19, 110.

134. For this reason, there would also be no end to citing further passages from Blanchot's novel that register the troubling effects of language. For example, when a woman whom Thomas encounters at the highest point of his own journey toward the upper floors of the house asks him to choose between her present company and his past in the house, he finds himself incapable of answering her, or even indicating his incapacity to answer, as the sweetness of her words and intonation throw him into an insurmountable, inexplicable "trouble": "Thomas could hardly overcome the confusion these words caused him. Such sweetness, such consideration! What a tone one used to speak to him! [*Sur quel ton on lui parlait!*] He had never heard anything so pleasant, so persuasive. He would have liked to merge with these words so as to know all their sweetness; he would have liked to be as true and as perfect as they were." Blanchot, *Aminadab*, 168 (trans. modified); cf. Blanchot, *Aminadab*, 245. The fact that "sweetness" is cited both as the cause of Thomas's trouble and as that which he wishes still to "know" indicates that the "cause" is not yet well known and that "sweetness" may not even be an adequate term for this unknown tonal factor in his experience. Similarly, the guardian whom Thomas confronts at the outset of the novel had seemed to speak in dulcet tones, only for this semblance to be revoked when the guardian repeats his question—"Where are you going?"—whereby it is said: "This time his

voice was not so gentle [*douce*]." Blanchot, *Aminadab*, 7; Blanchot, *Aminadab*, 18. At the same time, the suggestion that solely by merging with the woman's words could Thomas himself be "perfect" and "true" implies not only that no response he could give would be true but also that the only true response would fail to respond at all and would ultimately eliminate the responder. Meanwhile, the woman likewise vanishes into her words and intonation, becoming an anonymous "one [*on*]," as soon as it is a question of "sweetness." In all of these respects, the "trouble" that this experience of language entails thus resembles the unknown, anonymous, and unspeakable "prophecy" that affects the hearts of the inhabitants, just as they are said no longer to know how to understand the words that they believe themselves to pronounce and cannot even determine whether those words are their own. Blanchot, *Aminadab*, 85–86; cf. Blanchot, *Aminadab*, 129. For a further discussion of Thomas's encounter with this woman, see the last pages of this chapter.

135. Blanchot, *Aminadab*, 82; (trans. modified); cf. Blanchot, *Aminadab*, 124.

136. Blanchot, *Aminadab*, 27; cf. Blanchot, *Aminadab*, 46.

137. This is the exemplary topos that Aristotle cites in *The 'Art' of Rhetoric* 1358a 12–14. The methodical function of *topoi* is introduced in the first lines of the *Topics*, 100a 18–21, in Aristotle, *Aristotelis Topica et Sophistici Elenchi*. ed. W. D. Ross (Oxford Clarendon, 1958).

138. Scholars such as Allen have also stressed the importance of Paulhan's study for Blanchot's *Aminadab*; in both texts, he writes, "forms of ordinary language [. . .] persistently reappear as material refractions of meaning, suggesting that whether we take language for granted or not, it still holds the possibility of falling apart by exposing its words as shards of illegibility." Allen, *Aesthetics of Negativity*, 148–49.

139. Maurice Blanchot, "La Terreur dans les lettres," in *Chroniques littéraires du Journal des débats: Avril 1941–août 1944*, ed. Christophe Bident (Paris: Gallimard, 2007), 89–94, 90. All translations of passages from this text are mine.

140. Blanchot, "La Terreur dans les lettres," 91.

141. Jean Paulhan, *The Flowers of Tarbes, or Terror in Literature*, trans. Michael Sytotinski (Chicago: University of Chicago Press, 2006), 11 (trans. modified); cf. Jean Paulhan, *Les Fleurs de Tarbes, ou La terreur dans les lettres* (Paris: Cercle du Livre Précieux, 1967), 22.

142. These writers are several of those whom Paulhan lists in *The Flowers of Tarbes*, 32. But it is the passages that Paulhan cites from them which testify most pronouncedly to the violence of their efforts. Albalat, for instance, states: "If we allow ourselves to use these ready-made expressions once, [. . .] we will allow ourselves to use them twice, then three times, and once we're on that slippery slope, we let ourselves go." Paulhan, *The Flowers of Tarbes*, 19. Gourmont is cited shortly thereafter, proclaiming an aim to "destroy with merciless criticism the work of imitators," and thus to "smother these revolting creatures in their holes" (23).

143. Allen, *Aesthetics of Negativity*, 102.

144. Paulhan does, however, insist that this "malady affecting literature would, after all, be fairly insignificant if it didn't reveal a chronic illness of expression in general," before adding remarks on the deployment of duplicitous commonplaces by "political leaders." Paulhan, *The Flowers of Tarbes*, 6.

145. Blanchot, "La Terreur dans les lettres," 91.

146. Blanchot, *Aminadab*, 86; cf. Blanchot, *Aminadab*, 129.

147. Paulhan, *The Flowers of Tarbes*, 60–61; cf. Paulhan, *Les Fleurs de Tarbes*, 64.

148. Blanchot, *Aminadab*, 102; cf. Blanchot, *Aminadab*, 152.

149. Blanchot, *Aminadab*, 99 (trans. modified); cf. Blanchot, *Aminadab*, 147.

150. Paulhan will explicitly say: "But one thing we can say for sure is that *they [common places] are not common*. Despite their name. Despite the appearance. [*Malgré leur nom. Malgré l'apparence*]." Paulhan, *The Flowers of Tarbes*, 78 (trans. modified); Paulhan, *Les Fleurs de Tarbes*, 80.

151. The often-cited and discussed formulation appears in Aristotle's *Politeia* 1253a 10.

152. Especially in the "Notes et documents" that follow the end of his book, Paulhan characterizes the very notion of independent thought as the product of attempts to disengage thought from language and thus as a derivative phenomenon. Hence, whereas Nicolas Malebranche had claimed that truth could be attained by "rendering oneself attentive to the clear ideas that each of us discovers in himself [*de se rendre attentif aux idées claires que chacun de nous découvre en lui-même*]," Paulhan says that "it would rather be necessary for us to render ourselves attentive to hearing these clear ideas in the wake of the ungraspable, obscure, yet radiating idea from which they detach themselves, and from which comes any sense and clarity that fall to them [*plutôt faudrait-il nous rendre attentifs à entendre ces idées claires suivant l'idée insaisissable, obscure, mais rayonnante, dont elles se détachent, et d'où vient ce qui leur échoit de sens et de clarté*]." Paulhan, *Les Fleurs de Tarbes*, 139; my translation.

153. Blanchot, *Aminadab*, 141; cf. Blanchot, *Aminadab*, 207.

154. Blanchot, *Aminadab*, 142; cf. Blanchot, *Aminadab*, 208.

155. Philippe Lacoue-Labarthe, "The Contestation of Death," trans. Philip Anderson, in *The Power of Contestation: Perspectives on Maurice Blanchot*, ed. Kevin Hart and Geoffrey Hartman (Baltimore: Johns Hopkins University Press, 2004), 141–55, 152. Lacoue-Labarthe's essay develops this notion, however, through the way in which "death is *contested*" in Blanchot's last narrative, where "the 'always-already-deceased' in him," the subject of writing, "is summon(s)ed as the witness of a conversion, or of a radical break. And suddenly, as if miraculously, freed of death and of the *mortiferous*." This liberation, in turn, is said to give testimony to a "*survival* which is perhaps nothing other, nothing more in any case, than existence." Lacoue-Labarthe, "The Contestation of Death," 152.

156. Blanchot, *Aminadab*, 104 (trans. modified); cf. Blanchot, *Aminadab*, 155.

157. In the *Theaetetus*, Socrates will call "thinking" the "dialogue [διαλέγεσθαι]" that unfolds as the soul itself "asks and answers itself, affirming and not affirming." Plato, *Theatetus*. 189e–190a; my translation.

158. As Paulhan summarizes the desire of "the Terror," whose spokesmen range from Sainte-Beuve to Henri Bergson, the aim is to arrive upon "an expression which is infinitely transparent to the mind." Paulhan, *The Flowers of Tarbes*, 81; cf. Paulhan, *Les Fleurs de Tarbes*, 82.

159. Søren Kierkegaard, *Le concept d'angoisse*, trans. K. Ferlov and J-J. Gateau (Paris: Gallimard, 1948), 294; my translation. I have cited this version of Kierkegaard's text because this translation, originally published in 1935, is the one which would have been available to Blanchot. The likelihood of a resonance with Kierkegaard in Blanchot's novel is supported not only by the fact that Blanchot was engaging with Kierkegaard's oeuvre at the time, as is indicated by the essays collected in *Faux pas*, "De l'angoisse au langage" and "Le 'Journal' de Kierkegaard," but also by the fact that the treatment of the condemned in *Aminadab* includes silent treatment, where the punished are kept in solitary confinement, "sealed off from all sound" until they begin to speak again. Blanchot, *Aminadab*, 119; cf. Blanchot, *Aminadab*, 176. This punitive redoubling of the silence of the guilty is precisely the method that Kierkegaard claims to be most effective in breaking the self-enclosure of the demonic. See also Blanchot, *Faux pas* (Paris: Gallimard, 1943), 7–23, 25–30.

160. Blanchot, *Aminadab*, 120; cf. Blanchot, *Aminadab*, 177.

161. Blanchot, *The Infinite Conversation*, 67; cf. Blanchot, *L'entretien infini*, 96.

162. Blanchot, *The Infinite Conversation*, 77 (trans. modified); Blanchot, *L'entretien infini*, 108.

163. Smock similarly writes of the weakness involved in speaking: "But maybe it's with their weakness that men do more than they have the strength for," which also by no means turns "weakness" into a power, as she indicates next: "And maybe what they do ineptly thus, with weakness, doesn't thereby become any less impossible." Smock, *What Is There to Say?*, 30.

164. Blanchot, *The Last Man*, 76; cf. Blanchot, *Le Dernier homme*, 127.

165. While cleaning the woman's chamber, he will even ascend a ladder that reaches partway toward the vaults, where the "sparkling powder" that he sees upon looking upward creates the impression that "the arches, reaching their highest point, had been broken and that what seemed to be the key element of the structure was only a large opening through which poured the light of day." Blanchot, *Aminadab*, 163; cf. Blanchot, *Aminadab*, 237. An infinite height beyond the confines of the house is thus suggested at this point, which Thomas glimpses before redescending the ladder. This episode echoes, among others, Plato's allegory of the cave, where ascent leads to the light of truth, but unlike the brightness to which the prisoner rises in Plato's allegory, the phenomenon of light that Thomas observes may itself be illusory. See Plato, *Republic* 514a–517a.

166. Blanchot, *Aminadab*, 80; cf. Blanchot, *Aminadab*, 120.

167. Blanchot, *Aminadab*, 164 (trans. modified); cf. Blanchot, *Aminadab*, 240.

168. Blanchot, *Aminadab*, 241; my translation. This passage is omitted from the English edition.

169. Blanchot, *Aminadab*, 165; cf. Blanchot, *Aminadab*, 240.

170. Blanchot, *Aminadab*, 165; cf. Blanchot, *Aminadab*, 241.

171. Blanchot, *Aminadab*, 165; cf. Blanchot, *Aminadab*, 241.

172. Blanchot, *Aminadab*, 165 (trans. modified); Blanchot, *Aminadab*, 241. The erotic encounter Blanchot traces is at least as radically estranging as the one that Frieda and K. had shared, when they "rolled [*rollten*]" on the floor in Kafka's *The Castle* and erred into sheer "thoughtlessness [*Besinnungslosigkeit*]" and "foreignness [*Fremde*]." Kafka, *Das Schloss*, 1:109. As Michael G. Levine has most precisely and insightfully argued, Kafka's language of lovemaking in this scene unravels in such a way that "the more they lose themselves in each other, the more they forget who and where they are, the more they bump up against things and knock unwittingly on Klamm's door, the harder it is to tell them apart from their surroundings. Such is the heat of this scene, in which Frieda's little body is said to burn in K.'s hands, that the lovers not only exchange all manner of bodily fluids but themselves dissolve utterly intoxicated into the puddles of beer in which they lie. [. . .] What remains of the lovers—or rather of a separateness still to be overcome—is conveyed through a certain rhythm. Gone is the subject 'they,' the active verbs 'embraced,' 'rolled,' 'bumped,' and even 'lay'; gone are the precise spatial and temporal coordinates. In their place, it is said only that 'hours passed, hours breathing together with a single heartbeat [. . .].'" Michael G. Levine, "'A Place So Insanely Enchanting': Kafka and the Poetics of Suspension," *Modern Language Notes* 123, no. 5 (2008): 1039–67, 1042.

173. Merleau-Ponty, *The Phenomenology of Perception*, 191; cf. Merleau-Ponty, *La phénoménologie de la perception*, 872. For Husserl's descriptions of pairing, which are rhetorically closer to the experiences of Thomas and the woman than his argumentation otherwise would imply, see chapter 2.

174. Blanchot, *Aminadab*, 165; cf. Blanchot, *Aminadab*, 241.

175. Blanchot, *Aminadab*, 165; cf. Blanchot, *Aminadab*, 241.

176. Blanchot, *Aminadab*, 76; cf. Blanchot, *Aminadab*, 115.

177. Blanchot, *Aminadab*, 196–97 (trans. modified); cf. Blanchot, *Aminadab*, 286–87. This nocturnal "truth" can only be the truth of the withdrawal of truth from all experience, as Bataille had said in a commentary on these lines: "Utmost lucidity isn't given in immediate lucidity, but happens when lucidity fails: the night has to fall before knowledge is possible." Bataille, *Guilty*, 104; cf. Bataille, *OC* 5:349.

178. Blanchot, *The Unavowable Community*, 41.

179. Blanchot, *The Unavowable Community*, 41.

180. Even the room will appear "unharmed from the furious destruction," with the exception of the fallen desk. Blanchot, *Aminadab*, 165; cf. Blanchot, *Aminadab*, 241.

181. Fynsk, *Last Steps*, 133.
182. Blanchot, *Aminadab*, 168 (trans. modified); cf. Blanchot, *Aminadab*, 245.
183. Blanchot, *Aminadab*, 168; cf. Blanchot, *Aminadab*, 245.
184. Derrida, *Demeure: Fiction and Testimony*, 30.
185. After explicitly calling this association between the woman and the name "probable," rather than definitive, the woman will nevertheless be called "Lucie" for the remainder of the novel.
186. Blanchot, *Aminadab*, 168; cf. Blanchot, *Aminadab*, 246.
187. Blanchot, *Aminadab*, 168; cf. Blanchot, *Aminadab*, 246.
188. Blanchot, *Aminadab*, 114; cf. Blanchot, *Aminadab*, 168.
189. Blanchot, *Aminadab*, 169–70 (trans. modified); cf. Blanchot, *Aminadab*, 247.
190. Blanchot, *The Infinite Conversation*, 67; cf. Blanchot, *L'entretien infini*, 96.
191. Fynsk, *Last Steps*, 107.
192. Blanchot, *The Unavowable Community*, 49.
193. Blanchot, *Aminadab*, 170; cf. Blanchot, *Aminadab*, 249.
194. Blanchot, *Aminadab*, 171 (trans. modified; my emphasis); cf. Blanchot, *Aminadab*, 249. While the verb "s'étaler" surely signifies "stretch" here, as Fort renders it, the sense of self-display that the reflexive formulation may also imply underscores the separation of Thomas's initial from any self-presentation of his "own."
195. Blanchot, *Aminadab*, 171; cf. Blanchot, *Aminadab*, 250. The conditional verb that is rendered "cannot" in this passage ("devrais") also recalls the register of duty and obligation ("devoir").
196. Blanchot, *Aminadab*, 173 (trans. modified); cf. Blanchot, *Aminadab*, 253.
197. Blanchot, *Aminadab*, 171; cf. Blanchot, *Aminadab*, 249.
198. As before, "Lucie" will immediately follow her expression of satisfaction with demands, asserting that their "attachment" requires another "contract," whose terms would entail the avoidance of all speech, sight, and thought on Thomas's part, so as to avoid "expos[ing]" their "intimacy" to "any disturbance." Blanchot, *Aminadab*, 174–76; cf. Blanchot, *Aminadab*, 254–57. With these stipulations, "Lucie" not only seeks to enforce the self-abandon that let them touch on the floor and on the page; for she also admits despite herself the irrevocable loss of that abandon, which could therefore hardly be recovered but only contradicted by a self-imposed act of will.
199. Blanchot, *Aminadab*, 165; cf. Blanchot, *Aminadab*, 241.
200. Blanchot, *The Infinite Conversation*, 55; cf. Blanchot, *L'entretien infini*, 79.
201. Fynsk, *Last Steps*, 153.
202. Blanchot, *Aminadab*, 173 (trans. modified); cf. Blanchot, *Aminadab*, 253.
203. Blanchot, *The Writing of the Disaster*, 14; trans. modified.
204. Blanchot, *L'écriture du désastre*, 29–30.

Postscript

1. Augustine, *Confessions* X.3.3; Augustine, *On the Trinity*, 306; Husserl, *Cartesian Meditations*, 157.
2. Kafka, *Nachgelassene Schriften und Fragmente II*, 42.
3. Blanchot, *Aminadab*, 13, 43, 66, 96, 199; cf. Kafka, *Das Schloss*, 1:36, 40, 51.
4. Husserl, *Cartesian Meditations*, 29.
5. Friedrich Nietzsche, *On the Genealogy of Morality*, trans. Carol Diethe (Cambridge: Cambridge University Press, 2007), 3 (trans. modified); cf. Friedrich Nietzsche, *Zur Genealogie der Moral*, in *Jenseits von Gut und Böse. Zur Genealogie der Moral*, ed. Giorgio Colli and Mazzino Montinari (Berlin: de Gruyter, 1999), 247. The first "reason" that Nietzsche cites for our ignorance—"We have never sought after ourselves [*nach uns gesucht*] [. . .] our heart is simply not in it"—also echoes the reasons for self-ignorance that Augustine will provide: namely, the loves that draw our minds away from us. Nietzsche, *On the Genealogy of Morality*, 3 (trans. modified); cf. chapter 1.
6. Nietzsche, *On the Genealogy of Morality*, 26; trans. modified; Nietzsche, *Zur Genealogie der Moral*, 279.
7. Paul Celan, "You transfathom," in *Breathturn into Timestead: The Collected Later Poetry*, trans. Pierre Joris (New York: Farrar, Straus and Giroux, 2014), 360–61; trans. modified.
8. Nietzsche, *On the Genealogy of Morality*, 87.
9. Nietzsche, *On the Genealogy of Morality*, 88, 56.
10. Celan's word of "misknowledge [*Verkenntnis*]" alone echoes Nietzsche, who will write elsewhere: "we misknow ourselves [*wir verkennnen uns*]." Friedrich Nietzsche, *Morgenröthe*, in *Morgenröthe. Idyllen aus Messina. Die fröhliche Wissenschaft*, ed. Giorgio Colli and Mazzino Montinari (Berlin: de Gruyter, 1999), 108.
11. Celan, "Who Rules?" in *Breathturn into Timestead*, 112–13; trans. modified.
12. Nietzsche, *On the Genealogy of Morality*, 3.
13. Augustine, *Enarrationes in Psalmos*, XLI.13.
14. Blanchot, *Thomas the Obscure*, 25 (trans. modified); Blanchot, *Thomas l'obscur*, 44. For an incisive reading of this passage, which occurs within a scene of reading from Blanchot's novel, see Thomas Schestag, *Mantisrelikte* (Basel: Urs Engeler, 1998), 69–117.
15. Martin Buber, *I and Thou*, trans. Ronald Gregor Smith (Edinburgh: T. & T. Clark, 1937), 3–4.
16. Bataille, *Inner Experience*, 94; cf. Bataille, *OC* 5:111–12.
17. Buber, *I and Thou*, 3, 11.
18. Buber, *I and Thou*, 18.
19. Hamacher, "What Remains to Be Said," 217.

20. Gilles Deleuze, *The Logic of Sense*, ed. Constantin S. Boundes, trans. Mark Lester and Charles Stivale (London: Athlone, 1990), 261. An instance of such "internal resonance" and original "disparity" might also be found in Deleuze's invocation of "internal resonance," which at once resonates with and differs from Gilbert Simondon's use of the term to refer to the relational trait of individuating life that does not "spring forth between two terms that would already be individuals" but rather bears out as the "living being, which is both more and less than unity," and "conveys an *interior problematic* and *can enter as an element into a problematic that is vaster than its own being.*" Gilbert Simondon, *Individuation in Light of Notions of Form and Information*, trans. Taylor Adkins (Minneapolis: University of Minnesota Press, 2020), 8.

21. Hamacher, "What Remains to Be Said," 217.

22. Blanchot, *The Infinite Conversation*, 8. Here, Blanchot characterizes "the movement of signification" as a "relation of infinity" that follows from its structural "dissymmetry," and in so doing, he offers a variation upon the terms that Levinas had used to describe the relation to the Other, whose absolute transcendence entails "an asymmetrical relation" that "opens time," while the "infinity" of the other "transcends and dominates the subjectivity (the I not being transcendent with regard to the other in the same sense that the other is transcendent with regard to me)." Emmanuel Levinas, *Totality and Infinity*, trans. Alphonso Lingis (The Hague: Nijhoff, 1979), 225. In their resonance and difference, the passages of Blanchot and Levinas themselves register a "plural speech" that suspends "predominance and subordination," including the domination of the Other that Levinas affirms, despite his critique of violence.

23. Hamacher, "What Remains to Be Said," 217.

24. Hamacher, "For—Philology," 123 (trans. modified); cf. Werner Hamacher, "*Für*—Die Phillologie," in *Was zu sagen bleibt*, 20.

Works Cited

Abraham, Nicolas. "Le symbole ou l'au-delà du phénomène." In *L'écorce et le noyau*. By Nicolas Abraham and Maria Torok, 25–76. Paris: Flammarion, 1987.
Adler, Anthony Curtis. "The Biopolitics of Noise: Kafka's 'Der Bau.'" In *Thresholds of Listening: Sound, Technics, Space*, edited by Sander van Maas, 125–42. New York: Fordham University Press, 2015.
Adorno, Theodor W. "Notes on Kafka." In *Prisms*, 243–71. Translated by Samuel Weber and Shierry Weber. Cambridge, MA: MIT Press, 1981.
Agamben, Giorgio. *Infancy and History: The Destruction of Experience*. Translated by Liz Heron. London: Verso, 1993.
Allen, William S. *Aesthetics of Negativity: Blanchot, Adorno, and Autonomy*. New York: Fordham University Press, 2016.
Aquinas, Thomas. *Summa Theologiae*. Edited by Thomas Gilby. 61 vols. New York: McGraw-Hill, 1964–1981.
Arendt, Hannah. *The Life of the Mind*. 2 vols. New York: Harcourt, 1978.
Aristotle. *Aristotelis ars rhetorica*. Edited by W. D. Ross. Oxford: Clarendon, 1959.
———. *Aristotelis categoriae et liber de interpretatione*. Edited by L. Minio-Paluello. Oxford: Clarendon, 1949.
———. *Aristotelis Topica et Sophistici Elenchi*. Edited by W. D. Ross. Oxford: Clarendon, 1958.
———. *The 'Art' of Rhetoric*. Translated by John Henry Freese. Cambridge, MA: Harvard University Press, 1926.
———. *Categories, On Interpretation, Prior Analytics*. Translated by H. P. Cooke and Hugh Tredennick. Cambridge, MA: Harvard University Press, 2002.
Augustine. *Augustin d'Hippone: Sermons pour la Pâque*. Edited by Suzanne Poque. Paris: Cerf, 2003.
———. *The City of God against the Pagans*. Edited and translated by R. W. Dyson. Cambridge: Cambridge University Press, 1998.
———. *Les commentaires des Psaumes: Enarrationes in Psalmos, Ps. 37–44*. Edited by M. Dulaey et al. Paris: Institut d'Études Augustiniennes, 2017.

———. *Confessions*. Translated by Maria Boulding. New York: New City Press, 1997.
———. *Confessions*. Edited by James J. O'Donnell. 3 vols. Oxford: Clarendon, 1992.
———. *De Civitate Dei*. Edited by B. Dombart and A. Kalb. 2 vols. Turnhout: Brepols, 1955.
———. *De diversis quaestionibus LXXXIII. De octo Dulcitii quaestionibus*. Edited by A. Mutzenbecher. Turnhout: Brepols, 1975.
———. *De doctrina Christiana. De uera religione*. Edited by Joseph Martin. Turnhout: Brepols, 1962.
———. *De trinitate libri XV*. Edited by W. J. Mountain and F. Glorie. Turnhout: Brepols, 1968.
———. *Enarrationes in Psalmos I-L*. Edited by E. Dekkers and J. Fraipont. Turnhout: Brepols, 1956.
———. *Johannis Evangelium tractatus CXXIV*. Edited by Radbodus Willems. Turnhout: Brepols, 1954.
———. *Of True Religion*. In *Augustine: Earlier Writings*. Edited and translated by J. H. S. Burleigh, 218-83. London: SCM, 1953.
———. *On Order [De Ordine]*. Translated by Silvano Borruso. South Bend: St. Augustine's Press, 2007.
———. *On the Trinity*. Translated by Stephen McKenna. Washington, DC: Catholic University of America Press, 1963.
———. *Sermones de vetere testamento (1-50)*. Edited by C. Lambot. Turnhout: Brepols, 1961.
———. *Sermons, (1-19) on the Old Testament. Volume III/1*. Edited by John E. Rotelle. Translated by Edmund Hill. New York: New City Press, 1990.
———. *Tractates on the Gospel of John 1-10*. Translated by John W. Rettig. Washington, DC: Catholic University of America Press, 1988.
Austin, J. L. *How to Do Things with Words*. Edited by J. O. Urmson and Marina Shisà. Cambridge, MA: Harvard University Press, 1975.
Ayres, Lewis. *Augustine and the Trinity*. Cambridge: Cambridge University Press, 2010.
Badiou, Alain. *Being and Event*. Translated by Oliver Feltham. London: Continuum, 2007.
Barthes, Roland. "The Death of the Author." In *Image, Music, Text*, 142-48. Translated by Stephen Heath. New York: Hill & Wang, 1977.
———. "Outcomes of the Text." In *The Rustling of Language*, 238-49. Translated by Richard Howard. Berkeley: University of California Press, 1986.
———. "Les sorties du texte." In *Bataille*, edited by Philippe Sollers, 49-62. Paris: Union générale d'éditions, 1973.
Bataille, Georges. *L'Abbé C*. Translated by Philip A. Facey. London/New York: Marion Boyars, 1983.

———. *The Accursed Share. An Essay on General Economy*. Translated by Robert Hurley. New York: Zone, 1988.
———. *Eroticism: Death and Sensuality*. Translated by Mary Dalwood. San Francisco: City Lights Books, 1986.
———. *Guilty*. Translated by Bruce Boone. Venice: Lapis, 1988.
———. *Inner Experience*. Translated by Leslie Anne Boldt. Albany: State University of New York Press, 1988.
———. "The Language of Flowers." In *Visions of Excess: Selected Writings, 1927-1939*, 10-14. Translated by Allan Stoekl. Minneapolis: University of Minnesota Press, 1985.
———. *Literature and Evil*. Translated by Alastair Hamilton. London: Marion Boyars, 1973.
———. "Nonknowledge." In *The Unfinished System of Nonknowledge*, 196-205. Translated by Michelle Kendall and Stuart Kendall. Minneapolis: University of Minnesota Press, 2001.
———. *Oeuvres complètes* (= *OC*). 12 vols. Paris: Gallimard, 1970-1988.
———. *Story of the Eye*. Translated by Joachim Neugroschel. San Francisco: City Lights Books, 1987.
Bégout, Bruce. *La généalogie de la logique: Husserl, l'antéprédicatif et le catégorial*. Paris: Vrin, 2000.
Bennington, Geoffrey, and Jacques Derrida. *Derrida*. Paris: Seuil, 2008.
Bergmann, Hugo. *Untersuchungen zum Problem der Evidenz der inneren Wahrnehmung*. Halle: Niemeyer, 1908.
Bernheimer, Charles. *Flaubert and Kafka: Studies in Psychopoetic Structure*. New Haven, CT: Yale University Press, 1982.
Blanchot, Maurice. *Aminadab*. Paris: Gallimard, 1942.
———. *Aminadab*. Translated by Jeff Fort. Lincoln: University of Nebraska Press, 2002.
———. *De Kafka à Kafka*. Paris: Gallimard, 1981.
———. "Discours sur la patience (en marge des livres d'Emmanuel Lévinas)." In *Maurice Blanchot et la philosophie*, edited by Éric Hoppenot and Alain Milon, 403-20. Nanterre: Presses Universitaires de Nanterre, 2010.
———. *L'écriture du désastre*. Paris: Gallimard, 1980.
———. *L'entretien infini*. Paris: Gallimard, 1969.
———. *Faux pas*. Paris: Gallimard, 1943.
———. *The Infinite Conversation*. Translated by Susan Hanson. Minneapolis: University of Minnesota Press, 1993.
———. "La parole prophétique." In *Le livre à venir*, 109-19. Paris: Gallimard, 1959.
———. *Le pas au-delà*. Paris: Gallimard, 1973.
———. "Prophetic Speech." In *The Book to Come*, 79-85. Translated by Charlotte Mandell. Stanford, CA: Stanford University Press, 2003.

———. *The Step Not Beyond*. Translated by Lycette Nelson. Albany: State University of New York Press, 1992.

———. "La Terreur dans les lettres." In *Chroniques littéraires du Journal des débats: Avril 1941–août 1944*, edited by Christophe Bident, 89–94. Paris: Gallimard, 2007.

———. *Thomas l'obscur: Première version, 1941*. Paris: Gallimard, 2005.

———. *The Unavowable Community*. Translated by Pierre Joris. Barrytown: Station Hill, 1988.

———. *The Writing of the Disaster*. Translated by Ann Smock. Lincoln: University of Nebraska Press, 1995.

Boethius, *Commentarii in librum Aristotelis ΠΕΡΙ ΕΡΜΗΝΕΙΑΣ*. Edited by Charles Meiser. Leipzig: Teubner, 1877.

Boldt-Irons, Leslie. "Irony/Humor in the Fast Lane: The Route to Desire in *L'Abbé C*." *Romantic Review* 85, no. 2 (1994): 271–90.

Brentano, Franz. *Psychologie vom empirischen Standpunkt*. Edited by Oskar Kraus. 3 vols. Hamburg: Meiner, 1971–74.

Brod, Max. Afterword to *Der Prozess* by Franz Kafka, edited by Max Brod, 279–90. Munich: Deutscher Taschenbuch Verlag, 1997.

Brodksy, Claudia. "'A Now Not *toto caelo* a Not-Now': The 'Origin' of Difference in Husserl, from Number to Literature." In *Phenomenology to the Letter: Husserl and Literature*, edited by Philippe P. Haensler, Kristina Mendicino, and Rochelle Tobias, 283–307. Berlin: de Gruyter, 2021.

Buber, Martin. *I and Thou*. Translated by Ronald Gregor Smith. Edinburgh: T. & T. Clark, 1937.

Burnyeat, Miles. "The Inaugural Address: Wittgenstein and Augustine, *De Magistro*." *Proceedings of the Aristotelian Society* 61 (1987): 1–26.

Burton, Philip. *Language in the Confessions of Augustine*. Oxford: Oxford University Press, 2007.

Butler, Judith. "Who Owns Kafka?" *London Review of Books* 33, no. 5 (2011): https://www.lrb.co.uk/the-paper/v33/n05/judith-butler/who-owns-kafka. Accessed December 20, 2020.

Caputo, John D. *The Prayers and Tears of Jacques Derrida: Religion without Religion*. Bloomington: Indiana University Press, 1997.

———. "The Question of Being and Transcendental Phenomenology: Reflections on Heidegger's Relationship to Husserl." *Research in Phenomenology* 7 (1977): 84–105.

Cary, Phillip. *Outward Signs: The Powerlessness of External Things in Augustine's Thought*. Oxford: Oxford University Press, 2008.

Celan, Paul. *Breathturn into Timestead: The Collected Later Poetry*. Translated by Pierre Joris. New York: Farrar, Straus and Giroux, 2014.

Cicero, Marcus Tullius. *Tusculum Disputations*. Translated by J. E. King. Cambridge, MA: Harvard University Press, 1927.

Corngold, Stanley. "Ritardando in Das Schloß." In *From Kafka to Sebald: Modernism and Narrative Form*, edited by Sabine Wilke, 11–26. London: Bloomsbury, 2012.

Corngold, Stanley, and Benno Wagner. *Franz Kafka: The Ghosts in the Machine*. Evanston, IL: Northwestern University Press, 2011.

Cornille, Jean-Louis. "Georges Bataille: un rat dans la bibliothèque." *Revue de littérature comparée* 313 (2005): 35–50.

Courcelle, Pierre. *"Connais-toi toi-même," de Socrate à St. Bernard*. 3 vols. Paris: Études augustiniennes, 1974–1975.

Dastur, Françoise. "Finitude and Repetition in Derrida and Husserl." *Southern Journal of Philosophy* 32, no. 5 (1993): 113–30.

———. *Questions of Phenomenology: Language, Alterity, Temporality, Finitude*. Translated by Robert Vallier. New York: Fordham University Press, 2017.

Davies, Paul. "Kafka's Lesson, Blanchot's Itinerary." *parallax* 12, no. 2 (2006): 23–39.

Deleuze, Gilles. *Difference and Repetition*. Translated by Paul Patton. New York: Columbia University Press, 1994.

———. *Différence et répétition*. Paris: Presses Universitaires de France, 1968.

———. *The Logic of Sense* Edited by Constantin S. Boundes. Translated by Mark Lester and Charles Stivale. London: Athlone, 1990.

Deleuze, Gilles, and Félix Guattari. *Franz Kafka: Pour une littérature mineure*. Paris: Minuit, 1975.

———. *Kafka: Towards a Minor Literature*. Translated by Dana Polan. Minneapolis: University of Minnesota Press, 1986.

———. *A Thousand Plateaus: Capitalism and Schizophrenia*. Translated by Brian Massumi. Minneapolis: University of Minnesota Press, 1987.

Depew, David J. "Lyotard's Augustine." In *Augustine for the Philosophers: The Rhetor of Hippo, the Confessions, and the Continentals*, edited by Calvin L. Troup, 59–76. Waco: Baylor University Press, 2014.

Depraz, Natalie. *Transcendence et incarnation: Le status de l'intersubjectivité comme altérité à soi chez Husserl*. Paris: Vrin, 1995.

Derrida, Jacques. "Circumfession: Fifty-Nine Periods and Periphrases, Written in a Sort of Internal Margin, between Geoffrey Bennington's Book and Work in Preparation (January 1989–April 1990)." Translated by Geoffrey Bennington. In *Jacques Derrida*. By Geoffrey Bennington and Jacques Derrida. Chicago: University of Chicago Press, 1993.

———. "Composing Circumfession." In *Augustine and Postmodernism: Confessions and Circumfession*, edited by John D. Caputo and Michael J. Scanlon, 19–27. Bloomington: Indiana University Press, 2005.

———. *Demeure: Fiction and Testimony*. Translated by Elizabeth Rottenberg. Stanford, CA: Stanford University. Press, 2000.

———. *Demeure: Maurice Blanchot*. Paris: Galilée, 1998.

———. *L'écriture et la différence*. Paris: Seuil, 1967.

———. *Edmund Husserl's Origin of Geometry: An Introduction*. Translated by John P. Leavey. Lincoln: University of Nebraska Press, 1989.

———. "La forme et le vouloir-dire: Note sur la phénoménologie du langage." *Revue internationale de philosophie* 21, no. 81 (1967): 277–99.

———. "The Law of Genre." In *Parages*, edited by John P. Leavey, 217–49. Translated by Avital Ronell. Stanford, CA: Stanford University Press, 2011.

———. "La loi du genre." In *Parages*, 231–66. 2nd ed. Paris: Galilée, 2003.

———. *Mémoires d'aveugle: L'autoportrait et autres ruines*. Paris: Editions de la Réunion des musées nationaux, 1990.

———. *Memoirs of the Blind: The Self-Portrait and Other Ruins*. Translated by Pascale-Anne Brault and Michael Naas. Chicago: University of Chicago Press, 1993.

———. *Of Grammatology*. Translated by Gayatri Chakravorty Spivak. Baltimore: Johns Hopkins University Press, 1997.

———. "The Pit and the Pyramid: Introduction to Hegel's Semiology." In *Margins of Philosophy*, 69–108. Translated by Alan Bass. Chicago: University of Chicago Press, 1982.

———. *The Problem of Genesis in Husserl's Philosophy*. Translated by Marian Hobson. Chicago: University of Chicago Press, 2003.

———. *Speech and Phenomena, and Other Essays on Husserl's Theory of Signs*. Translated by David B. Allison. Evanston, IL: Northwestern University Press, 1973.

———. *La voix et le phénomène: Introduction au problème du signe dans la phénoménologie de Husserl*. Paris: Presses Universitaires de France, 1967.

———. *Writing and Difference*. Translated by Alan Bass. London: Routledge, 2001.

Dolar, Mladen. "The Burrow of Sound." *differences* 22, no. 2/3 (2011): 112–39.

Douchin-Shahin, Andrée. "Pardoxalement parlant: quelques réflexions sur *L'Abbé C.* de Georges Bataille." *Romantic Review* 78, no. 3 (1987): 368–82.

Dowden, Stephen. *Kafka's Castle and the Critical Imagination*. Columbia: Camden House, 1995.

Einstein, Albert. *Relativity: The Special and General Theory*. Translated by Robert W. Lawson. New York: Henry Holt, 1921.

Emrich, Wilhelm. *Franz Kafka: A Critical Study of His Writings*. Translated by Sheema Zeben Buehne. New York: Ungar, 1968.

Ernst, Gilles. *Georges Bataille: Analyse du récit de mort*. Paris: Presses Universitaires de France, 1993.

Fink, Eugen. *Sixth Cartesian Meditation: The Idea of a Transcendental Theory of Method*. Translated by Ronald Bruzina. Bloomington: Indiana University Press, 1995.

Fitch, Brian T. "L'Énigme faite texte: *L'Abbé C.* de Georges Bataille." In *Ecrivains de la modernité*, 43–64. Paris: Minard, 1981.

Fort, Jeff. Introduction to *Aminadab*, by Maurice Blanchot, vii–xvii. Translated by Jeff Fort. Lincoln: University of Nebraska Press, 2002.
———. "Rumors of the Outside: Blanchot's Murmurs and the Indistinction of Literature." *Angelaki: Journal of the Theoretical Humanities* 23, no. 3 (2018): 158–77.
Foucault, Michel. "Maurice Blanchot: The Thought from Outside." In *Foucault / Blanchot*, 7–58. Translated by Brian Massumi. New York: Zone Books, 1987.
———. *Les mots et les choses: Une archéologie des sciences humaines*. Paris: Gallimard, 1966.
———. *The Order of Things: An Archaeology of the Human Sciences*. Translated by Alan Sheridan. New York: Vintage, 1994.
———. "La scène de la philosophie." In *Dits et écrits 1954–1988*, edited by Daniel Defert, François Ewald, and Jacques Lagrange, 571–95. Vol. 3. Paris: Gallimard, 1994.
Franck, Didier. *Flesh and the Body: On the Phenomenology of Husserl*. Translated by Joseph Rivera and Scott Davidson. London: Bloomsbury, 2014.
Freud, Sigmund. *Civilization and Its Discontents*. Edited and translated by James Strachey. New York: Norton, 1961.
———. "Screen Memories." *The Standard Edition of the Complete Psychological Works of Sigmund Freud: Volume 3 (1893–1899): Early Psychoanalytical Publications*, edited and translated by James Strachey, 298–322. London: Hogarth, 1962.
———. *Das Unbehagen in der Kultur*. In *Gesammelte Werke: Vierzehnter Band: Werke aus den Jahren 1925–1931*, edited by Anna Freud et al., 419–506. London: Imago, 1948.
Fynsk, Christopher. *Infant Figures: The Death of the 'Infans' and Other Scenes of Origin*. Stanford, CA: Stanford University Press, 2000.
———. *Last Steps: Maurice Blanchot's Exilic Writing*. New York: Fordham University Press, 2013.
Gasché, Rodolphe. *Georges Bataille: Phenomenology and Phantasmatology*. Translated by Roland Végsö. Stanford, CA: Stanford University Press, 2012.
———. "On Re-presentation, or Zigzagging with Husserl and Derrida." *Southern Journal of Philosophy* 32, no. 5 (1993): 1–16.
———. *The Tain of the Mirror: Derrida and the Philosophy of Reflection*. Cambridge, MA: Harvard University Press, 1986.
Gellen, Kata. *Kafka and Noise: The Discovery of Cinematic Sound in Literary Modernism*. Evanston, IL: Northwestern University Press, 2019.
Gemerchak, Christopher M. *The Sunday of the Negative: Reading Bataille Reading Hegel*. Albany: State University of New York Press, 2003.
Giartosio, Tommaso. "'La vérité du bonheur': The Legitimation of Literature in Georges Bataille's *L'Abbé C.*" *Qui parle* 5, no. 2 (1992): 21–47.

Gilson, Étienne. *The Christian Philosophy of Saint Augustine*. Translated by L. E. M. Lynch. New York: Vintage, 1967.
Granel, Gérard. *Le sens du temps et de la perception chez Husserl*. 2nd. ed. Paris: Éditions T.E.R., 2012.
Hadot, Pierre. "L'image de la Trinité dans l'âme chez Victorinus et chez saint Augustin." In *Études de patristique et d'histoire des concepts*, 283–317. Paris: Belles Lettres, 2010.
Haensler, Philippe P. "Fort. The Germangled Words of Edmund Husserl and Walter Benjamin." In *Phenomenology to the Letter: Husserl and Literature*, edited by Philippe P. Haensler, Kristina Mendicino, and Rochelle Tobias, 85–112. Berlin: de Gruyter, 2021.
Hamacher, Werner. "Afformative, Strike." Translated by Dana Hollander. *The Cardozo Law Review* 13, no. 4 (1991): 1133–57.
———. "Bogengebeten." In *Aufmerksamkeit*, edited by Norbert Haas, Rainer Nägele, and Hans-Jörg Rheinberger, 11–43. Eggingen: Isele, 1998.
———. "For—Philology." In *Minima Philologica*, 107–56. Translated by Jason Groves. New York: Fordham University Press, 2015.
———. "Für—Die Philologie." In *Was zu sagen bleibt*, 7–49. Schupfart: Engeler, 2019.
———. *Pleroma—Reading in Hegel*. Translated by Nicolas Walker and Simon Jarvis. Stanford, CA: Stanford University Press, 1998.
———. "Ungerufen: Kommentar zu Kafkas Prüfung." *Die Neue Rundschau* 118, no. 2 (2007): 132–53.
———. "Was zu sagen bleibt: Twelve and More Ways of Looking at Philology." In *Was zu sagen bleibt*, 79–202. Schupfart: Engeler, 2019.
———. "What Remains to Be Said: Twelve and More Ways of Looking at Philology." Translated by Kristina Mendicino. In *Give the Word: Responses to Werner Hamacher's 95 Theses on Philology*, edited by Gerhard Richter and Ann Smock, 217–354. Lincoln: University of Nebraska Press, 2019.
Hansel, Georges. "Maurice Blanchot, lecteur de Lévinas." In *Maurice Blanchot et la philosophie*, edited by Éric Hoppenot and Alain Milon, 315–73. Paris: Presses Universitaires de Paris Nanterre, 2010.
Hart, Kevin. *The Dark Gaze: Maurice Blanchot and the Sacred*. Chicago: University of Chicago Press, 2004.
Hegel, G. W. F. *Enzyklopädie der philosophischen Wissenschaften im Grundrisse: Dritter Teil: Die Philosophie des Geistes*. Edited by Eva Moldenhauer and Karl Markus Michel. Frankfurt am Main: Suhrkamp, 1986.
———. *The Phenomenology of Spirit*. Translated by Terry Pinkard. Cambridge: Cambridge University Press, 2018.
———. *The Science of Logic*. Translated by George di Giovanni. Cambridge: Cambridge University Press, 2010.

Heidegger, Martin. "Augustin und der Neoplatonismus." In *Phänomenologie des religiösen Lebens*, edited by Claudius Strube, 160–299. Frankfurt am Main: Klostermann, 1995.

———. *Being and Time*. Translated by Joan Stambaugh. Albany: State University of New York Press, 1996.

———. "Language." In *Poetry, Language, Thought*, 185–208. Translated by Albert Hofstadter. New York: HarperCollins, 2001.

———. *Phenomenology of Religious Life*. Translated by Matthias Fritsch and Jennifer Anna Gosetti-Ferencei. Bloomington: Indiana University Press, 2004.

———. *Sein und Zeit*. Tübingen: Niemeyer, 2001.

———. *Unterwegs zur Sprache*. Edited by Friedrich-Wilhelm von Herrmann. Frankfurt am Main: Klostermann, 1985.

Heidsieck, Arnold. *The Intellectual Contexts of Kafka's Fictions: Philosophy, Law, Religion*. Columbus: Camden House, 1994.

———. "Physiological, Phenomenological, and Linguistic Psychology in Kafka's Early Works." *German Quarterly* 62, no. 4 (1989): 489–500.

Held, Klaus. *Lebendige Gegenwart: Die Frage nach der Seinsweise des transzendentalen Ich bei Edmund Husserl entwickelt am Leitfaden der Zeitproblematik*. The Hague: Nijhoff, 1966.

Hemmings, Clare. "Invoking Affect: Cultural Theory and the Ontological Turn." *Cultural Studies* 19, no. 5 (2005): 548–67.

Henke, Anna. "Sound and Unsound Advice: Unveiling Walter Benjamin's Umlaut." In *Playing False: Representations of Betrayal*, edited by Kristina Mendicino and Betiel Wasihun, 229–60. Oxford: Peter Lang, 2013.

Henry, Michel. *Phénoménologie matérielle*. Paris: Presses Universitaires de France, 1990.

Hill, Leslie. *Bataille, Klossowski, Blanchot: Writing at the Limits*. Oxford: Oxford University Press, 2001.

Holenstein, Elmar. *Phänomenologie der Assoziation: Zu Struktur und Funktion eines Grundprinzips der passiven Genesis bei E. Husserl*. The Hague: Nijhoff, 1972.

Holland, Michael. "Qui est l'Aminadab de Blanchot." In *Avant dire: Essais sur Blanchot*, 9–35. Paris: Hermann, 2015.

Hollier, Dennis. *Against Architecture*. Translated by Betsy Wing. Cambridge, MA: MIT Press, 1989.

Howells, Christina. *Mortal Subjects: Passions of the Soul in Late Twentieth-Century French Thought*. Cambridge: Polity, 2011.

Husserl, Edmund. *Analyses Concerning Passive and Active Synthesis: Lectures on Transcendental Logic*. Translated by Anthony J. Steinbock. Dordrecht: Kluwer, 2001.

———. *Briefwechsel. Band IV: Die Freiburger Schüler*. Edited by Karl Schuhmann. Dordrecht: Springer, 1994.

---. *Cartesian Meditations: An Introduction to Phenomenology.* Translated by Dorion Cairns. The Hague: Nijhoff, 1960.

---. *The Crisis of the European Sciences and Transcendental Phenomenology.* Translated by David Carr. Evanston, IL: Northwestern University Press, 1970.

---. *Erfahrung und Urteil: Untersuchungen zur Genealogie der Logik.* Edited by Ludwig Landgrebe. Prague: Academia Verlagsbuchhandlung, 1939.

---. *Experience and Judgment: Investigations in a Genealogy of Logic.* Translated by James S. Churchill and Karl Ameriks. London: Routledge, 1973.

---. *Formal and Transcendental Logic.* Translated by Dorion Cairns. The Hague: Nijhoff, 1969.

---. *Gesammelte Werke. Husserliana (= Hua).* Edited by Herman van Breda et al. 43 vols. Dordrecht: Springer, 1950–.

---. *Ideas Pertaining to a Pure Phenomenology and to a Phenomenological Philosophy: First Book: General Introduction to a Pure Phenomenology.* Translated by F. Kersten. The Hague: Nijhoff, 1982.

---. *Ideas Pertaining to a Pure Phenomenology and to a Phenomenological Philosophy: Second Book: Studies in the Phenomenology of Constitution.* Translated by Richard Rojcewicz and André Schuwer. Dordrecht: Kluwer, 1989.

---. *Logical Investigations.* Edited by Dermot Moran. Translated by J. N. Findlay. 2 vols. London: Routledge, 2001.

---. *The Phenomenology of Internal Time-Consciousness.* Edited by Martin Heidegger. Translated by James S. Churchill. Bloomington: Indiana University Press, 1964.

---. *Späte Texte über Zeitkonstitution (1929–1934): Die C-Manuskripte.* Edited by Dieter Lohmar. Dordrecht: Springer, 2006.

---. *Thing and Space: The Lectures of 1907.* Translated by Richard Rojcewicz. Dordrecht: Springer, 1997.

Jamison, Anne. *Kafka's Other Prague: Writings from the Czechoslovak Republic.* Evanston, IL: Northwestern University Press, 2018.

Jaspers, Karl. *Philosophie: Zweiter Band: Existenzerhellung.* Berlin: Springer, 1932.

---. *Philosophy: Volume 2.* Translated by E. B. Ashton. Chicago: University of Chicago Press, 1970.

Kafka, Franz. *Briefe: 1914–1917.* Edited by Hans-Gerd Koch. Frankfurt am Main: Fischer, 2005.

---. "A Country Doctor." In *Selected Stories*, edited and translated by Stanley Corngold, 60–65. New York: W.W. Norton, 2007.

---. *The Man Who Disappeared.* Translated by Ritchie Robertson. Oxford: Oxford University Press, 2012.

---. *Nachgelassene Schriften und Fragmente I.* Edited by Malcolm Pasley. Frankfurt am Main: Fischer, 1993.

---. *Nachgelassene Schriften und Fragmente II.* Edited by Jost Schillemeit. Frankfurt am Main: Fischer, 1992.

---. *Der Process: Faksimile-Edition (Franz Kafka-Ausgabe. Historisch-Kritische Edition sämtlicher Handschriften, Drucke und Typoskripte)*. Edited by Roland Reuß and Peter Staengle. Frankfurt am Main/Basel: Stroemfeld/Roter Stern, 1997.

---. *Das Schloss: Faksimile-Edition (Franz Kafka-Ausgabe. Historisch-Kritische Edition sämtlicher Handschriften, Drucke und Typoskripte)*. 6 vols. Edited by Roland Reuß and Peter Staengle. Frankfurt am Main: Stroemfeld, 2018.

---. *Tagebücher: Kritische Ausgabe*. Edited by Hans-Gerd Koch, Michael Müller, and Malcolm Pasley. Frankfurt am Main: Fischer, 1990.

---. *The Trial*. Trans. Mike Mitchell. Oxford: Oxford University Press, 2009.

---. *Der Verschollene*. Edited by Jost Schillemeit. Frankfurt am Main: Fischer, 1983.

---. "Wedding Preparations in the Country." In *Wedding Preparations in the Country and Other Posthumous Prose Writings*, 7–37. Translated by Ernst Kaiser and Eithne Wilkins. London: Secker and Warburg, 1954.

Kahnert, Klaus. *Entmachtung der Zeichen? Augustin über Sprache*. Philadelphia: John Benjamins, 2000.

Kierkegaard, Søren. *Le concept d'angoisse, simple éclaircissement psychologique au problème du péché originel*. Translated by K. Ferlov and J-J. Gateau. Paris: Gallimard, 1948.

Kleinwort, Malte. *Der späte Kafka: Spätstil als Stilsuspension*. Munich: Fink, 2013.

Klossowski, Pierre. *Such a Deathly Desire*. Translated by Russell Ford. Albany: State University of New York Press, 2007.

Koyré, Alexandre. "Notes sur la langue et la terminologie hégeliennes." In *Études d'histoire de la pensée philosophique*, 175–204. Paris: Gallimard, 1961.

Krell, David Farrell. *Contagion: Sexuality, Disease, and Death in German Idealism and Romanticism*. Bloomington: Indiana University Press, 1998.

---. *Of Memory, Reminiscence, and Writing: On the Verge*. Bloomington: Indiana University Press, 1990.

Lacan, Jacques. *The Seminar of Jacques Lacan: Book 1: Freud's Papers on Technique 1953–1954*. Edited by Jacques-Alain Miller. Translated by John Forrester. New York: W.W. Norton, 1991.

Lacoue-Labarthe, Philippe. "The Contestation of Death." Translated by Philip Anderson. In *The Power of Contestation: Perspectives on Maurice Blanchot*, edited by Kevin Hart and Geoffrey Hartman, 141–55. Baltimore: Johns Hopkins University Press, 2004.

Laporte, Roger. *Maurice Blanchot: L'ancien, l'effroyablement ancien*. Paris: Fata Morgana, 1987.

Lawlor, Leonard. *Derrida and Husserl: The Basic Problem of Phenomenology*. Bloomington: Indiana University Press, 2002.

Leibniz, Gottfried Wilhelm. "Meditations on Knowlege, Truth, and Ideas." In *Philosophical Papers and Letters*, edited by L. E. Loemker 291–95. Vol. 2. Dordrecht: Springer, 1989.

———. "Meditationes de cognitione, veritate et ideis." In *Die philosophischen Schriften von Gottfried Wilhelm Leibniz*, edited by Carl Immanuel Gerhardt, 422–26. Vol. 4. Hildesheim: Olms, 1965.

Levinas, Emmanuel. *Autrement qu'être ou au-delà de l'essence*. The Hague: Nijhoff, 1974.

———. *Otherwise Than Being, or, Beyond Essence*. Translated by Alphonso Lingis. Pittsburgh: Duquesne University Press, 1998.

———. *Totality and Infinity*. Translated by Alphonso Lingis. The Hague: Nijhoff, 1979.

Levine, Michael G. "'A Place So Insanely Enchanting': Kafka and the Poetics of Suspension." *Modern Language Notes* 123, no. 5 (2008): 1039–67.

Libera, Alain de. *Naissance du sujet*. Paris: Vrin, 2007.

Long, A. A. "Soul and Body in Stoicism." In *Stoic Studies*, 224–49. Berkeley: University of California Press, 1996.

Lyotard, Jean-François. *The Confession of Augustine*. Translated by Richard Beardsworth. Stanford, CA: Stanford University Press, 2000.

———. *Discours, figure*. Paris: Klincksieck, 1971.

Mackey, Louis H. "The Mediator Mediated: Faith and Reason in Augustine's 'De Magistro.'" *Franciscan Studies* 42 (1982): 135–55.

Marder, Michael. *Phenomena—Critique—Logos: The Project of Critical Phenomenology*. London: Rowman & Littlefield, 2014.

Marek, Johann Christian, and Barry Smith. "Einleitung zu Anton Martys *Elemente der deskriptiven Psychologie*." *Conceptus* 21, no. 53/54 (1987): 33–47.

Marion, Jean-Luc. *Being Given: Toward a Phenomenology of Givenness*. Translated by Jeffrey L. Kosky. Stanford, CA: Stanford University Press, 2002.

———. *In the Self's Place: The Approach of Saint Augustine*. Translated by Jeffrey L. Kosky. Stanford, CA: Stanford University Press, 2012.

———. *Reduction and Givenness: Investigations of Husserl, Heidegger, and Phenomenology*. Translated by Thomas A. Carlson. Evanston, IL: Northwestern University Press, 1988.

Markus, Robert A. "St. Augustine on Signs." *Phronesis* 2, no. 1 (1957): 60–83.

Marmande, Francis. "L'incitation ou l'oeil de l'histoire." In *Georges Bataille et la fiction*, edited by Henk Hillenaar and Jan Versteeg, 49–57. Amsterdam: Rodopi, 1992.

Marty, Anton. *Deskriptive Psychologie*. Edited by Mauro Antonelli and Johann Christian Marek. Würzburg: Königshausen & Neumann, 2011.

———. *Untersuchungen zur allgemeinen Grammatik und Sprachphilosophie*. Halle: Niemeyer, 1908.

Marx, Karl. *Das Manifest der kommunistischen Partei*. Edited by Theo Stammen and Alexander Classen. Munich: Fink, 2009.

Marx, Karl, and Friedrich Engels. *The Communist Manifesto. Collected Works*. Translated by Richard Dixon. Vol. 6. New York: International Publishers, 1976.

Mayer, C. J. "Signifikationshermeneutik im Dienste der Daseinsauslegung: Die Funktion der Verweisungen in den *Confessiones* X–XIII." *Augustiniana* 24 (1974): 21–74.

———. *Die Zeichen in der geistigen Entwicklung und in der Theologie des jungen Augustinus.* 2 vols. Würzburg: Augustinus Verlag, 1969–1974.

Merleau-Ponty, Maurice. *La phénoménologie de la perception.* In *Oeuvres*, edited by Claude Lefort, 655–1167. Paris: Gallimard, 2010.

———. *The Phenomenology of Perception.* Translated by Donald A. Landes. London and New York: Routledge, 2012.

Metzger, Arnold. "Die Phänomenologie der Revolution." In *Frühe Schriften*, edited by Karl Markus Michel, 13–104. Frankfurt am Main: Syndikat, 1979.

Mickunas, Algis. "Self-Identity and Time." In *Augustine for the Philosophers: The Rhetor of Hippo, the Confessions, and the Continentals*, edited by Calvin L. Troup, 107–125. Waco: Baylor University Press, 2014.

Montavont, Anne. *De la passivité dans la phénoménologie de Husserl.* Paris: Presses Universitaires de France, 1999.

Nancy, Jean-Luc. *Being Singular Plural.* Translated by Robert D. Richardson and Anne F. O'Byrne. Stanford, CA: Stanford University Press, 2000.

———. *Ego sum.* Paris: Flammarion, 1979.

———. *Ego Sum: Corpus, Anima, Fabula.* Translated by Marie-Eve Morin. New York: Fordham University Press, 2016.

———. *L'être singulier pluriel.* Paris: Galilée, 1996.

———. "L'excrit." *Alea* 15, no. 2 (2013): 312–20.

Neesen, Peter. *Vom Louvrezirkel zum Prozess: Franz Kafka und die Psychologie Franz Brentanos.* Göppingen: Kümmerle, 1972.

Neumann, Gerhard. "Franz Kafkas 'Schloss'-Roman: Das parasitäre Spiel der Zeichen." In *Franz Kafka: Schriftverkehr*, edited by Wolf Kittler and Gerhard Neumann, 199–221. Freiburg: Rombach, 1990.

Newman, Michael. "The Trace of Trauma: Blindness, Testimony, and the Gaze in Blanchot and Derrida." In *Maurice Blanchot: The Demand of Writing*, edited by Caroline Bailey Gill, 152–73. London and New York: Routledge, 1996.

Nietzsche, Friedrich. *The Gay Science.* Translated by Walter Kaufmann. New York: Vintage, 1974.

———. *Jenseits von Gut und Böse. Zur Genealogie der Moral.* Edited by Giorgio Colli and Mazzino Montinari. Berlin: de Gruyter, 1999.

———. *Morgenröthe. Idyllen aus Messina. Die fröhliche Wissenschaft*, edited by Giorgio Colli and Mazzino Montinari. Berlin: de Gruyter, 1999.

———. *On the Genealogy of Morality.* Translated by Carol Diethe. Cambridge: Cambridge University Press, 2007.

North, Paul. *The Yield: Kafka's Atheological Reformation.* Stanford, CA: Stanford University Press, 2015.

Noys, Benjamin. *Georges Bataille: A Critical Introduction.* London: Pluto, 2000.

Parain, Brice. *Essai sur la misère humaine.* Paris: Grasset, 1934.

---. *Recherches sur la nature et les fonctions du langage*. Paris: Gallimard, 1942.
Patocka, Jan. *The Natural World as a Philosophical Problem*. Edited by Ivan Chvatík and Lubica Ucník. Translated by Erika Abrams. Evanston, IL: Northwestern University Press, 2016.
Paulhan, Jean. *Les Fleurs de Tarbes, ou La terreur dans les lettres*. Paris: Cercle du Livre Précieux, 1967.
---. *The Flowers of Tarbes, or Terror in Literature*. Translated by Michael Sytotinski. Chicago: University of Chicago Press, 2006.
Plato. *Charmides*. In *Plato: Complete Works*, edited by John M. Cooper, 639–63. Translated by Rosamond Kent Sprague. Indianapolis: Hackett, 1997.
---. *Opera*. Edited by Jonathan Burnet. 5 vols. Oxford: Clarendon, 1900–1907.
Plotinus. *Ennéades*. Edited and translated by Émile Bréhier. Vol. 5. Paris: Belles Lettres, 1931.
Pynchon, Thomas. *Gravity's Rainbow*. New York: Penguin, 1973.
Rademaker, Adriaan. *Sophrosyne and the Rhetoric of Self-Restraint: Polysemy and Persuasive Use of an Ancient Greek Value-Term*. Leiden: Brill, 2005.
Rajan, Tilottama. *Deconstruction and the Remainders of Phenomenology: Sartre, Derrida, Foucault, Baudrillard*. Stanford, CA: Stanford University Press, 2002.
Rameau, Jean-Philippe. "Observations on Our Instinct for Music and on Its Principle." In *Essay on the Origin of Languages*, edited and translated by John T. Scott, 175–97. Hanover: University Press of New England, 1998.
Reuss, Roland. "Das Schloss: Zur Einführung." In *Franz-Kafka-Heft 9*, 2–23. Frankfurt am Main/Basel: Stroemfeld/Roter Stern, 2018.
Richter, Gerhard. *Verwaiste Hinterlassenschaften: Formen gespenstischen Erbens*. Berlin: Matthes & Seitz, 2016.
Ricoeur, Paul. "Étude sur les 'Méditations Cartésiennes' de Husserl." In *À l'école de la phénoménologie*, 161–95. Paris: Vrin, 1986.
---. *Oneself as Another*. Translated by Kathleen Blamey. Chicago: University of Chicago Press, 1992.
---. *Soi-même comme un autre*. Paris: Seuil, 1990.
---. "A Study of Husserl's Cartesian Meditations I–IV." In *Husserl: An Analysis of His Phenomenology*, 82–114. Translated by Edward G. Ballard and Lester E. Embree. Evanston, IL: Northwestern University Press, 1967.
Robert, Marthe. *L'ancien et le nouveau: De Don Quichotte à Franz Kafka*. Paris: Grasset, 1963.
Ronell, Avital. *Complaint: Grievance Among Friends*. Urbana: University of Illinois Press, 2018.
---. "Doing Kafka in *The Castle*: A Poetics of Desire." In *Kafka and the Contemporary Critical Performance: Centenary Readings*, edited by Alan Udoff, 214–35. Bloomington: Indiana University Press, 1987.
Rousseau, Jean-Jacques. "Examination of Two Principles Advanced by M. Rameau in His Brochure Entitled: 'Errors on Music in the Encyclopedia.'" In *Essay on

the Origin of Languages and Writings Related to Music, edited and translated by John T. Scott, 271–88. Hanover: University Press of New England, 1998.

———. "On the Principle of Melody, or Response to the 'Errors on Music.'" In *Essay on the Origin of Languages*. Edited and translated by John T. Scott, 260–70. Hanover: University Press of New England, 1998.

du Roy, Olivier. *L'intelligence de la foi en la Trinité selon Saint Augustin: Genèse de sa théologie trinitaire jusqu'en 391*. Paris: Études Augustiniennes, 1966.

Sartre, Jean-Paul. "Aller et retour." In *Situations I*, 175–225. Paris: Gallimard, 1947.

———. "Aminadab or the Fantastic Considered as Language." In *Literary and Philosophical Essays*, 60–77. Translated by Annette Michelson. New York: Collier, 1962.

———. "Aminadab ou du fantastique considéré comme un langage." In *Situations I*, 113–32. Paris: Gallimard, 1947.

Schestag, Thomas. *Mantisrelikte*. Basel: Urs Engeler, 1998.

———. *Namenlose*. Berlin: Matthes & Seitz, 2020.

Scholem, Gershom. "Über Klage und Klagelied." In *Tagebücher nebst Aufsätzen und Entwürfen bis 1923: 2. Halbband 1917–1923*, edited by Karlfried Gründer et al., 128–33. Frankfurt am Main: Jüdischer Verlag, 2000.

Schütz, Alfred. "Making Music Together: A Study in Social Relationship." *Social Research* 18, no. 1 (1951): 76–97.

Shaviro, Steven. *Passion & Excess: Blanchot, Bataille, and Literary Theory*. Tallahassee: Florida State University Press, 1990.

Simondon, Gilbert. *Individuation in Light of Notions of Form and Information*. Translated by Taylor Adkins. Minneapolis: University of Minnesota Press, 2020.

Smith, Barry. "Kafka and Brentano." In *Structure and Gestalt: Philosophy and Literature in Austria-Hungary and Her Successor States*, edited by Barry Smith, 113–59. Amsterdam: John Benjamins, 1981.

Smith, James K. A. *Speech and Theology: Language and the Logic of Incarnation*. London: Routledge, 2002.

Smock, Ann. *What Is There to Say? Blanchot, Melville, des Forêts, Beckett*. Lincoln: University of Nebraska Press, 2007.

Sng, Zachary. "Ablative Affinities." *Modern Language Notes* 133, no. 5 (2018): 1233–53.

———. *The Rhetoric of Error from Locke to Kleist*. Stanford, CA: Stanford University Press, 2010.

Spanos, William V. *Heidegger and Criticism: Retrieving the Cultural Politics of Destruction*. Minneapolis: University of Minnesota Press, 1993.

Steinbock, Anthony. *Limit-Phenomena and Phenomenology in Husserl*. Lanham, MD: Rowman & Littlefield, 2017.

Stock, Brian. *Augustine the Reader: Meditation, Self-Knowledge, and the Ethics of Interpretation*. Cambridge, MA: Harvard University Press, 1998.

———. *The Integrated Self: Augustine, the Bible, and Ancient Thought.* Philadelphia: University of Pennsylvania Press, 2017.
Strathman, Christopher A. "*Aminadab*: Quest for the Origin of the Work of Art." In *Clandestine Encounters: Philosophy in the Narratives of Maurice Blanchot*, edited by Kevin Hart, 91–118. Notre Dame, IN: Notre Dame University Press, 2010.
Stull, William. "Reading the *Phaedo* in Cicero's *Tusculan Disputations* 1." *Classical Philology* 107, no. 1 (2012): 38–52.
Sussman, Henry. *Franz Kafka: Geometrician of Metaphor.* Madison: Coda, 1979.
Taipale, Joone. *Husserl and the Constitution of Subjectivity.* Evanston, IL: Northwestern University Press, 2014.
Tell, David. "Beyond Mnemotechnics: Confession and Memory in Augustine." *Philosophy & Rhetoric* 39, no. 3 (2006): 233–53.
Teske, Ronald J. *Augustine of Hippo: Philosopher, Exegete, and Theologian: A Second Collection of Essays.* Milwaukee: Marquette University Press, 2009.
Theunissen, Michael. *Der Andere: Studien zur Sozialontologie der Gegenwart.* 2nd. ed. Berlin: de Gruyter, 1977.
Thiel, Detlef. "Husserls Phänomenographie." *Recherches Husserliennes* 19 (2003): 67–108.
Tobias, Rochelle. *Pseudo-Memoirs: Life and Its Imitation in Modern Fiction.* Lincoln: University of Nebraska Press, 2021.
Troup, Calvin L. *Temporality, Eternity, and Wisdom: The Rhetoric of Augustine's Confessions.* Columbia: University of South Carolina Press, 1999.
Vogl, Joseph. "Am Schlossberg." In *"Schloss"-Topographien: Lektüren zu Kafkas Romanfragment*, edited by Malte Kleinwort and Joseph Vogl, 23–32. Bielefeld: [transcript], 2013.
———. *Ort der Gewalt: Kafkas literarische Ethik.* Zurich: diaphanes, 2010.
———. "Vierte Person: Kafkas Erzählstimme." *Deutsche Vierteljahrsschrift für Literaturwissenschaft und Geistesgeschichte* 68 (1994): 745–56.
Wagner, Benno. "Kafka's Office Writings: Historical Background and Institutional Setting." In *The Office Writings*, by Franz Kafka, edited by Stanley Corngold, Jack Greenberg, and Benno Wagner, 19–48. Translated by Eric Patton and Ruth Hein. Princeton, NJ: Princeton University Press, 2009.
Waldenfels, Bernhard. *Grundmotive einer Phänomenologie des Fremden.* Frankfurt am Main: Suhrkamp, 2006.
———. "Hearing Oneself Speak: Derrida's Recording of the Phenomenological Voice." *Southern Journal of Philosophy* 32, no. 5 (1993): 65–77.
———. *Phenomenology of the Alien: Basic Concepts.* Translated by Alexander Korzin and Tanja Stähler. Evanston, IL: Northwestern University Press, 2011.
———. *Das Zwischenreich des Dialogs: Sozialphilosophische Untersuchungen im Anschluss an Edmund Husserl.* The Hague: Nijhoff, 1971.

Wall, Thomas C. *Radical Passivity: Levinas: Blanchot, and Agamben*. Albany: State University of New York Press, 1999.
Waltz, Matthew D. "The Opening of 'On Interpretation': Toward a More Literal Reading." *Phronesis* 51, no. 3 (2006): 230–51.
de Warren, Nicolas. "Augustine and Husserl on Time and Memory." *Quaestiones Disputatae* 7, no. 1 (2016): 7–46.
Whitney, Tyler. "Inside the Ear: Silence, Self-Observation, and Embodied Spaces in Kafka's 'Der Bau.'" *Germanic Review* 92, no. 3 (2017): 301–19.
Wolf, Burckhardt. "Die Nacht des Bürokraten: Franz Kafkas statistische Schreibweise." *Deutsche Vierteljahrsschrift für Literaturwissenschaft und Geistesgeschichte* 80 (2006): 97–127.
Zahavi, Dan. *Husserl and Transcendental Intersubjectivity: A Response to the Linguistic-Pragmatic Critique*. Translated by Elizabeth A. Behnke. Athens: Ohio University Press, 2001.
———. "Self-Awareness and Affection." In *Alterity and Facticity: New Perspectives on Husserl*, edited by Natalie Depraz and Dan Zahavi, 205–28. Dordrecht: Springer, 1998.
———. *Self-Awareness and Alterity: A Phenomenological Investigation*. Evanston, IL: Northwestern University Press, 1999.

Index

Abraham, Nicolas, 61, 213n99
affection, 1–3, 15, 39, 41–42, 48–50, 56, 58, 66–68, 77, 171n17, 196n98, 201n5, 203n20, 204n27, 209n59, 209n61, 214n105, 217n130, 218n132, 238n5
Agamben, Giorgio, 36–38, 193n79, 195n88, 196n95
alter ego, 23, 50–51, 56, 61, 66, 100, 203, 219
anamnesis. *See under* memory
appeal, 2–3, 6, 13, 15, 48–52, 55–58, 62, 70, 82, 94, 163, 165, 223n19, 229n59
apperception, 50, 56, 81, 206n41, 217n130
Aquinas, Thomas, 1, 169n3
Arendt, Hannah, 130–31, 180n82, 195n83, 255n9
Aristotle, 1, 4, 20, 24, 41, 58, 80, 152–53, 169n1, 173n35, 182n7, 186n23, 193n74, 198n108, 198n111, 211n78, 226n44, 227n55, 265n137, 266n151
association, 2, 8–11, 13–16, 19, 25, 47–52, 57–59, 69–70, 105, 123, 144, 146, 201n5, 202–203n15, 207n50, 210–11n72, 212n88, 213–14n102, 214n106, 215n111, 217n130

Augustine, 1–4, 9–10, 14–18, 21, 23–45, 51, 54–56, 58, 68, 73–75, 77, 80, 84, 86, 94, 97, 109, 118, 130–31, 169n4, 175n51, 177n54, 178–79n70, 180nn82–83, 183–85nn13–20, 186–87nn29–30, 187n32, 188nn33–34, 188nn36–37, 188nn40–41, 189nn43–44, 189nn46–50, 189–90nn54–58, 190–92nn60–66, 192–93nn69–78, 194n81, 195nn83–85, 196nn91–96, 196n98, 197–98nn99–105, 198–99nn109–11, 199–200nn118–26, 200nn130–31, 204n26, 207n49, 210n68, 211nn82–83, 219n134, 220n143, 224nn23–24, 224–25nn27–28, 226n45, 230n73, 236n126, 237n128, 239n17, 248n81, 255nn5–6, 255n10, 270n1, 270n5; *Confessions*, 14, 26, 37–43, 86, 94, 130–31, 161–62, 163–65, 169n4, 177n54, 178–79n70, 183n14, 184n16, 188n33, 190n58, 193n71, 195n84, 196nn91–96, 197–98nn99–103, 198–99nn110–11, 210n68, 211n82, 230n73, 236n126, 237n128, 255nn5–6; *De Civitate Dei*, 44, 56, 58, 80, 196n98, 200n126, 224–25n28, 226n45; *De doctrina christiana*, 198n105; *De*

Augustine *(continued)*
magistro (*On the Teacher*), 30–31, 68, 187n30, 187n32, 188n37, 188n40, 196n98, 197n104, 219n134; *De ordine* (*On Order*), 183n13; *De trinitate* (*On the Trinity*), 14, 26–37, 54–55, 118, 184n15, 184n18, 185n20, 186–87n29, 188n40, 189nn43–44, 189–90nn54–57, 190–92nn60–63, 193nn72–74, 195n83, 198n109, 207n49, 211n83, 224n27; *De uera religione* (*On True Religion*), 188n34; *Enarrationes in psalmos*, 43–45, 51, 199nn119–23, 200nn130–31, 204n26, 220n143
Austin, J. L., 260n56

Bataille, Georges, 9–13, 17–19, 21, 41, 64–65, 73–97, 99–107, 114, 116, 118, 125, 133, 161, 162, 176nn47–50, 177nn54–56, 177–78nn64–65, 181n91, 199n112, 222nn1–8, 222–23nn11–19, 225nn29–30, 225nn33–38, 226nn46–47, 226–27n49, 228–30nn59–65, 230nn67–68, 230nn70–71, 230–38nn74–149, 238–39nn1–10, 239nn12–14, 239–40nn16–21, 240nn23–24, 241nn28–30, 248n80, 248n82, 254n132, 258n15, 258n18; *L'Abbé C.*, 18–19, 87–97, 99–107, 110, 114, 116, 118, 125, 231–33nn80–86, 233–35nn88–103, 235nn106–113, 235–36nn115–22, 236nn124–26, 237nn128–30, 237–38nn134–40, 238n149, 238–39nn1–10, 240nn19–20, 240n23, 248n80, 248n82, 268n177, 270n16; *The Accursed Share*, 228n57; *Eroticism*, 64–65, 82–87, 228–30nn59–65, 230nn70–71, 231nn76–78, 235n105, 237n132, 238nn144–47; *Guilty*, 9–10, 176n47, 177nn54–56, 223n19, 230n74, 233n87, 237n133, 239n17, 268n177; *Inner Experience*, 41, 73–82, 176n50, 177n54, 199n112, 216n117, 222nn1–8, 222–23nn11–19, 225nn33–38, 226nn46–47, 231n79, 235n104, 237n128, 237n131, 238n141, 240n21, 258n18, 270n16; "The Language of Flowers," 226–27n49, 235n114; *Literature and Evil*, 105–107, 110, 181n91, 236n127, 238n148, 239n18, 240n24, 241nn28–30, 254n132; "Primitive Art," 103; *La Scissiparité*, 82, 228n58; *Story of the Eye*, 9, 11–12, 176n49, 177–78n64–65
Bergmann, Hugo, 108, 109, 243n40, 244n41
Blanchot, Maurice, 3, 9, 13, 17–21, 36–37, 60–61, 117–18, 132–62, 162, 163, 170n15, 173n33, 176n50, 180n79, 181–82nn94–96, 194–95n82, 212nn94–95, 212nn97–98, 213n100, 245–46n60, 248n79, 254n133, 255–57nn13–28, 258–60nn31–55, 260nn57–59, 260n61, 260n63, 260–61nn66–72, 262–63nn78–126, 264–65nn131–36, 265nn138–40, 266nn145–46, 266nn148–49, 266nn153–54, 267n156, 267–68nn159–72, 268nn174–77, 268n180, 269nn182–83, 269nn185–204, 270n2, 271n22; *Aminadab*, 18, 20–21, 60–61, 135–62, 163, 165, 166, 181–82nn94–96, 212nn94–95, 212nn97–98, 258–59nn39–42, 259nn44–45, 259–60nn47–55, 260nn57–59, 260n61, 260n63, 261nn70–72, 262nn80–83, 262nn86–95, 262nn97–98, 262nn101–102, 263nn104–106, 263n110, 263nn112–16, 263nn118–

20, 263nn122–26, 264n131, 264–65nn133–36, 266n146, 266nn148–49, 266nn153–54, 267n156, 267nn159–60, 267–68nn165–72, 268n180, 269nn182–83, 269nn185–89, 269nn193–99, 269n202, 270n2, 270n14; *The Book to Come*, 151, 264n133; *The Infinite Conversation*, 37, 117–18, 132, 155, 166, 181, 213n100, 248n79, 256n16, 263n111, 267nn161–62, 269n190, 269n200, 271n22; *The Instant of My Death*, 154, 266n155; *The Last Man*, 133, 256n14, 256–57nn17–21, 257nn23–24, 257n164; *The Step Not Beyond*, 3, 173n33, 259n43; *Thomas the Obscure*, 9, 36, 165, 176n50, 194–95n82, 270n14; *The Unavowable Community*, 132, 158, 256n15, 268nn178–79, 269n192; *The Writing of the Disaster*, 132–35, 143–46, 151, 161, 254n133, 255–56n13, 257nn26–28, 258nn31–37, 259n46, 262nn84–85, 262n100, 262n103, 263n107, 264n132, 269nn203–204
blindness, 9–12, 19, 178–79n70
body, 27–28, 50–51, 57–64, 70–71, 157, 180n81, 186n23, 188n36, 188n40, 192–93n70, 203–204n24, 206n41, 206–207n44, 211n79, 212n88, 216n125, 219–20n142, 221n146, 244n43
Boethius, 1
Brentano, Franz, 29–30, 108–109, 111, 126–27, 186n28, 242–43n37, 243n40, 244n42, 253–54nn126–27
Brod, Max, 19, 105–106, 108, 112, 115, 240–41nn25–26
Buber, Martin, 165–66, 270n15, 270nn17–18

chorus, 20, 129–34, 139–44, 150–52, 162, 255n12, 256n18
Cicero, Marcus Tullius, 27–28, 41, 109, 185–86nn21–24, 188n40
citation, 2–3, 6–7, 10–14, 24–31, 34–35, 41, 93–94, 102–103, 142, 151, 171n22, 189n46, 193n70, 220n144, 231–32n84, 236–37n127, 244n42, 261–62n78
cogito, 3, 10, 12, 15, 33, 49, 63–64, 66, 77, 84, 118, 173n35, 175n44, 179n73, 209n61, 218n133
coincidence (*Deckung*), 48, 52–54, 58–61, 63–66, 69–70, 117, 186n27, 212n96, 219n135, 247n74
commonplace, 24, 152–54, 159–61, 186n23, 286n144
communication, 15–16, 21, 48, 53, 56, 70, 75–78, 88, 92–94, 104, 133, 172n30, 179n77, 211n79, 223n19, 233n87
community, 5, 13, 16, 78, 112, 115, 130–32, 135–36, 143–44, 146, 149–52, 161, 201n5, 204n24, 256n15
confession, 2–3, 8–9, 11–14, 20–21, 31–32, 37, 40–44, 74, 76–77, 86, 96–97, 129–35, 145, 155, 158–62, 166, 189n46, 190n58, 193n71, 234–35n103, 237n128, 254–55n4, 255n10. *See also* Augustine
consciousness, 2, 4–5, 15, 26, 29–33, 43–44, 50–51, 54, 57, 62, 65–66, 78–79, 81, 85, 97, 108–109, 118–19, 142, 155, 165, 170n6, 170n10, 173–74n35, 184n16, 186n28, 200–201n1, 203n23, 204n27, 208n53, 208–209nn58–59, 209n61, 213n99, 216n118, 216n120, 217n127, 218–19nn132–33, 219n136, 225n32, 242–43n37, 243–44n41, 247n75, 248n78, 261n77

consonance, 49–52, 62, 69–70, 140–42, 202–203n15, 208n53, 218n132, 261n75

Deleuze, Gilles, 51, 166, 205n41, 205n35, 250n91, 279n20
Delphic oracle, 14, 23–28, 42, 109–110, 152, 183n10, 183nn12–13
Derrida, Jacques, 8, 10–13, 16, 18–19, 40, 44, 51–52, 54–56, 79, 145, 171n18, 172n32, 175n43, 176nn45–46, 177n58, 177n60, 177–78nn60–68, 178–79nn70–72, 179nn75–77, 180n79, 191–92n63, 198n106, 198–99n111, 200n127, 203n16, 205nn33–36, 207n48, 208n56, 210n69, 216n119, 220n144, 221nn146–47, 225nn39–40, 241n27, 262n96, 269n184; "Circumfession," 40, 44, 198–99n106, 200n127; *Demeure: Fiction and Testimony*, 4, 13, 145, 171n18, 179n72, 180n79, 262n96, 269n184; *Edmund Husserl's* Origin of Geometry, 16, 51–52, 176nn45–46, 205nn33–34; *Memoirs of the Blind*, 10–13, 172n32, 176n45, 177n58, 177n60, 177–78nn60–66, 177n68, 178–79nn70–71; *Speech and Phenomena*, 12, 54–56, 179nn75–77, 203n16, 208n56, 210n69, 216n119, 221n146, 241n27; *Writing and Difference*, 79, 225nn39–40, 241n27
Descartes, René, 26, 33–35, 173n35, 184–85n19, 189n45, 253n124
dialogue, 24–25, 27, 49–52, 54, 112, 115, 120–22, 154–55, 165–66, 203n16, 267n157
dissonance, 49–52, 64, 68–70, 131–32, 219n136, 261n75

epoché, 7, 23, 33, 36, 79–80, 106, 110, 171n22, 225–26n41, 241n27

evidence, 7–12, 17, 19–20, 23–27, 32, 67–69, 84, 86, 105, 110–11, 131, 142, 145, 155, 160, 162, 177n61, 184–85n19, 188n36, 202n15, 206–207n44, 216n125, 226n43, 242–43n37, 243n40, 250–51n93, 261n75
experience, 2–9, 11–21, 31–41, 47–70, 73–88, 90–91, 94–96, 107–11, 113, 116, 118–21, 124, 126–27, 129, 131, 133–34, 136, 144–45, 151, 154, 157–58, 162, 163–65, 171n17, 172–73n33, 173–74n35, 174n37, 175n44, 177–78n64, 187n32, 195n90, 196n92, 197n101, 200n129, 202n15, 205n28, 206n41, 206n44, 207n50, 208n56, 218n133, 225n39, 226–27n49, 228–29n59, 239n17, 242n36, 243n40, 244nn42–43, 252n102, 253n117, 256n18, 257n29, 261n75, 264–65n134, 268n177
expression, 3, 5–7, 15, 25, 29, 41–42, 52–53, 63, 70–71, 76, 103, 129, 139, 153, 172n32, 186n27, 205n36, 206n44, 207n50, 210n70, 265n142, 266n144

faith, 30–32, 36–37, 43–44, 101, 130, 150, 188n36, 188n38, 200n131, 255n10
Fink, Eugen, 23–24, 172n30, 182n4
Foucault, Michel, 17–18, 140, 175n44, 181nn88–90, 260n66
Freud, Sigmund, 8, 34, 62, 174–75n41, 213–14n102, 214n106, 254n130

Gasché, Rodolphe, 9, 70, 78, 176n48, 179n72, 220n144, 222n10, 224n27, 225n34, 227n49
gesture, 1, 15, 31–32, 35, 40–42, 47, 52–53, 56–57, 135, 141–43, 160, 206–207n44, 211n79, 251n98

Index | 295

givens / givenness, 2, 4–7, 12, 15–16, 18, 29–30, 39, 50, 54, 57, 62, 66, 69, 76–77, 79, 81–83, 88, 104–105, 142, 164, 171nn21–23, 172–73n33, 189n45, 197n101, 202n10, 203n19, 206–207n44, 213n100, 218–19n133, 219–20n142, 226–27n49, 233n87, 244n43

Hamacher, Werner, 4, 51–52, 59, 62, 70, 120, 166, 171n19, 175n43, 177n57, 204n25, 206n37, 212n87, 214n104, 219n140, 240n22, 251n95, 270n19
Hegel, G. W. F., 8, 74–76, 82, 102, 139–40, 148–49, 173n35, 175nn43–44, 222nn9–10, 222n13, 223nn19–20, 228n56, 239n11, 260n62, 263n117
Heidegger, Martin, 5, 10–11, 14–15, 21, 74, 76, 86, 136, 171n22, 177n59, 180n82, 200n129, 223n19, 230n72, 259n42
Husserl, Edmund, 2–18, 21, 23–26, 29–30, 33, 39, 42, 47–71, 73, 76–79, 81, 84, 97, 107, 109, 116–17, 130–31, 157, 161–65, 170nn6–11, 171nn20–22, 172n25, 172nn28–31, 172–73n33, 173–74nn35–39, 175n44, 177n53, 178n69, 180n84, 182nn1–6, 182–83n9, 184nn16–17, 186nn27–28, 189nn42–53, 195n90, 197n101, 197n103, 198n116, 200n132, 200–201nn1–7, 202–203nn15–22, 206–207nn38–47, 207–208nn50–54, 209n59, 209n61, 209–10nn63–67, 210–11nn71–74, 211nn79–81, 211–12nn84–86, 212n88, 212n91, 212n93, 212n96, 213nn100–101, 214n103, 214n105, 214–15nn107–108, 215–16nn112–16, 216n118, 216–19nn120–33, 219nn135–39, 219n141, 220n144, 221n146, 221–22n149, 224n23, 225nn31–32, 226n43, 227nn51–52, 229n64, 230n74, 240n22, 241n27, 242n33, 244n43, 247nn74–77, 255n8, 261nn75–77, 270n1, 270n4; *Cartesian Meditations*, 14–15, 23–26, 42, 44, 50, 56–60, 63–65, 81, 180n84, 182nn1–3, 198n116, 200n132, 203n19, 203nn21–22, 206n41, 210n66, 210–11nn72–73, 211–12nn85–85, 212n88, 212n93, 214–15n108, 215n114, 219nn137–38, 225n32, 227n51, 261n75, 270n1, 270n4; *Crisis of the European Sciences*, 4, 24, 33, 171n21, 175n44, 182nn5–6, 189nn42–53, 229n64; *Formal and Transcendental Logic*, 54, 207n50; *Ideas Pertaining to a Pure Phenomenology*, 3, 5–8, 10, 30, 79, 117, 170n8, 170n11, 171n20, 171n22, 172n25, 172nn28–29, 172n31, 177n53, 178n69, 185n28, 212n100, 216n125, 230n74, 240n22, 241n27, 247nn75–76, 261n75; and internal time-consciousness, 26, 65, 142, 184n16, 216n118, 216nn120–21, 261nn76–77; and intersubjectivity: *see under* intersubjectivity; lectures on passive synthesis, 5–6, 13, 15–16, 47–51, 60, 62–63, 66–70, 116, 161, 200–201nn1–6, 203n18, 209n61, 212n96, 214n103, 217nn128–29, 218–19nn132–33; *Logical Investigations*, 7–8, 12–13, 52, 54, 68, 78, 107, 173–74nn35–39, 186n27, 207–209nn51–54, 214n105, 218–19n133, 219nn135–36, 219n139, 221–22n149, 225n31, 226n43, 242n33, 247n74; and pairing: *see under* pairing

imaginative variation, 4, 87, 121, 126

infancy, 14, 35–42, 97, 193n71, 193n79, 194n81, 195n84, 195n86, 195n88, 195n90, 196n93, 196n96, 197n99, 197n101, 211n79
intention / intentionality, 5, 14–16, 23, 25, 29–30, 33, 52, 66–68, 73–75, 79, 107, 110, 114, 157, 161, 170n6, 173–74n35, 182–83n9, 184n17, 186nn27–28, 201n1, 205n33, 208n53, 208n56, 209n58, 211n74, 211n79, 213n100, 214n105, 215n110, 217–18n131, 218–19n133, 219n136, 225n41, 242–43n37, 247n75
intersubjectivity, 6, 15–16, 18, 20–21, 47–48, 50–52, 62–66, 81, 97, 100, 130–31, 195n90, 203n16, 203n23, 205n28, 206n41, 206–207n44, 207n47, 210n65, 210n67, 210n70, 211n74, 211n84, 213n99, 214n107, 216n116, 227–28n55, 255n8
intuition, 2, 5–17, 57, 74, 79, 164, 170n6, 172n32, 174n38, 177n61, 186n27, 216n125, 218–19n133, 225n40
Ionesco, Eugene, 3

Jaspers, Karl, 76–77, 85, 180n82, 223n19, 224n26, 230n69, 233n87

Kafka, Franz, 3, 10, 17–21, 44, 94, 105–27, 129–36, 140, 145–46, 150–51, 161–63, 170–71n16, 176–77n52, 177n54, 181nn92–95, 200n128, 236–37n127, 240–41nn25–26, 241–42nn31–32, 242–43nn35–38, 244–47nn45–73, 248n78, 248–53nn83–122, 254nn129–31, 255nn10–12, 256n18, 258–59n30, 260n55, 260n64, 262n95, 262n99, 263–64nn127–30, 270nn1–2; *The Burrow*, 111, 151, 254–55nn1–4, 263–64n130, 268n172; *The Castle*, 3, 18, 20–21, 112–27, 130–32, 135–36, 140, 146, 150–51, 170–71n16, 177n54, 181n92, 181n94, 245–46nn52–60, 246–47nn62–71, 247n73, 248–50nn85–89, 250–51nn91–94, 251–52nn97–102, 252–53nn104–16, 253nn118–22, 254nn129–30, 258–59n30, 260n64, 263n128, 268n172, 270nn1–2; diaries, 20, 94, 107–108, 245nn51–52, 248n78, 253n117, 254n131, 254n3; testament, 19, 105–107, 240–41nn25–26; *The Man Who Disappeared*, 255n12; *The Trial*, 19, 106, 119, 129–31, 249n87, 250n90, 254–55n4, 255n11, 256n18, 260n55
Kant, Immanuel, 2, 29, 164, 170n6, 174n36, 175n44, 186n28, 201n9, 248n78
Kierkegaard, Søren, 74, 154, 255n10, 267n159
Klossowski, Pierre, 17, 173–74n35
Koyré, Alexandre, 74, 76, 82, 222n9, 223n20, 228n56

Lacan, Jacques, 31, 42, 188n38, 199n115
lament, 108–10, 243n39, 244n44
language acquisition, 14, 37–42, 193n71, 195n84, 195n86, 196n93, 196n96, 197–98nn104–105
Leibniz, Gottfried Wilhelm, 7–8, 173n35, 174n36, 174n40, 175n42, 253n124
Levinas, Emmanuel, 3, 13, 15, 134–35, 170n14, 180n79, 257–58nn28–30, 271n22
love, 26–27, 33–36, 43, 54–56, 76–77, 92, 158–61, 191–92n63, 195n83, 224n24, 232n85, 234–35n103, 251n98, 268n172, 270n5

Lyotard, Jean-François, 15–16, 38, 41, 180n85, 193n71, 196n92, 198–99n111

Marion, Jean-Luc, 5, 14–15, 26, 33, 51, 130, 171n21, 171n23, 173n33, 180n82, 184–85n19, 189n46, 189n51, 190n60, 200n129, 205n30, 235n7
Marty, Anton, 108–111, 117–18, 125–27, 242–43n37, 243–44nn40–41, 248n81, 253nn123–25, 253–54nn127–28
Marx, Karl, 25, 182–83nn8–9
memory, 1, 3, 8, 12, 14, 27, 30, 32–41, 47–48, 51, 83, 109, 114, 118–19, 125, 139, 150, 154, 164, 174–75n41, 177–78n64, 184–85n19, 187n32, 190nn58–59, 190–91n61, 191–92n63, 192–93nn70–71, 193n77, 195n84, 196n93, 197n103, 198n109, 217n130, 244n42; anamnesis, 34, 187n32, 190n59; memory of the present, 32–35, 190n59, 190–91n61; screen memory, 8, 174–75n41
Merleau-Ponty, Maurice, 15–16, 51, 157, 205n29, 205n35, 211n79, 268n173
Metzger, Arnold, 25, 182–83n9
music, 139–44, 156, 159, 202–203n15, 203n23, 260n60, 260n65, 261n73; *see also* chorus, consonance, dissonance

Nancy, Jean-Luc, 34–35, 189n45, 192nn67–68, 213n100, 227n53
Nietzsche, Friedrich, 74, 94, 133, 163–66, 223n19, 236n123, 256n18, 270nn5–6, 270nn8–10, 270n12

pairing, 18, 21, 50, 57–65, 81–83, 91, 97, 100, 116, 157, 160, 206n41, 214–15n108, 215n113, 265n173; *see also* intersubjectivity
Parain, Brice, 7, 173–74n35
passive synthesis; *see under* Husserl
Patocka, Jan, 54–56, 208n55, 209n62, 217–18n131
Paulhan, Jean, 152–54, 265nn138–42, 266n144, 266n147, 266n150, 266n152, 267n158
Plato, 26–27, 34, 109, 154, 166, 173–74n35, 183nn11–13, 186nn23–24, 187n32, 193n74, 267n157, 267n165; *Charmides*, 26–27, 183nn11–12; *Meno*, 187n32; *Phaedo*, 186n24; *Republic*, 267n165; *Theatetus*, 154, 267n157
protest, 2, 4, 13, 49, 62, 66–70, 217–18n131; *see also* dissonance
Pynchon, Thomas, 55–56, 209n60
psychoanalysis, 17, 62, 174–75n41, 232–33n86; *see also* Abraham, Freud, Lacan

Rameau, Jean-Philippe, 142, 261n73
reduction, 4–5, 8, 23, 25, 42, 51–52, 62, 66, 79–80, 93, 106, 112, 119, 239n18, 241n27; *see also* epoché
repression, 66–70, 204n27, 219nn135–36
Ricoeur, Paul, 179n73, 204n27, 205n28, 208–209n58
Rousseau, Jean-Jacques, 140, 142, 260n60, 260n65, 261n74

Sartre, Jean-Paul, 21, 135, 151, 173–74n35, 181n94, 258–59n39
Scholem, Gershom, 109, 243n39
scissiparity, 18–19, 64–65, 82–88, 90–92, 97, 100, 114, 227–28n55, 228n57, 228–29n59, 229n63, 230n67, 230n75, 231–32n84, 232–33n86, 237n134

soul, 1, 20, 27, 39, 41, 43–44, 56, 58, 68, 70, 102, 139, 154, 155, 169n1, 180n81, 180n83, 183n13, 185–86nn20–22, 186–87n29, 189n46, 190n59, 192–93nn69–71, 193n74, 197n103, 198n105, 267n157
syncope, 34, 39

testimony, 4, 9, 12–13, 16, 19–20, 70, 82, 87, 95–97, 102, 109, 121, 145–46, 149–55, 158–59, 179n72, 196nn92–93, 234n95, 240–41n26, 244n42
Theunissen, Michael, 50–51, 57, 182–83n9, 203–204n24, 206n41, 210n70, 211n75, 212n88
time-consciousness, *see under* Husserl
trace, 3, 13, 19, 35–36, 55, 80, 96–97, 100–102, 105, 110, 112, 116–18, 120, 125, 143, 146, 151, 161, 166, 191–92n63, 195n86, 197n102, 200n131, 227n49, 239n8, 258n31
tropes, 2, 9, 11–12, 25, 108, 111, 170n10
truth, 4, 7, 10, 12, 14, 16, 19–21, 30–31, 34, 40, 48–49, 69–70, 86, 93, 96–97, 103–104, 106, 121, 123, 127, 129–36, 140, 145–51, 156–61, 176n45, 176–77n52, 187n32, 206–207n44, 225n32, 234–35n103, 255n10, 255n12, 266n152, 267n165, 268n177

Veranderung, 50–52, 62, 203–204n24, 212n88
Virgil, 33–34

Waldenfels, Bernhard, 5, 55, 171–72n24, 203n16, 207n48, 208–209n58

www.ingramcontent.com/pod-product-compliance
Lightning Source LLC
Chambersburg PA
CBHW031707230426
43668CB00006B/136